Assessment Practice
in Student Affairs

Assessment Practice in Student Affairs

An Applications Manual

John H. Schuh
M. Lee Upcraft
and Associates

JOSSEY-BASS
A Wiley Imprint
www.josseybass.com

Published by Jossey-Bass
A Wiley Imprint
989 Market Street, San Francisco, CA 94103-1741   www.josseybass.com

Jossey-Bass books and products are available through most bookstores. To contact Jossey-Bass directly call our Customer Care Department within the U.S. at (800) 956-7739, outside the U.S. at (317) 572-3986 or fax (317) 572-4002.

Jossey-Bass also publishes its books in a variety of electronic formats. Some content that appears in print may not be available in electronic books.

The exhibits included in this book (except those for which reprint permission must be obtained from the primary sources) may be freely reproduced for educational/training activities. There is no requirement to obtain special permission for such uses. We do, however, ask that the following statement appear on all reproductions.

Assessment Practice in Student Affairs: An Applications Manual by John H. Schuh, M. Lee Upcraft, and Associates. Copyright © 2001 by Jossey-Bass Publishers, San Francisco, CA.

Library of Congress Cataloging-in-Publication Data

Schuh, John H.
    Assessment practice in student affairs: an application manual/John H. Schuh, M. Lee Upcraft, and associates.—1st ed.
        p.   cm.—(The Jossey-Bass higher and adult education series)
    Includes bibliographical references and index.
    ISBN 0-7879-5053-X (alk. paper)
        1. Student affairs services—United States—Evaluation—Handbooks, manuals, etc. 2. Education, Higher—United States—Evaluation—Handbooks, manuals, etc. I. Upcraft, M. Lee. II. Title. III. Series.

LB2342.92 .S35 2001
378.1'98—dc21   00-048759

Printed in the United States of America
FIRST EDITION

PB Printing   10 9 8 7 6

The Jossey-Bass
Higher and Adult Education Series

Contents

Preface

IN THE PREFACE to *Assessment in Student Affairs: A Guide for Practitioners* (Upcraft and Schuh, 1996), we noted that colleges and universities had come under increasing pressure from their various constituencies to demonstrate their effectiveness in measurable terms. We also asserted that student affairs was under even more pressure from both external stakeholders (state legislatures, graduates, the general public, local communities, and others) and internal constituencies (faculty, students, other administrative units, institutional governing boards, and others) to justify its existence in an era of steady-state or declining resources. We concluded that a critical element in meeting these demands was a systematic and comprehensive approach to assessment that demonstrated the effectiveness and worth of student affairs services, programs, and facilities.

We have traveled widely over the past five years, conducting assessment workshops, presenting at regional and national conferences, teaching assessment courses, and consulting at individual institutions, and we have concluded that almost nothing has changed since our original assessment. The pressure on student affairs to demonstrate its effectiveness, for whatever purpose (survival, quality improvement, accreditation, enrollment management, affordability, strategic planning, policy development and decision making, local political contexts) still exists and is growing. Moreover, in addition to continuing internal and external pressures, regional accrediting agencies have become more serious about outcomes assessment as a criterion for accreditation. More often than not when we are asked to consult with an individual institution, part of the motivation for asking our assistance is its impending reaccreditation.

Our intention in *Assessment in Student Affairs* was to write a practitioner-focused book that gave readers the context within which to view assessment, along with some practical tools for developing selected assessments. Looking back, and in the light of our subsequent interactions with practitioners, we learned we were much more successful with the former than the latter. Although *Assessment in Student Affairs* provided some practical tools, it was not specific enough to enable most student affairs practitioners to develop systematic and high-quality assessments without considerable additional help. This book is an attempt to continue the dialogue about assessment in student affairs and provide practitioners with even more practical tools to develop and, in many cases, conduct assessments.

We should be very clear, however, that we are not advocating that all student affairs practitioners can or should conduct any and all assessments, all by themselves. Neither are we arguing that student affairs assessments should be conducted exclusively by social science researchers or institutional research personnel, based on the questionable assumption that most, if not all, student affairs practitioners lack the necessary skills to conduct rigorous and unbiased studies. Our middle ground is that some studies may, in fact, be conducted by student affairs practitioners if they have the appropriate education and training and if those studies meet acceptable assessment standards (see Chapter One for an elaboration of those standards and how they may differ from research standards). Other studies, whose designs and analyses may be more complex, require investigators with more assessment expertise. Either way, someone with assessment design and analysis expertise should review all assessment studies to ensure that these studies are rigorous, unbiased, and defensible.

The bias issue is especially problematic. On the one hand, we are asserting that student affairs practitioners in many instances can conduct and participate in every phase of their own assessment studies. We make this claim because we believe those involved in the delivery of student services and programs often are in the best position to define the problem, develop the design, collect and analyze the data, and suggest implications for practice. The prevailing counterargument, of course, is that staff involvement in their own assessment studies by definition creates biased and therefore flawed studies. Moreover, most student affairs staff are unqualified to conduct such studies in the first place.

We assert two basic arguments in response. First, many student affairs practitioners are qualified to conduct solid assessment studies based on their graduate education, which often includes research design as well as quantitative and qualitative assessment skills. These professionals should be used to the full extent of their education, training, and expertise. Second, since we argued that all assessment studies should be reviewed by assessment experts, one of their major tasks should be to identify and eliminate all bias (to the extent possible), including any that may have crept in as a result of practitioner involvement in their own studies.

We also faced some dilemmas in writing this book. The first one was whether to assume that readers had also read *Assessment in Student Affairs*. At first we tried to write a stand-alone manual, but very quickly became aware that the duplication required to bring the reader up to speed on the first book made this book redundant and excessively long. So we attempted a compromise: although it is desirable for the reader to have read *Assessment in Student Affairs* in its entirety, we attempted to write this manual in ways that summarized and updated this prior work and directed readers to selected parts of it when appropriate. Topics not included in this manual but covered in our book that are critical to a credible assessment effort include tracking the use of programs and services, using national standards to assess, quantitative methods, sampling procedures, comparable institution assessment, and reporting assessment results effectively.

We should note, however, that several important topics were not addressed in our first book. For example, we have added another component to our comprehensive assessment model: cost effectiveness. It became clear as we talked to practitioners that pressure to justify costs and defend against cutbacks was a major assessment issue, so we expanded our model to include this very important topic. We also added a discussion of accreditation, because it has become a major motivator for conducting assessments. Web-based data collection was not widely developed when we wrote our book, but now deserves attention because of its potential to streamline data collection procedures. And finally, we discuss the organizational aspects of initiating and conducting assessment in student affairs. Knowing how to do assessments is one thing; getting assessments done in varying organizational contexts is quite another.

Our second dilemma was how to design this manual for multiple audiences. The most obvious audience is student affairs practitioners. We wanted this manual to explain how to develop assessment studies and to promote awareness of specific tools to get that job done. However, we also wanted to design this manual in a way that would allow it to be used as a text for assessment courses in student affairs graduate training programs, an emerging topic in graduate curricula. A third audience is institutional research personnel who may be very well informed about assessment and evaluation but less about how they apply to student affairs.

A third dilemma, and the one that probably perplexed us the most, was which student services and programs to discuss in greater detail. It was impossible to include every student service and program, so we had to make some choices about which ones to include and which to exclude. We decided not to include chapters on services and programs that serve specific student subpopulations (for example, women, racial and ethnic minorities, adult students, veterans, disabled students, gay/lesbian/bisexual/transgendered students) as well as others (for example, academic advising, tutorial services, the registrar, commuter programs, child care). However, we believe that these student services and programs can develop systematic assessments by drawing on many different parts of this manual, including services and programs that may be similar to those not included.

A fourth dilemma was internal redundancy. We viewed this manual as a reference to be used in response to specific assessment issues, not a work to be read cover to cover. Thus, there is some repetition of material from chapter to chapter. For example, Astin's input-environment-outcome (IEO) model (1991) is included in chapters that discuss longitudinal studies and outcomes assessments. Similarly, although there are chapters on assessing needs, satisfaction, outcomes, and campus environments, these kinds of studies are often used in other chapters when case studies are discussed. And finally, for some readers, repeating the steps in the assessment process for each assessment example may seem particularly redundant. However, we believe that because each study presented is unique, the repetition allows for a more rigorous and thorough example.

A fifth dilemma was the extent to which we would discuss research methods in each chapter. This is not a book on research methods; however, understanding and applying research methods are necessary to conduct good assessment studies. We worried that if we included detailed descriptions of research methods, this manual would become too lengthy and lose the attention of readers. We have struck what we believe is a workable compromise. We have included a discussion of research methods in each chapter that deals with assessing individual student affairs units and then provided references to additional resources. No one should infer that our brief description of research methods is an endorsement of methodological shortcuts. That is not our position.

A sixth dilemma was how much information to provide in our case studies. Again, because of length limitations, we chose to provide only the most basic information. We assume that our audience is well informed about the basic operations of student affairs programs and services, and we determined that including such information would have been redundant.

Another dilemma is that there is some unevenness in our discussion of the assessment of various student affairs functions. This is because some student affairs functions have a longer and stronger history of assessment, while others are just beginning. For example, in student health services, there is a long history of quality control, attention to patient satisfaction, cost effectiveness, and accreditation. Assessment of recreation facilities and programs is a much newer and less developed endeavor.

Overview of Contents

This book was written on the assumption that it would not be read cover to cover at one sitting. We also assumed that our prior work, *Assessment in Student Affairs,* would serve as a resource for selected topics in this manual. With those caveats, we lead off with two chapters that essentially summarize our approach to assessment by offering an overview of assessment and steps in the assessment process. Part Two explores qualitative assessment methodologies, including a chapter with very specific advice about conducting focus groups. It also discusses quantitative methodologies, including instrument development, and compares locally developed and commercially developed quantitative instruments. It provides as well information about data collection and analysis and includes a discussion of mailed questionnaires, telephone surveys, and Web-based surveys.

Part Three is a more specific elaboration of various kinds of assessments discussed in *Assessment in Student Affairs,* including assessing needs, satisfaction, outcomes, environments, cost effectiveness, and accreditation. Part Three also covers several specialized assessment studies, including assessing dropouts, alumni, and group educational programs.

Part Four focuses on assessing selected student services and programs, including first-year programs, recreation programs, financial aid, admissions, residence life, college unions, health services, career services, counseling services, judicial affairs, and Greek life. Part Five gives attention to additional assessment issues, including getting started, arranging for a consultant, ethical issues, and strategies for implementing an assessment program.

The Resources section is an annotated bibliography of assessment instruments.

Some Important Caveats

Obviously we are strong advocates of the importance of assessment in providing high-quality student services and programs. We also believe that assessment is critical to the defense and survival of student affairs. But assessment is not a guarantee. As we have argued elsewhere (Schuh and

Authors and Contributors

Authors

John H. Schuh is professor of educational leadership at Iowa State University, Ames, Iowa, where he is also department chair. Previously he has held administrative and faculty assignments at Wichita State University, Indiana University (Bloomington), and Arizona State University. He earned his B.A. degree in history at the University of Wisconsin, Oshkosh, and his Master of Counseling and Ph.D. degrees at Arizona State University. Schuh is the author, coauthor, or editor of over 160 publications, including 14 books and monographs. He has served as editor and chair of *ACPA Media,* is editor in chief of the *New Directions for Student Services* series, and is associate editor of the *Journal of College Student Development.* Schuh has made over 150 presentations and speeches to campus-based, regional, and national meetings. He has served as a consultant to more than twenty-five colleges, universities, and other organizations.

Schuh has served on the governing boards of the American College Personnel Association, the National Association of Student Personnel Administrators, and the Association of College and University Housing Officers-International. He was chosen to join the Evaluator Corps of the North Central Association of Colleges and Schools in 1998.

Schuh has received the Contribution to Knowledge Award and the Presidential Service Award from the American College Personnel Association, the Contribution to Research or Literature Award from the National Association of Student Personnel Administrators, and the Leadership and Service and S. Earl Thompson Awards from the Association of College and University Housing Officers-International. The American College Personnel Association has elected him as a Senior Scholar Diplomate.

M. Lee Upcraft is a senior research scientist at the Center for the Study of Higher Education, assistant vice president emeritus for student affairs, and affiliate professor emeritus of higher education at Pennsylvania State University. He received both his B.A. degree (1960) in history and his M.A. degree(1961) in guidance and counseling from the State University of New York, Albany, and his Ph.D. degree (1967) in student personnel administration from Michigan State University. During his more than thirty-five years in higher education, Upcraft has served in various student affairs administrative and faculty positions. He is the author of eighty book chapters and refereed journal articles, and his published books include *Assessment in Student Affairs: A Guide for Practitioners* (1996, with J. H. Schuh), *Academic Advising for First-Year Students* (1995, with G. Kramer and Associates), *Designing Successful Transitions: A Guide for Orienting Students to College* (1993, with R. Mullendore, B. Barefoot, D. Fidler, and Associates), *New Futures for Student Affairs* (1990, with M. J. Barr and Associates), and *The Freshman Year Experience* (1989, with J. N. Gardner and Associates). He served as the associate editor of the *New Directions for Student Services* sourcebooks from 1986 to 1996.

Upcraft has received numerous awards and recognition, including the Outstanding Contribution to Literature or Research award from the National Association of Student Personnel Administrators, the Outstanding Contributions to the Orientation Profession award from the National Orientation Directors Association, and the Outstanding Contribution to the Profession awards from the college personnel associations of New York and Pennsylvania. He is a Senior Scholar Diplomate of the American College Personnel Association (ACPA) and was recognized as a Diamond Honoree by ACPA in celebration of its seventy-fifth anniversary in 1998.

Contributors

Jennifer L. Crissman is an assistant professor of counselor education at Pennsylvania State University. She holds a B.S. degree in elementary education from Millersville University, an M.S. in counseling and college student personnel from Shippensburg University, and a D.Ed. in higher education from Pennsylvania State University. Her student affairs experience includes residence halls and new student programs, and her teaching experience includes first-year seminars and graduate courses in student personnel. Her research interests encompass the first-year experience, assessment in student affairs, and seminars for first-year students.

Dennis Heitzmann is director of the Center for Counseling and Psychological Services and affiliate associate professor of counseling and clinical psychology at Pennsylvania State University. He holds a Ph.D. degree in counseling psychology from the University of Texas. He previously served as director of the Center for Student Development at the University of Memphis and director of Counseling Services at Rhodes College. He has served as the president of the Association for University and College Counseling Center Directors and president of the International Association for Counseling Services. He has been a teacher, consultant, and workshop presenter on topics that include the severity of client disturbance, students at risk, managed behavioral health care, and organizational development.

Brian R. Jara is a lecturer and undergraduate adviser in women's studies at Pennsylvania State University. He holds a B.A. degree in sociology from Johns Hopkins University (1992) and an M.Ed. degree in higher education from Pennsylvania State University (1993), where he is completing his Ph.D. in higher education with a graduate certificate in women's studies. He has previously worked in new student programs and has taught undergraduate courses in education, sociology, and women's studies. His research interests integrate feminist theory and higher education and include the construction of gender in college student culture, campus violence prevention programs, feminist pedagogy, and women's studies and interdisciplinarity in higher education.

Kirsten Kennedy is associate director of residential life for business operations at University of Missouri–Columbia. She formerly worked in residential life programs at Bloomsburg University and taught basic courses as an adjunct faculty member in the Business Administration Department at the Pennsylvania College of Technology. Kennedy received her B.S.B.A. degree in management (1987) and her M.B.A. degree (1988) from Bloomsburg University of Pennsylvania. Her professional and research interests include first-year interest groups, Continuous Quality Improvement, financial management in higher education and student affairs, and studies of student satisfaction.

Betty L. Moore has been at Pennsylvania State University for over twenty-six years and is currently the senior analyst and director for student affairs research and assessment. In this capacity, she has designed and implemented over seventy Pennsylvania State Pulse telephone surveys, the Class of 2000 Longitudinal Study, studies monitoring the educational impact of the Pennsylvania State Newspaper Readership project, and the 1999 Student Satisfaction study, which was implemented at twenty Pennsylvania State campuses. She has coauthored two publications at Pennsylvania State, *Quality of Instruction* and *Pennsylvania State as a Community of Learning,* as well as several articles and book chapters. Moore has a B.S. degree in industrial and

Part One

Principles and Purposes

agency effectiveness" (Upcraft and Schuh, 1996, p. 18). Effectiveness includes not only assessing student learning outcomes, but assessing other important outcomes, such as cost effectiveness, clientele satisfaction, meeting clientele needs, complying with professional standards, and comparisons with other institutions. Assessment in student affairs is not restricted to students, but may include other constituents within the institution, such as the faculty, administration, and governing boards, and outside the institution, such as graduates, legislators, funding sources, and accreditation agencies.

One further clarification is that for the purposes of this book, we are not including the assessment of an individual for the purposes of providing that person feedback for personal development or improvement. Our emphasis is on program or service assessment, not individual assessment. Nevertheless, assessing individual student or other clientele outcomes, *taken together*, is consistent with our definition of assessment. For example, we may not want any information about why an individual student may persist to graduation, but we will want to know why, in the aggregate, students graduate.

We have purposely omitted staff performance evaluations from our definition of assessment. In our context, assessment is limited to student services, programs, and facilities only, and should never include staff performance evaluations. Of course, we may gather assessment information that has indirect implications for the personnel involved, but this information should be used in the context of program or service assessment, not personnel evaluation.

Assessment must be contrasted with but linked to *evaluation*. Here there is less agreement about the definition. We assert that "evaluation is any effort to use assessment evidence to improve institutional, departmental, divisional, or institutional effectiveness" (Upcraft and Schuh, 1996, p. 19). In other words, assessment describes effectiveness; evaluation uses these descriptions in order to improve effectiveness, however that might be defined by an institution. For example, determining whether admissions criteria predict subsequent persistence and degree completion is assessment. Using that assessment to change admissions requirements is evaluation.

Another term also must be defined: *measurement*. Measurement refers to the methods we use to gather information for the purposes of assessment. Typically measurement methods are divided into two discrete categories: quantitative and qualitative. Quantitative methodologies assign numbers to objects, events, or observations according to some rule (Rossman and El-Khawas, 1987). Instruments with established psychometric properties are used to collect data, and statistical methods are used to analyze data and draw conclusions. For example, the ability to predict college success might involve gathering all the quantifiable data about the variables that are thought to predict persistence and degree completion, such as high school grades, scores on standardized tests, involvement in high school activities, and parents' education and income. These data might then be correlated with subsequent student behavior (dropping out or persisting) to determine which ones, and in which combination, best predict college success. (For a fuller discussion of quantitative methods, see Upcraft and Schuh, 1996.)

Qualitative methodologies are the detailed description of situations, events, people, interactions, and observed behaviors; the use of direct quotations from people about their experiences, attitudes, beliefs, and thoughts; and the analysis of excerpts or entire passages from documents, correspondence, records, and case histories (Patton, 1990). Using the admissions example again, admissions personnel might want to interview students who persisted and those who dropped out to determine the extent to which their backgrounds and experiences might have contributed to their success or lack thereof. Variables that seem to predict college success but are difficult to measure (for example, motivation) might be better understood through a qualitative approach. (For a fuller description of qualitative methods, see Upcraft and Schuh, 1996. For a discussion of how to do qualitative studies, see Chapter Three in this manual.) We should point out that the selection of an assessment methodology may not be an either-or decision; in fact, in many cases, the use of both methodologies is not only appropriate but also more powerful than a single one.

Another definition worth mentioning, although it will not be the focus of this manual, is *research*. In the 1960s and 1970s, it was fashionable to use the term *student affairs research* to refer to assessment and evaluation efforts. This term proved to be confusing, particularly to faculty, who had a much narrower definition of research. When comparing research and assessment, Erwin (1991) argues that although they share many processes in common, they differ in at least two important respects. First, assessment guides good practice, while research guides theory development and tests concepts. Second, assessment typically has implications for a single institution, while research typically has broader implications for student affairs and higher education.

The failure to understand the difference between research, on the one hand, and assessment and evaluation, on the other, can and often does lead to some strong differences of opinion between social science researchers and education assessors and evaluators. Chronbach (1982) was one of the first to distinguish between research and evaluation. He wrote:

Designing an evaluative investigation is an art. The central purpose of evaluation differs from that of basic social science research, and evaluations fit into different institutional and political contexts. The strategy of evaluative research therefore requires special consideration. Logic is necessarily the same in all disciplined inquiry, but the translation of logic into procedure should depend upon context, purpose, and the expected payoff. Many recommendations appropriate for long term programs of scientific research are ill suited to evaluation. Hence, general writings on design and scientific method are inadequate to guide the evaluator. For any evaluation many good designs can be proposed, but no perfect ones [pp. 1–2].

Does this mean that by definition, assessments and evaluations are flawed and therefore not to be relied on? No. Assessment and evaluation studies are useful and should be done even when they do not adhere strictly to the canons of social science research. Rossi and Freeman (1993) make the distinction between "perfect" and "good enough" assessments: "In many circumstances, it is difficult or impossible to conduct impact evaluations using what are in ideal terms, the best possible designs" (p. 220). We assert that the "perfect" research study (an impossibility) always evolves into a "good enough" assessment study for many of the following reasons.

Resource limitations. Most student programs and services lack the human and financial resources to conduct "perfect" assessments. Often already busy student affairs personnel are asked to participate in assessment studies in addition to their other responsibilities. Further, assessments cost money, but seldom is enough money available to conduct the "perfect study." Thus, resource compromises are often made which affect assessment designs.

Time limitations. Often decisions must be made, or policies addressed, or a problem solved before the "perfect" design can be implemented. The best example in higher education may be retention studies. A well-controlled, longitudinal, five-year study is ideal, yet few, if any, institutions can afford to wait that long to address retention problems. Our experience is that the window of opportunity to influence policies and practices may be open for as little as a month, and rarely more than a year. Assessment designs must be compromised to fit more realistic time expectations.

Organizational contexts. Organizations are not static; they are in a constant state of change, and therefore their assessment needs may vary over time. For student affairs, assessment needs might drastically change as a result of new leadership that requires different evidence of effectiveness, or sees new problems, or devalues old problems. In this changing environment, changes in initial assessment agendas must be made, perhaps further compromising the "perfect" design.

Implementation limitations. All assessment designs are based on certain assumptions that may or may not be correct. On the quantitative side, for example, a perfectly drawn random sample may yield a usable sample that is not representative of the population under study. Or the response rate may not be as high as desired, and thus the statistical analyses may be limited or the sampling error increased (or both). Or there may be problems with instruments that were poorly designed or failed to meet psychometric standards such as reliability ("the extent to which we are measuring some attribute in a systematic and therefore repeatable way"; Walsh and Betz, 1985) and validity (a test measures "what we intend to measure"; Walsh and Betz, 1985).

On the qualitative side, perhaps fewer people than expected showed up to participate in focus groups. Or the interview protocol did not yield the desired information. Or the interviewers failed to perform effectively. Or something as simple as a malfunctioning tape recorder limited precise analyses of participant voices. So again, "compromises" must be made. The social science researcher may have the luxury to discard a study whose flaws result from implementation limitations; the assessment investigator is under more pressure to salvage a study and report results based on design implementation flaws.

Political contexts. Social scientists attempt to conduct research that is, to the extent possible, apolitical, and they often have the luxury of conducting studies that "search for the truth no matter where it leads." Assessment, on the other hand, always occurs in a political context that must be taken into account in assessment designs. We have asserted that "all assessment is political" (Upcraft and Schuh, 1996, p. 16), and assessment designs can and often do reflect political realities. For example, an assessment study under discussion may never be done, a study in progress may be discontinued, and in rare instances, a study already completed may be kept confidential because the results may be politically or ideologically unacceptable to policymakers.

So where does this leave us? When does a study become so compromised that it should never be done, or discarded even if implemented? Rossi and Freeman (1993), while defending the "good enough" principle of assessment, also argue that the investigator has the responsibility to "raise the question whether to undertake the assessment at all, especially if meaningful results are unlikely" (p. 220). These choices, they say, always involve

answer is yes (see Pascarella and Terenzini, 1991; Kuh, Branch Douglas, Lund, and Ramin-Gyurnek, 1994), but this fact is limited in its application to practice, for two reasons. First, this research is often not well known among many higher education administrators and faculty, and second, even if it is, the question of local applicability always arises—for example, "OK, so the research evidence shows that students living in residence halls earn higher grades and are more likely to persist to graduation than students living else-where, but is that true at our institution?" National studies may be more elegant in design, more sophisticated in research techniques, and more lucid in the presentation and results, but locally produced studies, if done well, will have more impact on a particular campus. In this sense, all assessment is local.

In general, we believe that assessment efforts can and will demonstrate the effectiveness and worth of student services and programs, and show positive relationships between students' out-of-class experiences and use of student services and programs and student learning, including academic achievement and retention. However, local results may not be consistent with the findings of national studies, since students make their own environments based on interactions with their institutions. Further, even if local studies are consistent with national findings, local policymakers and decision makers may choose to ignore this evidence for other reasons. Thus, all assessment is a risk. We can never be certain that local assessment studies will have the desired impact of demonstrating the worth of student services and programs or ensuring their survival.

Quality

Although survival may be the primary motivator for assessment in student affairs, there are other equally valid reasons to assess. Even if it is demonstrated that student services and programs are essential and needed, a second question is, Are they of high quality? Assessment can be a powerful tool in linking goals to outcomes, helping define quality, and determining if quality exists in student affairs. We strongly believe that a fundamental responsibility of student affairs is to provide services, programs, and facilities that are of the highest quality. Assessment can help determine if we have been successful in fulfilling that responsibility.

Affordability

A third reason for assessment is to gauge affordability and cost effectiveness. The question faced goes something like this: "Sure, this program [or that service] is needed, and there is evidence of its quality, but in an era of declining resources, can we afford it? Can we continue to fund it at current levels? Can we afford it at all?" Decisions to eliminate services and programs based on their affordability may have to be made, but other affordability questions abound. Might it be less expensive to outsource this service or program? Are there other ways of providing the same service or program less expensively? Can this service or program generate income from fees? Can this service do more with less, or less with less? And how do we know? Unfortunately, these decisions are often made without adequate assessment, in part because there are few, if any, cost effectiveness models used in student affairs.

Strategic Planning

Strategic planning, according to Baldridge (1983), examines the big issues of an organization: its mission, purpose, long-range goals, relationship to its environment, share of the market, interactions with other organizations. Since many higher education institutions are seriously committed to strategic planning, it is important for student affairs to be an active and effective participant in this process. Assessment contributes to strategic planning by helping to define goals and objectives and pointing to critical issues or problems that must be resolved successfully if the organization is to achieve its goals. Assessment is especially important in the early phases of strategic planning to identify strengths, weaknesses, and opportunities for the future. It is also critical in the later stages of planning, when evaluation of policies and programs occurs.

Policy Development and Decision Making

What evidence do we have to help us make a decision or develop or revise a policy? Assessment can provide systematic information that can be critical in helping policymakers and decision makers make valid judgments about policy, decide on important issues, and make decisions about resource allocations. Making these kind of judgments based on systematic information is important not only within students affairs; it is also important to help student affairs influence policies and decisions within the institution and with stakeholders outside the institution, such as boards of control, legislatures, graduates, and the general public.

Politics

Assessment may be necessary for political reasons. Sometimes we must do assessment because someone or some institution of importance wants some information, which makes it politically important to produce. It may be the president of the institution, a faculty governing group, an influential board of control member, an outspoken legislator, or an influential graduate. We must also be concerned about the political impact of assessment findings. As we stated earlier, all assessment is political; thus, assessment investigators must be attuned to the impact of their studies from the moment an assessment idea emerges. If one of the purposes of assessment is to influence policy and practice, then the political context within which decisions are made must be accounted for in the assessment process.

Accreditation

According to the Commission on Higher Education's *Characteristics of Excellence in Higher Education* (1994), one of the criteria for accreditation is outcomes or institutional effectiveness: "The deciding factor in assessing the effectiveness of any institution is evidence of the extent to which it achieves its goals and objectives. The process of seeking such evidence and its subsequent use helps to cultivate educational excellence. One of the primary indications of the effectiveness of faculty, administration, and governing boards is the skill with which they raise questions about institutional effectiveness, seek answers, and significantly improve procedures in the light of their findings" (p. 16). This moves assessment from the "nice to have if you can afford it" category to the "you better have it if you want to stay accredited" category. Student affairs is expected to be an active participant in the accreditation process and therefore is required to contribute assessment evidence to this process.

These are among the many reasons for assessment in student affairs. They are important because we believe that the first step in the assessment process (see Chapter Two) is to determine why you are doing a particular study, because what you do will in large part be determined by why you are doing it. We also believe these questions are best answered within the context of a comprehensive assessment program.

A Comprehensive Assessment Model

Too often assessment is done piecemeal, without any real planning or consistency, in response to a crisis—or it is not done at all. Often we do not do anything because we do not know how to start or what to do. This comprehensive assessment model describes various types of assessment and offers advice about which assessments are appropriate.

Tracking

The first component of this model is *keeping track of who uses student services, programs, and facilities.* How many clients use services, programs, and facilities, and how are they described by gender, race, ethnicity, age, class standing, residence, and other demographic variables? For example, if we analyze the patient census in health services and discover that African Americans are underrepresented compared to their percentage of the student population, then we must uncover why this is so and make necessary changes.

This component is very important, because if the intended clientele do not use services, programs, or facilities, then our intended purposes cannot be achieved. However, sheer numbers do not tell the whole story, especially if users or participants are not representative of the clientele. The quantity and distribution of users have important implications for policy and practice and must be assessed.

Needs Assessment

The second component of this model is *assessing student and other clientele needs.* The basic principle that we should meet the needs of our clientele is a good one and well supported in the literature, but often it is not easy to accomplish. There are many questions to be answered. What kinds of services, programs, and facilities do students and other clientele need, based on student and staff perceptions, institutional expectations, and research on student needs? How do we distinguish between wants and needs? How do we know if what we offer fits our clientele? Assessing student and other clientele needs can provide answers to these questions. For example, a needs assessment could help determine if the educational programs offered in residence halls are consistent with residents' needs and what kinds of educational programs to conduct in residence halls (see Chapter Nine).

Satisfaction Assessment

The third component of this model is *assessing student and other clientele satisfaction.* Of those persons who use our services, programs, and facilities, what is their level of satisfaction? What strengths and suggestions for improvement do they identify? Clientele satisfaction is important because if users are not satisfied, they will not use what we offer again, and they will not recommend our services and programs to friends and colleagues. We are also interested in clientele satisfaction because it provides valuable information about how to improve our services, programs, and facilities. For example, a satisfaction study of users of recreational facilities may tell if the hours the facilities are open are consistent with students' available discretionary time (see Chapter Ten).

Student Cultures and Campus Environments Assessment

The fourth component is assessing *campus environments and student cultures.* It is critical to take a look at collective perceptions of campus environments and student cultures within which individuals conduct their day-to-day lives. This component of the assessment model can help answer such questions as, What is the climate for women on this campus? What is the academic environment, both inside and outside the classroom? What is the overall quality of life in residence halls? Is the campus environment receptive to and confirming of students of color (see Chapter Twelve)?

Outcomes Assessment

A fifth component is *assessing outcomes.* Of those who use our services, programs, and facilities, is there any effect on their learning, development, academic success, or other intended student learning outcomes, particularly when compared with nonusers? Can programmatic interventions be isolated from other variables that may influence outcomes, such as background, characteristics, and other experiences? For example, can we isolate living in residence halls as a unique, positive factor in students' grades and persistence to graduation? Do students who seek help from the counseling center for depression become less depressed as a result of receiving treatment?

Assessing outcomes, however, is not restricted to student learning outcomes. There may be other outcomes important to effective student services and programs, but not directly related to student learning outcomes. For example, a counseling center may determine that an important outcome is a reasonable wait time between when clients first seek treatment and when they actually receive treatment. Or an important outcome for a financial aid office is to ensure that students have access to the amount and types of financial aid consistent with institutional, state, and federal regulations.

These kinds of studies are very difficult to design, implement, and interpret, but in some ways they attempt to answer the most fundamental question of all: Is what we are doing having any effect, and, if so, is that effect the intended one? These studies are at once the most important we do yet most difficult to conduct (see Chapter Eleven).

Comparable Institution Assessment

A sixth component is *comparable institution assessment.* How does the quality of services, programs, and facilities compare with "best-in-class" comparable institutions? An important way of assessing quality is to compare one's own institution to other institutions that appear to be doing a better job with a particular service, program, or facility, often described as benchmarking. A particularly strong example of this approach is the work conducted by Taylor and Massy (1996); as a result of studying one thousand institutions, they developed over one hundred benchmarks for these institutions.

One purpose of comparable institution assessment would be to discover how others achieve their results and then to translate their processes to one's own environment. For example, if very few first-year students use the institution's career development services, can we look at another institution that has some success in getting those students to seek out career services and learn how it was done? The key to this assessment component is to select comparable institutions that have good assessment programs rather than relying on anecdotal or reputational information.

National Standards Assessment

A seventh component of this model is *using nationally accepted standards to assess.* How do our services, programs, and facilities compare to accepted national standards, such as those developed by the Council for the Advancement of Standards (CAS) for Student Services/Development Programs, various national and regional accrediting agencies, and professional organizations? For example, we might want to know from the CAS self-assessment instrument if our Center for Women Students is meeting minimal standards for women's centers in terms of its mission, goals, policies, funding, programs, services, and other dimensions.

Cost Effectiveness Assessment

The final component, added to the model since the publication of *Assessment in Student Affairs,* is *assessing cost effectiveness.* Are the benefits students derive from what we offer worth the cost, and how do we know that? For example, can we outsource health services and maintain the same level of quality and service at less cost to the institution and to students? There is very little guidance offered from current student affairs literature, except at the most basic level of analysis: divide the cost of a service by the number of students using the service. Such an "analysis" is often fraught with so many methodological problems that its conclusions may be meaningless. Cost-benefit analysis is difficult and somewhat imprecise in a nonprofit, service-oriented organization, but it should be attempted nevertheless (see Chapter Thirteen).

Conclusion

Assessment is not another educational fad that will disappear when newer fads emerge. For the many reasons discussed in this chapter, external pressures to assess, from accountability to accreditation, will continue for the near future. But even without these pressures, assessment must be done because if it is conducted properly, it is the best way to ensure our commitment to high-quality student services, programs, and facilities.

References

Baldridge, V. J. "Strategic Planning in Higher Education: Does the Emperor Have Any Clothes?" In V. J. Baldridge (ed.), *Dynamics of Organizational Change in Education.* Berkeley, Calif.: McCutchan, 1983.

Cage, M. C. "To Shield Academic Programs from Cuts, Many Colleges Pare Student Services." *Chronicle of Higher Education,* Nov. 18, 1992, pp. A25–A26.

Campbell, D. T. "Methods for the Experimenting Society." *Evaluation Practice,* 1991, *12*(3).

Chronbach, L. J. *Designing and Evaluating Social Programs.* San Francisco: Jossey-Bass, 1982.

Commission on Higher Education. *Characteristics of Excellence in Higher Education: Standards for Accreditation.* Philadelphia: Middle States Association of Colleges and Schools, 1994.

Erwin, T. D. *Assessing Student Learning and Development: A Guide to Principles, Goals, and Methods of Determining College Outcomes.* San Francisco: Jossey-Bass, 1991.

Kuh, G. D., Branch Douglas, K., Lund, J. P., and Ramin-Gyurnek, J. *Student Learning Outside the Classroom: Transcending Artificial Boundaries.* Washington, D.C.: George Washington University Press, 1994.

Marchese, T. J. "Assessment's Next Five Years." *Association of Institutional Research Newsletter,* Fall-Winter 1990, pp. 1–4 (special supplement).

Palomba, C. A., and Banta, T. W. *Assessment Essentials: Planning, Implementing, and Improving Assessment in Higher Education.* San Francisco: Jossey-Bass, 1999.

Pascarella, E. T., and Terenzini, P. T. *How College Affects Students: Findings and Insights from Twenty Years of Research.* San Francisco: Jossey-Bass, 1991.

Patton, M. Q. *Qualitative Evaluation and Research Methods.* (2nd ed.) Thousand Oaks, Calif.: Sage, 1990.

Rossi, P. H., and Freeman, H. E. *Evaluation: A Systematic Approach.* (5th ed.) Thousand Oaks, Calif.: Sage, 1993.

Rossman, J. E., and El-Khawas, E. *Thinking About Assessment: Perspectives for Presidents and Chief Academic Officers.* Washington, D.C.: American Council on Education and American Association for Higher Education, 1987.

Taylor, B. E., and Massy, W. F. *Strategic Indicators for Higher Education.* Princeton, N.J.: Peterson, 1996.

Upcraft, M. L. "Affordability: Responding to the Rising Cost of Higher Education." In C. S. Johnson and H. Cheathan (eds.), *Higher Education in the Next Century: A Research Agenda for Student Success.* Washington, D.C.: American College Personnel Association, 1999.

Upcraft, M. L., and Schuh, J. H. *Assessment in Student Affairs: A Guide for Practitioners.* San Francisco: Jossey-Bass, 1996.

U.S. Department of Education. *Digest of Education Statistics, 1998.* Washington, D.C.: U.S. Department of Education, 1999.

Walsh, W. B., and Betz, N. E. *Tests and Assessment.* Upper Saddle River, N.J.: Prentice Hall, 1985.

Chapter 2

Steps in the Assessment Process

IN OUR BOOK *Assessment in Student Affairs: A Guide for Practitioners*, we identified questions that should be answered for each assessment study regardless of its purpose, type, scope, setting, or methodology. In our subsequent assessment workshops, we converted these questions into steps to be followed as an assessment study is developed and implemented. In this chapter, we identify these steps, and offer specific examples of each step. This chapter roughly parallels Chapter Two in our earlier book, but the steps have been refined and slightly redefined so even readers familiar with our previous material may want to review this chapter. Also, the steps in the outcomes assessment process, identified in Chapter Ten in our previous book, are slightly different from the following steps.

Step 1: Define the Problem

All assessment flows from an attempt to solve some problem, so establishing a clear and concise definition of the problem is the first step in the assessment process. Another way of framing this step is asking the question, Why are we doing this assessment? Everything else flows from this question, for the "why" determines what we do, how we do it, and how we use the results. Other questions also might help define the problem.

What specific circumstances or situations are driving assessment efforts? Examples might include low enrollments, consideration of a policy to protect students from being discriminated against on the basis of their sexual orientation, pressures to reduce budgets, commitment to improving services and programs, and impending accreditation review.

What external pressures are driving assessment efforts? Pressures external to student affairs might include the general public (costs are rising more quickly than inflation), institutional boards of control (we need to increase minority enrollments), institutional leadership (too many problems are arising from students' abusing alcohol), graduates (the sinking feeling that student life just is not what it used to be), and, in state-supported institutions, legislatures, and governors (we need to cut state allocations by X percent), and from accrediting agencies (assessment is required for reaccreditation).

What internal circumstances are driving assessment? There is always a need to improve student services and programs, regardless of their quality, so improvement is a primary internal circumstance that drives assessment efforts. Other internally driven variables may include a concern that services and programs might not be meeting student needs or might not be equally accessible and used by all types of students. We may need to know more about whether our services and programs are achieving their intended outcomes, and if so, if they are being administered in cost-effective ways.

Step 2: Determine the Purpose of the Study

Recall from the definition in Chapter One that assessment is the process of gathering, analyzing, and interpreting evidence (information). Given the particular problem identified in Step 1, what information do we need to help solve it? What information will be critical to responding to external and internal pressure to do assessment? The answers to these questions then become the basis for determining the purpose of the study. For example, if we need more information about student satisfaction with health services, then we should conduct a study whose purpose is to measure that satisfaction.

Step 3: Determine Where to Get the Information Needed

Information can be retrieved from a wide variety of sources. The most obvious source is students or other clientele, but there are many other sources. Institutional or departmental records may well contain valuable information needed to solve a problem. For example, if our concern is the differential use of services by underrepresented groups, an analysis of student usage by gender, race or ethnicity, age, disability, and other categories may provide the information needed to verify the problem. Other sources of information might include institutional documents, student newspaper articles, and field observations.

Most student affairs assessment, however, focuses on gathering information directly from students, but they may not be the only sources of information. Others may have insight into the problem, including staff, faculty, administrators, community leaders, or even the general public. It may seem obvious, but defining the population precisely is important because the conclusions drawn from a particular inquiry apply only to those studied in the first place.

Step 4: Determine the Best Assessment Methods

Another way of framing this step is to answer the question, "What is the best way to get the information I need?" Of course, the best assessment method depends on the purpose of the study. Basically there are three choices: quantitative methods, qualitative methods, or a combination of both. According to Patton (1990), qualitative methods focus on gathering information from interviews, observations, and documents, and they require much smaller samples than quantitative measures. Quantitative measures include gathering data from a survey or other instrument and require much larger samples than qualitative methods.

In other chapters we discuss in greater detail how and when to use these methodologies. Given the information we need, what is the best way to retrieve it? Generally if we need information about "what" is occurring, quantitative methods are more appropriate. If we need information about "why" something is going on, qualitative measures are more appropriate. Our experience has taught us that a combination of methods may well best provide information to solve the problem that precipitated the study. For example, if one were studying the development of critical thinking in first-year students, a pre- and posttest measure of critical thinking would reveal if such a development did occur. Focus groups might best indicate why or why not.

Step 5: Determine Whom to Study

If the chosen population is narrowly defined, it may be possible to include the entire population in a study. But most often, a sample of the whole population must be selected in ways that ensure that those selected are representative of that population according to some criteria. The most typical criteria are the demographics of the population, such as gender, age, and race and ethnicity. In the collegiate setting, factors such as class standing, grades, place of residence, full-time or part-time enrollment, disability, and major field, among others, also may be important. If the sample is representative, then one can generalize with much more confidence to the whole population. In qualitative studies, however, although strict adherence to the representativeness of the sample is not required, it is nonetheless important within general parameters.

Step 6: Determine How Data Will Be Collected

Data can be collected in a wide variety of ways, including mailed questionnaires, telephone surveys, individual interviews, and focus groups. Although all are intended to include the desired number and type of participants in the study, each procedure has strengths and limitations. For example, mailed questionnaires may yield a low percentage of responses but can collect rich information. On the other hand, telephone surveys may yield a higher percentage of return but may be limited in the amount of information collected. Individual interviews and focus groups require a more personal touch, and incentives such as food or token monetary compensation may be helpful. (The advantages and disadvantages of each data collection method are covered in later chapters.) The method that is chosen should be consistent with the purposes of the study and should best collect the information needed.

Step 7: Determine What Instruments Will Be Used

The instruments used to collect data depend on several factors, including which methodologies are chosen. For quantitative methodologies, the instrument must be chosen that yields results that can be statistically analyzed. Beyond that, we need to decide whether to use an already constructed instrument with appropriate psychometric properties and standardized norms, or a locally constructed instrument that may be more appropriate to this particular study but lacks validity, reliability, and other psychometric properties. Generally instruments available from any one of several national test publishing houses are preferable if an opportunity is available to add locally developed items. But if the problem under study is unique to a campus, then test construction experts should be consulted when developing local instruments. (The pros and cons of using local or national instruments are discussed in Chapter Five.)

For qualitative methodologies, the interview protocol must consist of standardized, open-ended questions that retrieve the information needed for the study. According to Patton (1990), an item is standardized when it is written out in advance *exactly* the way it is to be asked during the interview. Clarifications or elaboration should be included, as well as any probing questions. Variations among interviewers can be minimized and comparisons across interviews can be made if the interview protocol is standardized. *Open-ended* means there are no prescribed answers (such as "yes" or "no"); respondents are free to provide any answer they choose. (The development and use of interview protocols are discussed in Chapter Four.)

Step 8: Determine Who Should Collect the Data

At first glance, this question may not seem to matter particularly. Obviously data should be collected by people who are competent to do so. But often the most qualified people are also those who have a personal stake in the outcome. This is less of a problem with quantitative methodologies, where bias is more likely to have occurred in the selection or development of the instrument. In qualitative methodologies, however, the data are collected and filtered by those who conduct the study and record the data, so bias becomes a larger issue. Can we really trust a study that was done entirely by those with a personal stake in the outcome? On the other hand, can we really trust a study that was done entirely by outside experts who know little or nothing about the context and nuances of the study? The solution, we believe, is that bias can be reduced if the overall design is reviewed by an assessment expert and student affairs staff are selected who have some background, education, and experience in assessment in general, and data collection in particular.

Step 9: Determine How the Data Will Be Analyzed

Analysis of quantitative data depends on the purpose of the study. Chapter Four of our earlier book and several chapters of this manual discuss appropriate statistical analyses in greater detail. Probably the most important first step is to determine if the respondents are in fact representative of the population to be studied. Then appropriate descriptive and inferential statistical analyses can be applied. Because many student affairs professionals lack the skills necessary to determine which statistical analyses are most appropriate and how to interpret statistically generated results, we recommend using statistical consultants familiar with social science research methodologies for both data analysis and interpretation.

Analysis of qualitative data is somewhat more consistent with the skills and abilities of student affairs professionals, but still must be done in systematic ways, including listening to and searching for meaning in interview and focus groups, audiotapes, or transcripts, and looking for themes, trends, variations, and generalizations. This process should be an inclusive one, with data gatherers collaborating with colleagues, students, and even subjects in the interpretation of the data.

Step 10: Determine the Implications of the Study for Policy and Practice

Too often investigators are content with reporting the findings and conclusions of a study, leaving its implications for policy and practice to various audiences. We believe that the report of assessment results should spell out the implications of the study. Here we are clearly crossing the line from assessment to evaluation. (Remember that assessment is the gathering and analyzing of information, and evaluation is using assessment information to solve the problem that precipitated the study.) What approaches to solving the problem should be considered in the light of the findings? What policies and practices need to be revised, eliminated, or created because of the findings? There should be clear calls for action in assessment reports that motivate the reader to do something about the problem that precipitated the study. Simply reporting the data without discussing the implications for policy and practice will almost certainly weaken the impact of the study.

Step 11: Report the Results Effectively

Once the findings have been reported and analyzed, and the implications for policy and practice identified, how do we report the results? In what form do we report the results? To whom should the study be reported? Should every stakeholder get the whole report? More studies end up filed under "I" for "Interesting" or gathering dust on someone's shelf because we fail to package results in ways that move decision makers to make changes based on the study. In fact, how a study is formatted and distributed may be more important than its results. The biggest formatting mistake is to format the results of a study on the basis of a typical academic research report, which among other flaws, is often boring, redundant, and without recommended actions.

Probably the biggest distribution mistake in our view is to send the full report to all audiences and hope for the best. There are several ways to overcome this problem. One way is to prepare multiple reports for multiple audiences, highlighting the results most applicable to each audience. Executive summaries, which summarize the study, its findings, and recommendations for policy and practice, are also effective. Getting results to the right people—those who can do something about the problem studied—also is very important. Offering to discuss the results in greater detail in person may be appropriate. Even going so far as to suggest how decision makers may make best use of the study is not out of the question. Clearly, if the purpose of the study is to solve a problem, then the report must not only report the results, but explore how the results can be used to solve the problem. (For further information on using assessment results effectively, see Chapter Thirteen in *Assessment in Student Affairs*.)

Conclusion

We have provided these steps early in this manual because we hope you use them in all the various types of assessment discussed in this manual. It has been our experience that these steps are necessary to all good assessment studies and that not giving each of them careful consideration will result in studies that are not be well conceived, designed, implemented, and analyzed.

Further, these steps should be addressed for each study *before* the study is conducted. To be sure, as the study progresses, changes may have to be made, but a major impediment to good assessment is the lack of planning, and following these steps helps ensure that the study will be a good one.

References

Patton, M. Q. *Qualitative Evaluation and Research Methods*. (2nd ed.) Thousand Oaks, Calif.: Sage, 1990.

Upcraft, M. L., and Schuh, J. H. *Assessment in Student Affairs: A Guide for Practitioners*. San Francisco: Jossey-Bass, 1996.

Part Two

Methods

Chapter 3

Qualitative Assessment

A VARIETY OF research approaches fit under the umbrella of qualitative assessment research methods. Qualitative research includes such studies as ethnographies, case studies, evaluations, historical research, policy research, market research (Birley and Morgan, 1998), as well as phenomenology, cultural studies, and semiotics (Gall, Borg, and Gall, 1996). Among the research techniques that are part of this research tradition are interviews (both individual and group), document analysis, and field observations of people. Although the amount of rigor attributed to this form of research has been debated, little question remains that this form of research is quite rigorous.

A number of definitions can be applied to the term *qualitative research methodology.* Denzin and Lincoln (1994, p. 2) define qualitative research as "multimethod in focus, involving an interpretive, naturalistic approach to its subject matter. This means that qualitative researchers study things in their natural settings, attempting to make sense of, or interpret, phenomena in terms of the meaning people bring to them." For the purpose of this chapter, we wish to use the definition inspired by Patton (1990) presented in Upcraft and Schuh (1996, p. 21): "Qualitative methodology is the detailed description of the situations, events, people, interactions, and observed behaviors, the use of direct quotations from people about their experiences, attitudes, beliefs, and thoughts; and the analysis of excerpts or entire passages from documents, correspondence, records and case histories." Whitt (1991, p. 406) cautions that "a precise and generally agreed upon definition of qualitative research is at this time—perhaps for all time—elusive."

This chapter provides a brief overview of qualitative research techniques. Many colleges and universities offer courses in qualitative methodology, and excellent books are available that discuss this topic in depth. At the end of this chapter, in addition to the References, we have added a list of suggested readings, which provide an excellent discussion of qualitative research techniques. Besides this list, reading good qualitative studies is helpful in developing these skills.

Key Assumptions of Qualitative Methods

Qualitative researchers are interested in understanding the meaning people have constructed, that is, how they make sense of the world and their experiences in it (Merriam, 1998). Making meaning, explaining their lives, reporting how various experiences have affected them, and other similar broad forms of how people interpret the world and their experiences are the basis for qualitative research. This form of research is not concerned with conducting studies that apply broadly to situations outside the case being studied. In this respect, this research tradition is the opposite of quantitative research, which often is interested in generalizing the findings of the study to a larger population. Qualitative research generally does not reflect this interest.

Whereas questionnaires and other kinds of instruments are used to collect information in quantitative research, in the case of qualitative methods, the researcher, often in the field, is the primary means by which data are collected and analyzed.

Qualitative research usually requires fieldwork. The persons conducting the research need to get out of their offices and into the field to collect their data. That may be accomplished through interviews on site, observing people in the field, or collecting and reviewing documents. Punch (1994, p. 83) describes qualitative researchers this way: "They should abandon the classroom in order to knock on doors, troop the streets, and join groups."

Qualitative research primarily is an inductive strategy—that is, the data lead to a theory rather than researchers' conducting an inquiry to test a theory. In going into the field to collect data, the researchers may have ideas as to what they may find, but they do not conduct the research project to test a theory. Rather, they may conduct the research project to develop a theory that explains the situation. "Theory evolves during actual research, and it does this through continuous interplay between analysis and data collection" (Strauss and Corbin, 1994, p. 273). This is the opposite of the deductive approach used in quantitative research.

The resulting product of a qualitative study should be descriptive and detailed. The report of the research findings is a rich, thick description of the situation studied in the field. Whitt (1991, p. 412) describes reports as "detailed descriptions of what was done and why, and of the phenomena studied, including contexts, behaviors, perceptions, feelings and insights. An important element of thick description is the use, to the extent possible, of verbatim quotations." One is never entirely sure when the project has been completed, but until a rich, thick description has been developed, the work has to continue.

Comparisons with Quantitative Methods

Qualitative methods reflect a substantially different approach to research from quantitative methods. Some individuals try to make the case that one approach is more rigorous than the other, that one is better than the other, and so on. What appears to be emerging in the literature about research methods, however, is that both research traditions are highly valued, and when they are used in combination with one another, the researcher can develop high-quality studies. Gall, Borg, and Gall (1996, p. 32), point out that "both approaches have helped educational researchers make important discoveries." Birley and Morgan (1998, p. 38) add, "It should never be forgotten that the choice of methodologies is dependent upon the subject of the research and the related aspects of the research design."

Actually, the two research traditions are not as distinctive as one might conclude. Qualitative researchers use computers, at one time thought to be the exclusive territory of quantitative researchers (Richards and Richards, 1994). Blaxter, Hughes, and Tight (1996, p. 61) offer the following observation on how the lines between these approaches to research have become blurred:

> *On the first consideration, the use of questionnaires as a research technique might be seen as a quantitative strategy, whereas interviews and observations might be thought of a qualitative techniques. In practice, however, it is often more complicated than that. Thus, interviews may be structured and analyzed in a quantitative manner as when numeric data is collected or when non-numeric answers are categorized and coded to numeric form. Similarly, surveys may allow for open-ended responses and lead to the in-depth study of individual cases.*

Table 3.1 compares the two research traditions. It is important to remember that the differences between these research traditions fundamentally have much more to do with assumptions about research than actual research techniques. For example, Gall, Borg, and Gall (1996, p. 30) assert that quantitative researchers "assume an objective social reality," while qualitative researchers "assume that social reality is constructed by the participants

TABLE 3.1

A Brief Comparison of Qualitative and Quantitative Methods

	Qualitative	Quantitative
Epistemological roots	Postpositivist research	Positivist research
Focus of research	Quality (nature, essence)	Quantity (how much, how many)
Philosophical roots	Postmodernism	Modernism
Key concepts	Meaning, understanding, description	Statistical relationships, prediction control, description, hypothesis testing
Associated terms	*Fieldwork, ethnographic, naturalistic*	*Experimental, empirical, statistical*
Sampling	Nonrepresentative, small, purposeful	Large, random, representative, stratified
Data	Field notes, people's own words	Measures, counts, numbers
Methods	Observations, reviewing documents	Experiments, surveys, instruments
Instruments	Researcher, tape recorder, camera, computer	Inventories, questionnaires
Data analysis	Ongoing, inductive (by researcher)	Deductive (by statistical methods)
Findings	Comprehensive, holistic, richly descriptive	Precise, numerical
Advantages	Flexibility, emphasis on understanding large groups, hard-to-explain anomalies	Ease of use, high acceptance
Disadvantages	Time, hard-to-reduce data, hard-to-study large groups, hard-to-explain anomalies	Controlling intervening variables, oversimplification

Sources: *Bogdan and Biklen, 1992; Worthen and Sanders, 1987; Gall, Borg, and Gall, 1996; and Merriam, 1998.*

in it." (We refer readers to Gall, Borg, and Gall, 1996, for a fuller discussion of the philosophical differences between these research traditions.)

Planning a Qualitative Study

Birley and Morgan (1998) posit a series of questions that need to considered in planning a qualitative study:

What are the research questions that are the focus of the interviews? From an assessment perspective, this question relates directly to the question, "What is the problem?" or "What is the purpose of our study?"

Who is the sample? In the development of the assessment project, this question could be reframed as, "What information do we need from our study?"

What interview structure should be used: structured, semistructured, or unstructured? The interview structure can vary from a highly structured format, with precise questions asked of the respondents, to a much more conversational approach, where only a general question might be asked (for example, "What is it like to be a student at this college?") and the interchange follows the direction the interviewees take it.

What should the format be of the different questions and any necessary prompts and follow-up questions? Generally the questions will be framed in such a way as to elicit rich, descriptive responses. Nevertheless, different types of questions generate different kinds of responses.

How will responses be recorded? Various ways of recording the data are available, including taking notes, audio- or videorecording, or some combination of these approaches.

Who should be interviewed (should they be typical of the targeted population, atypical, or both?), and how should they be interviewed? A wide variety of sampling techniques is available to the researchers. These range from simply asking people who can be identified conveniently to participate to other forms of sampling.

How are respondents contacted? Will they be invited by mail, by the telephone, in person, or through some other technique?

Where and how will the interviews be conducted? (formal? informal? at home?) Thought must go into determining where the interviews are conducted to ensure that they will not be disrupted by noise or distractions and or that the facility will prove inadequate (too small, too hot, poorly lit, or otherwise unsuitable). Especially thorough planning is necessary in providing sites for focus groups, for example (Morgan, 1998).

What protocols will be used in producing transcripts? How will the data be recorded. Will transcripts be developed? If so, will verbatim transcripts be developed (Birley and Morgan, 1998)?

Interviews: Individual or Group?

"The most common form of interviewing is individual, face to face verbal interchange, but it can also take the form of face-to-face group interviewing, mailed or self-administered questionnaires, and telephone surveys"

(Fontana and Frey, 1994, p. 361). Central to all forms of interviews "are the trust and rapport to be built with respondents" (Manning, 1992, p. 102).

Individual and group interviews have advantages and disadvantages. Individual interviews give each person interviewed an opportunity to answer each question completely. Rapport can be established more quickly in an individual interview, and the interviewer can focus completely on the respondent's comments rather than having to be concerned about the dynamics of the group. However, interviewing the entire pool of subjects individually can take a great deal of time. Moreover, if a person does not show up for the interview, the interviewer will be wasting an entire interview time period.

Focus group interviews are a structured process for interviewing a small group of individuals. They had their origins in market research but now are used widely in education and social science research (Witkin and Altschuld, 1995).

Group interviews are more efficient than individual interviews for obvious reasons. Among the advantages, according to Fontana and Frey (1994), are that this form of data collection is relatively inexpensive, data rich, flexible, and stimulating to respondents. The group can be conducted even if several people who were expected do not attend. However, group dynamics can be a bit difficult to manage if people are talking to each other, reading, or engaging in disruptive behavior. Fontana and Frey (1994) point out that this form of interviewing takes greater skill on the part of the interviewer, can be dominated by one person, and can lead to groupthink. On the other hand, people in a group can stimulate the thinking of each other, a process that can make for a very rich discussion.

Sampling

Miles and Huberman (1994) have described several key features of sampling. Sampling in this research tradition tends to be purposive, as opposed to random. Samples also tend to be small in number, as opposed to large data sets more commonly found in quantitative inquiries. Patton (1990) identifies a number of different kinds of purposeful sampling approaches:

Typical sampling—samples are selected because they reflect the average person, situation, or instance of the phenomenon of interest (Merriam, 1998). Key informants may be useful in identifying such subjects.

Extreme or deviant case sampling—cases that are rich because they are unusual or special in some unique way.

Intensity sampling—cases that are information rich but are not unusual.

Homogeneous sampling—a small sample of individuals who share common characteristics and describe it in depth.

Stratified, purposeful sampling—consists of taking a sample of above-average, average, and below-average cases.

Criterion sampling—selects subjects on the basis of certain predetermined criteria.

Confirming or disconfirming case sampling—includes subjects who will confirm what has been learned already, or will disconfirm what has been learned; that is, they will disagree with what has been learned.

Opportunistic sampling—requires that the researchers include an unexpected case in the sample because of something that occurs unexpectedly.

Politically sensitive case sampling—included because of the politically sensitive nature of the situation. In a study of student leaders, for example, it would make sense to make sure that the most prominent student leaders on the campus are included on the basis of the positions they hold.

Convenience sampling—a form of sampling that involves selected individuals because they are easy to identify and invite to participate in the study. These students, however, may or may not be able to contribute much to the study.

Snowball or chain sampling—respondents are asked who else among the potential respondent group may be knowledgeable about the subject under study. Merriam (1998) also refers to this form of sampling as *network sampling*.

Regardless of the sampling technique used, the sample should be information rich (Morse, 1994), that is, in a position to be knowledgeable about the topic under consideration.

Weiss's observations (1991, p. 228) are particularly instructive in drawing a sample for a study: "I am also heartened by the widespread recognition today among evaluators, as well as policy researchers and social scientists generally, that research has a political dimension." What this suggests is that in drawing a sample, important political considerations must be taken into account. Failure to do so can doom a study, no matter how pristine the methodology.

One of the questions that arises in sampling is how many individuals should be sampled before enough subjects have been identified. Mathematical formulas can be helpful in answering this question for quantitative studies, but the situation is more ambiguous for qualitative studies. Merriam (1998, p. 64) cites Lincoln and Guba (1985) on this matter and concludes that sampling continues until "a point of saturation or redundancy is reached." (This issue is developed in detail in Chapter Four.)

Developing Interview Questions

Interviews can range from being highly structured to having no structure at all. "Structured interviewing refers to a situation in which an interviewer asks each respondent a series of preestablished questions with a limited set of response categories" (Fontana and Frey, 1994). The nature of the interview structure will depend to a great extent on the nature of the problem. (Chapter Four on developing focus groups provides more information on this topic.)

The moderator of the interview needs to be well prepared for the session and have specialized skills. Not just any person can walk into a room with a group of people and conduct a focus group skillfully. People with academic course work in counseling or other forms of listening skills have good preparation for conducting focus groups. Merriam (1998, p. 85) observes, "Skilled interviewers can do much to effect positive interaction. Being respectful, nonjudgmental, and nonthreatening is a beginning."

Document Review

Documents can provide a rich source of information in the development of a qualitative study. Suppose you were studying the culture of a residence hall and noticed that a large percentage of students had moved to other residence halls on the campus. A review of the forms the students completed giving reasons for choosing to move potentially would be a useful source of information. The data might not provide a complete picture, but they would provide a good place to start the inquiry.

Documents can be divided into two categories: public records and personal documents (Lincoln and Guba, 1985, p. 277). Public records are such items as enrollment reports, magazines, and newspapers; personal documents include letters and photographs (Whitt, 1991, 1992).

Documents have advantages and disadvantages, as is the case for other qualitative methods. Among the strengths of documents are that they are readily available, provide a stable source of data, and are grounded in the setting in which they are found. Conversely, they may be incomplete, reflect the bias of the author, and be nonreactive, meaning that the researcher may not be able to sit down with the author and ask questions about the document (Upcraft and Schuh, 1996).

Determining the authenticity of a document is a crucial step in the use of this form of data for an assessment project. Authenticity refers to whether or not a document is reliable and can be trusted. A number of questions can be raised in determining the authenticity of a document, including the following, based on Whitt (1992) and Merriam (1998):

What is the history of the document?

How did it come into my possession?

What assurances are there that the document is what it purports to be?

Is the document complete? Has it been altered in any way?

Who was the author?

What is the author trying to accomplish?

What were the author's sources of information?

Are any biases evident?

Are there other documents that could provide additional information about the topic?

Additional questions related to documentary analysis are included in Exhibit 3.1.

In conducting a document review, one of the sources that should not be overlooked is the institution's database. The records of many offices can be very helpful in document review. For example, the office of financial aid has

---

EXHIBIT 3.1

Questions to Ask When Analyzing a Document

- What is the complete title of the document?
- Who produced the document?
- For what purpose was the document produced?
- What information is contained in the document?
- Do themes and patterns emerge from the document that are related to the questions guiding the investigation?
- What is the significance of the document for the study?
- Does the document generate further questions?
- Is the document consistent or inconsistent with other sources of information about this investigation?

Source: *Adapted from Whitt, 1992, with permission of the American College Personnel Association.*

information about the relative financial health of the student body, the registrar has materials related to the academic progress of students, and the student health service can provide information related to the physical health of students.

Observations

The third form of data collection that is used commonly in qualitative analysis is observations. "Observational research can vary considerably in its character among different practitioners, through the stages of a research project, in various settings, and depending on the relationship of the researchers to their subjects" (Adler and Adler, 1994, p. 379). Merriam (1998) distinguishes observations from interviews in two ways: observations take place in the field rather than in an interview room, and they reflect an encounter with the phenomenon of interest rather than a second-hand account of the circumstance through the view of an interviewee. Observations may take the form of attending special events, routine activities, or both, depending on the nature of the research (Whitt, 1991).

Researchers can be engaged with the subjects along a wide-ranging continuum. For example, the researchers simply might choose to observe their subjects in the setting and have no interaction with them. At the other end of the continuum is the participant observer, who is immersed in the setting and is engaged with the subjects intensively. Moffatt (1988), for example, lived with students in a residence hall for an extended period of time.

Merriam (1998, pp. 97–98) has identified the elements present in virtually any setting. These provide a good list of items of interest in conducting an observation and include the following:

The physical setting. What is it like, what is its context, how is the space allocated, and what objects are in the setting?

Participants. Who is on the scene, and what are their roles?

Activities and interactions. What is going on, and is there a sequence of activities? How do the people interact with one another?

Conversation. Who talks to whom, and what is the content of the conversation?

Subtle factors. What are the informal and unplanned activities, the symbolic meaning and connotation of words, and the nonverbal communication?

The observer's behavior. What role did the observer play in this setting, and how did he or she affect it?

Conducting an observation is a complex task because so much occurs simultaneously. As a consequence, it is useful to have a way of recording the observations quickly and accurately. At times, videorecording can be helpful, although the value of the use of this equipment has to be balanced with the presumed effect of the recorder on the people to be observed. Also, conversations might not be recorded without sophisticated microphones.

Data Analysis

Analyzing qualitative data is not an easy task. Although computer programs are available to assist in this activity, the process is dissimilar to the way that quantitative data are analyzed. Krueger (1998, p. 5) observes, "Consider the distinction between analysis of words and analysis of numbers. Analysis of numbers can be seductive, because the researcher gains a sense of accomplishment and confidence by knowing the exact nature of the results." On the other hand, Krueger asserts, "The analysis process is like detective work. One looks for clues, but in this case, the clues are trends and patterns that reappear among various focus groups" (p. 6).

Remember that qualitative research takes an inductive approach. That is, theories and hypotheses for explaining behavior and how people make meaning of their circumstances emerge from the data. The data are not gathered to test the hypotheses. As a consequence, looking for patterns and trends among the data, much like Krueger's detective, results in broad concepts about the case. But in the beginning, the data can be messy and difficult to sort.

Among the ways that Merriam (1998) identifies for analyzing data is the constant comparative method. The basic strategy of this method, according to Merriam (p. 159), "is to do just what the name implies—constantly compare." Bits of data are compared across interviews, documents, or observations, and the comparisons that emerge are used to develop categories that are compared with each other. "Comparisons are constantly made within and between levels of conceptualization until a theory can be formulated" (Merriam, 1998, p. 159).

As the interviews are conducted, it is important to look for trends and patterns in the responses from the interview participants. These preliminary constructions can be tested in other interviews and either confirmed or discarded.

Although the process of analyzing data may seem complex, our experience has been that depending on the complexity of the assessment, categories emerge without much difficulty, and trends and patterns are fairly easy to identify. When groups of people are engaged in the assessment, the power of stimulating each other is very helpful in identifying conclusions to draw from the study. As we asserted in our previous book on assessment, "All we can say is that in most instances, it is in fact easier done than said" (Upcraft and Schuh, 1996).

Ensuring Rigor

The question of whether qualitative methods are sufficiently rigorous has been raised from time to time. Lincoln and Guba (1994, p. 651) describe the situation in this way: "Clients and program funders ask whether naturalistic evaluations are not so subjective that they cannot be trusted." They define trustworthiness in this way: "The basic issue in relation to trustworthiness is simple: How can an inquirer persuade his or her audiences (including self) that the findings of an inquiry are worth paying attention to, worth taking account of?" (p. 290). Scott (1991, p. 421) adds, "Some confusion exists concerning the criteria for rigor in naturalistic research. It has been erroneously said that either naturalistic research or laboratory-experimental research is more rigorous than the other. Scientific rigor, however, lies not in the use of one method *versus* another, but in the soundness with which a given method is applied."

Scott (1991) recommends several principles in establishing rigor for a qualitative study:

- The research must be systematic, meaning that it is logical and orderly.

- The research is internally consistent.

- The specific procedures used should be at the highest level and be consistent with the question being asked.

- The research should be open to public inspection, that is, written down and subject to critique.

Adhering to these principles can involve a variety of techniques, among them the following (Lincoln and Guba, 1994):

Prolonged engagement—lengthy and intensive researcher contact with the phenomena or respondents in the field

Persistent observation—in-depth pursuit of salient elements through prolonged engagement

Triangulation of data—the cross-checking of data through different sources, methods, and investigators

Peer debriefing—exposing oneself to a disinterested professional to assist in working through hypotheses and developing and testing the emerging design

Negative case analysis—the active search for negative instances relating to developing insights and adjusting to them until none further are found

Member checks—the continuous testing of information by soliciting the reactions of respondents to the investigator's reconstruction of what has been found and a formal testing of the case report with stakeholders

For transferability, the narrative needs thick descriptive data. Thick descriptions are "detailed descriptions of what was done and why, and of the phenomena studied, including contexts, behaviors, perceptions, feelings, and insights" (Whitt, 1991, p. 412). With a thick description, judgments can be made about whether the findings could be applied in other cases.

To ensure dependability and confirmability, an audit trail needs to be established—that is, a person not associated with the study could review the evidence assembled by the researcher and would reach essentially similar conclusions. Among the elements of the evidence are raw data, products of data analysis, and process notes and intentions of the researcher (Whitt, 1991).

Conclusion

Qualitative methods are extremely effective in the use of assessment projects in student affairs. Although these studies are time-consuming, present challenges in data analysis, and require special skills, they will generate special insights into the object of the assessment. When used in combination with quantitative approaches, qualitative studies will produce assessment projects that will serve student affairs practitioners and the students they serve very well.

References

Adler, P. A., and Adler, P. "Observational Techniques." In N. K. Denzin and Y. S. Lincoln (eds.), *Handbook of Qualitative Research.* Thousand Oaks, Calif.: Sage, 1994.

Birley, G., and Morgan, N. *A Practical Guide to Academic Research.* London: Kogan Page, 1998.

Blaxter, L., Hughes, C., and Tight, M. *How to Research.* Bristol, Pa.: Open University Press, 1996.

Bogdan, R. C., and Biklen, S. K. *Qualitative Research for Education*. (2nd ed.) Needham Heights, Mass.: Allyn & Bacon, 1992.

Carnaghi, J. "Focus Groups: Teachable and Educational Moments for All Involved." In F. K. Stage and Associates, *Diverse Methods for Research and Assessment of College Students*. Washington, D.C.: American College Personnel Association, 1992.

Denzin, N. K., and Lincoln, Y. S. "Entering the Field of Qualitative Research." In N. K. Denzin and Y. S. Lincoln (eds.), *Handbook of Qualitative Research*. Thousand Oaks, Calif.: Sage, 1994.

Fontana, A., and Frey, J. H. "Interviewing: The Art of Science." In N. K. Denzin and Y. S. Lincoln (eds.), *Handbook of Qualitative Research*. Thousand Oaks, Calif.: Sage, 1994.

Gall, M. D., Borg, W. R., and Gall, J. P. *Education Research: An Introduction*. (6th ed.) New York: Longman, 1996.

Krueger, R. A. *Moderating Focus Groups*. Thousand Oaks, Calif.: Sage, 1998.

Lincoln, Y. S., and Guba, E. G. *Naturalistic Inquiry*. Thousand Oaks, Calif.: Sage, 1985.

Lincoln, Y. S., and Guba, E. G. "But Is It Rigorous? Trustworthiness and Authenticity in Naturalistic Evaluation." In J. S. Stark and Alice Thomas (eds.), *Assessment and Program Evaluation*. New York: Simon & Schuster, 1994.

Manning, K. "The Ethnographic Interview." In F. K Stage and Associates, *Diverse Methods for Research and Assessment of College Students*. Washington, D.C.: American College Personnel Association, 1992.

Merriam, S. B. *Qualitative Research and Case Study Applications in Education*. San Francisco: Jossey-Bass, 1998.

Miles, M. B., and Huberman, A. M. *Quantitative Data Analysis*. (2nd ed.) Thousand Oaks, Calif.: Sage, 1994.

Moffatt, M. *Coming of Age in New Jersey*. New Brunswick, N.J.: Rutgers University Press, 1988.

Morgan, D. L. *Planning Focus Groups*. Thousand Oaks, Calif.: Sage, 1998.

Morse, J. M. "Designing Funded Qualitative Research." In N. K. Denzin and Y. S. Lincoln (eds.), *Handbook of Qualitative Research*. Thousand Oaks, Calif.: Sage, 1994.

Patton, M. Q. *Qualitative Research and Evaluation Methods*. Thousand Oaks, Calif.: Sage, 1990.

Punch, M. "Politics and Ethics in Qualitative Research." In N. K. Denzin and Y. S. Lincoln (eds.), *Handbook of Qualitative Research*. Thousand Oaks, Calif.: Sage, 1994.

Richards, T. J., and Richards, L. "Using Computers in Qualitative Research." In N. K. Denzin and Y. S. Lincoln (eds.), *Handbook of Qualitative Research*. Thousand Oaks, Calif.: Sage, 1994.

Scott, M. M. "Naturalistic Research: Applications for Research and Professional Practice with College Students." *Journal of College Student Development*, 1991, *32*, 416–423.

Strauss, A., and Corbin, J. "Grounded Theory Methodology: An Overview." In N. K. Denzin and Y. S. Lincoln (eds.), *Handbook of Qualitative Research*. Thousand Oaks, Calif.: Sage, 1994.

Upcraft, M. L., and Schuh, J. H. *Assessment in Student Affairs: A Guide for Practitioners*. San Francisco: Jossey-Bass, 1996.

Weiss, C. H. "Evaluation Research in the Political Context: Sixteen Years and Four Administrations Later." In M. W. McLaughlin and D. C. Phillips (eds.), *Evaluation and Education: At Quarter Century*. Chicago: National Society for the Study of Education, 1991.

Whitt, E. J. "Artful Science: A Primer on Qualitative Research Methods." *Journal of College Student Development*, 1991, *32*, 406–415.

Whitt, E. J. "Document Analysis." In F. K. Stage and Associates, *Diverse Methods for Research and Assessment of College Students*. Washington, D.C.: American College Personnel Association, 1992.

Witkin, B. R., and Altschuld, J. W. *Planning and Conducting Needs Assessments: A Practical Guide*. Thousand Oaks, Calif.: Sage, 1995.

Worthen, B. R., and Sanders, J. R. *Educational Evaluation: Alternative Approaches and Practical Guidelines*. New York: Longman, 1987.

Suggestions for Further Reading

Banta, T. W., and Associates. *Making a Difference: Outcomes of a Decade of Assessment in Higher Education*. San Francisco: Jossey-Bass, 1993.

Banta, T. W., Lund, J. P., Black, K. E., and Oblander, F. W. *Assessment in Practice: Putting Principles to Work on College Campuses*. San Francisco: Jossey-Bass, 1995.

Denzin, N. K., and Lincoln, Y. S. (eds.). *Handbook of Qualitative Research*. Thousand Oaks, Calif.: Sage, 1994.

Palomba, C. A., and Banta, T. W. *Assessment Essentials: Planning, Implementing, and Improving Assessment in Higher Education*. San Francisco: Jossey-Bass, 1999.

Patton, M. Q. *Qualitative Research and Evaluation Methods*. Thousand Oaks, Calif.: Sage, 1990.

Stark, J. S., and Thomas, A. (eds.). *Assessment and Evaluation*. New York: Simon & Schuster, 1994.

Chapter 4

Conducting
Focus Groups

FOCUS GROUPS ARE an important research method used in many qualitative studies and an important tool in gathering information (although they are not appropriate for all situations). Morgan (1998a) identifies them as appropriate in conducting assessments. In this chapter we discuss how to apply focus groups to specific assessment questions and provide details about how to conduct these groups. As is the case with virtually any other investigatory tool, this approach requires a substantial level of knowledge and sophistication.

Assessors should not assume that they could apply this methodology without proper grounding in focus group techniques. We believe that with proper information and practice, however, those conducting an inquiry can employ focus groups with excellent results.

When to Use Focus Groups

Focus groups are not appropriate for all situations. They work best when the purpose of the assessment is to learn about the perceptions, beliefs, or opinions of the students or others who use campus facilities, services, or programs. They are less useful if the goal is to generate statistical data for comparison across large data sets or institutions. Too often, in our opinion, investigators choose to conduct focus groups because they are more confident in their expertise in this research tradition (qualitative) than in handling large numbers or using sophisticated statistical techniques. That is a poor reason to conduct focus groups. The technique has to fit the assessment problem.

Morgan (1998a) points out that focus groups should be avoided when statistical data are required, the researcher is trying to save time and money, or the topic involves something that the respondents may not be comfortable discussing. In these cases, a different data collection method is appropriate. On the other hand, using focus groups is appropriate when the goal is to pursue questions such as how or why the researcher wants to learn from respondents on the basis of their experiences or wants to plan for programs or other initiatives and is not quite sure where to start (Morgan, 1998a).

Under these guidelines, focus groups would serve an assessment project well if one were trying to determine the reasons that students choose to enroll in one college as opposed to another or choose to live off campus rather than on campus, or describing the culture of Greek letter organizations. Focus groups would not be too useful in a study to compare student perceptions on a specific campus with national norms.

Sampling and Recruiting Participants

Investigators have a wide variety of approaches to sampling. Probably the most fundamental question to ask is: "Who knows something about the topic we are investigating, and why?" From this question, the investigator can develop a sampling approach. Rea and Parker (1997) conclude that "focus groups are more effective when they consist of participants who share many of the same key characteristics. Homogeneous groups tend to exchange ideas and opinions more freely than do groups with widely divergent backgrounds" (p. 84). Birley and Morgan (1998) add that focus groups need to be composed of people who are interested in and knowledgeable about the topic being investigated.

Let us say that an investigator wished to study the effectiveness of the student government senate. In this case, the people to study would be the senators themselves, executive officers of the student government association, members of the student affairs staff who work with the senate, student newspaper reporters who cover the senate, and students at large. This form of sampling, referred to as *purposive sampling*, is used because the goal is to solicit the perceptions of specific groups of people who are well informed about the situation (Merriam, 1998). The investigator might also use *maximum variation sampling* (Merriam, 1998) and try to identify people who know little about the student senate in an effort to determine why they are uninformed. One of the best techniques to use in sampling is to ask participants to identify others who know about the topic under investigation. This form of sampling, referred to as *snowball, chain,* or *network sampling* (Merriam, 1998), has as an advantage that it involves potentially key informants about the topic who have not been invited to participate. In the case of the student senate study, included in this group might be former senators or student body officers who have graduated from the institution but still maintain close ties to student politics.

The number of people to include in a focus group and the number of focus groups is open to debate. Carnaghi (1992) suggests seven to ten people in a focus group, a size with which Gall, Borg, and Gall (1996) agree. Morgan (1998b) suggests that six to ten is a typical group size, although he points out that there may be reasons for having larger or smaller numbers in the group. Smaller groups might make sense when the topic is controversial or complex, if the members are expected to know a lot about the topic, or if they are emotionally caught up in the topic (Morgan, 1998b). For larger groups, the opposite is true.

The number of groups to conduct also is open to question. Rea and Parker (1997) report that the range can be from two to ten to fourteen. Krueger (1998b) indicates that the typical number of groups is three to five, although he notes that more or fewer groups may be conducted depending on the nature of the topic. Merriam (1998) provides excellent advice on this topic: "What is needed is an adequate number of participants, sites, or activities to answer the question posed at the beginning of the study (in the form of a purpose statement)" (p. 64), an observation with which Manning (1992) agrees. Manning adds that respondents can continue to be heard until the multiple perspectives present in the community are represented. Clearly, conducting just one group is a risky practice (Morgan, 1998b). Rather, groups should be conducted until redundancy is reached—that is, until nothing new is being learned.

Contacting people to participate in focus groups can be done in a variety of ways. One approach is to send letters to approximately three times as many volunteers as the study requires and ask that these people call to confirm that they will participate. After the people confirm that they will participate, a postcard reminder should be sent to them. Two days or so before the group is conducted, the people should be called and reminded of the time and place where the group is being conducted and queried as to whether they plan to participate. In spite of this thorough approach to recruiting volunteers, it is still possible that not everyone will participate. As a consequence, it is a good idea to oversubscribe the group by at least 50 percent (receive confirmations from twelve people for a group of eight, for example). Should everyone show up, it is possible to run two groups of six each, but the likelihood that everyone will participate is remote.

Rea and Parker (1997) suggest that 20 to 35 percent of confirmed participants (that is, those who have given assurances they will attend) will not attend focus groups, so that a number larger than the ideal number for the group should be invited. As a consequence, it is best to receive confirmations from a larger number of people for the group than the actual number planned. Since they suggest that a typical group is eight to twelve in size, confirmations should be received from fifteen participants. Morgan (1998a), on the other hand, recommends that six to ten persons form a typical focus group, although he reminds the group organizer that the larger the group is, the less time there will be available for each person to talk.

Krueger (1998b) offers several excellent suggestions about planning focus groups to make sure that participation is at a high level. He urges that the times of the focus groups do not conflict with events in the community. If Greek letter organizations have their chapter meetings on Monday nights, that is a poor time to schedule focus groups if participation by Greeks is important. Similarly, certain times in the academic calendar are inconvenient for students, such as just before midterm or final examinations or holiday breaks. Scheduling groups during homecoming or spring festivals also can be a poor time to conduct groups, especially if these events involve a large number of student participants. Krueger (1998b) recommends personalizing the invitation and also telephoning participants the day before the event to remind them of their intention to attend.

Managing Focus Groups

Rea and Parker (1997) suggest that the site of the focus group be easily accessible (and accessible for people with disabilities), convenient, and in a well-known place. Morgan (1998b) adds a series of items to consider in selecting a site:

- Make sure that parking is adequate.
- Check that participants are able to see and hear each other.
- Keep distractions, such as the noise level, to a minimum.
- Provide comfortable chairs.
- Determine whether sufficient electrical outlets are available for any equipment that will be used (for example, tape recorders).
- Develop a plan for handling late arrivals.
- Identify a process for serving refreshments if they are to made available to the participants.

Gall, Borg, and Gall (1996) offer several recommendations on how to encourage people to serve as volunteers for studies. Among these are to make the appeal nonthreatening, emphasize the benefit that others may realize from the study being conducted, and make the process as interesting as possible. Having snacks and drinks is always a good idea, and at times, the focus group can be built around a pizza party.

The length of time it will take the group to move through its discussion varies. Our general experience is that a group of six to ten students can complete its work in about an hour, a time frame with which Manning (1992) agrees.

Equipment

Rea and Parker (1997) advise that all equipment be in place before the session begins. Krueger (1998b) suggests a list of equipment that may be essential to the success of a focus group:

- Cassette tape recorder
- Microphone
- Microphone extension cord and electrical extension cord
- Blank index cards for "name tents" (outward-facing place cards)
- Extra batteries for tape recorder
- Blank cassette tapes
- Marking pens
- Writing tables and pens for the moderator and assistant
- Copies of the interview protocol
- List of names, addresses (postal and e-mail), and telephone numbers of participants
- Pens or pencils and small tablets for participants
- Handouts, prototypes, rating forms
- Duct tape to secure electrical cords
- Masking tape to hang material on walls
- Box of tissues
- Flip chart

Many things can go wrong with equipment. The batteries of the recorder can fail at just the wrong time, for example, or the tape can run out at a strategic moment. Krueger (1998b) lists some other equipment problems, including pushing the wrong button on the recorder, plugging the microphone into the ear jack, or the recorder gets unplugged and no one notices.

The point is that relying entirely on technology can be a problem, especially if an assistant is not available to take notes. We recommend that even if the session is recorded, that a person be available to take notes.

One of the equipment-related issues to be resolved in planning to lead groups is whether to tape-record the sessions. Some form of record needs to be kept as to what is going on in the group, and it can be very difficult for the moderator to take notes and lead the group simultaneously. Even if an assistant moderator takes notes, content might be missed. At times, concerns are expressed that students will not participate as openly if they know they are being recorded. On the other hand, it can be difficult to understand everything that is going on in the discussion without some form of record. For this reason, we advise that group sessions be tape-recorded, with the participants' permission. The recordings can be played back at another time and are available to be transcribed for further study and analysis. It can also be useful to have a student (not a member of the group) listen to the tape to help interpret what has been said. This is especially true if students speak in slang terms that might not be familiar to the moderator. Typically tapes are not transcribed due to cost and time, but in some cases, transcribing will be important if verbatim student quotations are to be used in the final report.

Compensation

At times, the question of whether to offer compensation for participation arises. We believe that compensation is appropriate, but we recommend that rather than offering cash payments, a coupon worth a certain value at the campus bookstore or snack shop is a good strategy. With this approach, the money stays within the institution. At times the proprietor of, say, the campus snack shop may offer a discount from the face value of the coupon to the department conducting the assessment; for example, a discount coupon worth a dollar is charged at a fifty-cent rate to the sponsoring department.

Interview Structure

The structure of the interview depends on the purpose of the study, the extent to which specific answers are sought from the participants, or whether the investigator is simply trying to develop some general ideas on the topic. Manning (1992) provides helpful advice on the amount of structure in developing an interview protocol. She observes that the role of the researcher is "to strike a balance between overstructuring the interview such that theory and a priori assumptions guide the research and understructuring the interview such that the interview is not focused and becomes useless as data collection" (1992, p. 96).

Highly structured or standardized interviews are those in which the wording of the questions and their order are predetermined. In many respects, this is the oral form of a survey. Highly structured interviews minimize interviewer errors (Fontana and Frey, 1994). More structured interviews include more questions, according to Krueger (1998b), and the role of the moderator is to be relatively directive in keeping the group on topic.

Unstructured and informal interviews "are particularly useful when the researchers does not know enough about a phenomenon to ask relevant questions. Thus, there is no predetermined set of questions. and the interview is essentially exploratory" (Merriam, 1998, pp. 74–75). An unstructured interview is more like a conversation and, according to Merriam (1998), can be used to learn enough to ask good questions in other situations. Morgan (1998b) suggests that it is unlikely that a focus group could be conducted with only one question. His view is that less structured focus groups should pose three to five questions.

Somewhere between these two ends of the continuum is the semistructured interview, with a mix of open-ended questions and semistructured questions. Our general view is that this middle ground serves the interviewer well and is the desired approach, consistent with the advice of Whitt (1991), who, agreeing with Merriam (1988), concludes that semistructured interviews, which suggest questions and issues that should be explored but do not prescribe their order or wording, are most typical of qualitative studies.

For example, Exhibit 4.1 sets out some typical unstructured and structured questions for focus groups in a study intended to explore senior students' perceptions of their academic experiences.

Wording of Questions

Good, easy-to-understand questions are essential in conducting interviews. Several concepts are useful in this process.

Clear Questions

The use of acronyms, abbreviations, or jargon may lose the respondents. Terms such as *self-actualization* and *identity development* may fit very nicely in an interview with people who are conversant about student development theory, but in an interview with students, it would be much more useful to ask what the students have learned from an experience or if their plans have

---

EXHIBIT 4.1

Typical Unstructured and Structured Questions for a Focus Group on Student Perceptions

Typical Unstructured Questions

When you think of your academics at the college, what pops into your mind?

Are there any special highlights of your academics that stick out in your mind?

As you reflect on your academics, what might have been disappointing to you?

What else would like to tell me about your academic experiences at the college?

Typical Structured Questions

Why did you choose to attend this college? What role did academic matters play in this decision?

What major did you choose? Why did you select this major?

What has been your favorite class? Why?

Can you pinpoint two or three things you found disappointing in your academic work?

What have been your experiences with computer support on campus?

In what ways do you use the library? How you been satisfied with the support available there?

If you were to identify three very important things you have learned in class, what would they be?

What would you say to a prospective first-year student about academics at the college?

---

changed based on their participation in an activity. Similarly, staff might refer to the Office of Counseling and Human Development Services as CHDS, but students may have no idea what the abbreviation stands for, so using the full name or a shortened version of it (the Counseling Center) is a much better strategy in an interview.

Open-Ended Questions

Open-ended questions allow the respondents to take the discussion in whatever direction they choose. For example, rather than asking, "How happy are you with the programs of the student activities center?" one might ask, "Tell me about the programs of the student activities center." If an evaluation of the student activities center is an important feature of the study, the discussion can be moved in that direction as the interview proceeds.

Merriam (1998) identified four types of questions that are useful in eliciting information from respondents, drawn from an interview of students regarding recreation programs on campus:

5. Summary questions follow an oral summary provided by the moderator of the interview. Example: "Did I correctly summarize what you told me about the counseling center?"

6. Final questions provide the last chance to gather information. Example: "Is there anything we should have discussed about the counseling center but didn't?"

Other classic questions have great utility for focus groups. Following are several, continuing with the example of a discussion of a counseling center:

"If you were in charge of the counseling center for a day and had the authority to change everything, what would be the one thing you would not change?"

"If you were in charge of the counseling center for a day and had the authority to change everything, what would be the first thing you would change?"

"If your brother or sister asked you if it was a good idea to use the counseling center, what would say?"

"What do you want to tell me about the counseling center that I have not asked?"

Conducting the Group

Rea and Parker (1997) and Krueger (1998b) advise beginning the group with a welcoming statement, a statement of the subject matter to be covered, and an explanation of the rules for the discussion. To this, we would add that this is an appropriate time to discuss the voluntary nature of participation in the group and to make sure that each person has completed a consent form before the discussion begins.

Krueger (1998b) provides some other information for guidelines for discussion. He notes that the moderator should indicate if the session is being recorded, should explain that observations of the participants will not be attributed to a specific person, and should identify the sponsor of the study. In a discussion of why students enrolled at a specific college, the introduction might go like this:

Welcome to our session. I am very glad that you have taken time out today to visit with us. This session is being tape-recorded so that I can make sure to be as accurate as possible in writing my report. What we are doing is visiting with a number of students at the college about why they chose to enroll here. I will be preparing a report for the college's steering committee on recruitment and admission, but I want to assure you that I will not attribute anything you say directly to you. Please understand that you may leave the group at any time and that your participation is strictly voluntary. You have a form in front of you that I ask you to sign before we move ahead. It indicates that you understand the voluntary nature of your participation and that you may leave at any time. Do you have any questions at this point?

Krueger (1998b) also indicates that at times he includes a brief discussion on the role of the moderator and explains that people can respond to one another but that only one person can talk at a time. Also, the concept that there are no wrong answers should be emphasized and that everyone is on a first-name basis.

Moderator Characteristics and Skills

Krueger (1998b) identifies several characteristics of focus group moderators:

The moderator must have an interest in the participants. An individual who cannot listen attentively and with sensitivity should not moderate a group. College students can have strong opinions that may or may not be based on fact—for example, "The faculty do not care about the students" or "Food service uses poor-quality ingredients in preparing the food." Even if the moderator knows better, this person needs to listen attentively and conduct the group with positive regard for the participants.

The moderator needs to be a moderator, not a participant. It is difficult to listen to students offer observations about college life when you know they are not informed—for example, "It is too bad we don't have anyone here to work with pre-med majors" when you know the pre-med adviser. The temptation to correct the participants must be resisted. The moderator conducts the interview and remains neutral regardless of the accuracy or tenor of the information.

Unpleasant views must be heard. Students can be highly critical about the campus in a pejorative way—for example, "Nobody knows what they are doing around here, and besides that, the faculty are way overpaid." Rather than debating these observations, the moderator might follow up with a simple question such as, "Tell us more about why you feel that way."

Not every person can moderate all groups. It is difficult to moderate groups when the topic is something about which the potential moderator has strong opinions. For example, it can be difficult for the chair of a department to moderate a group that deals with the evaluation of that person's department. In addition to the obvious conflict of interest, the temptation to respond to criticism can be especially difficult to overcome. Issues related to race or gender might get in the way of moderating a group, and so it might be difficult for a male to moderate a group dealing with the topic of what it is like to be a female student on campus. In these instances, it is appropriate to use other individuals as moderators.

Moderators must have good communications skills and an understanding of the group process. Individuals with training in counseling or psychology are excellent candidates to serve as moderators of groups, since their academic preparation has provided them with background information about group process.

Faculty members can be used as moderators of focus groups, but they need to be reminded that they are to act as group leaders, not educators. For example, suppose a student participant in the group indicates that one of the reasons that she is planning on transferring to another college is that this university does not have a major in forestry. The faculty member, knowing that the college has a major in forestry, might be tempted to correct the student and refer her to the appropriate office for information. That is not the role of the moderator, and the temptation to educate the group must be resisted. The focus group is not a classroom for the faculty member.

A useful strategy can be to have an assistant or co-moderator for the focus group. This person can take notes, help clarify when answers are difficult to follow, and provide technical assistance, such as if a tape-recorder breaks down. Students can be employed very effectively in this role. As they become more comfortable with the process, they might even switch roles with the faculty or staff member as moderator and lead a group.

Analyzing Focus Group Data

Data analysis after conducting focus groups is the next step in this process, although it is important to remember that data are collected and analyzed virtually simultaneously in conducting focus groups. It is very important to summarize notes and jot down impressions after each group. To wait until all the groups have been conducted to sharpen notes and begin to draw conclusions may result in important points being forgotten.

Assuming that an assistant has been present at the session, the moderator and assistant can debrief each other right after the session, always remembering to make notes of the debriefing. In this way, initial impressions can be captured and committed to the record. Krueger (1998a, p. 50) offers a list of questions to consider in the debriefing process:

- *What are the most important themes or ideas discussed?*
- *How did these differ from what we expected?*
- *How did these differ from what occurred in earlier focus groups?*
- *What points need to be included in the report?*
- *What quotes should be remembered and possibly included in the report?*
- *Should we do anything differently for the next focus group?*

Merriam (1998, pp. 183–184) identifies some guidelines related to developing categories in analyzing data. The categories should reflect the purpose of the research, and they should be exhaustive (meaning complete), mutually exclusive (meaning that no categories overlap), sensitizing (meaning that the category is as sensitive as possible), and conceptually congruent (meaning that all categories of information are at the same level of abstraction). Further discussion of data analysis is available from Whitt (1991).

We advise reading the section related to data analysis in Chapter Three for additional ideas about how to analyze focus group data.

Conclusion

Conducting focus groups takes a great deal of expertise. We believe that the best way for a person to gain this expertise is to serve as an assistant moderator working with an experienced person and observing his or her techniques. Collection of data through the use of focus groups can yield extremely useful information in the assessment process, and for that reason, we urge investigators to add this approach to their portfolio of assessment skills.

We want to acknowledge the Focus Group Kit, a six-volume set prepared by Morgan and Krueger (1998). This complete discussion of focus groups is particularly useful for those who are embarking on data collection using this technique.

References

Birley, G., and Morgan, N. *A Practical Guide to Academic Research.* London: Kogan Page, 1998.

Carnaghi, J. E. "Focus Groups: Teachable and Educational Moments for All Involved." In F. K. Stage and Associates, *Diverse Methods for Research and*

Assessment of College Students. Washington, D.C.: American College Personnel Association, 1992.

Fontana, A., and Frey, J. H. "Interviewing: The Art of Science." In N. K. Denzin and Y. S. Lincoln (eds.), *Handbook of Qualitative Research.* Thousand Oaks, Calif.: Sage, 1994.

Gall, M. D., Borg, W. R., and Gall, J. P. *Education Research: An Introduction.* (6th ed.) New York: Longman, 1996.

Krueger, R. A. *Analyzing and Reporting Focus Group Results.* Thousand Oaks, Calif.: Sage, 1998a.

Krueger, R. A. *Moderating Focus Groups.* Thousand Oaks, Calif.: Sage, 1998b.

Manning, K. "The Ethnographic Interview." In F. K. Stage and Associates, *Diverse Methods for Research and Assessment of College Students.* Washington, D.C.: American College Personnel Association, 1992.

Merriam, S. B. *Qualitative Research and Case Study Applications in Education.* San Francisco: Jossey-Bass, 1998.

Morgan, D. L. *The Focus Group Guidebook.* Thousand Oaks, Calif.: Sage, 1998a.

Morgan, D. L. *Planning Focus Groups.* Thousand Oaks, Calif.: Sage, 1998b.

Morgan, D. L., and Krueger, R. A. *The Focus Group Kit.* Thousand Oaks, Calif.: Sage, 1998.

Rea, L. M., and Parker, R. A. *Designing and Conducting Survey Research: A Comprehensive Guide.* (2nd ed.) San Francisco: Jossey-Bass, 1997.

Whitt, E. J. "Artful Science: A Primer on Qualitative Research Methods." *Journal of College Student Development,* 1991, *32,* 406–415.

Chapter 5

Designing and Selecting Quantitative Instruments

ONCE A DECISION has been made to use a quantitative approach to a study, the next decision is to identify what instrument will be used to gather data: a commercially developed instrument or a locally developed one. If a locally developed instrument is chosen, how do you go about developing a good one? This chapter provides a basis for making these very important decisions.

Criteria for Choosing Between Locally or Commercially Developed Instruments

Ory (1994) identified six factors by which locally developed instruments (LDIs) may be compared and contrasted with commercially developed instruments (CDIs): purpose, match, logistics, institutional acceptance, quality, and respondent motivation to return the instrument.

Purpose

Probably the most important criterion for determining which type of instrument to select is the purpose of the study. Why are we doing this study, and how will the results be used? If one of the reasons is to compare the results with other institutions or national standards ("We want to compare our students' overall satisfaction with their collegiate experience to students attending similar institutions"), then CDIs are the only choice. But if such comparisons are not relevant to the study ("We simply need to know our students' overall satisfaction with their collegiate experience so that we may target areas of improvement"), then an LDI may do just as well. Further, if the purpose is to track institutional patterns over several generations of students ("We want to know if students enrolled at our institution today are more or less satisfied with their collegiate experience compared to those five years ago"), then an LDI can be used.

Match

A second criterion for determining what type of instrument to select is whether there is a CDI available that well matches the purpose of the study. Sometimes there are no CDIs that meet the study's purposes, and sometimes a CDI is available but the match is not perfect; it may ask some questions that are irrelevant to the study or fail to ask questions pertinent to the study. For example, if the goal is to assess student needs in the broadest sense, then one of several CDIs available might serve this purposes. If, however, if the goal is to assess the needs of specific subpopulations of students unique to the institution (for example, working single mothers, biracial students, certificate program students) and there is no CDI, then an LDI that can be tailored specifically to these students is probably required. There are CDIs that allow for some locally developed questions, but that still does not overcome the problem of asking questions that are irrelevant to the study.

Logistics

Ory (1994) identifies ten logistical considerations in comparing LDIs with CDIs:

Availability. Is there a CDI that fits the purposes of our study? Is it readily available? Can it be easily adapted to meet our needs? If the answer to these questions is yes, a CDI may be the better choice.

Preparation time. Is there enough time to construct and pilot a LDI to conduct the study in a timely fashion? If we need to do a study by a certain deadline, we may not have enough time to construct a LDI. LDIs take a considerable amount of time to develop, sometimes even months.

Expertise. LDIs require substantial expertise in their development. Psychometric properties such as reliability, validity, and factor analysis of items require the use of professionals with considerable expertise in instrument development. One may expect that CDIs are psychometrically sound, although the test manual should be reviewed to make certain that this is the case.

Cost. Constructing LDIs requires a considerable expenditure of money for instrument development, ensuring appropriate psychometric properties, scoring and recording data, and reporting findings. CDIs can usually be purchased at a reasonable cost, and the price often includes scoring and reporting services. However, CDIs represent a continuing cost if they are used in repeated administrations, whereas constructing LDIs is a one-time expenditure.

Scoring. Scoring of LDIs can often be immediate if there are campus resources available to scan questionnaires. Scoring of CDIs often may be delayed for weeks if the instruments must be sent to the publisher.

Testing time. If LDIs are used, the testing time can be controlled, consistent with the purposes of the study and the respondents' time availability and tolerance. With CDIs, the testing time is fixed, which could affect the rate of return. Even a perfectly matched CDI may not be useful because it takes too long for respondents to fill out. Our experience has been that instruments that take longer than ten minutes to fill out will have a significantly lower rate of return.

Test and question types. LDIs allow flexibility in the type of test (objective or open ended) and the type of questions asked (multiple choice, rank ordering, true-false, agree-disagree, and so on), whereas with CDI, the type of test and questions are predetermined.

Ease in administration. LDIs allow for flexibility in administering the instrument, and test administrators may not need special training. Because CDIs often require standardized administration, test administrators may need to be specially trained.

Availability of norms. LDIs allow for intra-institutional comparisons only, while CDIs allow for national and interinstitutional comparisons.

Reporting. LDIs allow for institutionally tailored reporting of results, whereas CDIs use standard formats that are not necessarily appropriate to a particular institution.

Institutional Acceptance

A fourth important criterion that Ory (1994) suggested is which type of instrument will have the greater acceptability by intended audiences. LDIs can encourage local ownership and acceptance, but quality concerns may reduce their credibility. CDIs may have a national reputation for quality that may make them more respectable and therefore enhance local acceptance. Even if LDIs are well constructed and psychometrically sound, CDIs may have more face credibility with certain audiences, such as faculty, governing boards, graduates, and state legislatures.

Quality

In many ways, the quality of a study is very much dependent on the quality of the instrument used. Even if all the other parts of a study are credible (design, sampling, data analysis, and so on), a poor-quality instrument alone can ruin a study. Because CDIs almost always have better psychometrics (evidence of validity, reliability, item differentiation, and so on) than do LDIs, they are almost always of higher quality than LDIs. That is not to say that LDIs are always significantly lower in quality than CDIs. It does mean, however, that if LDIs are used, there must be some effort to ensure their quality by subjecting them to standard psychometric procedures, if time allows.

Respondent Motivation to Return the Instrument

Is an LDI or a CDI more likely to produce the highest response rate among potential respondents? While there may be no appreciable difference, there is the possibility that one or the other might lead to a higher response rate. For example, while CDIs may have more instant credibility with potential respondents, LDIs, because of their local specificity, may yield a higher response rate.

Overcoming the Limitations of the Choice

In the end, we must carefully consider all of the criteria, determining their priority based on the purpose of the study and local circumstances. But a choice has to be made, and then the problem becomes overcoming any limitations of that choice.

Let us assume that you have chosen a CDI. Prus and Johnson (1994) suggest the following ways of reducing the disadvantages of CDIs:

Choose the instrument carefully, and only after affected stakeholders (students, faculty, or others) have reviewed available instruments and determined a satisfactory degree of match between the test and the purpose of the study.

Request and review technical data, especially reliability and validity data and information on the normative sample from test publishers.

Use on-campus measurement experts to review reports of test results and create more customized summary reports for various audiences.

Choose tests that provide criterion-referenced results, that is, the extent to which the test measures some well-defined knowledge, skill, or competency.

Ensure that CDIs are only one aspect of a multimethod assessment approach in which no firm conclusions based on norm-referenced data are reached without cross-validation from other sources.

Prus and Johnson (1994) conclude that CDIs are relatively quick, easy, and inexpensive, but useful mostly when group-level performance and external comparisons of results are required. The are not as useful for individual student or program evaluation.

Now let us assume we have chosen a LDI but want to reduce its disadvantages. Prus and Johnson (1994) identify several ways:

Enter into a consortium with other departments or institutions with assessment needs as a means of reducing costs associated with developing LDIs. Such collaboration may also improve the quality of the instrument by adding an element of external review.

Use on-campus measurement experts for test construction and validation.

Contract with faculty members to consult on development and grading.

Involve faculty, students, community leaders, and other stakeholders in the instrument development process. This involvement will not only improve the quality of the instrument, but will help build local confidence in and acceptability of the instrument.

Validate the results through cross-validation from other data and sources. This will strengthen the credibility of the results with audiences who may lack confidence in findings generated from LDIs.

Prus and Johnson (1994) conclude that LDIs are most useful for individual student or program evaluation, with careful adherence to measurement principles, and must be supplemented for external validity.

Developing a Quantitative Instrument

Let us assume you have decided to develop your own instrument. Our first and strongest recommendation is that you do so under the guidance of a measurement expert. Such an expert can help you along the way, as well as conduct postinstrument analysis on psychometric properties such as reliability, validity, or other psychometric issues. (Since we do not cover this topic in this chapter, readers should consult Gall, Borg, and Gall, 1996.)

Suskie (1992) advises that a quantitative instrument should have the following qualities:

Is considerate of respondents. This includes length (the shorter, the better), clarity, sequencing of items, and ease of completion *and* return.

Appears professional to respondents. A professional instrument asks interesting and important-sounding questions, reproduces the instrument on high-quality paper with readable print, and avoids grammatical and spelling errors.

Has clearly stated and understood items. This includes keeping the items short, readable, interesting, and specific. Each item should ask only one question, and all assumptions, definitions, and qualifiers should be clear. Perhaps most important, items should not be loaded, leading, or biased.

Elicits consistent responses (has reliability). This usually means that similar questions should elicit similar responses. To determine reliability, one should ask at least two questions on the same subject. To keep the instrument short, however, this may not be possible.

Measures what it says it measures (has validity). Ideally, each respondent should interpret each question in the same way, which means that questions must be consistently clear. Also, items should have an intuitive relationship to the purpose of the study. This relationship can be tested by a pilot case.

Has properly ordered items. The first items should be chosen with care. They should be intriguing, easy to answer, general, and impersonal. This means that demographic inquiries such as gender, age, and major should *not* go first. Remaining items should follow a natural flow, both logically and psychologically.

Avoids contingency questions (those where if the respondent checks yes to one question, he or she is directed to go to another set of questions). Contingency questions can be frustrating and confusing. If you have several questions that you want only a small group to answer, put them at the end of the instrument, and tell everyone else to stop before reaching them. Even better, send this group a separate instrument.

Steps in the Development of a Quantitative Instrument

Step 1: Determine What Information Is Needed

Look at the purposes of the study, and determine what information is needed. The best way to make this determination is to ask: What information do we need to solve the problem that initiated the study? For example, if the problem is student alcohol abuse, then we will need specific information about this issue. Patton (1990) identifies six kinds of information that can be gathered:

Experience and behavior information—probes what a respondent does or has done, with the aim of eliciting descriptions of experiences, behaviors, actions, or activities. For example, it may be helpful to study students' alcohol use and abuse patterns or students' experiences as a person from a racial or ethnic minority in a predominantly white institution.

Opinion and values information—helps us understand the cognitive and interpretive processes of respondents. These questions tell us what people think about certain issues, including their goals, intentions, desires, and values. For example, we may want to know how students who use the recreation facility rate its effectiveness, or what students believe they have learned by participating in leadership positions in student government.

Information about feelings—the emotional reactions respondents have to their experiences and thoughts. In asking feeling questions, we are looking for adjectives that describe emotions such as anxiety, confidence, anger, frustration, and elation. Unfortunately, feelings and opinions are often confused. For example, "Did you feel you had difficulty getting an appointment at the counseling center to discuss your alcohol abuse problem?" is really an opinion, not a feeling (in this context *feel* means "believe" or "think"). "How did you feel when you had difficulty getting an appointment at the counseling center?" gets at the respondent's emotions in that situation.

Information about respondents' knowledge—helps the investigator find out what factual information the respondent has. This information is often important to student affairs practitioners who are concerned about whether students know about various services, programs, and facilities and whether their knowledge is accurate. For example, we may want to know if students are familiar with the fee structure in the health center, or if they have accurate information about how AIDS is transmitted.

Sensory information—what respondents have seen, heard, touched, tasted, and smelled. The purpose of gathering this information is to explore the respondents' sensory apparatus. Technically, sensory data are behavioral data, but they are sufficiently different to merit a separate category. For example, we might want to know if students have temporary problems with their hearing after attending a rock concert, or what kinds of smells emanate from the campus waste disposal plant.

Background and demographic information—identifies the characteristics of the respondent, such as age, major, race or ethnicity, gender, and class standing. If respondents have been selected from an institutional database, it may not be necessary to collect the information from the instrument questions.

Step 2: Decide the Format of the Questions

Although most quantitative surveys ask closed-ended questions that force the respondent to choose from a list of alternative answers, it is possible to ask a limited number of open-ended questions as well. However, for the purposes of this chapter, we will assume that we have decided to use only closed-ended questions.

Step 3: Decide on the Measurement Scale

According to Terenzini and Upcraft (1996), considerable thought must be given to how the array of possible answers in a quantitative instrument is constructed. They identify four measurement scales.

Nominal Scales

These scales categorize objects; they "name" them. Thus, gender, race or ethnicity, religious preference, and type of institution are all nominal variables. An object is in a category (and is "scored" accordingly because it possesses the trait or characteristic that defines the category), or it is not. No ordering along any dimension is implied. Yes-no responses also fall into this category. Obviously, if one responds yes to a question, then one cannot respond no.

Examples

I like the taste of beer.   ___ Yes   ___ No

Please indicate your gender.   ___ Female   ___ Male

In another form of a nominal scale, the respondent is asked to check off one or more characteristics from a list of several possible responses. In effect, we are asking the respondent to indicate yes (by checking off an item) or no (by leaving it blank).

Examples

When I am intoxicated, I generally feel (check more than one if appropriate):

___ Angry ___ Frustrated ___ Apathetic ___ Anxious

___ Elated ___ Relaxed ___ Confident ___ Assertive ___ Sleepy

___ Sexy ___ Pumped Up ___ Stupid ___ Embarrassed ___ Sick

___ Depressed

___ Other (Please specify) _____

Please indicate your race or ethnicity (check all that apply):

___ African American   ___ Hispanic

___ White   ___ Other (specify) _____

___ Asian American

___ Native American Indian

Ordinal Scales

These scales rank-order objects according to the amount they possess of the defining characteristic of the variable. For example, the order of finish in a horse race is an ordinal variable. Ordinal variables reflect varying amounts or levels on the variable (rankings from high to low), but the measure has no absolute zero (we do not know if an object has none of the property; does the horse finishing last never enter the race?). Moreover, the intervals between the ranking in ordinal variables are not the same from one point to the next: we know nothing about how far ahead the winning horse was from the one that finished second. Nor do we know if that distance was the same as between the third and fourth horse, and so on down the line.

Examples

Please rank-order the information you need to know about alcohol, with 1 being your first priority, 2 your second, and so on.

___ Factors that affect the rate of absorption of alcohol into my bloodstream

___ Penalties for violating under-age drinking laws

___ Percentage of alcohol in various drinks

___ Definition of alcohol abuse

___ Alcohol and sex

___ Alcohol and interpersonal relations

___ Other (please specify) _____

Please rank-order your on-campus living preferences for next year, with 1 being your first priority, 2 the second, as so on:

___ Single room

___ Double room

___ Suite (two double rooms separated by a bathroom)

___ One-bedroom apartment

___ Multiple-bedroom apartment

Interval Scales

Like ordinal scales, interval scales can be used to rank-order objects or people according to some trait they possess, but interval variables have the added advantage of equal interval score values. The numerically equal distances on such scales are presumed to reflect equal differences in the property being measured. Thus, the difference between 1 and 2 is presumed to be the same as that between 4 and 5. Although Likert-type scales (where, say, 1= strongly agree, 2 = agree, 3 = no opinion, 4 = disagree, and 5 = strongly agree) are, strictly speaking, ordinal scales, they are often treated like interval scales when conducting statistical analyses. In non-Likert interval scales, we define possible answers, but the distances between responses are still presumed to be equal.

Likert Scale Examples

Abortion should remain legal:

___ Strongly agree ___ Agree ___ Neither agree nor disagree
___ Disagree ___ Strongly disagree

Non–Likert Scale Example

The legal definition of driving while intoxicated is a blood alcohol content of:

___ 15 ___ 12 ___ 10 ___ 07 ___ 05

Please rate your satisfaction with the various services offered by the Career Placement Service on a scale of 1 to 5, with 1 indicating very dissatisfied, 2 indicating dissatisfied, 3 indicating neither satisfied nor dissatisfied, 4 indicating satisfied, and 5 indicating very satisfied:

___ Scheduling interviews

___ Interview facilities

___ Advanced screening of applicants

___ Information about companies

___ Clerical staff cooperation

___ Placement staff cooperation

___ Vacancy listings

___ Overall quality of placement services

___ Other (specify) _____

We advise against rating alternatives that are not defined. For example, we may ask students to rate their satisfaction with a particular service on a scale of 1 to 5, with 1 indicating "very dissatisfied" and 5 indicating "very satisfied." The problem is that when a respondent answers 3, we have no precise interpretation of what a 3 means. It could mean "somewhat satisfied," "somewhat dissatisfied, "neither satisfied nor dissatisfied," or even "no opinion."

We also advise against "forcing" a student to choose a positive or negative response. For example, we may ask students to rate their satisfaction with a particular service by indicating only degrees of satisfaction or dissatisfaction. There are almost always some students who are genuinely ambivalent about their satisfaction with a service or program, and forcing them to one side or the other yields invalid responses.

And finally, there may be some students who have used some services and not others, so they have no basis for rating their satisfaction with some services. When appropriate, items should allow respondents to indicate a "no basis" answer as well.

Ratio Scales

Ratio scales are the highest form of measurement. They have all the ordering characteristics of nominal, ordinal, and interval scales, plus the advantage of having an empirically meaningful zero. Family income, age, years of formal schooling completed, number of times a students meets with a faculty member—all are variables measured on a ratio scale. Also, for analysis purposes, ratio scales may be converted to ordinal scales. We may ask the respondent to indicate his or her age but we later aggregate these data by age categories, such as under 18, 18–22, 23–25, and over 25.

Examples

Please indicate the number of times you visited the student union in the last seven days: ___

Please indicate your age: ___

Choosing a Scale

When to use each of these scales is dependent on the purpose of the study, and it is possible to use one or more in a single study. However, as Terenzini and Upcraft (1996) point out, these measurement scales are also important because the types of statistical analyses chosen are in part determined by the measurement scales used. For example, if we want to know the average response to a question (mean), then we can use only interval or ratio scales. (For further information on this point, for both descriptive and inferential analyses, see Terenzini and Upcraft, 1996.)

Step 4: Determine the Wording of the Questions

Too often locally developed instruments fail because of the question wording. Blaxter, Hughes, and Tight (1996) offer the following hints on wording of questions.

Avoid ambiguous or imprecise questions. Nothing can wreck a response quicker or better than questions that are not clear. For example, if the purpose of the instrument is to determine the extent to which students use campus recreation facilities, we could ask:

My friends often use campus recreation facilities.

___ Yes ___ No ___ I don't know

This is an imprecise question in least two ways. First, the respondent has no clear definition of what "often" means: Twice a day? Twice a week? Second, on some campuses, there may be several campus recreation facilities, and thus the respondent may not clearly understand which facilities the question is asking about. Third, "my friends" is subject to a wide variety of interpretation: just student friends or all friends? A better question might be:

I use the Smith Recreation Facility:

___ Not at all ___ Once a semester ___ Once a month

___ Once a week ___ 2 to 4 times a week ___ Daily

In this question, the people who are using the facility are narrowed to the respondent, the facility is clearly identified, and the amount of usage is specified.

Avoid questions that require recalling things that occurred long ago. Let us assume that we want to know something more about student use of alcohol before they came to college. For students who admitted using alcohol, we could ask:

At what age did you first use alcohol?___

This questions assumes that the respondent can recall precisely the age at which he or she first used alcohol. The respondent may not remember the precise age, but may be able to recall more general time periods:

I first used alcohol when I was in:

___ Elementary school ___ Middle school

___ High school ___ College

This question gives the respondent some latitude in defining when he or she started using alcohol, thereby not forcing him or her to recall the exact age.

Avoid asking two questions in the same question. This error is probably the most common of all in developing instrument questions. If the purpose of the study is to learn more about a student's rating of services received at the counseling center, then we could ask:

The counselor I saw was friendly and helpful.

___ Strongly agree ___ Agree ___ No basis ___ Disagree
___ Strongly disagree

The problem, of course, is that the respondent may believe the counselor was very friendly but not very helpful so how should he or she answer the question? A better way of getting to this information is to ask two questions: one about counselor friendliness and another about counselor helpfulness.

Draft questions that do not presume a particular answer. Questions that make presumptions about the respondent's experience or behavior will be confusing to the respondent and make interpretation of the answer very difficult. For example, if we are interested in learning more about the respondent's sexual abuse behavior, a question might ask:

Do you still batter your spouse? ___ Yes ___ No

This question presumes that the person once battered his spouse. If that presumption is correct, then the appropriate answer is yes. But if the person never battered his spouse, how should this question be answered? A "no" answer presumes that he once battered his spouse but no longer does so. The question does not allow a response that indicates never battering his spouse. A better way to get at this information is to ask:

Did you ever batter your spouse? ___ Yes ___ No

Have you battered your spouse in the past year? ___ Yes ___ No

Rea and Parker (1997) add more advice to this list:

Avoid emotional words and phrases. Certain words and phrases can elicit powerful emotions. If we want to know more about students' moral attitudes toward homosexuality, we could ask:

Persons who engage in same-sex sexual relations are eternally damned.

___ Strongly agree ___ Agree ___ No opinion ___ Disagree
___ Strongly disagree

"Eternally damned" is an emotionally charged term. A better question might be, "Homosexuality is morally wrong," which is a more neutral and less emotional way of getting at students' moral attitudes toward homosexuality.

Provide information necessary to answer the question. At times, it may be necessary to provide accurate information about an issue before the question is asked. If we are interested in knowing more about students' attitudes toward the institution's residency requirement, we might ask:

> Do you agree with the university's residency requirement?
>
> ___ Yes ___ No

This question assumes that the respondent knows what the university's residency requirement is. A respondent who does not know will either answer the question based on ignorance or skip it. A better question might be:

> The university's current residency requirement requires that all first-year students must live in residence halls unless they are married, living at home, or more than twenty years old. Do you agree with this requirement?
>
> ___ Yes ___ No

This question informs the respondent of the requirement, and then asks if he or she agrees or disagrees with it, providing information that is much more accurate for the study.

Step 5: Determine the Sequencing of the Questions

Poor sequencing of questions can confuse respondents, bias their responses, and jeopardize the quality of the entire assessment effort. Rea and Parker (1997) suggest several guidelines for question sequencing:

Start with questions that are easy to answer. The first questions should be related to the topic of the study and elicit a straightforward and uncomplicated opinion or derive basic factual but not sensitive information. For example, if the purpose of the study is to assess student satisfaction with health services, the first questions might be about their frequency of use of these services, which is relatively nonthreatening and does not intrude on their privacy.

Place sensitive information late in the instrument. If some questions are of a more sensitive nature, they should be placed late in the instrument, for two reasons. First, if the respondent reacts negatively to such questions and decides to quit answering the questionnaire, the information obtained on all previous questions may still be used. Second, if the respondent becomes comfortable with the questions during the course of filling out the questionnaire, it is more likely that this person will answer sensitive questions that come later. In the previous example, intimate details about the nature of the medical condition that required the respondent to seek campus health services are best left to the end of the questionnaire.

Pose related questions together. Typically instruments are designed to get at categories of information. For example, if the purpose of the study is to assess the needs of adult learners, we probably want information about their academic needs and their personal needs. In this instance, proper clustering of questions around these topics helps the respondent to focus on each issue without being distracted by another topic.

Follow a logical sequence of questions. There is often a clear, logical order to a series of questions in a survey instrument. If we need information about employment or residence history, it may be important to follow an appropriate time sequence so that the respondent can answer in a sequential or temporal order, such as most recent to least recent over a specified period of time. For example, if we are assessing racial climate, we might ask students to recall a sequence of experiences based on their class standing.

Use filter or screen questions very carefully. Sometimes it is necessary to establish the respondent's qualifications to answer subsequent questions. The first question requires that some respondents be screened out of certain subsequent questions. The typical format is to ask a question, followed by a question: "If you answered yes to the previous question, please respond to the next series of questions. If not, skip to question [the appropriate question number is inserted here]." However, this approach can sometimes confuse the respondent and probably should be avoided if possible.

Consider reliability checks. Sometimes when a question is particularly important or controversial, the accuracy of the response may be in doubt. If so, it may be appropriate to ask virtually the same question in a somewhat different manner and at a different place within the instrument.

Ask demographic characteristics last. Starting off an instrument with a laundry list of demographic characteristics hardly engages the respondent and may, in fact, cause the respondent to become a nonrespondent. Demographic characteristics also should be kept to a minimum. Collect only the information that is important to the purpose of the study or necessary to determine the representativeness of the sample.

Step 6: Format the Instrument

In developing the format, two criteria should be used. First, the format should be such that the instrument is easily scored. For most quantitative studies, this means putting the instrument into machine-readable or scanning format. Second, the instrument should be formatted so that the respondent can provide the right responses without confusion. For example, if the instrument is machine scannable, there are two choices: provide the questions in one place and a generic scannable form in another, or provide the scannable responses next to the questions. The problem with the first alternative is that sometimes respondents can get on the wrong line and thus provide inaccurate information for all the questions that follow. Therefore, we recommend providing the scannable responses right next to the questions, although this means that the scanner will have to be programmed to read this format. Another alternative is to collect data on-line, thus eliminating scanning problems. (See Chapter Eight for a detailed discussion of on-line data collection.)

Step 7: Pilot-Test the Instrument

Another mistake that damages the credibility and accuracy of a locally developed instrument is to be in such a hurry to collect the data that pilot-testing the survey is abandoned. In a pilot test, a small number of respondents are asked to complete the instrument and provide comments on its overall efficacy. Specific issues to inquire about include those in Steps 3, 4, and 5. The overall goal is to ensure that the instrument does not confuse or frustrate respondents or miss the mark in terms of the purpose of the study.

The traditional means of piloting is to mirror the data collection procedures of the intended study. However, piloting instruments on-line has much potential and can be done more easily and quickly than traditional means. (See Chapter Eight.) Based on the pilot study, the instrument then can be improved through editing and revising the content, format, and other instrument characteristics. We recognize, however, that there may not be time to pilot instruments according to strict piloting guidelines, but some attempt should be made, even if on a small, informal scale.

Step 8: Conduct Psychometric Analyses on the Instrument

After the instrument has been administered to a sufficient number of respondents (at least one thousand), it should be subjected to rigorous psychometric analyses by qualified measurement experts, particularly if the instrument is to be used in subsequent assessments. However, assessment studies often are time limited. In the instance of instrument development, there may be insufficient time to pilot-test the instrument, administer it to a sufficient number of respondents, and determine psychometric properties such as reliability and validity. In fact, although locally developed instruments are used often, they are rarely subjected to rigorous psychometric analyses. They can still be used, but only if this serious limitation is clearly identified in reports based on the findings of the study.

Some Additional Considerations

The decision of whether to use locally developed instruments or commercially developed ones affects the quality of the study, its credibility, and ultimately the impact of the study on the problem, policy, or practice. There is some evidence that the use of LDIs has been increasing. El-Khawas reported in 1991 that 66 percent of colleges and universities were using local measures, primarily because of greater interest in collecting student portfolios and more use of assessment data for program evaluation purposes, and our experience over the past decade indicates that LDIs continue to account for a majority of the instruments used for assessment studies. However, deciding to use an LDI without thoughtful consideration can be a disaster. Let us illustrate a worst-case scenario.

Let us assume there is an urgent need to conduct a quantitative study based on a particular problem at an institution. Too often, under these circumstances, the conventional wisdom, supported by expediency, is to construct a locally developed instrument. The assumption is that almost anyone can write up a list of questions and send them to potential respondents. It is usually not until the responses begin to be tabulated and analyzed that it becomes clear that the instrument was not well thought out and organized, is poorly designed, and is yielding confusing and possibly misleading findings. Comments like, "If only we could have asked the question differently, we could have obtained the information we really needed," or "We should have used a different type of question," or "We should have consulted a measurement expert" are frequent reactions to a hastily constructed and sloppily prepared instrument. So the choice is to abandon the study because the instrument failed or try to salvage what little redeeming value it has once the limitations of the locally developed instrument are taken into account.

If we choose the latter, we run the risk of reducing the impact of the study considerably. Critics who do not like the conclusions reached by the study will immediately pounce on the limitations of the instrument as a reason for disregarding the findings. The credibility of the investigators will also be questioned. "If they really knew what they were doing, they would never have sent out such a poor instrument" is a typical reaction. In this scenario, it would probably have been better not to do the study at all rather than conducting a poor one because of sloppy instrumentation.

This is not to say that we discourage the use of LDIs. It is just that it has been our experience that often LDIs are not well constructed or psychometrically tested, thus limiting the quality and usefulness of the study. If, however, they are carefully constructed according to the criteria suggested in this chapter and developed under the supervision of a measurement expert, LDIs can have considerable merit, depending on the purpose of the study and the use of the results.

On the whole, however, we recommend using commercially developed instruments, in spite of their limitations. We are especially enthusiastic about those that allow several locally developed questions, thus overcoming one of their major disadvantages. We also like the ease of scoring and summarizing the findings that many publishers of CDIs offer. This is particularly of value if the results are returned on a computer disk that can be further analyzed locally. Use of CDIs also reduces the likelihood that the study will be criticized for poor instrumentation. CDIs have more face credibility with potential audiences than LDIs. That is not to say that locally developed instruments should never be used, but only if the institution has the time, resources, and expertise to develop psychometrically sound and credible instruments.

References

Blaxter, L., Hughes, C., and Tight, M. *How to Research.* Bristol, Pa.: Open University Press, 1996.

El-Khawas, E. "Assessment on Campus: Local Instruments Are Strongly Preferred." *Assessment Update,* 1991 3, 4–5.

Gall, M. D., Borg, W. R., and Gall, J. P. *Education Research: An Introduction.* (6th ed.) New York: Longman, 1996.

Ory, J. C. "Suggestions for Deciding Between Commercially and Locally Developed Assessment Instruments." In J. S. Stark and A. Thomas (eds.), *Assessment and Program Evaluation.* New York: Simon & Schuster, 1994.

Patton, M. Q. *Qualitative Evaluation and Research Methods.* (2nd ed.) Thousand Oaks, Calif.: Sage, 1990.

Prus, J., and Johnson, R. "A Critical Review of Student Assessment Options." In J. S. Stark and A. Thomas (eds.), *Assessment and Program Evaluation.* New York: Simon & Schuster, 1994.

Rea, L. M., and Parker, R. A. *Designing and Conducting Survey Research: A Comprehensive Guide.* (2nd ed.) San Francisco: Jossey-Bass, 1997.

Suskie, L. A. *Questionnaire Survey Research: What Works.* Tallahassee, Fla.: Association for Institutional Research, 1992.

Terenzini, P. T., and Upcraft, M. L. "Using Quantitative Methods." In M. L. Upcraft and J. H. Schuh, *Assessment in Student Affairs: A Guide for Practitioners.* San Francisco: Jossey-Bass, 1996.

Chapter 6

How to Conduct Mail-Out Surveys

PROBABLY THE MOST traditional way of gathering quantitative data is to mail a survey to the sample selected for inquiry. According to Rea and Parker (1997), "The mail-out format for collecting survey data involves the dissemination of printed questionnaires through the mail to a sample of pre-designated potential respondents. Respondents are asked to complete the questionnaire on their own and return it by mail to the researcher" (p. 6).

Nevertheless, this traditional approach is not necessarily the best way to gather quantitative data. This chapter offers advice on whether a mailed survey is the best data collection method, given the purpose of the study, and guidelines that will help maximize the advantages of mail-out surveys.

To Mail or Not to Mail?

Assuming that a quantitative survey best meets the needs of the purposes of the study, the next decision concern becomes how to collect these data. There are many choices, including telephone surveys (see Chapter Seven) and on-line data collection (see Chapter Eight). Distributing and collecting surveys in classes and making surveys available in central locations on or off campus are other alternatives, but they are the least reliable means of collecting data, and we do not recommend them. If consideration is being given to mailing out a survey, Rea and Parker (1997) identify several advantages of this data collection format:

Convenience. The survey may be filled out at the convenience of the respondent rather than at the specific time demanded by other formats, such as telephone surveys or focus groups.

Ample time. The respondent has time (within the time constraints identified by the survey instructions) to consult personal records and other sources of data necessary to complete the questions.

Anonymity. Because there is no personal contact with the investigator, and if the survey is done is such a way as to protect anonymity (although this is not always the case), respondents may be more inclined to be honest in their responses and to return the survey.

Reduced interviewer bias. The mail-out survey exposes each respondent to the same wording on each question, thus reducing interviewer-induced bias in questions. The respondent is not subject to interviewer-induced bias in terms of voice inflection, misreading of the questions, or other clerical or administrative errors.

There are, however, significant disadvantages to a mail-out survey. Rea and Parker (1997) identify several downsides to this data collection format:

Lower response rate than other methods. Many follow-ups and substitutions of sample respondents are required in order to achieve the appropriate sample size and adequate random distribution necessary for purposes of generalization. Just what kind of response rate to a mail-out survey (or any other survey, for that matter) is acceptable? The answer, of course, is that it all depends. Nevertheless, a useful rule of thumb is that one should require at least a 50 percent response rate of those sampled in order to ensure that the usable sample is representative of the population studied. If the follow-up guidelines described later in this chapter are used, it is possible to get a 50 percent or more response rate. However, it has been our experience that this becomes a problem in assessment studies, because they often have substantial time and money constraints that do not allow for adequate follow-up of nonrespondents.

Comparatively long time period. A mail-out survey generally requires a few weeks for questionnaires to be returned, especially if follow-up mailings to nonrespondents are done. Our experience is that time constraints may not make a mail-out survey a feasible alternative in assessment studies.

Self-selection. Mail-outs almost never achieve a 100 percent response rate. Thus, even in the best of cases (85 percent to 90 percent response rates), there can be bias in the sample. For example, our experience in assessment studies involving students is that women, underclassmen, younger students, on-campus residents, and majority students are more likely to respond to a mail-out survey than men, upperclassmen, older students, off-campus residents, and minority students. (For more information about volunteers, see Gall, Borg, and Gall, 1996.)

Lack of interviewer involvement. Because there is no interviewer, unclear questions cannot be explained, spontaneously volunteered reactions cannot be probed, and there is no certainty that the questions will be answered in the order written, which may be an important factor.

It has been our experience that the cost of doing mail-out surveys is somewhat of a mixed bag. Obviously postage is a factor, and depending on the size of the sample and the number of follow-ups, postage may present a significant cost expenditure. Further, if the survey is a commercially available instrument purchased at substantial cost, the expense of a follow-up mailing can be considerable.

If cost is a factor in data collection, we recommend comparing the cost of a mail-out survey with other forms of data collection. Generally it has been our experience that mail-out surveys often cost more than telephone or on-line surveys. But it has also been our experience that mail-out surveys may or may not be less expensive than focus groups or individual interviews, depending on the breadth and depth of these qualitative approaches and how much staff time can be devoted to data collection as part of their defined responsibilities. Of course, each of these alternatives has other disadvantages (see Chapter Three on qualitative methods, Chapter Seven on telephone surveys, and Chapter Eight for on-line surveys) to consider in the data collection format decision.

Another potential problem is the confidentiality and anonymity issues. One could argue that mail-out surveys yield candid information because respondents can choose to return the survey without identifying themselves. This may be especially important if the study asks respondents to reveal personal and private information. But guaranteeing anonymity does create some other problems. Obviously anonymity is compromised somewhat because the survey is sent to a specific person at a specific mailing address. Also, anonymity is further compromised if surveys are coded so that follow-up reminders are sent only to those who did not respond. If anonymity is especially critical to the study, we advise not coding surveys and sending reminders to the whole sample. The cover letter must be careful in informing respondents about the specific nature of the anonymity guarantees.

Confidentiality is a slightly different issue. In this instance, you are conceding that you will know who responded, but guarantee that responses will be held in strictest confidence, and results will reflect aggregate, not individual, responses. The advantage of this approach is that since you know who responded, you are able to determine if the returned sample is representative and to conduct analyses based on respondent characteristics. Coding of instruments is probably the best way to identify respondents. Sending reminders only to those who did not respond can save money.

Sometimes it is possible to carve out some middle ground on these issues. For example, if you ask respondents to provide confidential information about their characteristics (gender, race and ethnicity, age, place of residence, class standing, grade point, and so forth), you will have information that can be used to determine representativeness and conduct analyses based on respondent characteristics. Of course, reminders must be sent to the whole sample, regardless of whether they responded to the first mailing.

Another strategy is to ask respondents to give written permission to access institutional databases for purposes of the study, based on their student identification number. In this instance, information retrieved from institutional databases must be specifically identified. An advantage of this approach is that the investigator does not have to retrieve this information on the survey, thus saving space on the survey and time in filling it out. Also, money can be saved by sending reminders only to those who did not respond.

To mail or not to mail? The question is best answered depending on the purposes of the study, the advantages and disadvantages, and the time and resources available to conduct the study.

How to Develop a Mailed Questionnaire

We offer the following advice about how to conduct a successful mail-out survey, based primarily on Suskie (1992).

Cover Letter

The cover letter explains the purpose and importance of the study and its relevance to the respondent. This is not only desirable, but often required to comply with human subjects' regulations (see Chapter Thirty-Two). It should be written on institutional letterhead, signed by someone who has credibility with the student, and personalized unless the study is so sensitive that anonymity must be respected. The letter also should clearly identify the person and office responsible for the study, and an address, telephone number, and e-mail address where respondents may direct questions or comments.

Informed Consent

An informed consent form for respondents' written approval should include the purpose of the study, the confidentiality parameters, the use of the results, and other legally required information. (For a checklist of required information and a sample form, see Upcraft and Schuh, 1996.)

Disseminating the Results

Offer to make a copy of the results of the study available to respondents. One strategy is to mail a copy of the results to the respondents. However, if anonymity is a condition of the study, then the results can be made available at central campus locations, at student affairs offices, or on a World Wide Web page.

Incentives

Appealing to students' sense of educational or civic responsibility or their willingness to improve the institution is commendable, but not likely to yield the desired number of respondents appreciably. Incentives to consider offering include coupons for discounts at food services or the bookstore on campus, which can be especially attractive to students. Often vendors are willing to offer these discounts as an incentive to gain greater visibility among student customers. Cash incentives also work (if the amount is consistent with the time required to fill out the survey), but in our experience it must be at least five dollars, payable on receipt of the survey. In states where lotteries are permitted, a possibility is to put all respondents into a lottery with a cash prize or other incentive. We know of one institution that offered registration priority for the next semester and another that offered a premium parking space on campus for a semester.

Time Required to Complete the Survey

In mail-out formats, time may be everything, so it is important to estimate the amount of time required to complete the survey. Shorter instruments are received better by potential respondents. The instrument also must not be visually overwhelming, meaning that the page is not crowded with too many questions in tiny print, and students are not asked to fill out a survey of more than just a couple of pages. It has been our experience that a survey that requires more than ten minutes to fill out will be much less likely to be returned than one that requires less time.

Questionnaire Return

Include a stamped, self-addressed envelope for returning the survey. Asking the respondents to supply their own stamp and envelope is unrealistic.

However, rather than putting an actual stamp on the envelope, consider metered mail or business reply envelopes so that the institution is charged for only mailings that actually are returned. Also, imprinted envelopes are preferable to mailing labels.

Follow-Up

Follow up with nonrespondents. Often a vigorous follow-up with nonrespondents can be successful if time and resources permit. Suskie (1996) recommends several follow-up strategies:

Send another complete survey package: cover letter (amended to read, "We haven't heard from you yet!"), questionnaire, and return envelope.

Send a reminder postcard or letter, asking respondents to return the questionnaire package mailed earlier (and thanking those who have already responded). This follow-up is cheaper than sending another complete package but not as effective, since some potential respondents may have discarded or misplaced the original questionnaire.

Send a complete survey package by certified mail. This can be effective but is expensive, and it may irritate respondents who have to travel to a post office to collect the package.

Use a double tear-off postcard, asking the respondent to complete, tear off, and mail a postcard containing only the most crucial questions. This can generate a higher response rate than the whole survey, but preparing custom postcards can be expensive. Also, the data retrieved will be more limited than the original survey, thus limiting the scope of the study.

Call nonrespondents to remind them to return the survey. Obviously, if the survey guaranteed respondent anonymity, then both respondents and nonrespondents must be called.

Call nonrespondents to ask them the most critical questions. Again, the data retrieved will be more limited than the original survey. However, this follow-up procedure must not be used if the survey guaranteed respondent anonymity, because by definition those who are called are not truly anonymous.

Timing is also important in follow-up procedures. According to Rea and Parker (1997), assuming a target date has been designated for the return of the survey (usually two or three weeks from the initial mailing date), a first reminder (preferably a postcard) should be sent approximately two weeks after the initial mailing date. Four weeks after the initial mailing date, a second follow-up mailing, which includes the original survey package, should be sent to nonrespondents (except where anonymity was guaranteed, in which case all persons included in the original sample should be included).

It has been our experience that follow-ups rarely yield significantly more responses, and the more follow-ups there are, the smaller the response is. In other words, if the initial response is low (less than 10 percent), the potential of receiving the desired number of responses (typically, at least 50 percent) is low. Further, it has also been our experience that seldom do student affairs operations have the time or resources to conduct extensive follow-ups.

Conclusion

As we have gained experience with data collection formats, we have found that alternatives to mail-out surveys are more viable, given the limited time and resources available for most student affairs assessment surveys. A telephone survey may do just as well, particularly if the information solicited is not considered private or personal (see Chapter Seven). The same is true for on-line data collection (see Chapter Eight). Collecting data in academic classes should be considered only if all other forms of data collection are not practical. However, investigators must be certain that they have collected enough information about respondents to ensure a representative sample. Of course, this format requires the cooperation of faculty. Asking students to complete a survey and return it to the faculty member at the next class period is preferable to taking class time. Another option is to find out from a faculty member when a class will be canceled so that the students can complete the questionnaire in place of the class session. Yet another alternative is to use student leaders, student organizations, or resident assistants to distribute and collect surveys. The response rate is typically higher, but a larger response bias is likely to be introduced. Making surveys available at selected campus locations is probably the least desirable alternative to the others because the return rate will be low and a larger response bias more likely.

Two other issues need to be explored. First, although quantitative surveys are a more traditional (and respected) means of assessment, they are not necessarily the best. A qualitative study, rather than or in addition to a quantitative study, might better serve the purposes of the study. Second, if a quantitative approach better meets the needs of the study, consider other data collection alternatives before settling on a mail-out survey.

References

Gall, M. D., Borg, W. R., and Gall, J. P. *Educational Research.* (6th ed.) New York: Longman, 1996.

Rea, L. M., and Parker, R. A. *Designing and Conducting Survey Research: A Comprehensive Guide.* San Francisco: Jossey-Bass, 1997.

Suskie, L. A. *Questionnaire Survey Research: What Works.* Tallahassee, Fla.: Association for Institutional Research, 1992.

Suskie, L. A. *Questionnaire Survey Research: What Works.* (2nd ed.) Tallahassee, Fla.: Association for Institutional Research, 1996.

Upcraft, M. L., and Schuh, J. H. *Assessment in Student Affairs: A Guide for Practitioners.* San Francisco: Jossey-Bass, 1996.

Chapter 7

Telephone Surveys

Betty L. Moore

TELEPHONE SURVEYS are among the primary tools for data collection procedures in student affairs assessment. Application of this data collection procedure to student affairs was pioneered by Gary Malaney, who created Project Pulse at the University of Massachusetts more than twenty-five years ago. Based on the success of this project, many other colleges and universities have adopted some form of student polling to provide data for assessment studies. This chapter discusses the advantages and disadvantages of telephone surveys and then explains how to conduct them.

Advantages and Disadvantages of Telephone Surveys

Telephone surveys offer several distinct advantages over other forms of data collection:

Rapid data collection. Well-organized telephone surveys can be developed, implemented, and published within six weeks and even more quickly if the survey is kept simple and very focused. A mail-out survey or in-person interview usually takes months from start to finish (Rea and Parker, 1997).

Lower cost. Generally telephone surveys are less costly to conduct than mail-out surveys, although the cost may depend on institutional factors,

The information presented in this chapter is based on Penn State Pulse, a telephone data collection system at Pennsylvania State University coordinated by the author. Penn State Pulse was adapted from the University of Massachusetts' Project Pulse, which was established by Dr. Gary Malaney. The specific example used in this chapter is an adaptation of a Penn State Pulse survey of student smoking behaviors.

such as availability of student interviewers, computer terminals, statistical consultation, and telephone lines (Rea and Parker, 1997).

Anonymity. No telephone survey is really anonymous, because the name and telephone number of the person called are known. However, it is more anonymous than in-person interviews, because the interviewer may be able to gather sensitive data in a less threatening environment than in-person interviews (Rea and Parker, 1997).

Large-scale accessibility. Telephone surveys need not be restricted to local calls; it is quite feasible to conduct statewide, regional, or national surveys by telephone. Of course, when geographic accessibility is expanded, so is the cost (Rea and Parker, 1997).

Assurance that instructions are followed. The telephone interviewer can make certain that questions are answered in the intended order, thus maintaining the integrity of the questionnaire sequence (Rea and Parker, 1997).

Assurance that questions are clear to the respondent. The telephone interviewer can make certain that respondents understand the questions asked, increasing the chances that valid information will be collected. If computer software is used to record data, the flow of questions presented is related to the respondent's answers to earlier questions, saving time and increasing accuracy.

Telephone surveys are also limited in several ways:

Less control. The interviewer has less control over the interview process than in an in-person interview. Obviously, the respondent can end the interview at any time by hanging up the telephone (Rea and Parker, 1997).

Less credibility. The interviewer may have greater difficulty establishing credibility and trust with respondents, compared to an in-person interview. On the other hand, use of peer telephone interviewers often results in quicker credibility and potentially less emotionally charged interviews (Rea and Parker, 1997).

Lack of visual materials. Telephone surveys cannot use visual aids such as pictures or graphs, while mail-out surveys and in-person interviews can easily permit such aids (Rea and Parker, 1997).

Limited potential respondents. Only people with telephones can be contacted, and even then only those who are available at the times the survey is being conducted. This could be an important limitation because it may be difficult to reach representative samples of groups who cannot easily access telephones or are not available (Rea and Parker, 1997).

Inability to access telephone numbers. If the survey respondents are exclusively students, access to telephone numbers should be less of a problem than attempting telephone contact with dropouts or alumni. But even on campuses, students may change their residence frequently, and telephone directories are often not kept up to date.

Problems with answering machines. Sometimes students use answering machines to screen calls and decide not to participate on the basis of the message left rather than a full explanation of the purpose of the call.

Limited complexity of questions. Telephone surveys have limits on the complexity of questions and response modes. For example, it is inadvisable to ask respondents to rank more than three potential choices.

Limited open-ended questions. The number and breadth of open-ended questions is limited. A modest number of open-ended questions (no more than three) can be incorporated into the interview protocol, with careful attention to anticipated response categories that minimize pauses when the interviewer is typing in the responses.

The issue of response rates to telephone surveys is somewhat mixed. For example, Project Pulse at the University of Massachusetts and Penn State Pulse routinely garner a 65 percent to 70 percent participation rate. On the other hand, it has been the experience of some less sophisticated telephone surveys that response rates can be as low as 35 percent, even with extensive recalls. However, typically as students become more aware of telephone surveys and the impact they have on institutional policies, the response rate tends to increase.

Steps in the Telephone Interview Process

The following step-by-step process will provide a data collection process for one study and lay the groundwork for subsequent assessment studies.

Step 1: Determine If a Telephone Survey Is Appropriate

All assessment is driven by some problem. Defining that problem is the first step in the assessment process. The second step is deciding what information is needed to help solve the problem. Therefore, determining whether a telephone survey is appropriate depends on the problem and what information is needed to help solve that problem. For example, if the problem requires immediate attention, then the relatively quick turnaround time of a telephone survey is an advantage. Further, if the amount of information needed is relatively small, then the efficiency of a telephone survey will also be an advantage. Problems that require assessments that yield greater breadth and depth of information are less well suited to telephone surveys.

In the example used in this chapter, the institution was planning an extensive effort to reduce student smoking as part of an overall health education and prevention program. Recent national data showed that smoking appeared to be on the increase among college students, so it was important to determine if students at this institution followed that trend and, if so, to reconsider smoking prevention strategies in the light of the results.

Step 2: Determine What Information Is Needed

Given the problem that generated the assessment (the increase in student smoking), what information is needed to help solve this problem? The general rule of thumb in telephone surveys is that they should take no longer than seven minutes to complete. Can valid and reliable information be efficiently collected within this time frame? If not, then other forms of data collection should be considered. Nevertheless, a surprisingly vast amount of information can be collected within seven minutes if the interview protocol is designed properly and implemented by trained personnel.

It is often useful to review the research and literature as well as consult with faculty and staff who have expertise on the topic. This broader knowledge contributes to more focused questions and allows for the possibility of comparing the results with other studies. Based on consideration of all these factors, a telephone survey seemed most appropriate to explore student smoking behaviors.

Step 3: Design the Interview Protocol

The interview protocol should be designed in a way to gather demographic information about the respondent as well as the problem or issue under study. Further, the protocol should include an informed consent section that outlines the purpose of the study, any potential risks, confidentiality parameters, how the findings will be used, and other information (see Chapter Thirty-Two). Review by an institution's human subjects committee may be required.

The introduction of the protocol, once the telephone connection has been made, is especially important. A poorly worded introduction can lead to a negative response by the respondent and confusion on issues such as confidentiality, the purpose of the study, and how the results are used. An introduction should include the following elements:

- The issue or topic to be explored
- The anticipated time necessary to answer the questions
- Assurance that participation is voluntary and that the participant may choose not to answer specific questions
- Assurance of confidentiality of responses, including the reporting of aggregate, rather than individual, data
- Description of how the data will be summarized and used
- When and where the results may be used
- The name of a contact person or office in case of questions

The Student Smoking Behaviors interview protocol (see Exhibit 7.1) was designed after an on-line research literature search, consultation with the institution's health education staff members, residence hall staff, and members of the institution's Commission for the Prevention of Alcohol, Tobacco, and Other Drug Abuse, which was composed of faculty, staff, and student representatives. The final draft was submitted to the institution's office of regulatory compliance for its review in accordance with institutional and federal regulations established to protect human subjects.

If a survey assessment is planned on a regular basis, it might be useful to meet with the compliance staff to explain the goals of the telephone survey service, paving the way for a speedy turnaround time for individual survey approval.

Step 4: Pilot the Interview Protocol

An interview protocol must be piloted to ensure that respondents understand the questions. Piloting the survey helps verify the length of estimated response time, uncover unclear or confusing questions, discover terms that some respondents may not know (in the example, the use of Zyban medication to quit smoking), and screen questions that might trigger an intense emotional response (for example, death of a friend or family member related to smoking) or train interviewers to handle such responses.

One of the best ways to pilot-test a survey is to ask a small number of students to serve as mock respondents and provide feedback on the clarity of the questions. A focus group of no more than ten students can provide such responses. If students are used as interviewers, they can provide an excellent resource for piloting the protocol. Using the telephone interviewers to pilot an upcoming survey and incorporating their suggestions when

EXHIBIT 7.1

Student Smoking Behaviors Interview Protocol

Introduction

My name is [name of interviewer]. May I speak to [name of respondent]. I work with the [institution's telephone survey title] team, which makes calls on a regular basis to gather student responses on various issues. You are one of the randomly selected [institution] students to be called for this voluntary four-minute survey on student smoking. Please be assured that your responses are confidential and are reported as summarized data used in future planning efforts by the institution. No individual data will be identified. You may choose not to answer specific questions. You may also see the survey results in about three weeks. If you have any questions, contact [name of contact] in Student Affairs Research and Assessment in [address] or by telephone [telephone number], or by e-mail [e-mail address].

I hope you will take this opportunity for your voice to be heard. Are you willing to participate?

1. Do you think cigarette smoking among students on this campus has increased, decreased, or remained the same since you began college?
    ___ Increased
    ___ Decreased
    ___ Remained the same
    ___ Don't know

2. What factors do you think encourage students to smoke? (Indicate all that apply.)
    ___ Friends smoke
    ___ Stress
    ___ Part of being "cool"
    ___ Drinking events
    ___ Other social occasions
    ___ Advertisements
    ___ Rebelling against pressure not to smoke
    ___ Other _____
    ___ Don't know

3. What factors do you think discourage students from smoking? (Indicate all that apply.)
    ___ Cost
    ___ Smell
    ___ Friends do not smoke
    ___ Personal dislike of smoking
    ___ Environmental factors
    ___ Health risks
    ___ Have to go outside (smoking prohibited in campus buildings)
    ___ Other _____
    ___ Don't know

4. How often does your smoking coincide with drinking alcohol?
   ___ Don't smoke
   ___ Never coincides
   ___ Sometimes coincides
   ___ Always coincides
   ___ Don't know

5. Using a scale of 1 = very uninformed, 2 = somewhat uniformed, 3 = moderately informed, 4 = informed, and 5 = well informed, how informed are you about reported health hazards of smoking?

   1   2   3   4   5   Don't know

6. What percentage of students on this campus do you estimate smoke?
   ___ [Record number]   ___ Don't know

7. Do you consider smoking a problem on this campus?
   ___ Yes
   ___ No [Skip to question 9]
   ___ Don't know

8. If yes, what makes you feel it is a problem? [Indicate all that apply.]
   ___ Second-hand smoke is dangerous
   ___ Smell
   ___ Health risks
   ___ Litter/mess
   ___ Prevalence (number of smokers)
   ___ Cost (future health care costs for everyone)
   ___ Other _____
   ___ Don't know

9. Have you used any "smokeless" tobacco (for example, chewing tobacco or snuff) during the past thirty days?
   ___ Yes
   ___ No
   ___ Don't know

10. Have you smoked any cigars in the past thirty days?
    ___ Yes
    ___ No
    ___ Don't know

11. Have you ever tried cigarette smoking, even one or two puffs?
    ___ Yes
    ___ No [If no, skip to question 31.]
    ___ Don't remember

12. How old were you when you first smoked a whole cigarette?
    ___ Never smoked a whole cigarette [If never, skip to question 31.]
    ___ [Record number.]
    ___ Don't remember

EXHIBIT 7.1

Student Smoking Behaviors Interview Protocol, continued

13. How many days during the past thirty days did you smoke at least one cigarette?
    ____ None [If none, skip to question 15.]
    ____ [Record number.]
    ____ Don't remember

14. How many cigarettes did you average during the past thirty days?
    ____ [Record number.]
    ____ Don't remember

15. The Centers for Disease Control defines a "regular smoker" as someone who smokes at least one cigarette each day for a month. Would you say you are or have ever been a "regular smoker"?
    ____ Yes
    ____ No [If no, skip to question 17.]

16. How old were you when you started smoking regularly?
    ____ [Record number.]
    ____ Don't remember

The next set of questions focus on "quitting smoking."

17. Do you think you will ever quit smoking?
    ____ Have quit already
    ____ Yes
    ____ No
    ____ Don't know

18. How often have you ever tried to quit smoking?
    ____ Never [If never, skip to question 31.]
    ____ Number

19. What factors motivated you to try to quit smoking?
    ____ Personal health concerns
    ____ Concern of friend or family member
    ____ Concern of health care professional (physician/nurse, etc.)
    ____ Death or illness of friend or family member
    ____ Cost
    ____ Other _____
    ____ Don't know

Using a scale of 1 = very unhelpful, 2 = unhelpful, 3 = neither helpful nor unhelpful, 4 = helpful, and 5 = very helpful, how helpful were each of the following in your attempts to quit smoking?

20. Nicotine replacement patch	1 2 3 4 5	Don't know
21. Nicotine replacement gum	1 2 3 4 5	Don't know
22. Nicotine inhaler	1 2 3 4 5	Don't know
23. Internet (on-line) information	1 2 3 4 5	Don't know
24. Advice from health care professional	1 2 3 4 5	Don't know

25. Friend/family member		1	2	3	4	5	Don't know
26. Counseling		1	2	3	4	5	Don't know
27. Major public relations campaign such as Great American SmokeOut	1	2	3	4	5	Don't know
28. Quitting "cold turkey"		1	2	3	4	5	Don't know
29. Zyban medication		1	2	3	4	5	Don't know
30. Printed information/brochures		1	2	3	4	5	Don't know

31. And finally, using a scale of 1 = very unimportant, 2 = unimportant, 3 = neither unimportant nor important, 4 = important, to 5 = very important, how important do you think it is for your campus to provide some designated rooms for smokers so they don't have to go outside for a smoke?

1   2   3   4   5   Don't know

Background

This ends the survey, although we do need some background information.

Age: Would you tell me your age? ___ [Record age]

Residence: Do you live on or off campus ___ Off campus ___ On campus

Semester standing: What is your current semester standing? ___ (Record number)

College of enrollment: In what college are you enrolled? _____

Greek status: Do you belong to a sorority or fraternity? ___ No ___ Yes.

    If yes: ___ Fraternity ___ Sorority

We understand these last questions may be sensitive. You may feel free not to respond.

Ethnic group: How would you describe your ethnic background? [Record as many as apply.]

    ___ Caucasian

    ___ Hispanic

    ___ African American

    ___ Asian American

    ___ American Indian

    ___ Other

Grades: What is your current cumulative GPA?

    ___ [Record number. Use two digits with a decimal point. Example: 3.2 or 2.09. If asked, explain that there is research that indicates a connection between GPA and smoking.]

Gender

    ___ Male

    ___ Female

Conclusion

This brings us to the end. We want to thank you very much for your patience and cooperation. The results of this survey will be available in about three weeks and can be picked up in [campus location] or found on the Web at [Web address]. If you have any comments or concerns, feel free to contact [name of person] at [telephone number] or by e-mail [e-mail address].

possible encourages their own interest in the survey process. In the example, students suggested "smell," "litter/mess," and "prevalence of other smokers" as possible responses to the question, "Why is smoking a problem on campus?" Telephone interviewers can suggest wording changes and challenge questions they think are too complicated or wordy.

Step 5: Select the Interviewers

Interviewers should be members of the population under study (for example, students of surveys that target student respondents and graduates of surveys that target graduates).

In recruiting student interviewers, care should be taken to make certain that they represent the broad diversity of students at the institution. Other factors that contribute to a positive feeling on the part of interviewers, include an above-minimum-wage salary, evening hours, central campus location, the camaraderie that develops among student interviewers, and the feeling that they are doing something important and useful. Thus, current interviewers usually recommend the position and distribute applications to their friends. Often there are inquiries from students who have experience in telemarketing and like doing telephone interviews but dislike jobs with pressure to make sales.

Telephone interviewers should be selected by the telephone survey administrative team in consultation with current student interviewers. Candidates should be asked to complete a written application and to submit names of references. Next, there should be a meeting of candidates to assess their communication skills and to observe and evaluate a test reading of a survey introduction to check for variables such as voice clarity, reading ability, and ability to handle stress.

In the initial meeting with candidates, issues such as the importance of maintaining confidentiality, the expectation that interviewers will respect the integrity of the office facilities and computers used, and the reality of the potential boredom of repetitive work should be covered. Also, permission should be gained from applicants to access their records from the office of judicial affairs to determine if they have any behavioral problems that might disqualify them from becoming telephone interviewers. The administrative team should then select interviewers based on all these factors.

Step 6: Train the Interviewers

Training should consist of three sessions. The focus of the first training session should be communication skills, including voice tone, speaking speed, and how to encourage respondent participation. Interviewers should understand how various institutional decision makers need to have reliable data from survey responses. Survey elements, such as consistency and the importance of reading questions and response options exactly as written even if the interviewer feels the wording is too long or awkward, should also be reviewed. Resource materials that have been developed for student referrals also should be reviewed, and interviewers should be taught how to signal other interviewers or the evening supervisor for assistance. In addition, work expectations such as evening scheduling, the use of e-mail reminders of work schedules, responsibility to locate substitute workers, and wage payroll materials and time card dates should be discussed.

The second training session should address the survey process and record-keeping materials. In the smoking survey, survey interviewers rotated among work stations located at staff and student government desks in three adjacent buildings. Work station assignment records were maintained, as well as the respondents contacted by each interviewer, the number of those who agreed and who refused to participate, and the diskettes used by individual workers. Lists of potential respondents' names and telephone numbers were drawn randomly from institutional databases. New interviewers were shown how to keep records on these name sheets so that data could be corrected if necessary. Instruction materials were passed out for them to review. Trainees practiced uploading survey diskettes and completing a practice survey.

The third training session should involve shadowing experienced interviewers for an evening. Trainees should share a work station with experienced interviewers to learn the ropes. For the next several survey evenings, new interviewers should always be stationed near experienced workers who have demonstrated their ability to handle problems.

Step 7: Decide On and Retrieve Information About the Sample

Who is called? It depends. We must first determine the population of interest for the survey. Depending on the topic, this may be first-semester students (for an orientation survey), eighth-semester or above undergraduates (for a survey on postgraduation career plans,) on-campus undergraduates and graduate students (for a residence life newspaper readership program), those living in a specific residence location, or those who began their studies at another location. For the purposes of the Student Smoking Behaviors survey, all undergraduate students were the population of interest because smoking is not limited to a particular segment of the undergraduate student population.

Names were pulled from an institutionalized student data warehouse in two steps. First, the entire population who fit the criteria for the survey was downloaded. Then the number desired was pulled one at a time on a random basis using the Statistical Package for the Social Sciences (SPSS) random-draw instructions. In special circumstances, the sample of those to be called can be organized by strata so that there is an equal representation of certain subgroups in the population. For example, if the institution enrolls a disproportionately small number of racial and ethnic minorities, it would be wise to stratify the sample so that they are equally represented. The names and telephone numbers are then listed and printed out. (For those making telephone calls from a centralized location, telephone numbers can be handled by a computer program that tracks and assigns the next number to the telephone interviewer ready for a new call.)

In the smoking survey, a random sample of three thousand names, out of a total undergraduate student population of approximately thirty-five thousand students, was drawn. The printed list of random names and telephone numbers was then randomly divided into lists of two hundred (one each for ten interviewers). Each interviewer started at top of the random list and began to try to contact the respondents.

There were several possible outcomes for a call:

- The telephone number was incorrect. No attempt was made to determine the correct telephone number, so these persons were eliminated from the sample. It has been our experience that approximately 15 percent of an original sample have incorrect telephone numbers.

- The person was not at home. Usually three or four attempts were made to reach a potential respondent. Again, it has been our experience that we may be unsuccessful in contacting as few as 20 percent or as many as 45 percent of the remaining sample.

- The person was reached but was unwilling to participate. This was usually a very small number—no more than 2 percent.

- Some students from the original list of three thousand were never contacted because time ran out. That is, time did not permit each interviewer to call all two hundred persons on his or her list. This figure may vary from 20 percent to 40 percent of students on their lists.

- The call was connected to an answering machine. Interviewers are instructed to hang up without leaving a message, and the procedure for a person not at home is used.

So given these complexities, how do we determine a response rate? The answer is to calculate the response rate based on the number of original respondents whom interviewers attempted to contact. Of an original random sample of 3,000, 500 in a typical survey will have incorrect telephone numbers and another 1,000 will never be called, leaving approximately 1,500 students whom interviewers attempt to contact. Of these, it is typical to get approximately 850 to respond, for a response rate of about 57 percent, which translates into a margin of error rate of between 3 percent and 4 percent.

To determine if the sample is representative of the population from which it was drawn, we must compare the demographics of the actual respondent sample with the demographics of the population (using chi-square analysis) to determine its representativeness. These demographics typically include college and area of study, race and ethnicity, age, semester standing, and grade point average. Depending on the survey topic, other demographics may include on- or off-campus residence, fraternity or sorority status, or honors college status. For the purposes of the Student Smoking Behaviors survey, Greek affiliation was also included.

Most often the respondent sample is in fact representative of the population as determined by a chi-square analysis of the demographic variables. In those rare instances when one or more of the demographic characteristics of the sample are not representative of the population, two alternatives are recommended. First, the findings may be published with a caution that the sample is unrepresentative in specific ways. Second, the data may be reanalyzed, weighting responses of students who are underrepresented in the sample to accommodate their lack of representativeness.

Step 8: Select a Computer Software Package to Record Data

Interviewers may use a paper and pencil checklist to record responses or a computer software package that allows direct entry of data into a database. If computer software is used, each interviewer must have access to a computer that can handle it. In most instances, since surveys are done in the evening, interviewers can use computers in student affairs or student organization offices, so the cost of purchasing computers exclusively for telephone surveys is eliminated.

One popular and useful data recording software is Ci3, produced by Sawtooth Software, Inc. (info@sawtooth.com.info), a computer-aided survey program that runs on Windows 95 and NT 97. Ci3 allows for a variety of question and response options. Different versions accommodate 100, 250, or unlimited responses. Survey software is constantly being upgraded, so by the time this manual is published, there may be more sophisticated and efficient software packages available.

Step 9: Develop a Procedure for the Interview Process

Telephone interviews are best conducted in a relatively short period of time (about four hours), preferably on the same day of the week. Interviewers will also need access to a telephone. Again, since most surveys are done in the evening, interviewers can use telephones and computers in administrative offices.

Step 10: Merge the Data

At the end of the interview period, interview data from the floppy disks must be merged into one data file. When a survey is completed, all the diskettes used are merged by a data manager. Data are then cleaned and changed if necessary. This can be done very quickly in contrast to more time-consuming data management procedures, such as transferring data from a machine-readable form to a data management file.

Step 11: Analyze the Data

Because of the brevity of telephone surveys, sophisticated statistical analyses usually are not possible. However, in addition to descriptive statistics such as means, medians, and percentages, some selected inferential statistics may be useful. Once the data have been saved as an ASCII file, they can be opened by a data analyst into a data management file for data analysis.

Step 12: Publish and Disseminate a Succinct and Engaging Report

Too often assessment reports go unnoticed because they were not written in an engaging way, disseminated in a timely fashion, or targeted to the proper audiences. Reports should be published taking into account these criteria.

Telephone surveys are particularly adaptable to on-line and Web dissemination. This is particularly valuable in providing respondents with feedback on the survey, which is highly recommended as an incentive for respondents to participate. Exhibit 7.2 contains an adaptation of a single-page report that described the results of the student smoking survey.

In addition to this summary report, a more extended report was developed that included a data set with response totals, frequencies, and percentages for each question and response options and a complete summary by question of all differences between student groups found to be statistically significant. Both the concise and the extended report were available upon request. However, before any report was published, the office that initiated the survey reviewed the findings and had the opportunity to suggest additional dissemination of results.

EXHIBIT 7.2

Report on the Results of the Student Smoking Survey

Purposes

The purpose of this survey was to better understand college student smoking behaviors including factors that encouraged or discouraged their smoking and the effectiveness of various approaches to quitting smoking.

Implications/Highlights

Students report feeling "well informed" about health risks associated with smoking. A majority do not think student smoking is a problem on campus. Three-fourths said they had "tried" smoking, and over 40 percent fit the Centers for Disease Control definition of a "regular" smoker. Those who smoke have tried to quit an average of three times. "Quitting cold turkey" was cited as the most helpful means of stopping smoking.

Response Rate

Of the 3,000 randomly selected student sample, interviewers attempted to contact 1,500 students. Of the 1,301 contacted, 987 agreed to participate, for a response rate of 66 percent of those contacted and 33 percent of the original sample. Respondents were representative of students in general by gender, class standing, residence, race and ethnicity, and age.

Findings

About a third (37 percent) of students considered smoking a problem on campus. More of the women (42 percent) than the men (32 percent)* and more nonminority students (40 percent) than minority students (24 percent)*** thought smoking was a problem. Most had not seen an increase in smoking since they began college, a finding that did not differ significantly by class (freshmen, sophomores, juniors, or seniors).

Factors That Encourage Smoking

Nearly one-third (31 percent) of respondents report that "having friends who smoke" is the most common factor that encourages student smoking. Other factors include:

- Social drinking events—parties/bars/tailgates (27 percent)
- Stress (20 percent)
- "Being cool" (13 percent)
- Other social occasions—meals/sports (8 percent)

- Advertisements (3 percent)
- Rebelling against family/society pressure "not to smoke" (2 percent)

Other factors that encourage smoking include: feeling bored, being a smoker before college, thinking that smoking helps one stay awake, presence of ashtrays everywhere, and having parents who smoke.

EXHIBIT 7.2

Report on the Results of the Student Smoking Survey, continued

Factors That Discourage Smoking

Slightly more than half of students (51 percent) reported that awareness of health risks is the most important influential factor that discourages smoking. Other factors include:

- Costs (13 percent)

- Smell (11 percent)

- Personal dislike of smoking (11 percent)

- Friends don't smoke (7 percent)

- Having to go outside to smoke (3 percent)

- Environmental factors (1 percent)

Other factors that discourage smoking include: parental guidance, athletics, cigarettes not being sold on campus, yellowing of teeth, and awareness of side effects.

Informed About Health Hazards of Smoking

Most students (84 percent) reported they were informed or well informed about the health hazards associated with smoking. However, more nonminority students (86 percent) than minority students (77 percent) reported they were informed or well informed about health hazards.**

For further information, please contact [name], [address], [phone number], and [e-mail address], or access our Web site [Web site address].

*Statistically significant at the .05 level.

**Statistically significant at the .01 level.

***Statistically significant at the .001 level.

Not all the information gathered by telephone survey interviewers was included in this summary report. Judgments about which of the findings to report were made by the persons who conducted the study. Because the basic purpose of the study was to help guide an institutional effort to reduce smoking, only findings that were directly relevant to this purpose were reported in the summary.

Cost of Telephone Surveys

Generally telephone surveys are at least as cheap to conduct as other forms of data collection. The actual cost depends on such considerations as the kind of support and resources that are available without extra cost within the institution. For example, a full-blown telephone survey operation with no support or resources from the institution, may cost as much as $4,000 per survey. On the other hand, costs may average out to about $1,000 per survey. For example, in an institution that has a system that allows for repeated surveys, then the more surveys that are done, the lower is the per survey cost. Cost can also be reduced in other ways—for example:

- Using student volunteers as interviewers
- Collaborating with faculty to assign credit or internships
- Assigning a portion of a staff position to this project
- Having free in-house design and statistical consultation
- Using already available computers and telephones
- Using a server-based data entry system to eliminate use of disks

It is important to consider costs in relation to benefits. For example, if a survey is done that determined that students would support a mandatory student activities fee, which would increase revenue flow and provide students more control over student activities money, the potential benefits to students and the institution might well be worth the cost of the survey.

If a telephone survey system is developed that is used continuously, it is possible to establish an income flow from various customers, which can then help fund the total cost of the program. It is unlikely that these revenue sources will make the program completely cost independent, but this approach will help.

Some Practical Advice

Based on our extensive experience with telephone surveys, we offer some additional practical advice:

- Be aware of campus or community special events before scheduling evening telephone calls, and reschedule a survey based on these events.
- Do not make calls on Saturdays.
- Call between 6:00 and 9:00 P.M. Calling earlier or later tends to reduce participation rates.
- Allow interviewers breaks to rest their throats and reenergize their voices, and to converse with other interviewers to see how the calls are going.
- Do not schedule surveys for the first or last week of classes or during examination periods.

Conclusion

Overall, given the typical time and resource limitations of student affairs assessment, we recommend telephone surveys over other quantitative data collection methods. Telephone surveys are more desirable than mail-out surveys and offer limited opportunities for more qualitative, open-ended questions. Of course, the most important factor in the data collection method chosen is to reflect the best way to gather the information needed for the study. The study should drive the data collection method, not the other way around.

Reference

Rea, L. M., and Parker, R. A. *Designing and Conducting Survey Research: A Comprehensive Guide.* (2nd ed.) San Francisco: Jossey-Bass, 1997.

Chapter 8

Web-Based Data Collection

Thomas I. Wortman, M. Lee Upcraft

PERHAPS THE MOST exciting recent development in the assessment field has been Internet-based surveying. Contrary to what might be common opinion, using the Internet to collect assessment data gives the investigator the ability to reach many more people than most other forms of data collection. This method also offers the advantage of being accomplished quite quickly, sometimes within hours of an event or program.

As student affairs involvement in assessment has increased, so too has the technology available to collect the data necessary to conduct such assessment. According to Dillman, Tortora, and Bowker (1998), there is little doubt that the number of surveys being conducted over the World Wide Web is increasing dramatically. Although there are some disadvantages to Web-based data collection, on the whole the advantages outweigh the disadvantages. Web-based data collection differs dramatically from surveys sent by e-mail because it offers greater potential for reaching larger numbers of people with relative ease and speed, allowing for interactivity, reducing the time devoted to responding to the survey, and reducing the time spent recording data.

Web-based data collection is an important topic for many reasons. First, there is great interest in this topic (as well as much skepticism), so a thorough and balanced discussion is needed about this newest form of data collection. Is it just another fad, or is it the wave of the future in assessment? The reality in higher education is that students, faculty, and staff have the means, almost universally, to communicate with each other electronically. Personal computers with Internet access are available to nearly everyone involved in higher education. Among first-year students alone, nearly 83 percent report having used the Internet for research or homework during the final year of high school (Higher Education Research Institute, 1998), and these same students probably have even greater access to personal computers and the Internet upon matriculating. Similarly, anecdotal evidence suggests that only the most stalwart of old-time traditionalists among colleges' faculty and staff fail to have a computer on their desk or in their office, and use it daily. Consequently, Web-based data collection must be explored toward the purpose of helping investigators to determine if it can enhance or even replace other data collection techniques, such as mailed or telephone surveys.

This chapter offers a primer of terms relevant to electronic assessment and gives practical advice about designing Web-based instruments and conducting Web-based assessment. We encourage readers to explore a companion Web site that offers interactive, real-life examples of Web-based data collection: http://www.international.psu.edu/iss/surveyexample.html. (See Appendix 8A for more details.)

Advantages and Disadvantages of Web-Based Data Collection

Web-based surveys offer assessment investigators the opportunity to collect much the same information as mailed or telephone surveys.

Advantages of Web-Based Data Collection

Web-based data collection has the following advantages:

Both quantitative and qualitative information can be gathered. Similar to mailed surveys or telephone interviews, quantitative and qualitative information can be collected using the Web. Respondents can be asked to answer questions that are worded in any standard way, whether the response scales are nominal, ordinal, or interval (see Chapter Five for a more detailed discussion of response scales). Exhibit 8.1 shows an example of how quantitative questions can be asked on the Internet. Similarly, open-ended questions that allow the respondents to form and submit their own answers can be incorporated into the Web design (see Exhibit 8.2). Questions that collect data in either of these two forms can be combined, as is shown in Exhibit 8.3.

Data can be collected in a user-friendly manner. Web-based instruments can be used to collect a wide variety of information in a user-friendly, efficient manners. Instead of the drudgery of completing and returning a mailed questionnaire, Web-based instruments demand far less time and effort on the part of respondents. Furthermore, unlike telephone surveys, which require respondents to be in a particular time and place, Web-based surveys

EXHIBIT 8.1

Questions Asking for a Quantitative Response

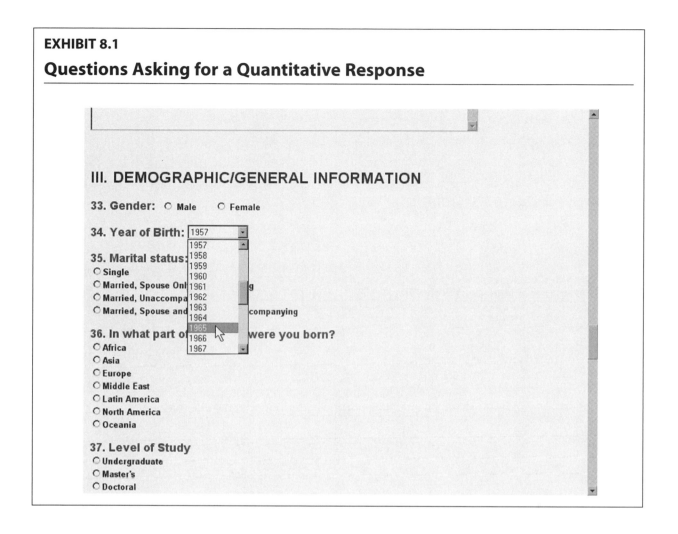

can be completed at a time and place convenient to respondents. Also, completing a Web-based survey requires no special skills beyond using a mouse to click on items and a keyboard to type some responses.

In Chapter Five, investigators are cautioned against using contingency questions that may be frustrating or confusing to the person completing the questionnaire. A Web-based instrument may eliminate these problems by electronically directing respondents to appropriate questions on the instrument. For example, students who answer no to a question inquiring about their attendance at an orientation session can be automatically directed to questions asking about their reasons for failing to attend, and students answering yes are provided with questions about the content of the sessions.

The return rate may be greater and more timely. Marine (2000) reviewed about two hundred articles in which the authors used multiple modes of survey delivery and collection to conduct surveys in business, education,

EXHIBIT 8.2

Open-Ended Question

		Not Satisfied	Somewhat Satisfied	Very Satisfied	Does not Apply
24	Accessible	O	O	O	O
25	Provide useful information	O	O	O	O
26	Understand my concerns	O	O	O	O
27	Allow sufficient time to discuss my concerns	O	O	O	O
28	Courtesy of adviser	O	O	O	O
29	Sensitive to international student issues/concerns	O	O	O	O
30	Accurate/correct information	O	O	O	O

31. What additional services or programs do you feel should be offered to assist international students at Penn State?

> Here, survey respondents can use their own words to answer questions that do not require a quantitative response.....

32. Please add any additional comments or suggestions you would like to share.

sociology, history, anthropology, health care delivery, and economics and identified some clear patterns of return rate. Seven of these studies provided direct comparisons of rates of response from all three survey modes: postal mail, e-mail, and Web-based surveys. A comparison of telephone survey response rates was not available from this work. Evidence from Marine and others seems to indicate that response rates can be quite high but are directly related to two factors: finding respondents to be at home and answering their telephone, and convincing the subject to respond to the survey.

Marine found that the rate of adoption of Web-based modes of survey distribution and collection is accelerating for two reasons. First is the low cost of distribution and collection to two disparate groups: very large ("broadcast") or tightly focused ("listserv" organization or discipline-based) populations, compared with either postal mail or e-mail. Second is the ability to automate distribution, collection, and data processing (including analysis).

Marine found as well that the effectiveness of each mode is directly related to the methods used to engage the audience in the survey process.

EXHIBIT 8.3

Questions Asking for a Quantitative Response, with an Option for a Qualitative Answer

○ American students sharing your same ethnic/racial background
○ American students with different ethnic/racial backgrounds from yours

44. Where do you live?
○ University residence hall
○ University apartment (or "family housing")
○ Off campus

45. How did you first hear about and consider attending Penn State?
○ Friend or relative
◉ An academic source such as a teacher or an advisor
○ Penn State's World Wide Web site
○ College Fair
○ Advising Center
○ Official Source (Government, industry, etc.)
○ Catalog or Printed material (example: ranking books)
○ For-Profit Agency
○ Other (please specify) [   ]

46. What are the main reasons you chose to study at Penn State? (Choose top 3 reasons.)
To choose more than one item, press the /CTRL/ key while clicking on your choice.

| Recommended by family/friend |
| Recommended by home institution |
| Reputation/quality of Penn State |

Other (please specify) [   ]

47. What is your main source of funds in the United States?
○ Personal funds

This may seem obvious, but the subtle side is a change in how this is done. Postal and in-person survey methods rely on appeals to group membership and social conditions. Web surveys can use multiple appeals simultaneously. Interface design, presentation of the survey tool, interactive forms, personalized messages, and subject behavior triggering survey delivery can all be simultaneously employed to engage the member of the population under study.

In the period 1995 through 1999, Marine found that Web surveys had increasing response rates (21 to 30 percent in 1995–1996 and 33 to 80 percent in 1998–1999). Postal mail surveys had stable to slightly decreasing response rates (30 to 60 percent, though in Marine's group of two hundred, the average was close to 40 percent). Those trends, however, understate the increased populations or sample sizes reached by the different modes. No surveys in the sample of two hundred studies were used for populations over five hundred. Meanwhile, Web surveys extended to over ten thousand.

The resulting numbers of participants, even at essentially equivalent rates of response by mode, are overwhelmingly demonstrative of the effectiveness of Web surveys.

So what does all this mean? Obviously, a higher rate of return increases the likelihood that the sample will be more representative of the population and the study will have greater credibility. On the whole, it has been our experience (although not necessarily the experience of other assessment investigators) that Web-based data collection often yields a higher rate of return than any of the other methods. Also, respondents seem to reply more quickly. For example, in a needs assessment of about twenty-four hundred international students at Penn State University, the response rate using a Web-based survey was 20 percent within twenty-four hours of its appearance on the Web. The final response rate for this instrument approached 50 percent.

Data collection time is reduced. Assessment studies using mailed surveys sometimes take months to complete the data collection process. Like telephone surveys, Web-based surveys can be turned around much more quickly if the amount of time required to complete the survey is reasonable (no more than six to eight minutes). This means that investigators can considerably reduce the time needed to complete the study, and thus increase the likelihood that information gathered can have a more immediate impact.

Anonymity can be managed. One of the major objections to Web-based surveys is that many people believe that respondent anonymity cannot be ensured, thus limiting the candidness of their responses, violating their privacy, or even compromising the integrity of the study. On the contrary, when placing an instrument on the Web, the investigator can choose the extent to which the identity of respondents is revealed. Results can be collected without any identifying information attached or with a user's specific e-mail address or computer location identified. Again the critic would argue that without knowing who responded, the representativeness of the usable responses cannot be determined. On the contrary, if proper demographic information is gathered, one can easily determine if the respondents differ from the population on variables such as race and ethnicity, gender, age, or other characteristics vital to the purposes of the study.

The respondent pool can be expanded. Web-based surveys allow the investigator to reach across boundaries of time and distance to reach the target audience. They allow persons to whom the investigator may not otherwise have access the opportunity to participate in an assessment effort. This is particularly important if the target audience is widely dispersed geographically.

Data can be more efficiently managed. Because the ease with which data collected over the Web can be aggregated electronically and compared with other electronic data, Web-based data collection creates more efficiency in the data analysis process. For example, data collected from a mailed or telephone survey must be transferred to a data management database by hand or machine-scored response forms. In contrast, Web-based data can be recorded and analyzed electronically, saving time and money.

Duplicate responses can be identified. One of the concerns that critics of Web-based data collection frequently express is that a rogue computer user might submit multiple responses to the same survey, thus compromising the integrity of the study. The reality is, however, that software programs that process responses may be able to identify if more than one survey is submitted by one respondent. Investigators may be well served, however, to limit access to the URL for the Web survey by asking intended participants to enter a code number, name, or e-mail address that allows the user to complete the survey only one time. Many end user applications do not allow this kind of control, however, and it may have to be built into the survey at the Web server level.

Our experience is that because of the relatively innocuous nature of most assessment instruments done in student affairs or higher education, users generally are not interested in submitting a survey more than one time. Uses of Web-based surveys assessing controversial programs or sensitive topics may wish to consider limiting access to the URL. At any rate, the URL for most Web-based surveys is best when not linked from other Web sites; the user then must purposefully enter the survey site. This procedure will virtually eliminate the possibility of unintended users' submitting the survey.

Instruments can be piloted more easily. Unless a commercially available Web-based instrument is being used, it is likely that an instrument must be developed that meets the specific purposes of an assessment. This means that the instrument should be piloted so that it may be refined and made more usable. Piloting an instrument by mail or telephone is a cumbersome and time-consuming process compared to the relative simplicity of piloting an instrument electronically. The piloting can be done through e-mail or Web-based approaches. Respondents are asked to fill out the survey and make comments on the relationship between the purposes of the study and the survey, as well as the clarity of the questions.

Instruments can be retooled to accommodate changes. Let us assume that the pilot results in needed changes in the instrument or individual items. Mailed surveys require significant time, effort, and money to revise, print, and resend, and old instruments must be discarded. In contrast, Web-based instruments can be easily and quickly modified, saving a lot of time, money, and inconvenience.

Certain costs may be lower. There may be some significant cost savings in using Web-based data collection. Compared to mailed surveys, Web-based data collection saves on costs such as printing, paper and envelopes, postage, and entering data into a data management or statistical software package. Compared to telephone surveys, Web-based data collection saves on wages for interviewers, telephone charges, and entering data into a data management software package. Of course, there are other costs associated with Web-based data collection, but overall it has been our experience that costs are lower.

Greater control over responses can be more easily achieved. Web-based data collection solves the problem of how to deal with questions that are answered improperly. For example, in a mailed survey, respondents may circle two choices instead of one. HTML coding allows investigators to ask for and receive specific responses without deviation. A survey may also be designed that does not allow respondents to skip questions by not allowing those respondents to continue until a field is filled in.

Disadvantages of Web-Based Data Collection

Overall, Web-based data collection procedures offer a lot of advantages compared to other data collection efforts, particularly ease of administration and analysis. However, there are some downsides to be considered.

Not all respondents have access to the Web. Although most colleges and universities provide computer access to the Web, there may be some that do not. There may also be some institutions where some students have access and others do not. If there is reason to believe that a significant number of potential respondents do not have ready access to the Web, then other forms of data collection should be used.

Not all respondents have the necessary computer literacy skills. There is some evidence that today's students are often very computer literate. However, this may not be the case for some students. At the most basic level, respondents may lack keyboarding skills. Even students with keyboarding skills and access to a computer may not have the skills necessary to complete a survey properly, resulting in invalid responses or the failure of the person to respond at all.

Web-based data collection requires different time and expertise. Web-based data collection adds some steps to the data collection process that are not required in more traditional data collection procedures. For example, finding Web space, authoring the Web pages, and linking the responses to a database or text file are not only extra steps, but require a level of computer expertise and time not needed in conducting assessment using other approaches.

The distrust of anonymity assurances may be a problem. While Web-based assessments can easily be structured to ensure the anonymity of responses, respondents may not believe the assurances and may not respond because they may not trust the ability of the computer or the investigator to protect anonymity and confidentiality. It must be noted, however, that this same problem may exist with mailed surveys that are individually coded for the purposes of tracking individual responses.

Return rate may be inconsistent. While is it generally assumed that return rates using Web-based techniques are consistently higher than those of mailed surveys and at least as high as telephone surveys, there are few systematic studies to confirm or deny these assumptions. There is some evidence that the return rate may be as much affected by the length of the survey as the fact that is Web based.

Certain costs may be more. Web-based surveys may incur some costs not normally associated with more traditional data collection methods—for example, computer processing time, wages for the HTML author, software and computer application costs, hardware purchases, cost for the Web space, and electronic security and storage fees. These costs may vary depending on the type of support and assistance provided by a institution.

Hardware, software, and server malfunctions may occur. There are certain realities in electronically based systems: hard drives crash, software glitches and failures occur, server malfunctions can happen, floppy disks can fail, and other problems can happen. It is also possible that human errors in programming, storing data, not having the proper expertise, and other problems can occur. Some of these problems can be prevented by making sure that those who manage the data collection are competent, while others (such as hard drives that crash) may not. If the proper expertise and equipment are not available, other forms of data collection should be considered.

How to Get Started

Let us assume that after weighing the advantages and disadvantages of Web-based data collection, the decision is made to use it.

Step 1: Assess the Coverage Among Potential Respondents

The investigator must be assured that the respondents will have access to the Web in order to complete and return a survey. If the instrument will not reach the audience, all other points are moot. Although we have made the argument that most college students are connected to the Internet, this may vary by institutional size and type and by the demographics of the student population. Assessing first-year students after their involvement in a summer orientation program, for example, may mean that a Web-based design may not be appropriate. Many of the students may not yet have access to their institution-issued Web accounts, or the students' home-based e-mail addresses may be too difficult to gather and use.

Step 2: Obtain Capable Personnel

Without individuals who are capable of creating and maintaining the necessary Web sites and collecting data for analysis, the process of a Web-based assessment must end at this point. Many administrators may be able to teach themselves the requisite skills or attend a few training sessions or courses to obtain the necessary knowledge. But often this process may require hiring a consultant or contractor to initiate, create, and maintain the instrument. Investigators should recognize and take advantage of the plethora of resources available to them at institutions of higher education. Computer science (or related) academic programs, for example, may be interested in placing undergraduate or graduate interns at little to no cost, and clerical staff members may have the knowledge necessary to perform in this role. Often graduate assistants can provide the necessary ambition and expertise.

Step 3: Determine Resource Availability

If a decision is made to conduct an assessment over the Web, the investigator must have the resources available to make the process work. Creation of Web-based assessment instruments requires both software (see Appendix 8B for some suggestions), and hardware. Upgrading or purchasing applications or equipment may create insurmountable financial barriers. Applications for analysis of either quantitative or qualitative data may also be costly. And permission may be needed to use institutional Web space for the purpose of conducting assessment surveys.

Step 4: Identify an Instrument

Many existing assessment instruments can easily be adapted for use in a Web-based environment, but permission is almost always required from the creator of the instrument. Regardless of the source of the instrument, it must be tested for bugs and piloted for usability on computers. The investigator must ensure that the data will be properly collected electronically and that respondents will be able to deliver completed instruments seamlessly. The data analysis process needs to be considered when creating an instrument; that is, the instrument needs to be coded for easy conversion into database or statistical software.

Step 5: Obtain Any Necessary Permission to Conduct Research on Human Subjects

Assessment investigators need to be very careful to respect the legal and ethical rights of respondents. Because Web-based surveys are relatively new, this data collection procedure should be discussed with the institutional human subjects committee to ensure that all appropriate laws and ethical guidelines are being followed. (See also Chapter Thirty-Two.)

Step 6: Test the Instrument

The instrument should be accessible to people with wide-ranging skill levels with computer equipment and usable across differing platforms, such as IBM-compatible and Apple-compatible personal computers, as well as able to be viewed on a variety of browsers. Clear and easy-to-understand instructions should be provided for all steps in the instrument. The instrument should be visually pleasing and easy to complete within a reasonable amount of time. The instrument should work well even at slow connection speeds. The instrument should be compatible with accessibility options that visually impaired or other users with disabilities use.

Step 7: Consider Data Security

Provision should be made for ensuring that the original instrument and accompanying code are properly stored and backed up in case of disaster. Data collected from the surveys should be backed up regularly and safeguarded to protect against compromise by outside hackers. The issue of data security is particularly critical when respondents' responses are not anonymous but confidentiality has been promised or when particularly sensitive data are being collected.

Step 8: Set a Reasonable Time Line

Even with the speed that is available for assessment using Web-based instruments, they cannot be done instantaneously. Consult with the personnel responsible for the instrument in setting data collection and analysis time lines.

Step 9: Determine Delivery Procedures and Collect Addresses

To make potential respondents aware of the Web-based survey, we recommend sending an e-mail notice to all possible subjects, with an in-line link to the Web site that contains the instrument. In this situation, the users are already using their computers and may take that moment to complete and return the questionnaire. In some circumstances, investigators may wish to send an additional announcement by postal mail that encourages users to complete the survey. In other cases, respondents may be directed to a computer immediately after taking advantage of a program or service to complete an evaluation of that endeavor. A reminder notice or notices may be necessary.

Step 10: Keep Notes Throughout the Process

As with any other new endeavor, this will be a learning process. Keep notes about what happens at each step and suggestions for improving subsequent deliveries. Revisit those notes when a Web-based assessment project is done again.

Step 11: Assess the Assessment

Following the process, everyone who was involved in the process should evaluate the entire project. Myriad materials are available that can provide specifics about evaluating an assessment project.

Some Practical Advice

Based on our experience with Web-based data collection, we offer some additional practical advice.

Design instruments that are deliverable and usable in multiple modes. HTML is a programming language used to create Web pages on the Internet. Since it was developed in 1989, it has been constantly improved and upgraded, but not everyone with access to a computer will have the hardware or application software necessary to view all of the advanced features that are available for use on a Web page written using HTML. Consequently, the investigator should seek to maintain the simplest yet most functional design elements in the assessment instrument. Even then, users should be given the option of accessing the assessment tool in other media. By making the instrument available in alternate forms, including e-mail and paper copies, some concerns about coverage can be alleviated.

Include access to a live person or some other communication point. Invariably, persons receiving a survey that is delivered in any form may have questions or comments relevant to the survey. At the least, the name, address, and telephone number of a person who can respond to questions and comments must be included in all correspondence with potential subjects. An e-mail link to that contact person is advisable. Messages delivered for contact information should be monitored throughout the assessment process so that specific concerns or problems can be addressed as they arise. Exhibit 8.4 contains an example of how this contact can be listed at the top of a Web page that introduces a survey.

Plan for future studies. It is important when conducting Web-based research to document all steps of the process. Provisions should be made that allow for investigators other than the Web author to be aware of the process and capable of accessing the data, replicating or changing the instrument, and responding to questions or concerns. Working in isolation in conducting Web-based surveys could lead to the elimination of future editions of the research or duplication of work that has already been done in creating or maintaining the surveys and the Web sites.

EXHIBIT 8.4

A Link to a Contact Person

 PENNSTATE

INTERNATIONAL STUDENTS AND SCHOLARS
THE PENNSYLVANIA STATE UNIVERSITY
INTERNATIONAL STUDENT NEEDS ASSESSMENT

Informed Consent

Contact Person:
Thomas I. Wortman
Interntional Students and Scholars
University Office of International Programs
The Pennsylvania State University
222 Boucke Building
University Park, PA 16802-5900
USA

Voice: 814.865.6348
Fax: 814.865.3336
E-Mail: twortman@psu.edu

Dear International Student:

We need your help. Please complete the following survey to help us assess international student concerns and needs at Penn State.

The survey asks you to answer questions regarding your concerns and needs as an international student as well as how offices and organizations are addressing them. The answers will be used to assess and to influence new directions for present programs and services.

Your participation in this research will take approximately 30 minutes. It is crucial to shaping and improving

Use qualified computer personnel. Just because someone knows how to use a computer does not mean he or she is an expert in Web-based designs. Dillman, Tortora, and Bowker (1998) expressed this point succinctly: "The task of responding to a Web questionnaire requires that respondents think simultaneously about how to answer a questionnaire and how to operate their computer. An effective bridge must be developed between the skills needed for sending commands to their computer and the cultural expectations that one brings to the questionnaire answering process" (p. 5). Web designers should strive to make that bridge as short as possible by maintaining plain instead of elaborate site designs and offering clear instructions for answering the questions and following the process for completing the survey. Exhibit 8.5 shows an example of a question that includes instructions about how to go about responding to a question that asks for multiple responses. Similarly, as is illustrated in Exhibit 8.6, the use of buttons and hyperlinks should be explained to users (see Exhibit 8.6).

EXHIBIT 8.5

Instructions for Responding to a Question

13) How did you first hear about and consider attending Penn State?
- ○ Friend or relative
- ○ An academic source such as a teacher or an advisor
- ○ Penn State's World Wide Web site
- ○ College Fair
- ○ Advising Center
- ○ Official Source (Government, industry, etc.)
- ○ Catalog or Printed material (example: ranking books)
- ○ For-Profit Agency
- ○ Other (please specify) [ ]

14) What are the main reasons you chose to study at Penn State? (Choose top 3 reasons.)
   To choose more than one item:
      PC USERS: Press the /CTRL/ key while clicking on your choice.
      MAC USERS: Press the /SHIFT/ key while clicking on your choice.

   Recommended by family/friend
   Recommended by home institution
   Reputation/quality of Penn State

Other (please specify) [ ]

15) What is your main source of funds in the United States?
- ○ Personal funds
- ○ Support from home government
- ○ Graduate/teaching assistantship
- ○ Support from international organization
- ○ Current employment
- ○ Support from U.S. government
- ○ Penn State scholarship
- ○ Other (please specify) [ ]

EXHIBIT 8.6

Explaining Hyperlinks and Buttons

---

83) What additional services or programs do you feel should be offered to assist international students at Penn State?

84) Please add any additional comments or suggestions you would like to share.

Thank you for your help!

| Click here to Submit Survey | | Click to Clear Form |

Click on these links to return to: Penn State Home   UOIP Home   ISS Home

Web Author: Thomas I. Wortman (click on name to send e-mail).
Copyright © 2000, The Pennsylvania State University. All rights reserved.
Revised: August 17, 2000.

☒ Hit Counter

Use expandable, text-wrapped boxes. Persons who fill out forms or surveys on-line that call for responses to open-ended questions are more likely to respond when the interface is user friendly. If a typed response to such a question does not stay on the respondents' computer screen, the user may become frustrated and discontinue responding or not provide a response that completely reflects her intention. Web designers must ensure that text boxes wrap the text that is entered. Text wrapping is a feature that allows all text to fit within a defined space. When a user reaches the end of a line, the words automatically jump to the next line; it is not necessary to press the Return key after each line. Text boxes should also be expandable. An expandable text box automatically increases in size so that lengthy responses can be entered. Exhibit 8.7 illustrates a box of this type.

Test the interface. Despite regular review of the survey and the Web interface, errors or design problems can be overlooked. It is imperative to have the survey tested repeatedly by users with differing levels of computer expertise. Surveys should also be assessed across different computer platforms.

EXHIBIT 8.7

Expandable, Text-Wrapped Box

---

83) What additional services or programs do you feel should be offered to assist international students at Penn State?

84) Please add any additional comments or suggestions you would like to share.

```
As you can see from this entry, when a respondent reaches the end of a
line, the text automatically starts again on the next line, instead of
running off of the screen.  The writer does not need to press
the /RETURN/key at all.
```

Thank you for your help!

| Click here to Submit Survey | | Click to Clear Form |

Click on these links to return to: Penn State Home   UOIP Home   ISS Home

Web Author: Thomas I. Wortman (click on name to send e-mail).
Copyright © 2000, The Pennsylvania State University. All rights reserved.
Revised: August 17, 2000.

☒ Hit Counter

Keep appropriate documentation. As in any other administrative process, it is critical when using Web-based surveys to maintain records in both electronic and print media. Although one may be tempted to archive resources, codebooks, and even the HTML code itself solely on a computer system, sometimes electronic files are lost or corrupted, resulting in significant costs in time and money to recover or rewrite. The investigator responsible for Web-based data collection may resign or otherwise be unavailable to provide the correct location and passwords necessary to access electronic documentation. Consequently, process notes, administrative manuals, and hard copies of instruments and coding should be kept together in one accessible yet secure location.

Stay away from custom programming. Hiring an expert in computer programming or Web design to write proprietary programs may be preferable in some cases, but in most instances it is more reasonable to use the simplest methods to create Web-based surveys. Using off-the-shelf application and Web-authoring software allows for easier and less costly revisions, fixes, changes, and perhaps most importantly, upgrades. Appendix 8B contains a list of many available applications packages. In addition, some investigators or organizations may find it useful to use commercially available Web survey design and collection sites or sites devoted to the analysis of Web pages. Appendix 8C contains a sampling of these sites.

Recognize that even electronic surveys may not be perfect. Despite the significant advantages of using the Internet to conduct assessment activities among college students and staff, even this process is subject to some of the same limitations as other forms of survey research. Keeping reasonable expectations and recognizing that any kind of research in the social sciences carries with it certain compromises is important here as well.

Conclusion

The proliferation of technology that is available to the entire higher education community makes this an exciting time for investigators in student affairs who are conducting assessment. Concerns about representativeness and coverage have been eased by recent advances in the availability of computers and Internet service providers among college students and staff alike. Using Web- or Internet-based surveys offers some distinctive advantages over more traditional methods of collecting survey data. Chief among these advantages are the speed and ease with which assessments can be accomplished. Web-based instruments may be more desirable than either mail or telephone surveys for some specific purposes. They also can collect extensive quantitative and limited qualitative data. It is imperative to remember, however, that not all types of assessment easily lend themselves to a Web-based delivery. Researchers should carefully analyze the specific needs and purposes of the study and choose the data collection method that best suits each particular study.

References

Dillman, D. A., Tortora, R. D., and Bowker, D. *Principles for Constructing Web Surveys.* [http://survey.sesrc.wsu.edu/dillman/papers/websurveyppr.pdf]. 1998.

Higher Education Research Institute. *The American Freshman: National Norms for Fall 1998.* Los Angeles: Higher Education Research Institute, University of California, 1998.

Marine, R. J. "Evolution of Survey Modes During the 1990s. Unpublished manuscript, Pennsylvania State University, 2000.

APPENDIX 8A

Sample Instrument

INTERNATIONAL STUDENTS AND SCHOLARS
THE PENNSYLVANIA STATE UNIVERSITY
INTERNATIONAL STUDENT NEEDS ASSESSMENT

Informed Consent

Contact Person:

Thomas I. Wortman

International Students and Scholars

University Office of International Programs

The Pennsylvania State University

222 Boucke Building

University Park, PA 16802-5900

U.S.A.

Voice: (814) 865-6348

Fax: (814) 865-3336

E-mail: twortman@psu.edu

Dear International Student:

We need your help. Please complete the following survey to help us assess international student concerns and needs at Penn State.

The survey asks you to answer questions regarding your concerns and needs as an international student as well as how offices and organizations are addressing them. The answers will be used to assess and to influence new directions for present programs and services.

Your participation in this research will take approximately 30 minutes. It is crucial to shaping and improving international student life at Penn State.

Your participation is voluntary. All information gathered is strictly confidential. If you do not wish to complete the survey, simply discard it. You also are free to decline to answer any of the questions in the survey. If you have questions, please contact Thomas Wortman, University Office of International Programs, 222 Boucke Building, Penn State, phone number (814) 865-6348.

Please remember that this survey is not simply to collect data, but to improve the quality of programs and services for international students. A few minutes of your time will help us to improve international student services and programs.

In order to return a completed survey, simply click once on the SUBMIT button at the bottom of the survey.

Thank you for your help.

Sincerely,

Jim Lynch

Director

International Students and Scholars

This instrument is available on the Web at http://www.international.psu.edu/iss/surveyexample.html.

I. Student Concerns

We are interested in finding out _how important_ each of the following is to you rather than how satisfied you are with services that you receive in these areas. Please answer each question by indicating your choice

How important is each of the following issues to you?

	Not of Concern	Insignificant Concern	Moderate Concern	Great Concern
1. Having adequate financial support				
2. Managing my personal finances				
3. Having work opportunities while a student				
4. Finding satisfactory housing				
5. Receiving good, affordable medical care				
6. Keeping up with news from home				
7. Maintaining contact with family at home				
8. Dealing with conflict between my goals and my family's goals for me				
9. Finding familiar groceries/foods				

	Not of Concern	Insignificant Concern	Moderate Concern	Great Concern
10. Understanding my U.S. tax obligation				
11. Finding employment after graduation				
12. Meeting others from my country				
13. Dealing with homesickness				
14. Finding a place of worship				
15. Making friends				
16. Communicating so that I am understood				
17. Understanding spoken American English				

	Not of Concern	Insignificant Concern	Moderate Concern	Great Concern
18. Understanding American slang/idioms				
19. Making American friends				
20. Learning how to interpret and respond to Americans of the opposite sex				
21. Learning how to interpret and respond to American behaviors/norms				
22. Understanding American values				

II. International Students and Scholars (ISS)

23. Did you attend the orientation programs offered by ISS?   ___ Yes ___ No

    a) *If you attended, which part of orientation was most useful?*

       Immigration responsibilities and procedures

       Employment responsibilities and procedures

       Academic life at Penn State

       Academic requirements and procedures

       Social and adjustment issues

       Medical care and health insurance

       Social activities

       Housing

    b) *If you did not attend all or substantial portions of orientation, it was because you*

       did not know one was offered

       arrived late

       were busy

       did not feel the need to attend

Please rate your level of satisfaction with each of the following items:

FOREIGN STUDENT ADVISERS

	Not Satisfied	Somewhat Satisfied	Very Satisfied	Does Not Apply
24. Accessible				
25. Provide useful information				
26. Understand my concerns				
27. Allow sufficient time to discuss my concerns				
28. Courtesy of adviser				
29. Sensitive to international student issues/concerns				
30. Accurate/correct information				

31. What additional services or programs do you feel should be offered to assist international students at Penn State?

32. Please add any additional comments or suggestions you would like to share.

III. Demographic/General Information

33. Gender: Male   Female

34. Year of birth:

35. Marital status:

    Single

    Married, Spouse Only Accompanying

    Married, Unaccompanied

    Married, Spouse and/or Children Accompanying

36. In what part of the world were you born?

    Africa

    Asia

    Europe

    Middle East

    Latin America

    North America

    Oceania

37. Level of Study

    Undergraduate

    Master's

    Doctoral

    Exchange (IEPS)

    Nondegree

    IECP

38. College

    Agricultural Sciences

    Arts and Architecture

    Communications

    Division of Undergraduate Studies (DUS)

    Earth and Mineral Sciences

    Eberly College of Science

    Education

    Engineering

    Health and Human Development

    Liberal Arts

    Smeal College of Business Administration

    Undecided

    Interdisciplinary

39. Do you have a graduate or teaching assistantship (RA or TA)?   ___ Yes ___ No
    a) If you answered yes, how satisfied are you with your assistantship?
       Very Dissatisfied
       Somewhat Dissatisfied
       Neither Satisfied nor Dissatisfied
       Somewhat Satisfied
       Very Satisfied
    b) If you answered yes, do you feel you are treated as well as your American RA/TA counterparts?
       Very Unequal Treatment
       Somewhat Unequal Treatment
       Neither Equal nor Unequal Treatment
       Somewhat Equal Treatment
       Very Equal Treatment
    c) If *unequal,* what could make it better?

40. How long have you been in the U.S.?
    Less than 1 year
    1–3 years
    3–5 years
    More than 5 years

41. Did you attend other colleges or universities in the U.S. prior to Penn State?   ___ Yes ___ No

42. How long have you been at Penn State?
    Less than 1 year
    1–3 years
    3–5 years
    More than 5 years

43. What group of students do you find yourself spending the most time with?
    Own nationality
    Other international students
    American students sharing your same ethnic/racial background
    American students with different ethnic/racial backgrounds from yours

44. Where do you live?
    University residence hall
    University apartment (or "family housing")
    Off campus

45. How did you first hear about and consider attending Penn State?
    Friend or relative
    An academic source such as a teacher or an adviser
    Penn State's World Wide Web site
    College fair
    Advising center
    Official source (government, industry, etc.)
    Catalog or printed material (example: ranking books)
    For-profit agency
    Other (please specify)

46. What are the main reasons you chose to study at Penn State? (Choose top 3 reasons.)
    To choose more than one item, press the /CTRL/ key while clicking on your choice.

    Other (please specify)

47. What is your main source of funds in the United States?
    Personal funds
    Support from home government
    Graduate/teaching assistantship
    Support from international organization
    Current employment
    Support from U.S. government
    Penn State scholarship
    Other (please specify)

Thank you for your help!

Return to: Penn State Home   UOIP Home   ISS Home.
Web Author: *Thomas I. Wortman.*
Copyright © 2000, The Pennsylvania State University. All rights reserved.
Revised: April 18, 2000.

APPENDIX 8B

Applications and Packages for Conducting Web-Based Assessment

There are myriad applications and software packages available to assist in conducting Web-based assessment. This list can serve as a primer in identifying the most commonly used or most accessible packages.

Web Authoring, HTML Editing

Office suites such as MS Office, Corel Suite, or others

Lotus Notes

Your browser (such as Netscape Communicator, Microsoft Internet Explorer)

Microsoft Front Page

Microsoft Visual Interdev

Any text editor

Allaire Coldfusion

Pervasive Software Tango

Flashlight (the University of Virginia's on-line instructional system)

Databases, Statistical Packages

Oracle

Office suites such as MS Office and Corel Suite

Decisive (survey research)

NUD*IST (qualitative analysis)

SPSS

SAS

MINITAB

Any company's version of SQL databases

APPENDIX 8C

Resources on the Web

Coomber, R. "Using the Internet for Survey Research." *Sociological Research Online,* 1997, *2*(2). [http://www.socresonline.org.uk/socresonline/2/2/2.html]. This article reviews the issues and process involved with conducting research over the Web and the Internet. Focuses discussion primarily on the problem of sample bias centered around sociological research. [http://www.soc.surrey.ac.uk/socresonline/2/2/coomber.htm].

Dillman, D. A. *Mail and Other Self-Administered Surveys in the 21st Century: The Beginning of a New Era.* [http://survey.sesrc.wsu.edu/dillman/papers/svys21st.pdf]. 1998.

Dillman, D. A., Tortora, R. D., and Bowker, D. *Principles for Constructing Web Surveys.* [http://survey.sesrc.wsu.edu/dillman/papers/websurveyppr.pdf.]. 1998. Tables are available at http://survey.sesrc.wsu.edu/dillman/papers/websurveyfigs.pdf.

Dillman, D. A., Tortora, R. D., Conradt, J., and Bowker, D. *Influence of Plain vs. Fancy Design on Response Rates for Web Surveys.* [http://survey.sesrc.wsu.edu/dillman/papers/asa98ppr.pdf]. 1998.

Doctor HTML. "Doctor HTML is a Web page analysis tool which retrieves an HTML page and reports on any problems that it finds." [http://www2.imagiware.com/RxHTML/]. 1998.

J&H Communications Group, Ltd. Creates and sells online surveys and their data collection. "Our iNet1 online survey software gives you control over the survey process from planning through reporting." [http://www.hr2000.com/hrbain30.htm].

Jakob Nielsen's Alertbox for Jan. 10, 1999, provides practical advice from Web users in response to the issue of how to get feedback from users to determine usability and future design directions for a large Web archive of historical documents. [http://www.useit.com/alertbox/990110.html].

M. Slinn Engineering designs and administers Internet surveys. [http://www.mslinn.com/web/surveys/].

Malcolm Duncan and Purdue Research Foundation markets TestPilot, software that "creates Internet or Intranet based tests and surveys. The tests are designed to be retrieved and displayed using most common Internet browsers like Netscape Navigator or Netscape Communicator." [http://www.clearcut-soft.com/TestPilot/].

Mediamark Research Inc. designs and sells proprietary survey software. [http://www.mediamark.com/pages/americom.htm].

Power Knowledge Software LLC sells PowerTab, software for designing and executing your own online surveys. [http://www.powerknowledge.com/comcanada/n1ccrv02.htm].

Rinaldi, A. H. "The Net: User Guidelines and Netiquette." [http://www.fau.edu/netiquette/netiquette.html]. 1999.

SiteInspector assesses Web pages and advises on any problems that are found. [http://siteinspector.linkexchange.com/].

SurveySite offers a variety of research methods including e-mail surveys, on-line focus groups, Web-based surveys, and Internet panel research." [http://www.surveysite.com/indexnew.htm].

SurveyTracker is a commercial site that offers to manage survey sites with distribution and data collection services. [http://siteinspector.linkexchange.com/].

Web Site Garage solutions focus on services for maintaining and improving Web sites. It automates site maintenance checks, optimizes graphics, and analyzes traffic. This is a free service. [http://www.websitegarage.com/].

Part Three

Basic Approaches

Chapter 9

Needs Assessment

NEEDS ASSESSMENT is a central element in a student affairs assessment program. It is very difficult to develop student affairs programs, activities, and services without an awareness of client needs. In spite of the centrality of needs assessment, the number of routine needs assessments that are conducted is inadequate. Buttram (1990, p. 207) concludes, "Although most program planners would probably argue that they know what their clients need, too many programs have failed because of mismatched services." We would also assert that before any new program, service, or activity begins, a systematic needs assessment ought to be conducted. We fear such is the case too infrequently.

Kaufman and English (1979) assert that needs assessment helps provide precision in addressing various problems, issues, and concerns: "Needs assessment is a tool by which one may be increasingly assured that the intervention, once selected, is related to basic gaps and problems, not just to the obvious symptoms or to problems poorly defined" (p. 55). Soriano (1995, p. 2) adds, "Needs assessments are used to collect data on the need for or current use of services, products or information. The information gained from needs assessment is typically used to make decisions about the allocation of program resources and services." Needs assessment, in our view, is closely linked with satisfaction assessment. In effect, needs assessment helps define problems so that they can be acted on, while satisfaction assessment helps determine if the interventions have been successful.

This chapter discusses the needs assessment process by using a case study that demonstrates how such an assessment was central to an overall decision-making process.

Definition of Needs Assessment

In *Assessment in Student Affairs,* we identified a number of definitions of needs assessment. One caution we offered was to distinguish between student wants and student needs. At times students think their needs can be met only through an expensive, elaborate intervention on the part of their institution, which could involve the addition of staff, new equipment, and so on. This may not always be the case. Consider the following example.

Student leaders report, after considerable input from their constituents, that a number of students with young children are unable to attend classes when their children are ill. The work of the leaders has been thorough; nobody on campus disputes their claims. Day care centers will not provide service to sick children for fear of contagion, and parents seem to have no alternative. Students need to attend class, they cannot leave their children in traditional day care, and they cannot leave them at home. What can be done?

This is a situation where the needs are clear: find a way to provide care for sick children so that their parents can attend class. One way of dealing with the problem would be to develop a day care program strictly for sick children. But this kind of care could prove to be costly for the parents since there would be no way to predict when the care would be needed or how many children would have to be served daily.

A far less costly alternative would be to develop a cooperative program among parents so that they could take care of each other's children on an emergency basis. That may or may not solve the problem. Another approach would be to form a partnership with businesses in the university area so that a program could be developed to serve the needs of working parents who face the same problem when their children are ill. Another possibility might be to work with a local hospital with empty beds to provide drop-in care for sick children.

Whether any or all of these approaches might be successful depends on local exigencies, although the approach with the local hospital was successful in one setting. Nevertheless, the examples demonstrate that there is a difference between student needs and student wants. Moreover, it is important to the institutional responses to the institution's mission. At a residential college that enrolls traditional-age students almost exclusively, it might not make sense to provide a response to this problem since very few students have children. Developing a complex system to meet the needs of a handful of students may fall outside the mission of the college. Harsh though it may seem, colleges and universities cannot provide services to meet the needs of everybody all the time. At times, it makes much more sense for institutions to narrow their focus and use their assets to advance their stated mission rather than to broaden their focus and dilute what they do best.

After reviewing a number of elements that potentially could be part of a definition of needs assessment, we agreed on the following: assessing student needs is the process of determining the presence or absence of the factors and conditions, resources, services, and learning opportunities that students need in order to meet their educational goals and objectives within the context of an institution's mission (Upcraft and Schuh, 1996).

Purposes of Needs Assessment

More than fifteen years ago, George Kuh developed a scheme for needs assessment that is still contemporary in its approach. He identified five different kinds of needs assessments and outlined the advantages and disadvantages of each (see Table 9.1).

We think that needs assessment, as depicted in this scheme, is especially useful in the justification of program policy. The purpose of the activity is to examine an expressed need and develop alternatives to address it. With the example of sick children of students, a need had been expressed, and no one disputes it. In an attempt to respond to it, a variety of alternatives are developed, and one or more may be tried on an experimental basis to determine which is most effective, given its various dimensions of cost effectiveness, service to parents, and enabling students to attend class. Consider the following case related to developing an institutional response to potential student needs.

Evening Student Concerns at Metro Community College: A Case Example

You chair one of the most prestigious councils on your campus, a community college that serves a large metropolitan area. This council is concerned with academic operations, such as registration, academic advising, and collecting fees. You have wide latitude to discuss academic matters on the campus, although the group does not address such faculty issues as curriculum, and tenure and promotion in academic rank. Representatives from every academic college sit on the committee, as well as staff from the registrar's office, faculty council, and so on.

At a recent meeting, questions were raised about how long offices ought to remain open during the day. The college has a night program with several thousand students, and so there may be a need for evening services.

TABLE 9.1

Purposes of Needs Assessments

Kind	Purpose	Advantages	Disadvantages
Monitor stakeholder perceptions	Generate ideas and document perceptions about various issues	Exploratory in nature; relatively threat free	Needs and wants may not be differentiated; not linked directly to action
Program policy justification	Collect information to support likely alternatives	Allows input into decision making	Needs and wants may not be differentiated
Satisfaction index	Estimate relative acceptability of various alternatives	Allows input; helps identify potentially controversial issues	Tends to emphasize wants over needs; may generate support for questionable or controversial activities
Participating policymaking	Select the most acceptable policy or program from alternatives	Allows stakeholders to influence institutional response to needs	Potential to generate support for questionable or controversial practices
Measurable improvement	Determine whether needs have been met	Documents effectiveness of unit; assesses client functioning	May not attend to existing problems or needs; focus on concerns previously functioning

Source: *Kuh, 1982, p. 205. Reprinted with permission of the American College Personnel Association (ACPA).*

What you do know is that over two thousand students out of a total enrollment of eighty-five hundred students are enrolled in classes only at night. The assumption is that these students work all day and probably could not conduct business on campus except during the evenings.

The discussion ranges from some offices being open for long evening hours and doing little business, to others that do a brisk business at night, to still others that close at 5:00 P.M. The discussion reflects anecdotal information about the question before the group. No one knows with any degree of certainty what services evening students need or for how long. As chair, you see that the discussion could go on indefinitely. Is there a way of getting a handle on this matter? What action steps might be taken?

The needs assessment in this case is a thorny issue. What are the needs of students who attend classes only at night at Metro CC? How could one determine these needs? These questions and others require a response from the college before programs and services are developed, modified, or eliminated.

A Quantitative Approach

The students involved in this case attended class only at night, took just a class or two, tended to work full time, and were rarely on campus. One strategy was to use a telephone poll. Two thousand students fit the definition of the students in the case, so a random sample of 959 was drawn (Rea and Parker, 1997), and these students were then queried over the telephone. The registrar's office or institutional research supplied a list of students who were enrolled only at night, along with their addresses and telephone numbers. The investigators then developed a questionnaire, trained people to collect data, and analyzed the information.

Using the telephone has two disadvantages. First, students do not always provide their up-to-date information for the institution's database, and the telephone numbers for some of them may be incorrect. Students seem to change residences frequently, and often they do not keep their telephone number after they move. The other problem is that it may be difficult to contact some of these students. We know by definition that they work all day and attend classes at least one night per week. Contacting them may be a challenge. The weekend might be the best possibility, although they may not want to engage in a telephone conversation on a Saturday or Sunday (see Chapter Seven for a detailed discussion of the advantages and disadvantages of telephone surveys).

The alternative to a telephone poll was to mail questionnaires to the students. We knew that the response rate would probably not be as high if we used a telephone survey, and we also knew that it would take a number of weeks to complete the data collection process since it was almost certain that a follow-up mailing or two would be needed (see Chapter Six for a detailed discussion of the advantages and disadvantages of mailed surveys).

Given the alternatives, a telephone poll seemed to be the better strategy. Before any data were collected, the design of the study was submitted to Metro Community College's Institutional Review Board, which reviewed the study to determine if the rights of participants were protected. Permission was granted, so the study was implemented (for a more detailed discussion of protection of human subjects, see Chapter Thirty-Two).

The first alternative in this case study was to consider using a commercially developed instrument, such as the College Student Needs Assessment Survey, developed by the American College Testing Program (1989) (www.act.org), or the satisfaction assessment instrument developed by Noel-Levitz (www.noellevitz.com). Still other instruments can be found on the American College Personnel Association World Wide Web site (www. acpa.nche.edu). In this instance, however, a locally developed instrument better fit the purpose of the study. (For a more complete discussion of locally developed instruments and commercially developed instruments, see Chapter Five.) Exhibit 9.1 contains a telephone survey, which determined if students knew about the student service and if they used it, the number of times they did.

Data analysis of this survey was quite simple. Reporting frequencies and percentages was sufficient. It would be possible to conduct additional analyses by using the demographic data as independent variables. Since this is a project designed to determine what student needs have gone unmet by the institution, more sophisticated quantitative data analyses were not necessary. For the open-ended question, data were analyzed by reporting the services identified by the participants.

"Conducting a needs assessment and undertaking appropriate analyses are meaningless if information is not presented in an appropriate manner" (Soriano, 1995, p. 84). The report developed based on the data collected was prepared for the committee charged with oversight responsibility for services for these students. Each of the committee members would receive a full report. Executive summaries would go to the senior academic and student affairs officers of the college to make them aware of the activities of the committee and the committee's efforts to meet the needs of students on campus better. Based on the results of the report, changes may or may not be made.

A Qualitative Approach

An alternative to the quantitative approach would be to employ a qualitative approach. Berkowitz (1996, p. 54) asserts that "the most salient reason to use qualitative methods in needs assessment is that they offer the opportunity to probe an issue or question in depth, and to explore respondents' views and perspectives in their own terms and framework of understanding." Should the committee have decided that the questions required more in-depth responses from the students that a telephone poll would yield, a qualitative approach would have provided a good alternative.

In this case, instead of contacting a random sample of 959 students, the committee could have decided to conduct five focus groups of approximately seven students each. Students would be invited to participate in the focus groups using criterion sampling (Patton, 1990). That is, the focus groups would consist of people who represented the kinds of students who took classes at night, based on their demographic characteristics. The groups would also represent proportions of students who took these classes by gender, race, class standing, and major. So, for example, if 60 percent of

EXHIBIT 9.1

Telephone Interview Protocol

Good evening. My name is _____ . May I speak to _____ ? I work with a committee at Metro Community College that is attempting to determine the needs of adult students such as you. You were one of the randomly selected Metro students to be called for this voluntary, eight-minute survey. Please be assured that your responses are confidential and will be reported as summarized data used in future planning efforts of Metro. No individual data will be identified. You may choose not to answer specific questions. If you have any questions, contact Dr. I. M. Doingastudy, at 403 Administration Building, Metro Community College, Metro, Pennsylvania, or by telephone (999) 555-1938, or by e-mail (imd5@metro.edu).

I hope you will take this opportunity for your voice to be heard. Are you willing to participate? Good. Here is my first series of questions.

Have you used the following student services, after 5:00 P.M., during the previous semester? And if so, how many times have you used this service? Have you:

Used the services of the admissions office?
    Yes ___ No ___ If yes, how many times? ___

Used the services of the financial aid office?
    Yes ___ No ___ If yes, how many times? ___

Sought career counseling from the career services center?
    Yes ___ No ___ If yes, how many times? ___

Used the placement services at the career services center?
    Yes ___ No ___ If yes, how many times? ___

Looked at the part-time job listings at the career services center?
    Yes ___ No ___ If yes, how many times? ___

Sought treatment from the student health service?
    Yes ___ No ___ If yes, how many times? ___

Purchased medication from the student health service?
    Yes ___ No ___ If yes, how many times? ___

Dropped or added a course at the registrar's office?
    Yes ___ No ___ If yes, how many times? ___

Gotten an identification card from the registrar's office?
    Yes ___ No ___ If yes, how many times? ___

Ordered a transcript from the registrar's office?
    Yes ___ No ___ If yes, how many times? ___

Paid fees at the controller's office?
    Yes ___ No ___ If yes, how many times? ___

Sought help from an academic adviser?
    Yes ___ No ___ If yes, how many times? ___

Sought help from the staff at the learning resource center?
    Yes ___ No ___ If yes, how many times? ___

EXHIBIT 9.1

Telephone Interview Protocol, continued

Used the math lab at the learning resource center?
    Yes ____ No ____ If yes, how many times? ____

Used the writing lab at the learning resource center?
    Yes ____ No ____ If yes, how many times? ____

Sought help from the counseling center?
    Yes ____ No ____ If yes, how many times? ____

Gotten a parking decal from the parking office?
    Yes ____ No ____ If yes, how many times? ____

Sought help from the disability services center?
    Yes ____ No ____ If yes, how many times? ____

Used the computer lab?
    Yes ____ No ____ If yes, how many times? ____

Ate a meal at the student union?
    Yes ____ No ____ If yes, how many times? ____

Used the commuter lounge at the student union?
    Yes ____ No ____ If yes, how many times? ____

Used the facilities at the recreation center?
    Yes ____ No ____ If yes, how many times? ____

Used services at the child care center?
    Yes ____ No ____ If yes, how many times? ____

Made purchases at the bookstore?
    Yes ____ No ____ If yes, how many times? ____

Used the library?
    Yes ____ No ____ If yes, how many times? ____

Studied on campus?
    Yes ____ No ____ If yes, how many times? ____

My second question is, given your daily schedule, are you able to access these student services during the day, from 8:00 A.M. to 5:00 P.M.?
    Yes ____ No ____

Thinking about these many services or others you believe you need that are not currently available, what services would you use if they were available after 5:00 P.M.?
[Record responses.]

Thank you very much for your help with this project. The results will be available in about six weeks on Metro's Web site: www.metro.edu.

the students who took classes at night were women, about 60 percent of focus group participants should be women.

The purpose of using this qualitative sampling technique is to ensure that the study will have credibility among prospective audiences and should not be confused with stratified random sampling in quantitative studies. There is no assertion of statistical representativeness in using this sampling procedure, but we recognize that there should be a logical similarity between the characteristics of students participating in focus groups and those of the general population of adult students.

One issue related to sampling would be left unresolved until the focus groups were completed: five groups may not be enough, but we will not know that until the information we have learned from our groups becomes redundant. Redundancy is reached when the information gleaned from a group is so similar to what has been gleaned from previous groups that nothing new is learned.

Focus Group Protocol

Exhibit 9.2 contains the focus group interview protocol that was used in conducting focus groups with Metro Community College students.

Data analysis began as the groups were conducted. For example, based on information gathered from early focus groups, the protocol could be modified for the later groups. Patterns, themes, and trends were sought from the groups and formed the basis of the report. In conducting the groups, the assistant moderator kept notes. All groups were tape-recorded and analyzed based on repeated listening to the tapes. If resources are available and time permits, the tapes could be transcribed for the purposes of data analysis.

Other qualitative approaches also were used to collect data. Evening students were observed on campus. Did they park their cars, go straight to class, and then go home, or did they detour to the library, the computer center, or the student union? Observations helps the investigators understand these students' behavior patterns while they are on campus.

Document and record analysis also was useful in this project. Did evening students drop or add classes at a rate different from day students? Did annual reports of the recreation center compare usage between day and evening students? Did these students use other services in campus and, if so, to what extent? Assuming campus services and programs track their student users, this information could be useful in this assessment.

The report from the qualitative study was developed for similar audiences as the quantitative approach. The oversight group had a copy of the

EXHIBIT 9.2

Student Needs Focus Group Protocol

Thanks very much for joining me today for this discussion. My name is _____ and I am _____ at Metro. We are here to visit for a few minutes about services for evening students at Metro. I would like to ask you folks a few questions about the services you use at Metro as evening students. Your participation in this group is voluntary. You may leave at any time. I will not attribute anything said to any specific person. If these conditions are agreeable to you, let us begin.

1. Why did you enroll at Metro?

2. How long have you been an evening student at Metro?

3. If you could do it all over again knowing what you know now, would you enroll at Metro? Why?

4. What is it like being an evening student at Metro?

5. Have you had any particular problems or challenges being an evening student at Metro?

6. What services and resources do you use at Metro at night?

7. Are there other services or resources you wish Metro would provide to evening students?

8. If you were in charge of all the services available for evening students at Metro, what would be the one service you would not change? What would you change immediately?

9. What should I ask you about services for evening students at Metro that I have not?

10. Is there anything else you would like to tell me?

If you have any questions, contact Dr. I. M. Doingastudy, at 403 Administration Building, Metro Community College, Metro, Pennsylvania, or by telephone (999) 555-1938, or by e-mail (imd5@metro.edu). Thank you very much for your help with this project. The results will be available in about six weeks on Metro's Web site: www.metro.edu.

complete report, and the senior officers of Metro received an executive summary. What was learned from the study became the basis for reconsidering the needs of evening students and the hours of operations of student services. Changes were thus dependent on what was learned from the study. While report preparation is discussed in much greater detail in Upcraft and Schuh (1996), it is important to remember just how crucial the presentation of the data is. Dillman (1987, p. 206) reminds us that "more needs assessments probably fail because of inadequate data presentation than for any of the other reasons so far discussed."

Combining Methods

Rather than choosing to do either a quantitative study or a qualitative study, what might make the most sense is to do both. One analysis of needs assessment is that using a combination of methods is quite rare. Witkin (1994) reports that in her study of 125 needs assessment reports, 86 percent used only one method. Of these studies, "the most widely used method was the written survey questionnaire followed by the structured interview" (p. 24). She urges the use of multiple methods since, in her view, "the data gathering instrument or method often constrains the kinds of data that emerge particularly in the case of surveys, in which case the [needs assessment] cannot reveal anything beyond what the questions ask; and . . . there is some evidence that different methods yield noncomparable results" (p. 24), an observation with which Wayman and Savaya (1997, p. 236) agree: "Mixed methods may provide divergent and even contradictory findings regarding a single phenomenon." They also point out that mixed methods require more personnel and time, and as a consequence they are more costly than using a single method.

Conclusion

Elsewhere (Upcraft and Schuh, 1996) we have noted that student affairs practitioners are tempted to implement programs and services based on what they learn at conferences, read in the literature, or talk about with their colleagues, but without carefully determining if there is need for a new intervention. Needs assessment becomes an essential tool in making sure that the programs that are offered are needed and that new interventions will meet an unaddressed need of students and other clients. Our view is that unless systematic needs assessments are conducted, precious resources are wasted addressing problems that do not exist.

References

American College Testing Program. *College Student Needs Assessment Survey.* Iowa City, Iowa: American College Testing Program, 1989.

Berkowitz, S. "Using Qualitative and Mixed-Method Approaches." In R. Reviere, S. Berkowitz, C. C. Carter, and C. G. Ferguson (eds.), *Needs Assessment: A Creative and Practical Guide for Social Scientists.* Washington, D.C.: Taylor & Francis, 1996.

Buttram, J. L. "Focus Groups: A Starting Point for Needs Assessment." *Evaluation Practice,* 1990, *11*(3), 207–212.

Dillman, D. A. "Elements of Success." In D. E. Johnson, L. R. Meiller, L. C. Miller, and G. F. Summers (eds.), *Needs Assessment: Theory and Methods.* Ames: Iowa State University Press, 1987.

Kaufman, R., and English, F. W. *Needs Assessment: Concept and Application.* Englewood Cliffs, N.J.: Educational Technology Publications, 1979.

Satisfaction Assessment Described and Defined

A satisfaction assessment seeks to determine if student or client experiences with programs, services, or learning opportunities are of high quality and consistent with the institution's mission. In effect, higher education has a challenge to be accountable from a consumer satisfaction perspective (Sanders and Burton, 1996). There are many ways to measure satisfaction on a college campus, and much of this work is consistent with Total Quality Management (TQM) or Continuous Quality Improvement (CQI).

In their study of alumni and student satisfaction, Hartman and Schmidt (1995, p. 214) found that "students' satisfaction with an educational program is dependent on that program's success in meeting students' needs." Thus, needs assessment and satisfaction assessment are linked.

Bryan (1996) asserts that the principles and practices of TQM can have a place in student affairs. These principles and practices have to do with providing a high-quality experience for students, which we believe needs to be consistent with the mission of the institution. Scott (1996) adds that assessment can be used to determine how quality is achieved in higher education. Toward that end, we have developed a case that illustrates how satisfaction can be assessed in student affairs.

A Satisfaction Assessment Case Study

Low Ridge College (LRC) is a medium-sized, residential state university with a mission to serve students whose hometowns are within one hundred miles of the college. Its roots are as a teachers' college. Although the curriculum broadened after World War II, the college takes its heritage seriously. Teacher education is still the primary focus of the curriculum, but the college also offers programs in the liberal arts and business, with a special emphasis on hotel and institutional management, given the strength of the tourism industry in the area.

LRC has had a contract food service provide food service to the student union building for the past ten years. General observations about the food service at the union are that it is mediocre at best. The student union handles all campus catering except for sporting events. Since the college is primarily residential, LRC has operated its own residence hall food service. Residential students seem to like the food service provided for them, but the catering operation is lackluster. Concessions for sporting events have been provided by various concessionaires that also operate local restaurants, and this approach has realized very little revenue for the college. Opinions about the quality of food served at sporting events are both positive and negative.

A new president was appointed at LRC two years, and she was surprised to learn about the food service operations at LRC. Previously she worked at colleges with a single campus food service, either self-operated or contracted, that was responsible for all food service on campus. What LRC has in the way of food services, in her view, is very inefficient, probably generates less revenue than it should, and has clients who are unhappy with it.

The president has proposed that the college study all of its food service operations, and toward that end she has appointed a committee to conduct a study and make various recommendations. The committee decides that the first thing it needs to determine is the level of satisfaction of various constituencies with the food service operations on campus. This is a crucial decision. Hobbs (1987) observes that a clear statement of purpose is crucial in the assessment process. The committee decides that there are four elements that need to be studied: student union food service, residence hall food service, catering services, and athletic concessions.

A Qualitative Approach

The problem to be analyzed by this assessment is the extent to which clients are satisfied with the various food services at Low Ridge College. Certainly the food service may have organizational problems, but the president is a fair-minded person who can be persuaded by data. In this case, she wants to know just how satisfied various consumers are with the various food services. If problems are identified in the level of satisfaction, then she is prepared to act. But if the food services are providing services that are meeting the expectations of the various consumer groups, she may choose to stay the course.

One of the challenges in this kind of assessment is that the populations to be studied for the three food services are very different. In a qualitative approach, one would want to conduct focus groups, study documents, and observe behavior. For this problem, there are three very different groups of people to study: those who live in the residence halls form a discrete group; those who use the union building food services primarily are members of the campus community; and many visitors and guests, in addition to students, faculty, and staff, attend sporting events.

One approach would be to conduct focus groups of students who live in the residence halls to get a sense of their views of the food service in student housing. This will be fairly easy to accomplish. Students will be invited to participate in focus groups. Criterion sampling (Patton, 1990) will be used to invite students to participate in focus groups, with the criterion being the student's place of residence. The goal is to make sure that students from all the residence halls with food service have an opportunity to participate in the focus groups.

For the people who use the student union building, primarily faculty and students, a combination of convenience sampling (people who are readily available to participate) and sampling politically important cases (such as faculty and student leaders) might be used.

The focus groups of people who use the stadium concessions present a special problem. No one knows for sure who goes to the games since many people buy punch-card passes that allow them to attend games or they buy individual tickets for games. Nonetheless, one might want to start with season ticket holders (which could include students and faculty who buy season tickets) and individuals who are members of athletic booster organizations, which would be a combination of sampling politically important cases as well as convenience sampling since these people are known by name.

What is most important is to keep on interviewing individuals who have a story to tell or knowledge about food service so that the point of redundancy of the information is reached. Morgan (1998, p. 79) observes, "Trying to understand a more diverse population means conducting more focus groups. . . . It will take longer to achieve a sense of completion or repetition when there are more points of views to hear."

Interview Protocols

The interview protocols to be used in this assessment could be quite similar (see Exhibit 10.1). They would need to be developed consistent with the purpose of the study, that is, to determine what various consumer groups think about the food services provided.

Data Collection

Clearly one person will not be moderating all of these focus groups, so a cadre of people would need to be trained in moderating the focus groups. At LRC, some of the possibilities would be graduate students in education, members of the student life staff, and perhaps some faculty. Training of the moderators would have to be done with care since the data likely will determine in large part the course the president sets with respect to food service.

Other forms of data collection also could be used for this study. One that is particularly appealing is the use of secret shoppers. Secret shoppers—

EXHIBIT 10.1

Focus Group Interview Protocol for Assessing Satisfaction with Residence Halls Food Services

Welcome to our session. I am very glad that you have taken time out today to visit with us. This session is being tape-recorded so that I can make sure to be as accurate as possible in writing my report. What we are doing is visiting with a number of students at LRC about their satisfaction with various food service operations on campus. Today we will be discussing residence hall food services. I will be preparing a report for the college's food service operations, but I want to assure you that I will not attribute anything you say directly to you. Please understand that you may leave the group at any time and that your participation is strictly voluntary. You have a form in front of you that I ask you to sign before we move ahead. It indicates you understand the voluntary nature of your participation and that you may leave at any time. Do you have any questions at this point?

You live on campus in the residence halls and eat regularly in the food service. Is that right?

- Please tell me what you think of the presentation of the food items, for example, the salad and dessert bars, the fountain drinks, and so on.

- I would like you to talk about the various entrees that are served. Could you speak to issues such as the variety of entrees, the tastiness of the food, and the size of the portions.

- Do you get enough to eat? Please elaborate.

- What do you think of the people who work for the food service—the servers and other people who provide service to you?

- When you talk with your friends from other colleges, what do you say about the residence hall food service?

- If you had a brother or sister considering LRC, would you recommend living in the residence halls because of the food service?

- Do you consider the residence hall food service a good value? Please explain.

- What haven't we asked you about the food service that you think we ought to know?

Thank you very much for your participating in our group today.

people who assume the role of consumer and report their experiences—often are used in commercial activities. In the case of the food service study, secret shoppers would be commissioned to make food purchases at the student union, athletic events, or the residence hall food service. Of course, the food service should be fully informed of this form of assessment in advance of the data collection and should know the purpose of the study and how the results will be used. The shoppers report their experiences through the use of a report protocol (see Exhibit 10.2).

A third form of data collection is to observe people who use the various food service operations. Through the use of these observations, additional

Instrumentation

There seem to be two choices in collecting data: use mail-out surveys or conduct a telephone poll. (A third option, a Web-based assessment, would be advisable only if the technology at all campuses involved is sufficiently sophisticated.) A mail-out survey would be lucky to generate a response rate of more than 30 percent, it might require several follow-up mailings to nonrespondents. This approach also will take a considerable amount of time. Because the study needs to be completed fairly quickly, the better option is a telephone survey. A simple survey can be developed for data collection purposes (see Exhibit 10.3). To make sure that the questions are easily understood, a pilot study can be conducted with some students and perhaps faculty members.

We make no claims about the psychometric properties of this brief questionnaire. A pilot test can provide some assurance that the respondents understand the meaning of the items. In developing local instruments, it is quite important to employ the services of an expert on campus, such as a faculty member in educational psychology specializing in psychometrics. (See Chapter Five for a more thorough discussion of instrument development.)

One of the choices that must be made by those planning the assessment is to prepare an instrument specific to the study or to use a commercial instrument, such as the Student Satisfaction Inventory, developed by USA Group/Noel-Levitz (n.d.) (www.noellevitz.com), or the Student Opinion Survey, produced by the American College Testing Program (1994) (www.act.org).

Another approach that might be considered for this study would be to analyze spending patterns of people who use the student union food services and stadium concessions. This approach would be to compute how much money is spent at the various food venues with similar food operations. For example, how much is the gross spending per person at football games? How does this amount compare with other schools in LRC's conference? What about basketball? How much is the gross revenue per day at the student union? How does this compare with peer institutions? Without some sense of context, it would be difficult to determine if LRC has come close to maximizing its revenue or has room for growth. This information will not answer the questions completely, but it will help in the decision-making process. Most institutions are members of athletic conferences or have peer institutions from which obtaining such information could be accomplished fairly easily, assuming LRC has good relationships with other institutions.

EXHIBIT 10.3

Telephone Interview Protocol for Assessing Food Services at the Football Stadium

Good evening. My name is [name of interviewer]. May I speak to [name of respondent].

I am working with the Food Services Department to gather information about student satisfaction with food services at the football stadium. You are one of the randomly selected LRC students to be called for this voluntary ten-minute survey. Please be assured that your responses are confidential and are reported as summarized data used in future planning efforts by the institution. No individual data will be identified. You may choose not to answer specific questions. You may also have access to the survey results. If you have any questions, contact [name of contact] at [address] or by telephone [telephone number], or by e-mail [e-mail address].

I hope you will take this opportunity for your voice to be heard. Are you willing to participate?

I will ask you a series of yes-no questions about the food service at the stadium. Please feel free to elaborate on any of your answers.

1. I have attended football games at LRC.   ___ Yes ___ No
   [If no] Thank you for your time. [If yes, please continue.]

2. When I go to the games, I buy something to eat at the stadium.   ___ Yes ___ No

3. When I go to the games, I buy something to drink at the stadium.   ___ Yes ___ No

4. I rarely have to wait more than two minutes to be   ___ Yes ___ No
   served at the concessions stands.

5. The people who serve me at the concessions stands are courteous.   ___ Yes ___ No

6. Hot food is served hot at the concessions stands.   ___ Yes ___ No

7. Cold food is served cold at the concessions stands.   ___ Yes ___ No

8. The concessions stands have the items I want to purchase.   ___ Yes ___ No

9. The items available at the concessions stands are a   ___ Yes ___ No
   good value for the money charged.

10. The concessions stands are located in a place convenient   ___ Yes ___ No
    to my seat at the stadium.

11. People who sit around me purchase items from the concessions stands.   ___ Yes ___ No

12. What else would you to let me know about the food service at the stadium?

Thank you very much for participating in this study.

Data Collection

Individuals need to be trained to place the calls in the telephone survey. Students can do this very well. After the training has been completed, the calls are placed and the data collected.

The secret shopper approach also could be used in combination with the telephone interviews. For the purposes of this study, such a strategy could provide very useful data.

Data Analysis

Assuming the appropriate software is available, data collection and analysis could be done simultaneously. If the software is not available, the interviewers should complete "bubble sheets" as they conduct their telephone interviews. The bubble sheets are then machine scored. Measures of central tendency as well as frequency distributions are computed on an item-by-item basis for each food service. To determine if members of different groups regarded the food service differently, an appropriate approach is to calculate t-tests, again on an item-by-item basis. For example, those conducting the survey might want to determine if faculty members thought the servers at the concessions standards were more courteous than members of booster clubs (item 5). Or they might want to compare those who purchase food items at the concessions stands with those who only occasionally purchase drinks (item 2). A t-test could be computed to determine if there was a significant difference.

Final Reports

As was the case with the qualitative study, a report should be prepared for each of the three food services assessed. Executive summaries can be prepared for senior administrators, and an umbrella report should be crafted that brings all the data together, along with recommendations of the committee.

Regardless of approach, it is crucial to receive permission from the institution's human subjects committee before collecting data.

A Combination of Methods

Rather than having to choose either a quantitative or qualitative approach to the assessment, a better option would be to use both methods. Reichardt and Rallis (1994, p. 11) observe that "at the most global level, the two traditions have a common goal: to understand and improve the human condition." Using both methods has advantages and disadvantages (Reichardt and Cook, 1979), but the value of using multiple methods seems to outweigh using just one approach.

Conclusion

Satisfaction assessments form the cornerstone of improvement efforts. Systematic and continuing assessment of student and other clientele perceptions can provide valuable insights into what works, what does not work, and what needs to be improved.

References

American College Testing Program. *Student Opinion Survey.* Iowa City, Iowa: American College Testing Program, 1994.

Bean, J. P., and Bradley, R. K. "Untangling the Satisfaction-Performance Relationship for College Students." *Journal of Higher Education,* 1986, *57*(4), 393–412.

Bryan, W. A. "What Is Total Quality Management?" In W. A. Bryan (ed.), *Total Quality Management: Applying Its Principles to Student Affairs.* New Directions for Student Services, no. 76. San Francisco: Jossey-Bass, 1996.

Garland, B. C., and Westbrook, R. A. "An Exploration of Client Satisfaction in a Nonprofit Context." *Journal of the Academy of Marketing Science,* 1989, *17*(45), 297–303.

Hartman, D. E., and Schmidt, S. L. "Understanding Student/Alumni Satisfaction from a Consumer's Perspective: The Effects of Institutional Performance and Program Outcomes." *Research in Higher Education,* 1995, *36*(2), 197–217.

Hobbs, D. "Strategy for Needs Assessment." In D. E. Johnson, L. R. Meiller, L. C. Miller, and G. F. Summers (eds.), *Needs Assessment: Theory and Methods.* Ames: Iowa State University Press, 1987.

Levine, A., and Cureton, J. S. *When Hope and Fear Collide.* San Francisco: Jossey-Bass, 1998.

Morgan, D. L. *Planning Focus Groups.* Thousand Oaks, Calif.: Sage, 1998.

Patton, M. Q. *Qualitative Evaluation and Research Methods.* (2nd ed.) Thousand Oaks, Calif.: Sage, 1990.

Pike, G. R. "The Effects of Background, Coursework, and Involvement on Students' Grades and Satisfaction." *Research in Higher Education,* 1991, *32*(1), 15–30.

Rea, L. M., and Parker, R. A. *Designing and Conducting Survey Research: A Comprehensive Guide.* (2nd ed.) San Francisco: Jossey-Bass, 1997.

Reichardt, C. S., and Cook, T. D. "Beyond Qualitative Versus Quantitative Methods." In T. D. Cook and C. S. Reichardt (eds.), *Qualitative and Quantitative Methods in Evaluation Research.* Thousand Oaks, Calif.: Sage, 1979.

Reichardt, C. S., and Rallis, S. F. "The Relationship Between the Qualitative and Quantitative Research Traditions." In C. S. Reichardt and S. F. Rallis (eds.), *The*

affect the outcomes (see Upcraft and Schuh, 1996). This is often considered to be overwhelming, because we cannot imagine doing a highly sophisticated study with complicated statistical analyses, so any hope of conducting outcomes assessments is abandoned. However, it is also possible to conduct outcomes studies using a qualitative design, particularly if the number of subjects is too small to use a quantitative approach. Qualitative designs for outcomes studies are often simpler and more within the skill range of student affairs professionals who are properly informed and trained. Better yet, some problems are best addressed by using both methodologies. Therefore, in this chapter, we provide an example of a quantitative and a qualitative outcomes assessment based on the same case study.

The second caveat is that not all outcomes important to student services and programs are student learning outcomes. There may be other outcomes important to effective student services and programs that are not directly related to student learning outcomes. For example, an outcome for health services may be the delivery of care in a timely and efficient manner. An important outcome for financial aid may be to develop a financial aid package that ensures that students have enough money to enroll and stay enrolled in college. These are not student learning outcomes, but nevertheless are outcomes that are important to students' success in college. In fact, for most student services and programs, assessing outcomes will involve both student learning outcomes and other learning outcomes.

Assessing Student Learning Outcomes

Astin's input-environment-outcome (IEO) framework (1991) provides the most credible design for assessing outcomes. Astin believes than any educational outcomes are the result of the wide variety of personal, background, and educational characteristics that students bring to the college (inputs) and the wide variety of student experiences once they enroll (environment). Only when both inputs and experiences are taken into account may one explain a particular outcome.

Terenzini and Upcraft (1996, p. 219) assert, "The primary purpose of Astin's IEO model is to identify and estimate institutional effects on how students grow or change during the college years. In particular, this model is a useful tool for identifying and estimating effects of those college experiences over which institutions have some programmatic or policy control, such as student experiences, which can be shaped to educational advantage through an institution's programmatic or policy action, both inside and outside the classroom."

Terenzini and Upcraft argue that the most important aspect of the outcomes assessment is determining outcomes. Next is to select which inputs and experiences may be relevant to those outcomes, based on previous research and other factors relevant to the purposes of the study. There are any number of taxonomies of learning outcomes, but perhaps the most relevant to student affairs is the work completed by a group of educators under the auspices of the National Association of Student Personnel Administrators (see Upcraft, 1999). Their purpose was to develop broad categories of learning outcomes, based on the Student Learning Imperative. This group identified six outcomes, embedded in current literature and research, on which student learning might be assessed:

Complex cognitive skills—Reflective thought, critical thinking, quantitative reasoning, and intellectual flexibility

Knowledge acquisition—Subject matter mastery and knowledge application

Intrapersonal development—Autonomy, values, identity, aesthetics, self-esteem, and maturity

Interpersonal development—Understanding and appreciating human differences, ability to relate to others, and establishing intimate relationships

Practical competence—Career preparation, managing one's personal affairs, and economic self-sufficiency

Civic responsibility—Responsibilities as a citizen in a democratic society and commitment to democratic ideals

Kuh, Branch Douglas, Lund, and Ramin-Gyurnek (1994, p. 13) argue, "The closer students come to attaining their educational objective, the greater their learning and personal development gains." Therefore, to this list of essentially behavioral and psychosocial outcomes, we would add two more categories:

Academic achievement—The ability to earn satisfactory grades in courses

Persistence—The ability to pursue a degree to graduation or achieve personal educational objectives

These general categories of student learning outcomes can serve as a framework for developing more specific learning objectives, depending on the program, service, or facility being assessed, remembering that there are other, equally valid outcomes specific to student affairs functions that should be assessed.

Leadership Development Case Study

The Student Activities Office of Cuttingedge College has identified leadership development for student leaders as an important program consistent with its goal to promote civic responsibility. For several years, this semester-long program was offered on a noncredit basis, taught by the student activities staff.

Recently the director of student activities persuaded Cuttingedge's business department to offer this program, on a trial basis, for two credits, team-taught by student activities staff and business faculty. When the course was taught on a noncredit basis, several systematic studies showed that students were highly satisfied with the content, methodologies, and instructors. In fact, these studies were critical in convincing the business department faculty that the course should be offered on a trial basis. The department chair, however, believed that student satisfaction, although important, was no substitute for "systematic, clear and credible" evidence that students in the course improved their leadership skills. He insisted on such evidence before he would recommend that the course be offered on a permanent basis.

The principal assessment investigator for this project must design and implement an appropriate assessment study that provides the department chair and the director of student activities with the information they will need to determine whether this trial course should be made a permanent part of the business curriculum.

Steps in the Quantitative Outcomes Assessment Process

According to Terenzini and Upcraft (1996), a basic yet credible quantitative outcomes assessment design should proceed according to twelve steps.

Step 1: Define the Problem

The problem is that the business department chair wants "credible empirical evidence" that this trial leadership development course results in specific student learning outcomes before the course is approved on a permanent basis. Without such evidence, it is very unlikely that this program would be continued as a credit course.

Step 2: Determine the Purpose of the Study

The purpose is to determine to what extent, if any, students in a class on leadership development showed improvement in their leadership skills.

Step 3: Determine the Appropriate Assessment Approach

Astin's IEO model was selected because there was an attempt to show the impact of a particular environmental intervention (a leadership development course) on a selected outcome (leadership development skills), taking into account initial differences and other environmental experiences.

Step 4: Determine the Outcomes

The outcomes selected for this study were leadership skills as defined by Kouzes and Posner (1990):

- Challenging the process
- Inspiring a shared vision
- Enabling others to act
- Modeling the way
- Encouraging the heart

These outcomes were chosen because they formed the basis for the leadership development course.

Step 5: Identify the Input or Control Variables

Astin (1993) identified 146 possible input or precollege variables. However, since most institutions have access to far fewer input variables, only those that had direct relevance to the purpose of the study and were readily available could be used. Since there is some evidence that leadership skills may be influenced by participant characteristics, the control variables selected for this study included race and ethnicity, gender, and class standing. A precourse measure of leadership skills was also included as an input variable, so that the leadership skills of participants before they enrolled in the course could be taken into account in analyzing pre- to posttest changes.

Step 6: Identify the Environmental Variables

This step is quite challenging, since so many other participant experiences might well have influenced the development of students' leadership skills. Astin (1993) identified some 192 possible environmental or during-college variables. However, since all of these variables would be impossible to gather, we must select the ones that appear to be the most relevant and available. In this instance, the extent of past and current involvement in student leadership positions was identified as the most important environmental variable, along with place of residence, number of hours worked per week, and grade point average.

EXHIBIT 11.1

Interview Protocol for Assessing Leadership Skills

1. How, if at all, have you improved each of the following leadership skills during this semester?
   - Challenging the process
   - Inspiring a shared vision
   - Enabling others to act
   - Modeling the way
   - Encouraging the heart

2. What factors contributed to your improvement (or lack of improvement) in these leadership skills? (Include both course-related and non-course-related factors)

3. How might this course be improved?

4. Should this course be offered for credit on a permanent basis?

---

the above-average, average, or below-average cases. In this study, ten students were chosen who received an A as the final grade in the course, ten students who received a B, and ten students who received a C, based on the recommendations of the instructors of the course.

Step 7: Determine How the Information Will Be Collected

Postclass individual interviews were conducted by professional staff who did not teach the course, asking students about their experiences in the class, based on the interview protocol.

Step 8: Determine How the Information Will Be Codified

Typically, individual interviews yield an enormous amount of data that must be codified, organized, and sequenced in ways that make analyses possible. (For a comprehensive discussion on techniques to manage qualitative data, see Patton, 1990.)

Step 9: Conduct the Appropriate Analyses

Unlike quantitative analyses, according to Patton (1990), there are few agreed-on rules for qualitative data analysis: no formulas for determining significance, no ways of replicating the researcher's analytical thought processes, and no straightforward tests for reliability and validity. The challenge of analyzing qualitative data is to try to make sense out of data, identify significant patterns, and construct a framework for communicating the essence of what the data reveal (Patton, 1990). Upcraft and Schuh (1996) suggest that investigators keep discussing, probing, and thinking until a consensus is reached on what it all means. It is also possible that more data will need to be collected from those interviewed in order to make the analysis complete. (For discussions of qualitative data analysis, see Upcraft and Schuh, 1996, or Chapter Three in this book.)

In this study, interviews with students revealed that most perceived improvements in each of the leadership skills identified in the interview protocol and attributed much of that improvement to the course. They suggested several ways in which the course might be improved, including more hands-on experience, and they were unanimous in recommending that the course continue to be offered for credit.

Evaluation: Two Additional Steps

Both studies suggested that students improved their leadership skills as a result of enrollment in a leadership development course. There are two final steps in the outcomes assessment process.

Step 1: Evaluate the Analyses for Policy and Practice Implications

The findings of these two studies provided evidence of improved leadership skills as a result of taking the leadership course, taking into account other precollege and during-college factors that might also have contributed to this improvement. In addition, the participants unanimously recommended that the course should be offered for credit on a permanent basis.

Step 2: Report the Results Effectively

Multiple reports to intended audiences are recommended to maximize the impact of assessment studies. A summary of the design and findings of these studies was published for general consumption, including students, administrative staff, and the general public. Since the primary skeptic of the course was the business department chair, a separate report was written for him, focusing on the "systematic, clear, and credible" evidence he said he needed to make his decision. Since it was well known that the chair valued quantitative evidence highly, the results of the quantitative study were highlighted first. The second study was framed with some information on the differences between quantitative and qualitative assessments, so that he could better evaluate the findings from the qualitative study. Another report was written for the faculty of the business department that focused on the findings of the study relevant to the criteria for making a course a permanent part of the curriculum. And finally, yet another report was written for the faculty and staff who taught the course, focusing on learning outcomes and how the course might be improved.

Conclusion

The purpose of assessing outcomes is to try to determine if a relationship exists between some intentional intervention and some desired outcome, taking into account those precollege and during-college factors that might influence the desired outcome. Quantitative methods most often are used in outcomes assessment, statistically controlling for input and environmental variables as possible, but more simplified qualitative approaches can also be used. Too often, when we are intimidated by the overwhelming complexities of a quantitative study, we abandon our efforts to conduct outcomes assessments. However, in many instances, a simple, "What did you learn?" and "How did you learn it?" may provide great insight into whether what we did resulted in the desired outcome. But as demonstrated in this chapter, using both methodologies often provides the greatest and most complete insights into the impact of programs and services.

References

American College Personnel Association. *The Student Learning Imperative: Implications for Student Affairs.* Washington, D.C.: American College Personnel Association, 1994.

Astin, A. W. *Assessment for Excellence.* Old Tappan, N.J.: Macmillan, 1991.

Astin, A. W. *What Matters in College: Four Critical Years Revisited.* San Francisco: Jossey-Bass, 1993.

Kouzes, J. M., and Posner, B. Z. *The Leadership Practices Inventory (LPI): A Self-Assessment and Analysis.* San Francisco: Pfeiffer, 1990.

Kuh, G. D., Branch Douglas, K. B., Lund, J. P., and Ramin-Gyurnek, J. *Student Learning Outside the Classroom: Transcending Artificial Boundaries.* Washington, D.C.: School of Education and Human Development, George Washington University, 1994.

Patton, M. Q. *Qualitative Evaluation and Research Methods.* (2nd ed.) Thousand Oaks, Calif.: Sage, 1990.

Terenzini, P. T., and Upcraft, M. L. "Assessing Program and Service Outcomes." In M. L. Upcraft and J. H. Schuh, *Assessment in Student Affairs: A Guide for Practitioners.* San Francisco: Jossey-Bass, 1996.

Upcraft, M. L. "Assessing Student Learning." In F. K. Stage, L. W. Watson, and M. Terrell (eds.), *Enhancing Student Learning: Setting the Campus Context.* Washington, D.C.: American College Personnel Association, 1999.

Upcraft, M. L., and Schuh, J. H. *Assessment in Student Affairs: A Guide for Practitioners.* San Francisco: Jossey-Bass, 1996.

Chapter 12

Environmental Assessment

EVERYONE INTERESTED in environmental assessment owes a debt of gratitude to two foundational sources. First, Kurt Lewin developed the theoretical approach to environmental assessment with his formula $B = f(S)$, meaning that behavior is a function of the whole situation or circumstance of a person. This was later represented in the formula $B = f(PE)$, meaning that behavior is a function of the interaction of the person with the environment (Paul, 1980). This formula elegantly asserts that behavior is a function of the interaction of persons and their environment. Although others have tinkered with and added to this formula over the years, Lewin's foundation continues to support the environmental assessment movement.

The other foundation of environmental assessment was the work of the Western Interstate Commission for Higher Education (WICHE). Environmental assessment was operationalized in the 1970s as a result of the leadership of the Western Interstate Commission for Higher Education, specifically under the direction of Ursula Delworth. WICHE's assertion was that every campus has a design, intentional or unintentional, and student behavior is affected by this design. WICHE has the following elements (Aulepp and Delworth, 1976, pp. vii, ix):

1. *A campus environment consists of all the stimuli that impinge upon the students' sensory modalities, including the physical, chemical, biological and social stimuli.*

2. *A transactional relationship exists between college students and their campus environment.*

3. *For the purposes of environmental design, the designing properties of the campus environment are focused on [the aggregate].*

4. *Every student possesses the capacity for a wide spectrum of possible behaviors.*

5. *Students will attempt to cope with any educational environment in which they are placed.*

6. *Because of the wide range of individual differences among students, fitting the campus environment to the students requires the creation of a variety of campus subenvironments.*

7. *Every campus has a design, planned or unplanned.*

8. *Successful campus design is dependent upon participation of all campus members.*

One of the ways of thinking about WICHE's approach to campus environments is that students and their environment have a transactional relationship, that is, one affects the other, and vice versa. The assertion of this model is that if students do not fit with their environment, it is up to campus ecologists to determine ways to reshape that environment and provide a better fit. To determine student fit with the environment, the environment needs to be assessed periodically. Hence, the ecosystem model of environmental assessment was developed, and it remains a unique way of assessing students and their environment.

This chapter defines environmental assessment, presents a case study in which environmental assessment is described, and then provides alternative approaches to dealing with the issues described in the case.

Environmental Assessment Defined

One of the ways to think about environmental assessment, a somewhat elusive term to define, is to conceive of it as a collection of individual perspectives about the campus environment, both physical and psychological. Every person's environment is different from every other student's, because the constellation of factors that comprise an individual's environment will vary from person to person. The courses a student takes, a student's friends, a student's residence, and so on accumulate to create a unique environment.

We have defined environmental assessment as a process that "determines and evaluates how the various elements and conditions of the college campus milieu affect student learning and growth" (Upcraft and Schuh, 1996, p. 167). In effect, an environmental assessment develops a collage of perspectives about the campus environment. In the end, what one has is a consensus that may or may not reflect the experiences and perspectives of any specific student.

Contributions of Environmental Assessment to Student Affairs

Evans (1983, pp. 294–295) identifies five potential contributions of environmental assessment to student affairs:

1. *Environmental assessment can be a powerful change strategy.*

2. *Environmental assessment can be adapted to gather information relevant to many different kinds of questions and settings.*

3. *Environmental assessment is an approach that can enhance the status and functional role for student affairs across the campus.*

4. *Intervening in the environment allows student affairs practitioners to do more with fewer resources.*

5. *Environmental assessment techniques have the potential to be particularly useful when combined with knowledge of student development theory. Theory identifies the potential changes students will undergo during their college experience; environmental assessment is a technique to determine if the environment is encouraging these outcomes.*

Evans (1983, p. 294) concludes, "Environmental assessment has great potential for student affairs, especially during periods of accountability and declining resources."

Environmental assessments can be conducted in a variety of settings and can range from specific units (Schuh, 1979) to an entire campus (Treadway, 1979).

Huebner (1979, pp. 14–15) asserts that environmental assessment is based on a series of assumptions:

1. *Students can and will accurately report their perceptions of their environment.*

2. *Dissatisfaction and self-reported stress are negative and counterproductive and need to be eliminated.*

3. *Closing the gap between goals and perceived reality will result in better functioning for students.*

4. *Aggregation of data by subgroups is a valid procedure.*

One of the challenges that environmental assessment can address is the matter of campus climate for historically underrepresented groups. Student affairs staff and other members of the campus community are interested in assessing the climate for these students. The process outlined in this chapter can be applied to virtually any population of students. Besides the approach presented here, investigators may wish to look at several quantitative instruments developed specifically for this purpose. One instrument worth considering is that developed by Harrold and Hanson (n.d.).

Consider the challenges faced by the new director of residence life in the case study presented here. An environmental assessment might be the answer to developing a picture of what life is really like in the residence halls.

Residence Life Quality Issues at State University: A Case Study

This fall you were appointed the director of the residence life department at a major state university. The department is large and complex, with hundreds of staff and thousands of students for whom you provide oversight.

During your interview on campus, you had heard some concerns expressed about the quality of life in the residence halls and the level of supervision provided. Some people thought that the residence halls were out of control; the study atmosphere was terrible, they said, and drinking and general carousing were the norm. Students did not think this was the situation, and staff disagreed with the assertions of the critics, but powerful faculty and some administrators took the other point of view.

After about one month on the job, you were summoned to the vice president's office for a meeting with two senior professors, one of whom held the rank of distinguished professor. The two faculty members explained in no uncertain terms that the residence halls were out of control. Students could not study in their rooms when they wished to, and often they were too tired in class to participate since they were kept up all night by the noise. Moreover, students did poorly on exams since the nonexistent study atmosphere got in the way of their preparation.

The professors explained that they had pointed out their concerns to the previous director but all they received in return was some educational mumbo-jumbo. The time for explanations was over, in their opinion. They made it very clear to you: either clean up this mess, or they would find someone who would. With that, the meeting was declared over, and they left.

A Quantitative Approach

In this case, the residence life staff is under significant pressure to develop a strategy to answer complaints about the residence hall environment. The faculty members are quite unhappy with their perception of study conditions in the residence halls, but they are willing to examine a data-based analysis of the problem. You decide to conduct an environmental assessment that is designed to examine the quality of life in the residence halls. The ecosystem approach developed by WICHE lends itself well to this problem.

In a situation like this, one of the issues to explore is the composition of the team that will conduct the assessment. Reviere and Carter (1996) outline the advantages and disadvantages of using insiders and outsiders. Outsiders have no preconceived expectations of the organizational culture and provide a fresh view. However, they will need to be compensated for their expertise, especially if they are from outside the institution. Insiders are familiar with facilities, personnel, and the style of the organization, but may have a fixed perception of what is right and wrong with the institution.

The ecosystem approach may include the use of a survey, either locally developed or available from commercial test publishers (see Resources at the end of the book for such environmental assessment instruments). In this instance, the development of a questionnaire with features unique to State U's problem seems appropriate. The development of a local questionnaire encourages respondents to become partners with the investigators in the process by which the environment is changed.

The first step is to identify the object of the assessment. In this case, the students residing in the campus residence halls form the population for the study. A random sample of students who live in each residence hall should be drawn so that the data can be analyzed by each residence hall, rather than just the residence hall system in the aggregate. The exact number of students in each sample will vary depending on the size of the residence hall. Rea and Parker (1997) identify sample sizes based on the level of confidence selected by the investigator and provide a good reference in selecting sample size.

Now we look at the questionnaire itself. Many questionnaires have been developed over the years using forced-choice formats. In the ecosystem model, the first part of the questionnaire uses a forced-choice format. Exhibit 12.1 provides a few sample items.

After a draft questionnaire has been prepared, it is important to conduct a pilot test along the lines recommended by Rea and Parker (1997). This step helps improve the psychometric properties of the instrument.

Once students complete the forced-choice items, they are asked to go back through the instrument and select a limited number of items about which they feel strongly. They are asked to identify the items, explain why they feel strongly about each one, and provide ideas on what they would recommend to improve the situation. This is true whether the students feel positively about the item or negatively about it.

EXHIBIT 12.1

Questionnaire for Determining Student Satisfaction with Residence Halls

Listed below are a series of questions about life in the residence halls. Please indicate your response to each item by placing an X in the appropriate blank. *Living unit* refers to the floor, house, or wing where you live.

	Strongly Agree	Agree	Neutral	Disagree	Strongly Disagree
1. I am satisfied with the services provided at the main desk.	_____	_____	_____	_____	_____
2. The custodian keeps my living unit clean.	_____	_____	_____	_____	_____
3. My resident assistant is available to my needs in the living unit.	_____	_____	_____	_____	_____
4. I am satisfied with the meals provided by the food service.	_____	_____	_____	_____	_____
5. Study conditions in my unit are adequate.	_____	_____	_____	_____	_____
6. I am satisfied with the social activities available in my unit.	_____	_____	_____	_____	_____

This part of the questionnaire is referred to as environmental referents. These environmental referents force students to identify the elements of the environment about which they are especially concerned, and they also become partners with the investigators in developing strategies to improving the environment. Exhibit 12.2 shows this part of the questionnaire.

Data collection in this case most commonly means using a mailed survey. We have asserted elsewhere in this book that we prefer other ways to collect information from student to mailed surveys. In this case, however, a mailed survey makes sense because we know all the members of the sample, residential staff can deliver questionnaires directly to the students in their rooms, and collection places can be established in a number of places in the residence halls, such as the main desk, food service area, or hall director's office. Follow-up surveys can be delivered to those who do not respond very easily, and the cost of mailing is eliminated. So in this situation, a mailed survey is an appropriate approach. Regardless of the methodology, the proposed methods must be approved by the institutional review board before any data are collected.

Data analysis was done not only for the entire residential system, but also by each residence hall and possibly by smaller units than that. The unit of data analysis can be whatever you as investigator choose. Descriptive sta-

---

EXHIBIT 12.2

Environmental Referents

Now that you have completed the first part of the questionnaire, please go back and identify not more than three items about which you feel very strongly—either positively or negatively. In the grid below, list each item number in the box to the left, and provide the additional information about the item in the boxes to the right.

Item Number	Why do you feel strongly about the item?	What do you recommend to enhance the situation?
3.	I can't find my RA when I need him.	Provide a list of on-call RAs so I can get help when I need it.
5.	I have to go to the library to study because of the noise.	Establish study hours rather than relying strictly on an honor system.
6.	I have plenty to do and the floor activities are great.	Just keep it up. Have more of the same activities.

Thank you very much for completing the questionnaire.

tistics and measures of central tendency can be computed on an item-by-item basis for the entire residential system as well as for each residence hall or each residential unit. The environmental referents require an analysis technique not unlike document analysis in qualitative methods. Each response needs to be read and analyzed and themes and patterns identified.

Forced-choice items and environmental referents can be analyzed together. Essentially the items are ranked by number of responses (see Exhibit 12.3). The forced-choice items are ranked from those that received the highest mean scores to the lowest. For the environmental referents, the numbers are ranked in inverse order, from those that received the fewest comments to those that received the most. From this point, if a specific item received a low mean score and a larger number of comments (for example, ranking in the top quartile of most frequent comments), that is an item that needs

---

EXHIBIT 12.3

Analyzing the Responses

On the left side of this sheet, rank the forced-choice items from most favorable mean scores to least favorable mean scores. On the right side of this sheet, rank the environmental referents from those that received the least number of comments to the most. Draw lines across the page at the 25th, 50th, and 75th percentiles. First analyze the numbers that appear in the 25th percentile first, then the 50th, and so on.

Most Favorable Mean Scores	**Least Number of Comments**
_____	_____
_____	_____
_____	_____
_____	_____
_____	_____
_____	_____
_____	_____
_____	_____
_____	_____
Least Favorable Mean Scores	**Greatest Number of Comments**

immediate attention. Scores with very positive mean scores and relatively few comments are those that probably need little to no attention.

In developing action strategies, the best approach is to produce an action plan by each residence hall. Conditions and perceptions potentially will vary widely from residence hall to residence hall, and an overall system report is not particularly useful for policymakers, senior administrators, and others with an interest in campus residence halls. Nevertheless, for the purpose of having a benchmark for the system, an overall report should be prepared and provided to the faculty and others who had expressed an intense interest in the quality of life in the residence halls.

A Qualitative Approach

This case also could be addressed through qualitative methodology. The use of focus groups, perhaps organized residence hall by residence hall, seemed appropriate.

Sampling for the use of focus groups would use a selection of students from each residence hall. Since the concern is to make sure that each residence hall has students involved as respondents, theoretically you need to conduct several focus groups for each residence hall. This form of criterion sampling (Patton, 1990) is an appropriate approach given the nature of the study.

Focus groups continue until the people conducting the groups encounter redundant information from the participants. Morgan (1998) claims that typically three to five groups are needed, although he concedes, "In most cases, it is difficult to anticipate exactly how many groups it will take to reach saturation" (p. 78).

The data for the study were collected through the use of a number of focus groups. Conducting a number of such groups, however, would require the involvement of many people, since a steering committee for the assessment project would have to devote substantial time, and perhaps discharge other responsibilities, to complete the project. It is possible that graduate students on campus, advanced undergraduate students, interested faculty, and perhaps some administrators could be trained to conduct the groups. The point to emphasize is that this approach can be labor intensive. Exhibit 12.4 shows a sample interview protocol to use as a guide with the focus groups.

The institution's database also might be a useful source of information. For example, if interviews are conducted with students who have withdrawn from the university, this information could be used to determine if students who withdrew provided observations about the residence halls during their exit interviews.

EXHIBIT 12.4

Residence Halls Environment Interview Protocol

Thanks very much for joining me today for this discussion. My name is _____ and I am _____ at State U. We are here to visit for a few minutes about what life is like in the residence halls here at State U. Your participation in this group is voluntary. You may leave at any time. I will not attribute anything said to any specific person. If these conditions are agreeable to you, let us begin.

1. Why did you choose to live in a residence hall at State?

2. Has living in a residence hall turned out the way you expected?

3. What do you like best about living in a residence hall?

4. How might residence hall life be improved?

5. What effect, if any, has living in residence halls had on your academic work?

6. Are you able to study and sleep when you want to? If not, please explain.

7. What would you tell your friends who go to other colleges about residence hall life at State?

8. Is there anything else you would like to tell me about residence hall life at State?

Thanks very much for being a part of this group. A report of the findings of this study will be available in approximately six weeks on State U.'s Web site: www.statu.edu.

Observations of students could be conducted. This might be accomplished by periodic visits to the residence halls during times when students presumably would be studying or sleeping. Anecdotal evidence of the kind that would be generated from this kind of activity never provides a complete picture of the floor or hall environment, but it can point to the tone that has been set in the unit and can provide a basis for further analysis.

Reports, as was the case for the quantitative approach, should be developed on a hall-by-hall basis. These reports then form the basis for the development of strategies to improve the quality of life in the residence hall. An overall report also could be developed for the reasons expressed above.

Conclusion

Environmental assessment is a particularly useful technique when the goal is to gain a sense of the total experience of students and their interaction with the institution. What is important to remember in using this approach is that it is designed to develop a partnership between those being assessed, typically students, and the institution. This form of assessment is designed to lead to change. When it is done effectively, the quality of student life can improve as a result of this form of assessment. As WICHE concluded nearly three decades ago (1973, p. 18), "The hope is to design and fit environments to people so they can achieve their greatest potential."

References

Aulepp, L., and Delworth, U. *Training Manual for an Ecosystem Model.* Boulder, Colo.: Western Interstate Commission for Higher Education, 1976.

Evans, N. J. "Environmental Assessment: Current Practices and Future Directions." *Journal of College Student Personnel,* 1983, *24,* 293–299.

Harrold, R., and Hanson, G. *Campus Diversity Survey.* Unpublished questionnaire, n.d.

Huebner, L. A. "Editor's Notes." In L. A. Huebner (ed.), *Redesigning Campus Environments.* New Directions for Student Services, no. 8. San Francisco: Jossey-Bass, 1979.

Lewin, K. *Principles of Topological Psychology.* (F. Heider and G. M. Heider, trans.) New York: McGraw-Hill, 1936.

Morgan, D. L. *Planning Focus Groups.* Thousand Oaks, Calif.: Sage, 1998.

Patton, M. Q. *Qualitative Evaluation and Research Methods.* (2nd ed.) Thousand Oaks, Calif.: Sage, 1990.

Paul, S. C. "Understanding Student-Environment Interaction." In W. H. Morrill and J. C. Hurst, with E. R. Oetting and others, *Dimensions of Intervention for Student Development.* New York: Wiley, 1980.

Rea, L. M., and Parker, R. A. *Designing and Conducting Survey Research: A Comprehensive Guide.* (2nd ed.) San Francisco: Jossey-Bass, 1997.

Reviere, R., and Carter, C. C. "Planning a Needs Assessment." In R. Reviere, S. Berkowitz, C. C. Carter, and C. G. Ferguson (eds.), *Needs Assessment: A Creative Guide for Social Scientists.* Washington, D.C.: Taylor & Francis, 1996.

Schuh, J. H. "Assessment and Redesign in Residence Halls." In L. A. Huebner (ed.), *Redesigning Campus Environments.* New Directions for Student Services, no. 8. San Francisco: Jossey-Bass, 1979.

Treadway, D. M. "Use of Campus-Wide Ecosystem Surveys to Monitor a Changing Institution." In L. A. Huebner (ed.), *Redesigning Campus Environments.* New Directions for Student Services, no. 8. San Francisco: Jossey-Bass, 1979.

Upcraft, M. L., and Schuh, J. H. *Assessment in Student Affairs: A Guide for Practitioners.* San Francisco: Jossey-Bass, 1996.

Western Interstate Commission for Higher Education. *The Ecosystem Model: Designing Campus Environments.* Boulder, Colo.: Western Interstate Commission for Higher Education, 1973.

Chapter 13

Assessing Cost Effectiveness

Kirsten Kennedy, Linda Moran, M. Lee Upcraft

ASSESSING COST EFFECTIVENESS may be the most neglected form of assessment in student affairs. We seldom assess cost effectiveness, and when we do, it tends to be haphazard rather than systematic. Typical student affairs professionals have little in their background or training that provides the knowledge and skills necessary to assess cost effectiveness, so decisions are often made on the basis of personal intuition, institutional realities, or historical precedent.

But as challenges to the breadth and depth of student services and programs increase, so do cost effectiveness questions. Most of these questions arise from what the public perceives as cost increases that are way out of line compared to overall cost increases in our society. For example, from 1987 to 1996, the gross per student cost of attendance at a four-year public institution increased 109 percent, compared to a 37 percent increase in median family income (National Commission on the Cost of Higher Education, 1998). Even taking into account growth in financial aid programs, the price of attendance minus all financial aid increased 95 percent from 1987 to 1996 at four-year public institutions, 64 percent at four-year private institutions, and 169 percent at public two-year institutions (National Commission on the Cost of Higher Education, 1998). Clearly we must be prepared to answer cost effectiveness questions better than we have in the past, and one important way is to develop more systematic ways of assessing cost effectiveness.

The harsh reality is that if we in student affairs do not adequately answer these questions, others will. Some of these others may be internal to the institution and might well include business officers with little or no understanding of the mission and goals of student affairs ("We could save the institution a bundle of money if we eliminated counseling services"), faculty with self-interested agendas ("The less we spend on student affairs, the more we can spend on academic functions"), or private entrepreneurs ("We can provide the same service for less cost"). But even if there are no pressures from others, we should be interested in assessing cost effectiveness systematically because we can provide greater breadth and depth of services and programs for students if we are using our financial resources efficiently and wisely.

This chapter provides a framework within which to assess the cost effectiveness of student services and programs. We examine some key questions in assessing cost effectiveness and present a case study based on cost effectiveness issues that arise in student health services.

Key Questions to Ask Before Assessing Cost Effectiveness

Before actually conducting the cost effectiveness assessment, some essential questions need to be considered as a background for the analysis.

How does the service or program contribute to the institution's mission? Defining what role the program or service plays in the achievement of the institution's mission will make a difference in the way in which the assessment of cost effectiveness is approached. The mission of the institution will aid in the assessment by identifying what is important to the entire institution. For example, the role of health services may be less prominent in an urban, commuting institution where abundant medical services are available off campus compared to a residential college located in a small town.

In what direction is the institution headed? What are the strategic plans of institution? The institution's direction and goals will aid in the analysis by identifying what is important to the institution as a whole. Even if you believe the service or program is important to the institution now, it may be that it will be more or less important depending on the direction in which the institution is headed. For example, the role of health services may be increasing in importance if the institution plans to expand enrollment and build more on-campus residence halls.

What are the institution's budget policies? Before embarking on a cost effectiveness assessment, you should make sure you are operating within your institution's overall budget policies and practices. These policies will make a difference in how you can use the information after the analysis is completed. For example, is the entire budget process closed (that is, none of the information is to be made available to the general public), or is it open (the public has the right to know what is in the budget)? Or the process could be open, but general practice is not to publicize the figures. Knowing what these boundaries are before beginning is very important.

Cost Effectiveness at State University: A Case Study

State University is located in a small, mostly rural area of the Southeast. The current enrollment is 13,500 students, 40 percent of whom are commuters, 40 percent of whom are resident students on campus, and 20 percent are a growing population of continuing and distance-education students. There are 204 full-time and 88 part-time faculty and 98 full- and part-time staff, with 36 occasional employees supporting the college operations.

The health service employs one nurse practitioner, three full-time registered nurses, one part-time practical nurse, one physician on retainer, and one physician's assistant, who maintains clinic hours four times per week and is paid under the physician's contract. One full- and one part-time pharmacist and one pharmacy technician manage the on-site pharmacy service.

Health services provided are for chronic or nonacute illnesses and minor traumatic injuries. The majority of illnesses are colds, viruses, minor illnesses, and other maladies that can be treated with standing orders from a physician or by a nurse practitioner or a physician's assistant. Educational programs, averaging approximately thirty hours annually, are provided for students and staff and are offered by health service personnel. The patterns of use for the health services have fluctuated seasonally, with highest use in the winter and spring semesters. The highest percentage of users is resident students and staff; commuter students rarely use the service unless they have no other health insurance coverage. Many of the staff and faculty seek health care from their managed care or private health care providers. The average age of the user of health services is twenty-nine. Emergency care situations involving life-threatening events are referred to the local health care system emergency department, with local ambulance transportation arranged according to contract and billed through the individual's health insurance plan.

The health service hours of operation are from 8:30 A.M. to 5:30 P.M. serving the daytime population. Health services are available to the evening students (36 percent of the total population) four evenings each week. Faculty and staff use of health services on site has declined in the past year because the college's board of trustees approved an employee health coverage plan through a managed care plan with providers in the local community. The faculty and staff do, however, use the on-site facility for the treatment of minor emergencies and injuries on the job, and the pharmacy to purchase prescription drugs and some over-the-counter medications. The physical plant space for health service functions includes three clustered rooms in the Block Building, which houses the Adult Education, Women's Center, and the Continuing and Distance Education Department.

The physical plant that houses the health service is coveted by the Continuing and Distance Education (CDE) Department, which has expanded due to a 25 percent increase in enrollees from local business partnerships that have been forged with the college. The CDE Department has shown a 15 percent profit margin increase in the past fiscal year and projects a 28 percent profit margin increase in the current fiscal year. The CDE has shown significant financial profit margins for the past two years.

Upon the recommendation of the president, the board of trustees voted recently to examine several of the college departments and services to determine their efficiency and are encouraging division managers to explore outsourcing services to contain operations costs not directly related to the educational mission. The Health Services Department falls under the vice president for student affairs who has requested an evaluation of the efficiency and effectiveness of the current services, and the presentation of alternatives for health service delivery to meet the needs of users.

Steps in Assessing Cost Effectiveness

Because financial management is most often a linear, step-by-step process, this same approach is necessary in assessing cost effectiveness. The cost assessment process considers the institutional context and then determines the reason for assessing cost effectiveness, which will help determine the purpose of the study. Then the cost of the service or program and revenue sources will be identified. After analyzing one year's worth of data, the past year's data will be looked at to determine trends and benefits of the program to the constituents and to consider alternatives.

Step 1: Examine the Institutional Context

There are key questions to be asked before embarking on a cost effectiveness assessment. First, how does the university's health service contribute to the institution's mission? If the mission is examined and the wholeness of the student is valued, then the health service can be assessed as integral to the mission. A student's good health may enhance learning and social and personal development and thereby influence the student's persistence.

Second, in what direction is the university headed? It is clear that the institution is searching for ways in which to make services and programs more efficient and cost-effective. It is unlikely that it would totally eliminate health services provided, given the needs of its students and the inability of the community to absorb the heath care needs of students. However, adjustment of some of the costs is a realistic consideration and may lead to outsourcing of selected health service functions.

Third, what are the university's budget policies? By state law, the university is required to have a completely open budget process. Any citizen may review the institution's budget, including the individual salaries of all employees.

Step 2: Determine the Reasons for Assessing Cost Effectiveness

All assessment starts with a problem. There is always at least one important reason for initiating any assessment. In this case study, the president and board of trustees are looking for more cost-effective ways of delivering health services, and chief among them is the idea of outsourcing some or all services currently offered. These decisions cannot be made without first knowing much more about the costs and the benefits of the current way of delivering health services. Only then will the institution be in a position to decide among suggested alternatives.

Step 3: Determine the Purpose of the Study

Based on the problem described in Step 1, the purpose of this study is to determine and analyze the costs and benefits of State University's health service and consider alternative means of delivery of health services based on that analysis.

Step 4: Determine the Cost of the Service or Program

How is the cost of delivering the university's health service determined? Although it may seem logical simply to look at the bottom line of this budget ($296,990 for FY 98, shown in Exhibit 13.1) and hand that over as the cost of running this program, it is not an accurate reflection of the actual cost. To assess this budget, costs must be calculated in three ways: (1) split budget line items between fixed and variable costs, (2) determine those costs within the control of health services and those over which it has no control, and (3) determine the direct and indirect costs of this health service. Using

parking. Indirect costs often are difficult to define and determine. The problem is that at times, indirect costs are charged back to service or program budgets from the institutional unit responsible for the service, or the service or program is charged a general percentage for all indirect costs. For example, staff benefits costs may or may not be charged back to the service or program budget. So depending on the budget policies at an institution, staff benefits may be a direct cost (specifically line items in your budget) or an indirect cost (covered by institutional resources).

The direct and indirect costs of the university's health service budget are shown in Exhibit 13.3. The direct expenses are the personnel, salaries and benefits, and the minor and capital equipment, amounting, respectively, to $296,990 (FY 98), and $315,870 (FY 99) and a projected $339,637 (FY 00). All of the direct costs can be controlled. Indirect costs are heat, light, and maintenance of the building, amortization, and depreciation, which either cannot be controlled or may be able to be controlled to some minor extent, like the use of utilities, based on hours of service.

Controllable and Uncontrollable Costs A controllable cost is one over which the health service has some control. For example, the health service has some control over how much it spends in office supplies, as well as the

---

EXHIBIT 13.3

Direct and Indirect Expenses

	FY 98	FY 99	FY 00 (Projected)
Direct Expenses			
Salaries	$133,000	$142,180	$157,731
Benefits	46,220	48,341	53,625
Supplies	58,000	60,900	63,945
Equipment	27,500	31,746	31,123
Subtotal	$264,795	$283,167	$306,414
Indirect Expenses			
Amortization	$11,545	$11,545	$11,545
Utilities	7,500	7,613	7,727
Subtotal	$19,045	$19,158	$19,272
Depreciation			
Equipment	$2,650	$2,730	$2,811
Physical plant	10,500	10,815	11,139
Subtotal	13,150	13,545	$13,951
Total expenses	$296,990	$315,870	$339,637

amount of supplies and equipment used. It is possible to hold off purchasing the power stapler, eliminate the duplicate paper calendar in lieu of exclusively using the computer calendar, reuse folders, and so on in an attempt to control costs. An uncontrollable cost is one over which health services has no control. Examples are staff benefits, debt retirement, and merit raises. These costs are directly related to health services operations, but the amounts and increases are beyond its control. Uncontrollable costs include those mandated by the institution. For example, administrative overhead charges paid back to the institution are uncontrolled costs. Other examples are parking for health services staff, food services for students and staff, housekeeping, and other assigned expenses based on the number of employees or staff full time equivalents (FTEs).

In Exhibit 13.4, controllable costs total $264,795 for FY 98, including salaries, benefits, supplies, and equipment, and uncontrollable costs total $7,500 for utilities.

Step 5: Identify Revenue Sources

Student affairs services and programs, including the health service, are typically funded from a wide variety of sources.

Direct Institutional Allocation The institution, usually on a year-to-year basis, provides all or part of the funds necessary to deliver a service or program. This usually means justifying a budget request on an annual basis through the institution's budget allocation process.

Required Fees for Services and Programs The institution mandates that the costs of certain services or programs will be covered by a separate student

---

EXHIBIT 13.4

Controllable and Uncontrollable Expenses

	FY 98	FY 99	FY 00 (Projected)
Controllable Costs			
Salaries	$133,000	$142,180	$157,731
Benefits	46,220	48,341	53,625
Supplies	58,000	60,900	63,945
Equipment	27,575	31,746	31,123
Subtotal	$264,795	$283,167	$306,414
Uncontrollable Costs			
Utilities	$7,500	$7,613	$7,727

fee, regardless of whether the individual student actually uses those services or programs. Typical examples are student activity fees, health service fees, computer fees, and laboratory fees.

Optional Fees for Services and Programs   The institution provides services and programs only to students who pay the service fee. Those who pay the overall fee are permitted to use the service or program; those who do not are denied access. Typical examples are room and board fees, parking fees, bus passes, health services fees, and recreation facilities fees.

Fees for Services Rendered   Students pay for only those services and programs they actually use, but may pick and choose within a service or program. For example, in health services, the student is charged only for specific services rendered, which means separate fees for a physician's examination, laboratory analyses, blood pressure screening, and so forth. Fees for services rendered also include fees charged to other institutional units. For example, if a health service provides blood pressure screening for faculty and staff, the cost of the program may be legitimately charged off as a staff benefit that is paid for by the institution.

Grants and Other External Funding   Occasionally a student services unit pursues a grant to fund a specific program or service, usually for some specified period of time. Sometimes these funds originate from within the institution, but often they come from sources outside the institution. For example, for many years colleges and universities received federal or state grants to support alcohol and other drug programs. The problem with these sources of revenue is that they eventually dry up, and the services or programs that were funded also dry up, except in that rare circumstance where the institution picks up the funding.

Funding Sources Unique to the Service or Program   Certain student services and programs may have sources of funding unique to their operation. A typical example is the funding of selected health services by health insurance carriers. Costs such as drugs, x-rays, and laboratory tests may be covered by an institution-based student insurance program or by the student's health maintenance organization, preferred provider organization, or other third-party providers.

Often a service or program may have several funding sources. For example, a mandatory health fee may include a physician's examination, but additional fees may be charged for laboratory analyses and x-rays, often covered by health insurance providers. Exhibit 13.5 identifies the sources of funding for the university's health services.

Revenue sources are important because in an era of declining resources, an institution may want to shift the ways in which it funds various student services and programs in an effort to reduce direct institutional allocations. Or the institution may intensify its efforts to seek external grants. Or students may resent paying for services that they do not use, and pressure the institution to eliminate selected mandatory fees.

Step 6: Determine Trends

There are several ways of determining trends.

Compare Costs from Year to Year The simplest trend analysis is to analyze costs over time by comparing this year's budget with those of previous years. This analysis can help in determining how the percentages of costs have changed. Have variable costs remained fairly constant while fixed costs have soared? Have direct costs increased while indirect costs have remained constant? On the other hand, this analysis may be misleading if a one-time or rare cost is included in one fiscal year. For example, if a capital investment is made (an outdated x-ray machine is replaced) in one fiscal year, resulting in a 15 percent increase in costs for that year, it is essential to identify that cost as a one-time item, not to be repeated in subsequent years.

Compare to Benchmarks It is often useful to compare costs, cost increases, fees, and fee increases over time to other units within the institution or to the total increases of the institution. For example, the annual cost increases

---

EXHIBIT 13.5

Funding Sources for the University's Health Services

	FY 98	FY 99	FY 00 (Projected)
Student health services fees	$258,250	$268,370	$285,660
Health fees	2,460	2,950	3,600
Co-pay fees	6,580	8,800	9,500
Grants	5,000	6,500	8,150
Preferred provider organization member fees	9,800	10,780	11,858
Pharmacy revenues	6,000	7,600	8,000
Additional revenues	8,900	10,790	12,869
Total	$296,990	$315,870	$339,637

in the health service may be compared to the overall cost increases of other units in the institution to determine if health services increases are in line with other increases. Or the health service's fee increase may be compared to the increase in tuition. However, such comparisons, when made public, may create difficult relations with the units with which comparisons are made, and thus should be very carefully planned and considered.

It is often useful to make comparisons to external benchmarks. The Consumer Price Index (CPI) attempts to measure changes in the prices of a market basket of some four hundred goods and services. It measures changes in the costliness of a constant (adjusted for inflation) standard of living (McConnell, 1984). This analysis provides a means of comparison in relationship to the U.S. economy. The Higher Education Price Index (HEPI) is similar to the CPI but takes into consideration the changes in constant cost of higher education. It serves as a comparison for the health services in relation to others at a national level. It may be necessary to explain why increases may have exceeded or not quite met the increases of those indexes used as benchmarks.

Benchmarking and determining trends are almost always specific to a particular institution. Nationwide benchmarks may not apply to regional facilities of health services delivered by a college or university. Rather than comparing national to institutional rates or trends, it is more appropriate to compare the structure, function, and usage patterns of health services to other similar institutions. When examining trends of costs, budget line items in the budget should be analyzed to identify supply and equipment usage, abuse, and misuse. Also unusual illnesses such as an outbreak of meningitis or measles on a campus should be considered as a historical effect on the budget, a one-time occurrence that must be identified as budget trends are supported or defended.

Compare Student Usage Rates In looking at trends, it must be determined how many students have been served and will be served in the future. What are student usage rates? What events have precipitated an increase or decline in usage? For example, have the number of students using the university's health service increased, and if so, why? Can community health care services provide comparable health services to students for less cost and thus affect usage rate? It is also possible that while overall usage rates may stay the same, student use of specific health services may vary. For example, there may be an increase in student use of women's health services but a decline in students attending health education programs.

Changes in the source of funding can also affect usage rates. For example, if the required health services fee is eliminated in favor of an optional fee (only students who pay the fee receive services), then we might expect usage to drop. If the credit hour eligibility for service policy is changed from twelve credit hours to nine credit hours, we might expect usage to increase. These are the kinds of questions that should be asked when past, current, and future usage rates are compared.

It is sometimes argued that services and programs that receive institutional funding can afford to be less concerned about student usage rates than those that depend on user fees. Although there is some truth to this argument, no student service or program will be in business long, even if it is institutionally funded, if students do not use it. Furthermore, institutionally funded units may argue for increased funding based on increased student use. Because health services are often funded by required fees, fees for services, institutional funds, or some combination of these funding sources, student use is especially important.

Attempt to Project the Future As important as using past history for comparison is projecting change within a department. Some premises will be predictions of what will occur in the future, while others will be formalizing plans for the future and the costs associated with them. If periodic capital investments have been made, projections should include the years when they will occur again, and for what purpose. If certain expenses will end within the coming fiscal year (for example, the retirement of a bond), they should also appear in projections. In addition, any projected changes in the number or type of students served should be taken into account. If new services or programs are anticipated that will increase or decrease student usage, they should be reflected in cost projections.

Health services usage rates on campus may be affected by student or staff use patterns. Special attention to separating the user populations may be of interest as the budget is examined. Services for each user group may vary, altering staffing patterns and affecting equipment and supplies. The need for equipment for preventive measures such as the administration of flu shots may be offset by external sources of revenue. On the other hand, to meet public health guidelines, health centers operated at state-assisted institutions may support some screening and preventive or maintenance costs such as screening for and treatment of tuberculosis or other contagious diseases.

Changes in the student population such as enrolling more international students may lead to changing patterns in student health services use, so we must look to the future of health services and usage trends, such as admissions projections, population shifts from census trends, and other incidental yet important information. Health services are specific for different age populations. The trends of user needs for the age group eighteen to twenty-four years are going to be different from those of the age group twenty-five to fifty years. Equipment and supplies needed for the treatment of acute illnesses and reproductive and adolescent conditions differ from the supplies and even hours of service for the middle-aged group of users who present with chronic lower back, upper respiratory, and incidental injuries or conditions of their developmental stages.

As the institution changes curricular offerings to meet the needs of adult and part-time students, health services may need to change their hours of operation. Opportunities may also develop with a population change. The adult users who require evening hours may be served by practitioners who offer a variety of services for sliding-scale fees, thus providing a revenue opportunity. For people who do not have health insurance coverage, fees may be charged for the treatment of minor injuries, illnesses, or group counseling support by licensed or certified personnel. Hiring these credentialed personnel may change the position descriptions and salary scales, but may provide the institution with a wider range of services and coverage than previously staffed.

Step 7: Determine Benefits

Benefits are the less tangible portion of assessing cost effectiveness. A student service or program usually cannot be easily identified or quantified. In some settings in student affairs, there is a tangible benefit. For example, in admissions, we know how many students applied, were accepted, paid a deposit, and enrolled at the institution. However, the benefits derived from most student affairs units are less tangible and therefore much less measurable. This problem is confounded by the fact that users may include not only students but also faculty staff, other institutional units, and sometimes the general public.

Benefits to Students   All services and programs in student affairs are designed to benefit students, but how will those benefits change if costs were reduced? The starting point for looking at benefits is to list the services and programs provided to students and then describe how students benefit from them, both tangibly and intangibly. Although most benefits are somewhat intangible, they can often be assessed (most importantly through outcomes assessments), and thus it may be possible to attach a dollar value to the benefit. Would the benefits change if those services or programs were eliminated, reduced, or outsourced? How would these benefits change if fees were added? Does the institution currently provide the service less expensively than a private provider does? Are services that are provided off campus as conveniently accessed as on-campus services?

For the university's health service, for example, the importance of providing flu shots to the students (an excellent preventive measure that decreases acute service costs in the long run, as well as improves classroom attendance and student learning) may take precedence over eliminating the service. Providing the equipment for the flu shots may be subsidized by the local health department, funded by the state and federal government, and even staffed by health care students as part of their educational practice at the institution.

Benefits to Staff Is the service one that also benefits staff? Again, the starting point is to list all the services and programs the department provides to staff. For example, does the health service provide emergency or routine services to faculty and staff? If so, is the cost comparable to services provided elsewhere? If the cost is less, is this considered an employee fringe benefit? After answering these types of questions, it is important to project how these benefits will change if health services eliminates services to faculty and staff, reduces the budget and tries to retain these services, reduces the budget and reduces services, outsources, or finds alternative revenue sources.

Benefits to the Institution The institution also benefits by having quality services for students, staff, and the public. Listing all the benefits to the institution can be a helpful starting point, followed by attempts to assess those benefits. For example, an institution can gain tuition and other revenue when student use of student services and programs is related to their retention, and there are many studies that show such a relationship (Pascarella and Terenzini, 1991). Thus, an institution may generate increased tuition revenues because of increased student retention. Also, having student services may be a public relations advantage. And perhaps most important, students may well select an institution based on the breadth and depth of its student services and programs. A high-quality health service may well contribute in these many ways.

Benefits to the Public and Graduates The public may benefit from student affairs services. The general public, as well as graduates, may access food service outlets, recreation centers, emergency medical services, career and placement services, and others. These benefits should be listed and taken into account in considering changes in student services and programs, because these stakeholders may be important to the institution. Although it is rare that graduates or the general public are eligible for health services (except for minor health emergencies), other student services such as placement may well benefit these constituencies.

The point here is that whenever cost cutbacks are suggested, they must be considered in the light of the corresponding loss of benefits. For example, if the pharmacy at the health service is eliminated, the projected savings to the institution would be the direct and indirect benefits costs of the employees, totaling $219,000. However, if faculty, staff, and students must now pay full rates for the pharmacy supplies that the university's health service buys in bulk and at a considerable discount, the net effect may be to increase their pharmacy costs, creating staff morale problems and increasing costs of attendance for students. So what was an attractive cost savings measure might well turn out, when the loss of benefits is considered, to be not so attractive or in the best interests of the institution.

Step 8: Consider the Alternatives

An assessment of a service and its effectiveness is generally nonthreatening; nevertheless, it may have some colleagues and subordinates on pins and needles. Challenging and difficult questions may be asked about why and how services are delivered to students. These questions may revolve around the elimination of service, providing the same service with less money, providing a pared-down service with a reduced budget, outsourcing the service, or finding alternative revenue sources. The difference between analyzing student services and programs and many of the examples found in business textbooks is that student services and programs do not usually produce a tangible product. At the end of the academic day, we in higher education cannot point to fifty widgets at the end of the production line, with two defects beyond tolerance. Student affairs units may face a number of issues as pressures rise to reduce costs or redirect resources.

Should This Service or Program Be Eliminated? Is this service or program really needed? The university's health service may be considered obsolete because the institution has made a commitment to serve primarily nontraditional, commuter students. Another scenario is that the health service is considered nonessential because it is not contributing directly to the academic mission of the institution. The service may be viewed as using valuable resources that could be directed to units that contribute more directly to student learning.

Could This Program or Service Provide the Same Service for Less Money? In other words, could the budget be cut without greatly affecting service to students, or could the service be offered for less money? Most would agree that if we could provide the same service for less money, we would strive to that end. A reduction in budget would most likely mean a reduction in service. For example, if more part-time employees are used in lieu of full-time, benefit-eligible employees, money would be saved in reduced salaries and in paying minimal benefits. However, service could decline in continuity and therefore in quality. Reduction of budget will not always equate with reduced service. Restructuring a department can sometimes lead to a cost savings while providing a comparable service. Demands for service should dictate a more efficient staff mix or pattern. For example, in the university's health service, readjusting hours to student use patterns has the potential of maintaining the quality and convenience of service while reducing costs.

Could This Service or Program Be Downsized? Could a particular service or program be reduced in scope or depth and thereby reduce costs as well? For example, could the health service staff be redeployed to meet the peaks and valleys of usage patterns? After assessing the usage patterns, it may be reasonable to decrease one FTE of a registered nurse position and split the licensed practical nurse positions into two part-time positions. The overall savings would be $36,000 of direct salary costs and $12,240 in associated benefits savings to the direct expenses category of your budget.

Typically, the highest expense in any health service budget (or the budget of any other student service or programs) is the direct costs for personnel. The staff mix and staffing patterns could include rearranging the schedules of the physician's assistant and nurse practitioner or the licensed practical nurse. The staffing patterns could be examined to determine if the rearrangement of personnel per shift is appropriate, based on the peak usage times of the health services. For example, if the personnel who can write prescriptions or orders are needed at other times and standing orders for nonacute or acute conditions can be followed, then staffing with registered nurses rather than the physician's assistant or the nurse practitioner is appropriate. If the nonacute illnesses demonstrate a pattern (for example, all showing up on a Monday morning), then registered nurses could be staffing these peak times rather than physician's assistants or nurse practitioners. By adapting staff schedules to meet the demand for service, a full-time licensed practical nurse and a half-time registered nurse position could be eliminated, realizing a $32,000 savings.

Could This Service or Program Be Outsourced? Increasing numbers of outsourcing service agencies argue that they can offer student services programs at less cost to the institution while maintaining comparable quality. The best example in student services is food services, which are often outsourced for both residential dining and fast food service. Other top candidates for outsourcing are housing and residential life, health services, counseling services, and student bookstores. The key in making the outsourcing decision is not only to preserve quality but to compare institutional costs with the cost of outsourcing, and that assumes that both the institution and the potential outsourcing agency have accurate cost and benefit information.

The outsourcing of the university's health services can be considered on a partial basis as well as a total basis. Rather than eliminating or outsourcing all health services, one possibility is to purchase supplies at a discounted rate from regional or statewide suppliers rather than local or regional manufacturers. Another possibility is to form a partnership with a local health maintenance provider, preferred provider organization, or local health system to offer health insurance plans at a group rate, given the size of the faculty, staff, and student population. Often institutional governing board members are valuable resources for networking to ascertain these sources.

Are There Ways This Service or Program Could Be Funded Differently? The usual source for most student services is direct allocation from the institution. But there are other possible sources of revenue—for example, a fee-for-service policy where students pay for only the services that they actually use. Some examples include having students pay each time they visit the counseling center, recreation center, or other service, or charging for voice mail or Internet service in student rooms. Further, health education for various services could be funded by federal or state monies from grant programs.

In this case study, the new health maintenance policy for staff and faculty had decreased the number of health education programs needed for the year. This eliminated the cost of materials purchased for these programs and was no longer an institution expense of $5,600 annually. In addition, elimination of services that were provided free of charge through the local community, such as tuberculosis screening, could provide a significant savings.

Another alternative is to charge students fees directly for a specific service or program. For example, a student's orientation fee may be included in the deposit that the student pays to secure admission to the institution. Other examples are computing fees, health fees, and student activity fees. The difference in these fees is that they are assessed on all students, not just those who choose to use the service. In the university's health services, departmental revenue could be increased by $45,000 annually by assessing a co-pay fee of $10 per visit for each full-time student.

There are also variations on these two alternatives. In the early stages of a new service, students who use it could pay a fee. As the service becomes more popular and students are using it as the rule rather than the exception, then the service may become incorporated into the fee structure. In this case study, the university's health service had a fee for testing for sexually transmitted diseases, but as more students became concerned about STDs, this testing was eventually incorporated into the health service fee paid by all students.

Another alternative is to consider dual uses of space or service. For example, in this case study, using the combined space of the health services area and the CDE may not be the best use of space given the growth of CDE. Technology wiring and construction may require that the CDE move into a more modern facility on campus. The downtime of the health services geographic floor space may create a space usage plan for sharing the common, unsecured areas for seminars held in the evening, community projects, or business partnerships the institution has with local businesses that pay a fee for the use of the space.

Step 9: Apply Findings to Policy and Practice

It is important to understand how cost effectiveness assessment can be used to affect policies and practices. Because there may be institutional policies that restrict public access to budget information, care must be taken when disseminating cost effectiveness assessment results. At many state-supported institutions, budget information is in the public domain. At some state-supported institutions and at most private institutions, budget information may be more closely guarded. So the dissemination of cost effectiveness information must be within institutional policies. There also may be some middle ground. For example, while discussing salaries in aggregate categories (support staff, managers, custodians, dishwashers, counselors, and so on) may be appropriate at a particular institution, singling out salaries by

Chapter 14

Assessment and Accreditation

ONE OF THE UNIQUE aspects of higher education in the United States is the accreditation process, one of the three major processes used to ensure public accountability and continuous improvement. The others are governmental regulation and the marketplace (Council for Higher Education Accreditation, 1998). Whereas in other countries accreditation is a governmental function, accreditation in the United States is voluntary and is conferred by nongovernmental bodies (North Central Association of Colleges and Schools, 1997). The New England Association of Schools and Colleges (1998) emphasizes that accreditation provides a service to a variety of constituencies, including the public, students, and the professions.

The Council for Higher Education Accreditation serves as a voice for colleges and universities on matters related to accreditation. This organization was founded in 1996 and succeeded the Council on Postsecondary Accreditation (COPA), which had been in existence since 1975. Six regional accrediting bodies exist in the United States. These bodies are the heart of the accreditation process in that they accredit entire institutions. Exhibit 14.1 contains a list of these associations, their addresses and telephone numbers, and the geographical areas they serve.

It is important to emphasize that institutions voluntarily seek accreditation from their regional body. No institution has to seek accreditation. From a practical point of view, however, lack of accreditation for a college or university would result in serious problems for the institution. For example, a college or university must be accredited for students to be eligible to participate in federal financial aid programs (Middle States Association, 1998).

EXHIBIT 14.1

Regional Accrediting Bodies

Middle States Association of Colleges and Schools

Delaware, District of Columbia, Maryland, New Jersey, New York, Pennsylvania, Puerto Rico, Virgin Islands

   Address: 3624 Market Street, Philadelphia, PA 19104

   Telephone: (215) 662-5606

   Internet: http://www.msache.org

New England Association of Schools and Colleges

Connecticut, Maine, Massachusetts, New Hampshire, Rhode Island, Vermont

   Address: 209 Burlington Road, Bedford, MA 01730

   Telephone: (617) 271-0022

   Internet: http://www.neasc.org

North Central Association of Colleges and Schools

Arizona, Arkansas, Colorado, Illinois, Indiana, Iowa, Kansas, Michigan, Minnesota, Missouri, Nebraska, New Mexico, North Dakota, Ohio, Oklahoma, South Dakota, West Virginia, Wisconsin, Wyoming

   Address: 30 North La Salle Street, Suite 2400, Chicago, IL 60602

   Telephone: (312) 263-7462

   Internet: http://www.ncacihe.org

Northwest Association of Schools and Colleges

Alaska, Idaho, Montana, Nevada, Oregon, Utah, Washington

   Address: 11130 Northeast Thirty-Third Place, Suite 120, Bellevue, WA 98004

   Telephone: (206) 827-3395

Southern Association of Colleges and Schools

Alabama, Florida, Georgia, Kentucky, Louisiana, Mississippi, North Carolina, South Carolina, Tennessee, Texas, Virginia

   Address: 1866 Southern Lane, Decatur, GA 30033

   Telephone: (404) 679-4500

   Internet: http://www.sacs.org

Western Association of Schools and Colleges

California, Hawaii, Guam, American Samoa, Federated States of Micronesia, Republic of Palau, Commonwealth of the Northern Marianas Islands, Pacific Basin, East Asia

   Address: Box 9990, Mills College, Oakland, CA 94613

   Telephone: (510) 632-5000

   Internet: http://www.wascweb.org

Typically institutions are reviewed for accreditation purposes every ten years (North Central Association of Colleges and Schools, 1997; Middle States Association of Colleges and Schools, 1998; New England Association of Schools and Colleges, 1998), although they may be evaluated more frequently than that depending on institutional exigencies. For example, the North Central Association (1997) conducts "Focused Evaluations" to review specific developments and changes at an institution or to follow up on concerns identified by a previous evaluation process.

Assessment is very important in the accreditation process since the associations expect accredited institutions to demonstrate the effectiveness of their various programs. This chapter identifies how accreditation and assessment are linked so that student affairs practitioners are aware of how accreditation and assessment are associated and to gain an understanding of how to prepare in general for an accreditation visit. (More specific information about the accreditation process for a specific region can be obtained from the accrediting body for the region in which an institution is located.)

A number of special types of accreditation that apply to specific programs also are part of the higher education accreditation process. Often specialized accreditation is linked to licensure in a specific field such as law or medicine. In these cases "specialized accreditation is recognized as providing basic assurance of the scope and quality of professional or occupational preparation" (New England Association of Schools and Colleges, 1998). This chapter will not discuss that aspect of the accreditation process.

General Aspects of Accreditation

Each accrediting body has slightly different purposes, takes slightly different approaches to accreditation, and has different criteria for membership than the others, but in the main they approach accreditation similarly. The New England Association of Schools and Colleges (1998), for example, identifies the general purposes of accreditation as follows:

> *Accreditation has two fundamental purposes: to assure the quality of the institution or program, and to assist in the improvement of the institution or program. Accreditation, which applies to institutions or programs, is to be distinguished from certification and licensure which apply to individuals.*
>
> *The goals are school effectiveness, improvement and public assurance. Unlike popular magazines, this does not involve ranking institu-*

tions, but rather, establishes a level of acceptable quality for all accredited institutions.

The Western Association of Schools and Colleges (1998b) describes its role as a regional accrediting body in this way:

It is the purpose of the Commission to validate to the public the ongoing credibility of an institution of higher education. It is the responsibility of the institution to demonstrate it has the resources, organizational arrangement, academic standards and processes necessary to give assurances of continuous self-monitoring, as well as the continued stability of its purposes, its programs, its faculty and staff, and its financial and physical resources for a minimum of five years. Unless an institution clearly exhibits such characteristics, the Commission is unable to express confidence in the institution through recognition as a Candidate for Accreditation or an accredited institution.

Accreditation bodies do not recommend colleges or universities to specific students. What they attempt to do is strengthen and sustain the quality and integrity of institutions and make judgments about how effectively institutions meet their stated missions and the accrediting body's standards (Southern Association of Colleges and Schools, 1998).

Who Are the Evaluators?

Professional staff conduct the daily business of the accrediting bodies; the persons who conduct the accreditation visits and provide direct feedback to the institutions under consideration for accreditation are members of the higher education community, typically faculty and administrators. The North Central Association of Colleges and Schools (1997) indicates that individuals who meet five criteria (official, full-time employees of accredited North Central institutions; have appropriate training, experience, and accomplishments; meet the projected needs of the commission; represent a diversity of people; and are willing and able to devote their time and energy to the process) may be invited to join the group of individuals who make accreditation visits (in the case of this body, they are called consultant-evaluators). The Southern Association of Colleges and Schools (1998) adds that "individuals selected to be included among the corps of evaluators from which accreditation committees are normally created must be individuals representing the highest level of competence and professional standards in their representative areas of expertise, and must be committed to the significant and sensitive role of the peer reviewer within the accreditation process."

General Criteria for Accreditation

Standards for accreditation vary from region to region, but in the main, institutions have to demonstrate that they have accomplished certain general criteria if they are to be accredited. The standards from the New England Association of Schools and Colleges (1998) provide a good example:

1. *The institution has appropriate resources.*

2. *The institution has the resources needed to accomplish its purposes.*

3. *The institution can demonstrate that it is accomplishing its purposes.*

4. *The institution gives reason to believe that it will continue to accomplish its mission.*

The third item is particularly important since demonstrating the accomplishment of its purposes leads to assessment activities. In this case, outcomes assessments would be particularly useful in demonstrating that the institution is accomplishing its purposes.

Standards for Accreditation

As was the case with the general criteria for accreditation, the more specific standards for accreditation vary from region to region. The North Central Association of Colleges and Schools (1997, pp. 64–67) has identified five specific criteria for accreditation:

1. *The institution has clear and publicly stated purposes consistent with its mission and appropriate to an institution of higher education.*

2. *The institution has effectively organized the human, financial, and physical resources necessary to accomplish its purposes.*

3. *The institution is accomplishing its educational and other purposes.*

4. *The institution can continue to accomplish its purposes and strengthen its educational effectiveness.*

5. *The institution demonstrates integrity in its practices and relationships.*

The New England, Western, and Middles States associations' standards are outlined in more detail in Exhibits 14.2, 14.3, and 14.4.

EXHIBIT 14.2

New England Association of Schools and Colleges: Standards of Effectiveness

---

Standard One: Mission and Purposes

Standard Two: Planning and Evaluation

Standard Three: Organization and Governance

Standard Four: Programs and Instruction

Standard Five: Faculty

Standard Six: Student Services

Standard Seven: Library and Information Resources

Standard Eight: Physical Resources

Standard Nine: Financial Resources

Standard Ten: Public Disclosure

Standard Eleven: Integrity

Note: *Under each one of these standards are specific criteria.*

Source: *Used with permission of New England Association of Schools and Colleges.*

Accreditation and Assessment

Assessment is an important part of the accreditation process. According to a survey of institutions in New England in 1997, of the 149 institutions participating, 135 reported that student outcomes assessment as an indicator of institutional effectiveness in academic programs is somewhat or extremely important to the governing board, 144 indicated that this process was somewhat or extremely important to the campus administration, and 138 reported that this form of assessment was important to faculty (New England Association of Schools and Colleges, 1998). With such a level of importance placed on outcomes assessment for academic programs, one can safely conclude that a similar level of emphasis will be placed on outcomes related to student affairs programs and services in the near future.

The various accrediting bodies provide specific recommendations regarding assessment as it applies to the accreditation process. A number of these items are identified in this section of the chapter to provide illustrations of how institutions need to respond to the requirements of the accreditation process.

- "Principle #3: Greater emphasis is needed on evidence of educational effectiveness and student learning" (Western Association of Schools and

EXHIBIT 14.3

Western Association of Schools and Colleges: Eligibility Criteria

1. A charter and/or formal authority to award degrees from the appropriate governmental agency in the region and operate within its authority. Such authority must be obtained in each state or jurisdiction in which programs are offered. In California approval is required for each degree program.

2. A formally adopted statement of institutional purposes, demonstrating that the fundamental purposes of the institution are education, appropriate to a degree-granting institution, and suited to the needs of the society it seeks to serve.

3. A governing board that operates as an independent policy-making body, and includes representation reflecting the public interest. If a separate institutional governing board is not possible or appropriate, the Commission may approve alternative means by which this criterion may be met.

4. A chief executive officer whose full-time or major responsibility is to the institution, and sufficient administrative staff to conduct the affairs of the institution.

5. One or more educational programs leading to the baccalaureate degree or beyond, educational objectives for each program that are clearly defined and published, as well as appropriate to higher education in level, standards, and quality, and a clear statement of the means for achieving the state educational objectives.

6. A coherent and substantial program of general education as either a prerequisite to or an essential element of the programs offered.

7. Faculty sufficient in terms of number, background, and experience to support the programs offered, and including a core of faculty whose primary responsibility is to the institution. In addition, a clear statement of faculty responsibilities must exist.

8. Evidence of adequate learning resources to support the programs offered on or off-campus. To supplement these resources beyond the core library of the institution, there may be specific long-term written arrangements for student access to readily available resources. The institution must also be able to demonstrate that library use is a fundamental part of all curricula.

9. Admissions policies and procedures consistent with the institution's stated objectives and appropriate to the degree level offered.

10. Evidence of basic planning for the development of the institution. Planning should identify and integrate plans for academic, personnel, library, and financial development, as well as procedures for program review and institution improvement.

11. An adequate financial base of funding commitments, with sufficient financial reserves, to assure future stability. A copy of the current budget and the prior two years' audited financial statements, prepared by an outside certified public accountant that has no other relationship to the institution, must be submitted.

12. A published policy and procedure, in keeping with generally accepted practices, for refunding fees and charges to students who withdraw from enrollment.

13. An accurate and current catalog or other comparable publication available to students and the public, setting forth purposes and objectives, entrance requirements and procedures, rules and regulations for conduct, programs and courses, degree completion requirements, full- and part-time faculty and degrees held, costs, and other items relative to attending the institution or withdrawing from it.

Source: *Used with permission of Western Association of Schools and Colleges.*

EXHIBIT 14.4

Commission on Higher Education of the Middle States Association of Colleges and Schools: Common Characteristics of Excellence

- Integrity in the institution's conduct of all its activities through humane and equitable policies dealing with students, faculty, staff and other constituencies

- Clearly stated mission and goals appropriate to the institution's resources and the needs of its constituents

- Clearly stated admissions and other student policies appropriate to the mission, goals, programs, and resources of the institution

- Student services appropriate to the educational, personal and career needs of the students

- Faculty whose professional qualifications are appropriate to the mission and programs of the institution, who are committed to intellectual and professional development, and who form an adequate core to support the programs offered

- Programs and courses which develop general intellectual skills such as the ability to form independent judgment, to weigh values, to understand fundamental theory, and to interact effectively in a culturally diverse work

- Curricula which provide, emphasize, or rest upon education in the arts and sciences, even when they are attuned to professional or occupational requirements

- Library/learning resources and services sufficient to support the programs offered and evidence of their use

- Policies and procedures, qualitative and quantitative, as appropriate, which lead to the effective assessment of institutional program and student learning outcomes

- Ongoing institutional self-study and planning aimed at increasing the institution's effectiveness

- Financial resources sufficient to assure the quality and continuity of the institution's programs and services

- Organization, administration, and governance which facilitate teaching, research and learning and which foster their improvement within a framework of academic freedom

- A governing board actively fulfilling its responsibilities of policy and resource development

- Physical facilities that meet the needs of the institution's program and functions

- Honesty and accuracy in published materials and in public and media relations

- Responsiveness to the need for institutional change and renewal appropriate to institutional mission, goals and resources

Source: *Commission on Higher Education, Middle States Association of Colleges and Schools.* Characteristics of Excellence in Higher Education: Standards for Accreditation. *Philadelphia: Author, 1994, pp. 4–5. Available in PDF format on the World Wide Web at http://www.msache.org/msachar.pdf. Used with permission.*

Colleges, 1998b). This principle from the Western Association speaks directly to the value of assessment in the accreditation. In effect, this regional body is asserting that institutions must develop better studies that report that their education programs are effective. They also must demonstrate that they are able to provide evidence that their students learn.

Clearly the way to get at such data is to conduct outcomes assessments. The process of outcomes assessment is discussed elsewhere in this book, but as a strategy to speak to this point, institutions will have to conduct outcomes assessments.

The Western Association also has published an institutional standard related to student services and the cocurricular environment (1998a). This standard requires that the institution demonstrate that it meets a number of standards and identifies supporting documents for the standard, including a student handbook and other data that will help provide a concept "of the nature of the student body" (p. 70).

• "Through a program of regular and systematic evaluation, the institution determines whether the co-curricular goals and needs of the students are being met. Information obtained through this evaluation is used to revise these goals and improve their achievement" (New England Association of Schools and Colleges, 1998). The New England Association is seeking several products as a result of this assertion. First, it wants assessment regularly incorporated in the institution's routine. Second, it wants these assessments to focus on learning outcomes as well as student needs. Third, these assessments are used to refocus goals and programs to meet the general mission of the institution better. Fourth, these assessments are to focus on the domain of what commonly has been assigned to the division of student affairs.

As a consequence, to address what the New England Association is seeking, an assessment program has to be developed that is a routine element of the institution's activities rather than an activity conducted on an occasional basis. Needs assessments must be developed to make sure that programmatic offerings are consistent with student needs. And outcomes assessments need to be conducted so that the institution can ensure that its programs work.

For a student affairs practitioner, say a department head or senior divisional leader, to respond to this guidance in the New England region, a regular assessment program focusing on needs and outcomes assessment would have to be in place. Anything less potentially would lead to problems in preparing the institutional case that accreditation should be renewed.

- Implement "policies and procedures, qualitative and quantitative, as appropriate, which lead to the effective assessment of institution, program and student learning outcomes" (Middle States Association Colleges and Schools, 1998). The Middle States Association is clearly seeking systematic data that demonstrate the effectiveness of general and specific institutional programs on student learning.

From a student affairs perspective it is obvious that to meet this standard, outcomes assessments will have to be conducted routinely to identify the benefits, if any, that students derive from their various experiences. Do students who live in residence halls demonstrate greater growth than those who commute? Do leadership development programs make a difference? Does membership in certain organizations inhibit or facilitate intellectual development? These questions and others will have to be examined routinely to stay within the spirit of this aspect of accreditation.

- Find "patterns of evidence" that show that the institution is accomplishing its educational and other purposes (North Central Association of Colleges and Schools, 1997, p. 50). The North Central Association is seeking evidence that student services support the institution's purposes. The institution must demonstrate that it has organized student services appropriate for its mission, so, for example, an open admissions, commuter institution that primarily enrolls students with children would have to configure services and programs that meet demonstrated student needs, such as making supplemental instruction services and day care facilities available to students. Descriptive materials can address one dimension of this matter, but the issue is more than simply providing services or facilities.

The institution also would have to demonstrate that these programs work. Does supplemental instruction actually contribute to persistence to graduation? Does the day care facility result in more students' being able to enroll at the institution, stay enrolled, and graduate? How does one know? In each of these cases, outcomes assessment projects would be necessary to provide compelling evidence. Since these areas typically are assigned to student affairs, the directors of the units responsible for these services are responsible for making sure that assessments are conducted, in concert with leadership from the senior administrators in the division.

- "Student development services *are essential* to the achievement of the educational goals of the institution and should contribute to the cultural, social, moral, intellectual and physical development of students" (Southern Association of Colleges and Schools, 1998, p. 60). The Southern Association of Colleges and Schools provides substantial information about conducting student development services on accredited campuses. In addition to describing a general framework for student affairs and appropriate resources, it also speaks specifically to student government, student conduct, residence halls, student financial aid, health services, and intramural athletics.

The overall framework suggests that these services need to contribute to the growth of students in a variety of ways. Outcomes assessment activities would seem to be logical way to provide information that would ensure external reviewers that the student development services and programs of a specific institution would in fact contribute to student growth. Outcomes assessments would need to be conducted on a routine basis to provide data necessary to paint an appropriate picture of the value of these services in the context of student growth.

• "The institution systematically identifies the characteristics and learning needs of its student population, and then makes provision for responding to them. It assists students to resolve personal, physical, and educational problems" (New England Association of Schools and Colleges, 1998). This standard indicates that institutions seeking accreditation have appropriate programs and services in the campus's portfolio to address student needs. It recognizes that student needs and characteristics may vary from institution to institution. Addressing learning needs might include the development of special programs to address deficits in study skills, mathematical skills, time management, and other skills related to academic success. How would one determine what these needs might be? The answer, quite obviously, is through needs assessment.

Through this assertion, the New England Association is urging institutions to conduct appropriate needs assessments so that programs and services are in place to address student needs. It also is urging them, after conducting needs assessments, to make sure that appropriate services have been established to meet the identified needs of students.

• "Assessment methodology is critical to an analysis of student experience and the impact of the institution resulting from the co-curricular environment. In this section, institutions need to pay particular attention to the experiences of different student groups, such as minority and majority students, returning adult students, disabled students" (Western Association of Schools and Colleges, 1994, pp. 761–762). This assertion emphasizes the importance of assessment. It seeks that assessments be conducted to measure the growth of students resulting from experiences outside the classroom. It also seeks assessment related to the impact of out-of-class experiences on specific groups of students. Blanket assessments of student experiences will not suffice to meet this standard. Outcomes assessments of specific experiences of identifiable segments of the student population are sought as well. As a consequence, in planning for accreditation, a variety of assessments will need to be conducted with a specific student group serving as the unit of assessment.

Assessment Strategies

From the concepts identified, typical assessments conducted to meet accreditation standards are either needs assessments or outcomes assessments, which are discussed in Chapters Nine and Eighteen. Here we examine various strategies related to assessment.

One form of assessment that is insufficient by itself is satisfaction assessment, an approach discussed in Chapter Ten. The North Central Association (1997, p. 52) makes the following observation: "An institutional assessment program relies almost solely on student satisfaction surveys. Such evidence alone is insufficient to support the institution's claims that it appropriately documents student academic achievement." Thus, institutions will have to develop other ways of measuring student achievement, such as outcomes assessment, to meet the requirements of the North Central Association of Colleges and Schools.

The North Central Association (1997, p. 53) identifies five factors that are key to the long-range assessment of student learning:

- *The governing board supports the assessment of student learning across the institution's educational programs.*

- *Senior executive officers provide leadership and support for assessment.*

- *Sufficient resources are allocated to sustain ongoing assessment efforts.*

- *Funds are available to support changes that need to be made to enhance student academic achievement.*

- *All planning and budgeting processes include ways in which assessment information can influence institutional priorities.*

These factors, which provide a framework for assessment on campus, are followed by specific strategies for assessment. The Western Association of Schools and Colleges (1994) provides a series of suggestions for assessment that are appropriate to undergraduate programs. Although they are suggested in the context of general education, they are also appropriate to assessment in student affairs.

Doherty and Patton (1991) advocate the use of multiple measures in the accreditation process. The Western Association observes that a single source of information is insufficient to make the case that goals are being achieved.

In the student affairs context, for example, sources of information might include questionnaires that students complete, telephone interviews conducted with students, or focus groups designed to elicit specific information about students' experiences.

What is assessed is consistent with what is taught. Questionnaires and other data-gathering techniques need to determine if the purposes of the learning experience have been achieved. Appropriate instruments, interview protocols, and other methods of data collection must measure what the activity is about.

Assessment and evidence-gathering practices are developed and applied largely by teaching faculty. Certainly faculty will not provide the leadership on assessment in student affairs, but the point is that the people who are responsible for programs and experiences should be the ones who conduct the assessments. In short, assessment should not be assigned to an administrative office outside the division of student affairs. This is consistent with advice that we have provided elsewhere (Schuh and Upcraft, 1998). Assessment needs to be conducted by the offices that are engaged in program planning and service delivery.

Evidence obtained and presented allows sufficient disaggregation so that the performance of different kinds of students can be identified. This recommendation is consistent with that of the Western Association. To measure the growth of the entire student body without paying attention to important subpopulations is to overlook critical aspects of the undergraduate experience on campus.

Assessment allows, whenever possible, direct feedback to participating students. Assessment reports should be provided to stakeholders in the process. No other group has greater stake in student affairs programs and services than students themselves.

The Western Association (1994) also provides advice in terms of how to conduct these reviews. The first of three principles is that reviews are systematic. The Western Association defines this element in the following way: "The review process should be a recognized, distinct process that is formally identified in some way." What this means, in our opinion, is that reviews are conducted on a routine basis rather than irregularly. Too often assessments are conducted as a result of a crisis or because of the calendar (decennial accreditation is just around the corner, so an assessment is conducted to satisfy the requirements of the accreditation visit). This approach is incorrect, from our perspective. Assessments need to be conducted on a routine basis, meaning annually or biannually. Any other approach is hollow, in our point of view.

The second principle is that reviews are regular. The Western Association (1994, p. 760) concludes, "Once is not enough. Nor is it sufficient to examine programs only at the point where visible problems arise." This point builds on the previous one. Routine assessments need to be conducted. Simply conducting an assessment because it is time to get ready for accreditation misses the point that is emphasized in this assertion.

The third principle is that the reviews need to be comprehensive, meaning that they are applied to a wide range of programs and that the process includes all aspects of a program's operation. Looking at this principle through a senior student affairs administrator's lens, this means that all of the programs in the division should be part of the review and that each program should be assessed in depth. That encompasses carefully assessing student needs, measuring student satisfaction with programs and services, and, most of all, measuring their impact on students through an outcomes assessment. The Western Association also provides assistance in defining how institutions can measure their overall effectiveness through assessment (1992).

Getting Started

Since accreditation visits are scheduled on a routine basis, preparation for them can follow a deliberate process. Quite obviously, accreditation for student affairs is part of a larger process by which the overall institution is accredited, so student affairs will need to work within the framework determined by the institution.

Normally the institution appoints an accreditation coordinator who will coordinate the institution's self-study. In turn, the student affairs division might appoint a person to coordinate the accreditation effort. We recommend that this person be a senior-level individual with a sense of the division's history and broad knowledge of the division, its units, and staff members. It would make good sense for the senior officer to serve in this role.

If a division of student affairs collects routine assessment information, preparation for accreditation will be smooth and fairly routine. Generally an accreditation team will be focusing on the following questions on assessment:

- Do you have an assessment plan?

- Are you doing assessment, and if so, what have you done or are you doing?

- Has what you have done led to improvement of services and programs?

Based on these questions, the coordinator will collect assessment reports from the various units and make judgments about what, if anything, is lacking for the institutional self-study. It may be that some information will need to be collected to round out the division's portfolio, but with good planning this extra effort should be kept to a minimum.

The student affairs coordinator also may need to do some work in coordinating the visit by the members of the accreditation team. It is important for this person to notify all staff of the division about when the accreditation team will visit and to ask them to be sure to be available should a team member wish to meet with them.

An accreditation visiting team of student affairs relating to assessment typically will ask the following questions and possibly institution-specific questions as well:

- What is your student services mission, and do your services and programs reflect this mission?

- Who are your students, and is there evidence that your student services and programs match well with the needs of these students?

- What evidence is there that your students are satisfied with the student services and programs you offer?

- Is there a relationship between use of your student services and programs and intended student outcomes?

- How would you describe your campus climate?

- Can you demonstrate that your student services and programs meet accepted national professional standards and service-specific accreditation?

- Do the breadth, depth, and quality of your student services and programs compare well with institutions similar to you?

- Are your student services and programs cost-effective?

If one or more of these questions cannot be answered with systematic studies, they should at least be part of an assessment plan to be implemented in the future. The key is that assessment data be collected regularly so that preparation for the self-study can be accomplished easily. Failure to have such information available can result in a potentially hollow portfolio being developed for student affairs.

Functional Unit Accreditation

In addition to accreditation within the overall context of an institution as guided by regional accrediting organizations, some student affairs functions are accredited by professional organizations. For example, the International

Association of Counseling Services accredits psychological counseling services through a rigorous review process described in Chapter Twenty-Seven. Also, the American Psychological Association, through its Office of Program Consultation and Accreditation Education Directorate, accredits doctoral internship programs located in psychological counseling centers.

In the health services field, both the Joint Commission for Accreditation of Healthcare Organizations and the Accreditation Association for Ambulatory Health Care accredit student health services. (See Chapter Twenty-Five for a detailed discussion of these accreditation processes.) It is expected that other professional organizations may follow suit in the near future by establishing accreditation mechanisms that will apply to additional student services and programs.

Conclusion

Student affairs plays an important role in the accreditation process, and the regional accreditation bodies are very interested in seeing evidence that indicates that programs and services contribute to student learning. It is also important to point out that assessments are to be conducted on a routine basis so as to contribute to institutional improvement.

The future of accreditation appears to be moving in the direction of quality improvement. The North Central Association, for example, has developed a quality improvement project, which may be accessed at http://www.ncacihe.org/AQIP/index/htm, and the Western Association (1999) is focusing on educational effectiveness as an accreditation framework. These initiatives are likely to require additional assessment activities to demonstrate that institutions accomplish what they profess.

Routine assessments demonstrating how various student affairs units contribute to making a difference in student learning and growth are essential in meeting accreditation requirements. Anything less from a student affairs division may cause problems in the accreditation process.

References

Council for Higher Education Accreditation. "About CHEA." Dec. 1998. [http://www.chea.org].

Doherty, A., and Patton, G. W. "Criterion Three and the Assessment of Student Academic Achievement." *NCA Quarterly*, 1991, *66*(2), 406–414.

Middle States Association of Colleges and Schools. "Commission on Higher Education." Dec. 1998. [http://www.msache.org].

New England Association of Schools and Colleges. "Welcome to the Web Site of the New England Association of Schools and Colleges." Dec. 1998. [http://www.neasc.org].

North Central Association of Colleges and Schools. *Handbook of Accreditation.* (2nd ed.) Chicago: North Central Association of Colleges and Schools, 1997.

Schuh, J. H., and Upcraft, M. L. "Facts and Myths About Assessment in Student Affairs." *About Campus,* 1998, *3*(5), 2–8.

Southern Association of Colleges and Schools. "Commission on Colleges." Dec. 1998. [http://www.sacs.org].

Western Association of Schools and Colleges. *Achieving Institutional Effectiveness Through Assessment.* Oakland, Calif.: Western Association of Schools and Colleges, 1992.

Western Association of Schools and Colleges. "Principles of Good Practice in Assessment." In J. S. Stark and A. Thomas (eds.), *Assessment and Program Evaluation.* New York: Simon & Schuster, 1994.

Western Association of Schools and Colleges. *Handbook of Accreditation.* Oakland, Calif.: Western Association of Schools and Colleges, 1998a.

Western Association of Schools and Colleges. "The Senior College Commission." Dec. 1998b. [http://www.wascweb.org].

Western Association of Schools and Colleges. *Invitation to Dialogue II: Proposed Framework for a New Model of Accreditation.* Oakland, Calif.: Western Association of Schools and Colleges, 1999.

Chapter 15

Dropout Assessment

STUDYING PERSISTENCE to graduation (or not) has become an important assessment agenda. Persistence is a recurring concern for higher education. For example, 24.4 percent of students who began their postsecondary education by enrolling at a four-year institution in 1989 were no longer enrolled in 1994 and had not earned a degree, and dropout rates at institutions that enroll nontraditional students are even higher (National Center for Education Statistics, 1999). Thus, a major issue at many institutions is how to improve persistence to graduation rates, and there are many possible solutions. For example, an institution might focus on enhancing the first-year experience (see Chapter Nineteen), improving academic achievement (see Chapter Eighteen), or considering other interventions such as looking at hard-to-pass "killer" courses, which may contribute to student attrition.

Another important way of explaining retention is to conduct assessment studies that gather information from students who have dropped out. Unfortunately, many, if not most, dropout studies are poorly done, often because they do not take into account the many factors that contribute to student success (see Chapter Eighteen). Further, we often study just those students who survive until graduation, while ignoring those who drop out, yielding a tainted view of student success (and failure) at the institution. Institutions with perceived "low" retention rates are often more motivated to study dropouts than those with "high" retention rates, however that is defined and determined.

This chapter discusses the problems of assessing students who fail to persist to graduation, identifies the reasons that they should be studied, and offers several ways of assessing dropouts, from the most basic to the most comprehensive.

Problems with Dropout Assessment

The technical definition of *dropout* is a student who initially enrolls at an institution and fails to graduate within some specified period of time, usually three years for two-year institutions and five or six years for four-year institutions. However, this definition is much too broad to be meaningful and may, as pointed out in Chapter Eighteen, provide a misleading way of defining student success. This overly broad definition encompasses many different types of students, including those who "stop out" (drop out with the intention of returning to the institution), transfer to another institution, take longer than the defined period of time to graduate (part-time students now account for nearly 40 percent of those enrolled in higher education), enrolled but never intended to graduate, as well as the small number of students who are dismissed from the institution for academic or disciplinary reasons. So the first task is for each institution to define just what *dropout* means and take that definition into account when studying this population.

The second problem is that dropouts often are very difficult persons from whom to gather meaningful information. Some students leave the institution during the semester without going through the formal withdrawal process; they just fade away. It may not be until the next semester that the institution even learns they have left. But even students who leave during the semester and do go through this withdrawal process may be reluctant to discuss their reasons for leaving in any meaningful way. For example, the simple question, "Why are you leaving the institution?" may yield more socially acceptable reasons (for example, financial problems or academic problems) rather than more accurate but personally sensitive reasons (such as personal or family problems). Further, students who withdraw between semesters typically do not need to go through a formal withdrawal process (they complete one semester and fail to attend the next), thus preventing the institution from gathering any data at all. These students often are difficult to locate after they have left, and if they are found, they may not be willing to discuss why they left.

The third problem is deciding what information is needed from those who left. The simplest and most basic question, "Why did you leave?" provides a great deal of information to ponder. This information is important, but it is not enough. A second basic question is, "What, if any, plans do you have for continuing your education?" At a minimum, any dropout study should focus on these two questions.

The fourth problem is a methodological one. On the one hand, the dropout study should be designed so that it requires dropouts to take as little time and effort as possible to participate. Conversely, it should provide a breadth and depth of information about those who leave. Striking a balance between these two goals often involves considerable methodological compromise that may limit the usefulness of the findings. So many methodological questions arise. Should information be gathered with an in-person interview, a telephone interview, or a written instrument? Regardless of which data collection procedure is used, should the approach be quantitative (questions that allow the participant to select from a predetermined list of possible answers) or qualitative (open-ended questions that allow the participant free rein to provide information)?

Because of these challenging problems, systematic, thorough dropout assessments rarely are conducted. And some institutions evince little interest in studying their "failures" because they fear the results might be embarrassing from a public relations standpoint. In fact, one institution we are aware of had an absolute prohibition against studying students who left and refused to provide any information about their whereabouts, let alone gather information from them. This attitude is self-defeating if an institution is serious about improving the chances of student persistence to graduation. Studying those who stay while ignoring those who leave provides the institution with what cannot be tolerated: only half the story.

Reasons for Assessing Dropouts

Many reasons underscore why those who leave institutions should be studied. First and foremost, these studies can provide insight into the educational experiences of all students, telling us where institutions are helping students succeed and where they are impeding student success. If we have any commitment at all to maintaining and improving the quality of our institutions, we need information from those who have left as well as those who graduate.

Second, dropouts can help determine if the institution can (or cannot) do anything about their reasons for leaving. In other words, institutions may criticize themselves needlessly because of what they consider to be alarming dropout rates, but students may be leaving for reasons far beyond the institution's control. For example, some students may be leaving because in a good economy, jobs are plentiful and well paying, and as a consequence, work is more desirable than going to college. Or they may be leaving because of personal circumstances, such as a job transfer or transfer to another institution that has an academic program that the institution does not offer. Clearly the institution does not control the economy or have unlimited resources to develop new academic programs. On the other hand, if students are leaving because academic advising is ineffective, or the quality of instruction is poor, or courses are not offered in a timely fashion, or financial aid programs are poorly administered, then the institution does have some control over these things and may alter policies and practices accordingly.

Third, dropout studies can help analyze the reasons for leaving within the context of why these students enrolled at the institution in the first place. As Shibley argues in Chapter Eighteen, this connection between educational goals and outcomes provides a much better and more accurate picture of student success rates and may in fact reveal that an institution's so-called retention problem is not really a problem after all. For example, let us assume that the mission of a two-year institution is to prepare students to transfer to a four-year institution, and let us further assume that the graduation rate is 50 percent after three years. A good dropout study may reveal that of those who leave, half are transferring to a four-year institution without an associate degree. So although the retention rate may seem low, in fact the mission of the institution is being fulfilled for 75 percent of its students.

Fourth, dropout studies can provide greater insight into possible differences among different types of students. For example, if an institutional study shows that African Americans drop out at a higher rate than white students (while controlling for precollege characteristics and during-college experiences; see Chapter Eighteen), a good dropout study can provide possible reasons for this differential attrition, and the institution can reconsider its policies and practices accordingly. The same may be true for age, gender, socioeconomic status, enrollment status (full or part time, degree-seeking or non-degree-seeking), and other student variables.

Finally, dropout studies sometimes are conducted because of severe retention problems that result in not only declining enrollments but declining revenues as well. Institutions may be able to improve their retention rate as well as their fiscal health by making improvements based on what dropouts report.

There are many reasons for studying dropouts, but they all boil down to an attempt by the institution to improve quality and enhance students' chances of success. Institutionally based reasons might hasten a dropout study, such as a drastic change in its mission, a reconfiguration of the demographics of the community surrounding the campus, or severe financial difficulties. But whatever the reasons are, these studies should be done, and done well.

Steps in the Dropout Assessment Process

All of the approaches to conducting dropout assessments, from the simplest to the more complex, assume that the institution has, or can retrieve, accurate names and addresses and other pertinent information about dropouts. Often this is not an easy task. At a minimum, when students drop out during the semester, a formal withdrawal process should be in place that gathers this information. If students drop out between semesters or a within-semester withdrawal process is not in place, home or family addresses may provide a way of contacting these students. It also may be possible to contact dropouts using e-mail addresses, although many institutions discontinue institutionally provided e-mail service once students leave the institution. Keeping students on institutionally based e-mail for some short period of time after they withdraw from the institution may help in maintaining contacts with dropouts.

Dropout Assessment Case Study

Traditional College is a four-year, church-related, residential, tuition-driven liberal arts college with an enrollment of approximately three thousand undergraduate students. Over the past few years, more and more students have been leaving before they graduate. Current data show that of those students who enroll in a given fall semester, only about 55 percent persist to graduation compared to about 75 percent for peer institutions.

Theories abound on campus about why students leave. Some faculty say it is because they have maintained rigorous academic standards and refused to "dummy down" their courses and inflate grades. Others say that costs have risen to a point where students must leave for financial reasons. Still others believe that many students are suffering from personal problems that preclude them from continuing their studies. But, in fact, no one really knows why students are leaving, because no systematic studies of dropouts have ever been conducted.

The president of Traditional is concerned because increased dropout rates decrease revenue, and in a tuition-driven institution, continued high dropout rates can eventually produce a fiscal crisis. He is aware that declining retention rates probably have multiple causes (see Chapter Eighteen), but he also knows that the first step in solving the problem is to determine why students are leaving. He asks the vice president for student affairs to conduct a study that will uncover the reasons students are leaving and recruits an educational psychology professor with assessment expertise to help design the study.

Step 1: Define the Problem

Students are failing to persist to graduation at Traditional College at rates unacceptable to the institution and lower than those of comparable institutions. Although the college has some guesses about why students leave, there have been no systematic studies of dropouts to help frame policies and practices designed to increase retention.

Step 2: Determine the Purpose of the Study

The purpose of this study is to determine why students left the institution, the future educational plans of students who left, and what the institution could do to increase persistence to graduation.

Step 3: Determine Where to Get the Information Needed

Information will be gathered from all students who dropped out of the institution during the fall semester or failed to reenroll for the subsequent semester. The fall semester is chosen because there is evidence that students are more likely to drop out during or after immediately after their first semester, compared to subsequent semesters (Upcraft and Gardner, 1989). Another approach is to conduct a three-year longitudinal study that is likely to yield even greater insight into student success or failure. In this approach, students who graduated will be compared to students who dropped out, taking into account precollege characteristics and during-college experiences that may affect persistence to graduation.

Step 4: Determine the Best Assessment Methods

In the short run, a brief quantitative study will be conducted to determine the reasons that students left the institution. A qualitative study will be conducted to gain greater insight into why they left. For the longitudinal study, both quantitative and qualitative methods will be used.

Step 5: Determine Whom to Study

All students who left the institution during or immediately after the fall semester are included in the short-term quantitative study. A purposeful, random sample of students who dropped out during the same time period will be selected for the short-term qualitative study. For the longitudinal study, all students who dropped out and all students who persisted to graduation during the three-year time period will be included in the quantitative part of the study, and a purposeful, random sample of both persisters and dropouts will be included in the qualitative part of the study.

Step 6: Determine How the Data Will Be Collected

For the short-term quantitative study, the names, addresses, telephone numbers, and e-mail addresses of dropouts should be retrieved from institutional records. Depending on the reliability of this information, there may be a short mailed survey, a telephone survey, or a Web-based survey, or some combination of all these data collection methods. There is often difficulty in locating dropouts, so multiple data collection methods may be needed to ensure a usable sample. If a mailed survey is used, we recommend a double-sided postcard to all dropouts: one side with the instructions and the other with a list of reasons for dropping out. The returnable side of the postcard can be metered postage, saving the respondent the time and money to send it back.

For the short-term qualitative study, student interviewers will be trained to conduct telephone interviews. For the longitudinal study, Chapter Eighteen provides a fuller discussion of how data might be collected.

Step 7: Determine What Instruments Will Be Used

Exhibit 15.1 contains the survey for the short-term quantitative study, which can be used for mailed, Web-based, or telephone data collection procedures. It could also be used for a brief exit interview.

The qualitative study demands more time and effort on the part of the institution and the student and assumes a more personalized approach. After covering the basic information contained in the first side of the postcard, the student is asked questions contained in Exhibit 15.2. (This interview protocol could also be used for an exit interview.) (Chapter Five contains instrumentation guidelines for the longitudinal study.)

Step 8: Determine Who Should Collect the Data

For personal or telephone interviews, who is gathering the information may be crucial. (For the mailed postcard, e-mail, or Web-based surveys, this is not an issue.) Our experience has been that for telephone interviews, current students are the best information gatherers, because former students seem to be more candid with them. If face-to-face interviews are used and verbal and nonverbal communication is therefore important, professional staff are preferred. But this decision should be made on the basis of which persons will generate the most accurate and complete information.

Chapter Two provides guidance on determining who should collect the data for the longitudinal study.

EXHIBIT 15.1

Sample Postcard/Web-Based Telephone Dropout Survey

Side 1:

Dear [insert name]: According to our records, you withdrew recently from Traditional College. We are asking you for some important information about why you left and what, if any, educational plans you have. The purpose of gathering this information is to learn more about why students leave, in order to help us improve our educational programs and help you with any future educational plans you might have. All responses are confidential. Findings will be reported to President I. M. Committed, who will review current academic and student affairs policies and practices in the light of your collective responses. Please take a minute to fill out this survey, and return it to Dr. Committed's office. Thank you for returning this survey, and if you need information about reenrollment, please contact our Admissions Office [address, telephone number, and e-mail address].

Side 2:

I withdrew from Traditional College because I:
(check as many as apply):

___ Transferred to another institution
___ Returning to Traditional College next semester
___ Needed some time off to reconsider my educational goals
___ Had health-related problems
___ Had problems financing my education
___ Had personal problems
___ Had family problems
___ Found a job
___ Entered military service
___ Was dismissed by the college
___ Did not obtain desired grade point average
___ Got what I needed without finishing
___ Other (please specify) _____

My future educational plans:
(check as many as apply):

___ Returning to Traditional sometime in the future
___ Transferring to another institution immediately
___ Transferring to another college in the future
___ I have no immediate plans to continue my education

EXHIBIT 15.2

Telephone Interview Protocol

Good evening. My name is [name of interviewer]. May I speak to [name of respondent]?

I am working with the president of Traditional College to gather information about why students leave TC. According to our records, you were enrolled at TC for the fall semester but did not reenroll for the spring semester. Is that true? I am asking you to participate in this voluntary ten-minute survey. We would like to audiotape this conversation, but please be assured that your responses are confidential and are reported as summarized data used in future planning efforts by the institution. No individual data will be identified. You may choose not to answer specific questions. You may also have access to the survey results. If you have any questions, contact [name of contact) at [address] or by telephone [telephone number] or e-mail [e-mail address].

I hope you will take this opportunity for your voice to be heard. Are you willing to participate?

1. Why did you decide to leave Traditional College?

2. What, if anything, did you like about Traditional College?

3. How might Traditional College be improved?

4. What, if anything, might Traditional College have done better to help you obtain your educational goals here?

5. What, if any, educational plans do you have?

6. How, if at all, might Traditional College be helpful to you in the future?

7. Any other comments?

Step 9: Determine How the Data Will Be Analyzed

For the brief quantitative study, the data will be entered into a database where the analysis may be done. The first level of analysis should be to determine if the respondents are representative of the population under study. If they are not, responses can be weighted to account for the lack of representativeness, or this fact should be included as a limitation of the study. Next, frequency counts of the percentages of responses should be calculated. Further analysis by gender, race and ethnicity, age, and other demographic variables might also be useful.

For the qualitative part of the study, data recorded on the audiotapes of telephone conversations should be analyzed by reviewing transcripts or repeated listening to the audiotapes. In either case, we recommend involving selected representatives from any part of the institution who might be affected by the results in the analysis process, such as faculty and students.

Upcraft and Schuh (1996, Chapter Four) provide guidance for determining how the data should be analyzed for the longitudinal study.

Step 10: Determine the Implications of the Study for Policy and Practice

What students who dropped out of an institution have to say undoubtedly will cut across many different institutional policies and practices, including administrative procedures, student support services, admissions, instruction, the curriculum, academic advising, financial aid, and many others. A team of selected faculty, staff, and students should be involved in determining policy and practice implications, and forming recommendations for change.

Step 11: Report the Results Effectively

The findings of dropout studies are often controversial and sometimes threatening to parts of the institution. Therefore, the way in which the results are reported is very important and must be done in order to promote change, not create defensiveness.

On the whole, we recommend a full and complete disclosure of any assessment study, but dropout studies may be the exception. For example, if one of the findings is that the financial aid office is seen by dropouts as unresponsive, ineffective, and unfriendly, it may be more prudent to report those results to a more limited audience rather than publish the results publicly and run the risk of embarrassing that office. Public humiliation of an office rarely results in an eagerness on the part of that office to make changes. As we have argued elsewhere (Upcraft and Schuh, 1996), assessment reports targeted to specific audiences are usually more effective than complete reports distributed widely.

Conclusion

Assessing dropouts can provide invaluable information to an institution and lead to improving the educational experience of students, the institution's quality, the retention rate, and the fiscal bottom line. Although a longitudinal study is probably the most desirable dropout assessment approach, there is rarely the time or the resources to conduct such studies. Thus, the quantitative and qualitative approaches suggested in this chapter will probably be more timely and useful to an institution that cannot wait three to five years to gain insight into this problem.

Ignoring those who leave is foolish. Without their perceptions, an institution cannot maintain a quality educational program, let alone maintain enrollments and ensure fiscal integrity.

References

National Center for Education Statistics. *1998 Digest of Education Statistics*. Washington, D.C.: U.S. Department of Education, 1999.

Upcraft, M. L., Gardner, J. N., and Associates. *The Freshman Year Experience: Helping Students Survive and Succeed in College*. San Francisco: Jossey-Bass, 1989.

Upcraft, M. L., and Schuh, J. H. *Assessment in Student Affairs: A Guide for Practitioners*. San Francisco: Jossey-Bass, 1996.

Chapter 16

Postgraduation Assessment

FOR MANY INSTITUTIONS, gathering information from former students who have graduated is very important. Although many of the assessment procedures suggested in this book also apply to postgraduation assessments, these studies do present a unique set of problems that must be taken into account. This chapter discusses the reasons for postgraduate assessments, explores issues unique to this assessment, and suggests categories of information that may be gathered.

Why Assess Graduates?

A major factor in determining what and how to assess is why the assessment is being carried out. So the first step is to look at the many reasons to do postgraduation studies. First, the institution may want feedback from graduates in order to improve the institution in general and the educational experience of current students in particular. This feedback can then become the basis for reconsidering policies and practices or helping to solve problems. For example, if it turns out that a majority of graduates have a poor opinion of the help they received in finding a job, then improving this service might take on a much higher priority. Or if one of the goals of general education is to enhance critical thinking and graduates say that critical thinking was not high on their list of perceived learning outcomes, then the institution might want to reconsider how that skill is integrated into the curriculum.

Assessing for institutional improvement is tricky, because the feedback may be very much affected by how long the respondents have been away from the institution. Students who graduated thirty years ago will relate their perceptions of the institution based on their experiences thirty to thirty-five years ago. Undoubtedly the institution has changed a great deal in that time; the faculty, curriculum, out-of-class environment, and administration are different, as are institutional policies, practices, and even mission. So conducting postgraduation assessments for improvement reasons is probably best restricted to more recent graduates. How recent depends on the purpose of the study. For example, if the purpose is to gather information from graduates on orientation programs, and these programs have not changed very much in the last ten years, then studying those who graduated within the past seven years would be appropriate. (Seven years is the time period because those who graduated in the first three years were not subject to the orientation program under review.)

Second, postgraduation assessments may be done for public relations or image reasons. The institution may want to highlight the success of its graduates by letting the public and prospective students know that graduates do well in graduate school, find rewarding and well-paying jobs, and are making significant contributions to society politically, economically, socially, and internationally. These success stories may enhance the institution's ability to maintain and improve its overall reputation, facilitate recruitment of new students, and strengthen its relationship with the corporate world and governmental agencies and other publics.

Third, the institution may do these studies to strengthen graduates' contributions to the institution. Knowing that the institution cares about its graduates by gathering information about them may encourage graduates to recruit prospective students, help the institution to make important economic and political connections, serve on boards of control, and, perhaps most important, contribute time and money to the institution.

One or all of these reasons may motivate a postgraduation assessment, which affects the purpose and design of the study.

Problems Unique to Postgraduation Assessment

Assessing those who have graduated from the institution can be difficult for several reasons. The first problem may be finding them. For graduates who have chosen to become a member of the institutional alumni association, finding names, addresses, and telephone numbers will be relatively easy. However, if the percentage of graduates who join the alumni association is low, then getting enough responses may be a problem. A second problem is that if the postgraduation population is restricted to only alumni association members, the sample may be very biased. We may assume that most members have a more positive attitude toward the institution than those who do not belong. It may be that only those who can afford to belong sign on, thus further biasing the sample.

A truly representative sample will have to go beyond alumni association members, and this is often very difficult. One way is snowball sampling, a technique described in Chapter Three. That is, the institution contacts graduates it does know about and asks them for pertinent information about how to find other graduates they know who may not be members of the alumni association. These graduates are contacted and asked for the same information, and so on.

Second, how long the graduate has been away from the institution can be a problem. As the years roll by, recollections may fade or become embellished, and thus the information retrieved may not be as valid as perceptions of more recent graduates. On the other hand, it may take some time away from the institution for graduates to truly appreciate the benefits of the education they received, so following up too quickly may provide an inaccurate picture as well. Once again, we return to the purpose of the study. If the purpose is to assess career and employment success, for example, it may be better to wait longer to follow up than if the purpose is to assess current student support services, which would dictate a shorter follow-up time.

Third, including only graduates in the study will present another bias. In a sense, postgraduation assessments study only "successful" students. Students who have failed to complete their degrees (for whatever reasons) might also have something very important for the institution to know, especially if the purpose of the study is institutional improvement. So a consideration is to follow up these students as well. The major problem here is that persons who left the institution are even more difficult to track down than graduates. This may be overcome in part by following up fairly soon after they leave (within three months), although this does not allow for much time for longer-term reflection on their collegiate experiences (see Chapter Fifteen for a discussion of dropout assessments).

Assessing Graduates of Comprehensive University

Comprehensive University is a state-supported research university with an enrollment of twenty-five thousand students. Recent *U.S. News and World Reports* rankings of comprehensive universities ranked CU among the lower third of comparable institutions. Based on this and other information, CU's newly appointed president has been directed by the board of trustees to explore ways in which the institution might improve its overall rank among comparable institutions. Among the many initiatives included in the president's plan for improvement is an alumni survey. She believes graduates could provide valuable information about their experiences at CU that might help determine strategies for improving the institution's overall quality and, she hopes, its ranking among comparable institutions. She is particularly interested in students' perceptions of both their in-class and out-of-class experiences. What kind of study should be developed to meet the president's need for information from graduates?

Step 1: Define the Problem

The institution wants to improve its overall quality because of concerns about its ranking in relation to other comparable institutions. One source of information about how to improve is its graduates, but to date there has been no systematic study of graduates on which to base improvements.

Step 2: Determine the Purpose of the Study

The purpose of this study is to gather information from CU graduates about their in-class and out-of-class undergraduate experiences, toward the goal of seeking to improve the quality of the institution.

Step 3: Determine Where to Get the Information Needed

Information will be gathered from students who graduated from CU.

Step 4: Determine the Best Assessment Method

Because the president believed that a survey of graduates would have the most credibility with faculty and the board of trustees, a quantitative approach was chosen. She did not preclude a subsequent qualitative study of graduates using individual interviews, but determined that CU's first priority should be a quantitative survey.

If a qualitative study is more appropriate to the purposes of the study, there are two choices: individual interviews or focus groups. We recommend individual interviews because they can be done over the telephone. Focus groups are not recommended because it is very difficult to get graduates together all in one place, and if there is success, the gathering is most often on an alumni weekend or at a regional alumni event, thus biasing the sample.

Step 5: Determine Whom to Study

All students who graduated from CU within the last four years were part of the study. Four years was chosen because enrollments, the curriculum, and the out-of-class activities, programs, and services have been relatively stable over this time period and because information from students who graduated more than four years ago is often less useful.

Step 6: Determine How the Data Will Be Collected

Probably the best way of collecting data from graduates, all things considered, is a telephone survey with both closed- and open-ended questions, locally developed consistent with the purposes of the study (see Chapters Five and Seven). The closed-ended format should be as brief as possible (no more than seven minutes; see Chapter Seven), collect only the data the institution does not already have (if the respondents' telephone number is known, the institution should know some background information from institutional records), and ask very few open-ended questions (several questions will lengthen the time of the conversation). However, CU decided to use a mailed survey to collect data from graduates. Although there are some limitations to this data collection procedure (see Chapter Six), given the population selected and the length of the survey, a mailed survey seemed most appropriate. Several strategies were employed to ensure an acceptable response rate. First, the survey was widely publicized in CU's alumni newsletter, which is sent to all CU graduates, stressing the importance of the information gathered for the institution. Second, CU was prepared to conduct intensive and frequent follow-ups with graduates to encourage them to fill out the instrument. And finally, CU offered a free one-year membership in the Alumni Association for both current association members and nonmembers if the survey were returned.

Step 7: Determine What Instruments Will Be Used

This decision proved difficult because there was no consensus, at least initially, among students, faculty, and administrators about what information was needed from graduates. In the end, a two-step process was decided on. First, a consensus was reached about what information was needed, and then the decision about instrumentation was reached based on the information needed. Information in a number of categories was deemed desirable.

Background Information

Beyond the usual data such as gender, race and ethnicity, age, and so on, CU wanted other information pertinent to the study, some of which it could retrieve from institutional records:

- Advanced degrees
- Grade point average upon graduation

- Undergraduate major field
- Citizenship
- Year of graduation
- Enrollment status (part or full time)
- Type of degree (for example, B.A., B.S., B.E.)
- Transfer from another institution
- Length of time to graduation

Employment History

Since a major goal of CU was preparing students for a career, CU wanted information about the graduates' employment history since graduation, such as:

- Current job
- Current annual income
- Employer
- Past job history

Educational Outcomes

Both CU faculty and staff were interested in what students learned from their CU experience. Self-reporting of educational outcomes can provide the institution with valuable information about its effectiveness. CU identified several categories of educational outcomes that were relevant to the mission and goals of the institution:

Cognitive Development (Skills Learned in College)

- Critical thinking
- Problem solving
- Creative thinking
- Writing skills
- Reading skills
- Computational skills
- Speaking skills
- Computer literacy
- Reflective judgment
- Learning how to learn

Content Mastery (Knowledge Acquired and Mastered During College)

- Major field content
- General education content

Interpersonal Development (Interpersonal Skills Learned in College)

- Relating effectively with others
- Working effectively in teams
- Leadership skills
- Relating to those with different racial and ethnic backgrounds
- Maintaining intimate relationships

Intrapersonal Development (Individual Development)

- Identity development
- Aesthetic appreciation
- Autonomy
- Moral development
- Spiritual development
- General mental health
- Physical health
- Gender role development
- Self-awareness
- Self-esteem

Career Development (Graduates' Career Preparation and Patterns)

- Satisfaction with career
- Satisfaction with current job
- Preparation for career
- Preparation for graduate school

Civic Responsibility (Graduate's Involvement in Community and Societal Issues)

- Participation in community affairs
- Awareness of global issues
- Participation in governmental affairs
- Advocacy for equity issues
- Voting in elections

- Participation in education
- Awareness of economic, social, and political issues

CU recognized that it must be very careful in the educational outcomes it selected, for two reasons. First, a postgraduation assessment should never ask about an outcome that is not reasonably related to the educational outcomes claimed by the institution. For example, many institutions would assert that intrapersonal outcomes were not and are not within their mission and educational programs. As one wag put it, "Don't promise your students eternal life if you don't have evidence that they go to heaven!" Second, postgraduation assessment must respect the privacy of the graduate. For example, graduates may not want to share information about income or self-esteem, even if confidentiality is assured. If such information is relevant to the study, then a clear rationale for retrieving this information must be included, and confidentiality must be explicitly defined.

Educational Experiences

CU also wanted to know what students did while they were in college and how they now reflect on those experiences. Several categories of educational experiences were determined to be important for the CU study:

Reflections on Classroom and Faculty Experiences

- Overall classroom experience
- Courses in major
- General education courses
- Quality of academic programs
- Quality of faculty in general
- Quality of faculty in major
- Relevance of courses to job or career
- Faculty-student relationships
- Preparation for graduate study
- Class size
- Inclusiveness of curriculum
- Class facilities

Participation in and Satisfaction with Academic Support Services

- Library
- Computer laboratories

- Academic advising
- Tutoring
- Registration
- Financial aid
- Admissions

Participation in and Satisfaction with Student Services and Programs

- Residence halls
- Orientation
- Health services
- Career counseling
- Personal counseling
- Student activities
- Student union
- Health education
- Services for racial and ethnic minorities
- Commuter services
- Cultural programs
- Judicial affairs
- Disabled student services
- Veterans' services
- International student services
- Placement services

Involvement and Satisfaction with Out-of-Class Activities and Experiences

- Student government
- Intramurals
- Academically related student clubs
- Greek life
- Intercollegiate athletic
- Student organizations
- Academic governance
- Community organizations

- Part-time employment
- Full-time employment
- Religious involvement
- Peer educator

Perceptions of and Satisfaction with the Overall Collegiate Environment

- Climate for women
- Intellectual environment
- Safety and security
- Climate for minorities
- Climate for adult students
- Residence hall environment
- Climate for commuter students
- Climate for disabled students
- Climate for part-time students
- Social environment

After much deliberation, CU decided to use a commercially developed instrument to gather relevant data, for several reasons. First, there was not enough time or money available to develop a psychometrically sound local instrument. Second, because CU wanted to improve itself in relation to other comparable institutions, a commercially developed instrument could provide norms for comparison purposes. Third, CU thought a commercially developed instrument would have more credibility with faculty and other important constituencies than a locally developed one. Fourth, publishers of commercially developed instruments typically provide scoring and report services, which save the institution the task of these procedures.

CU decided to use the Comprehensive Alumni Assessment Survey (CAAS), published by the National Center for Higher Education Management Systems (NCHEMS), because the items were generally consistent with the information CU needed, and because there was an opportunity for CU to add locally relevant questions (see Resources for how to obtain more information about this and other credible alumni instruments).

Step 8: Determine Who Should Collect the Data

CU's Office of Institutional Research assumed responsibility for distributing and retrieving the surveys, in close coordination with the alumni association.

Step 9: Determine How the Data Will Be Analyzed

NCHEMS scored the surveys and presented a report to the institution. This material then was interpreted to a wider campus audience.

Step 10: Determine the Implications of the Study for Policy and Practice

Because of the comprehensive nature of the survey, there were implications for virtually every part of the institution, including faculty, administrators, student affairs,

Use of Commercially Developed Instruments

If the choice is to use any one of many commercially available postgraduation surveys, several excellent ones are available, most of which allow for locally developed questions. Of course, this probably means collecting the data through the mail. (See Chapter Six for the advantages and disadvantages of this data collection procedure.) Commercially available instruments are reviewed in the Resources at the back of this book.

Conclusion

Postgraduation assessments are often important to an institution. Gathering data from graduates can provide critical information for institutional policies and practices, as well as generally enhancing the relationship between graduates and the institution. However, these studies are difficult to do, for reasons discussed in this chapter. We reiterate the notion discussed at the beginning of this chapter: first decide why you are studying graduates; then design and conduct the study, preferably a telephone survey using a open- and closed-ended questions.

Chapter 17

Assessing Group Educational Programs

WE IN STUDENT AFFAIRS rely heavily on group educational programs to educate students. Our assumption is that if we bring together a group of students and address a topic of importance or interest to them, led by "experts" on the topic, good things will happen. We do group programs on topics such as alcohol and drug education, sexually transmitted diseases, roommate relationships, academic skills, blood pressure screening, multicultural diversity, résumé preparation, date rape, long-distance relationships, student aid, and many, many others. It has become a cornerstone of efforts to help students succeed both inside and outside the classroom. But typically there is precious little evidence to suggest that these efforts are effective.

This chapter suggests several ways in which group educational programs may be assessed and gives concrete examples of assessment tools and strategies.

Some Overall Considerations

There are several considerations when exploring how to assess group educational programs:

Choosing an Assessment Method

Investigators must consider whether to use qualitative methods, quantitative methods, or both. Several options are available when considering the assessment of group educational programs. Investigators may develop a quantitative instrument that asks some closed-ended questions that can be easily recorded and analyzed. This approach is efficient but usually does not provide participants with an opportunity to go into greater detail about their answers. They may use a qualitative instrument that asks more general open-ended questions, but these are very time-consuming to record and interpret. Or they may use an instrument with both closed- and open-ended questions.

Another approach is to take some time at the end of the program for participants to give feedback on it. In this case, participants have an immediate opportunity to give feedback and often become a part of the educational process itself. One drawback is that participants may not want to give feedback publicly while the presenter is present. Another is that they may not want to spend the time required to complete a lengthy questionnaire.

If this approach is taken, the feedback items might include these:

- What were the strengths of this program?

- How might this program be improved?

- Any other comments?

It has been our experience that the question, "What were the weaknesses of this program?" is not a good one for two reasons. First, it may send participants on a downward spiral of unproductive negativity. Second, improvements tend to be mirror images of weaknesses; thus negative comments are framed in a more positive way and more useful.

Determining When to Gather Assessment Data

The most obvious time to gather feedback from participants is just before they leave the program, and that is often also the optimal time. After students leave the program, the response rate will be far lower. If, however, the nature of the program was such that participants need some time to mull over their experience before they give feedback or if the effect of the program may be more long term than immediate, then following up at a later date with a telephone or Web-based survey may be more appropriate. This assumes, of course, that students are willing to provide their telephone number or e-mail address. In some types of programs participants may want to remain anonymous (such as AIDS awareness), and thus this delayed assessment approach may not be appropriate.

Determining Whether the Number of Participants Is a Valid Assessment

For years educational programmers have argued this issue, with little resolution. Programmers who believe that number of participants is irrelevant argue that if the few participants who attend get something out of the program, then it was well worth doing. On the other hand, one of the reasons to do group educational programs is the efficiency of affecting a larger number of participants. Further, programmers who believe the number of participants *is* a valid assessment criteria would argue that if the same program fails to attract a critical mass of students over several iterations, then the program is failing, for whatever reasons: marketing, design, presenters, or others.

We tend to come down on the side of those who believe attendance is a legitimate criteria for assessing group educational programs. Our experience has been that if a program consistently attracts fewer than ten participants, another approach should be considered. On the other hand, attendance should not be the sole criterion for assessing group educational programs.

An Educational Programming Case Study

Midstate College is a public, regional college with an enrollment of about four thousand students, about half of whom live on campus. There was a time when the student affairs staff offered group educational programs on issues such as sexuality, alcohol and drug abuse, roommate relationships, study skills, and others, but attendance was so low that the effort was dropped. However, the new vice president for student affairs, B. N. Educator, believes strongly in the learning potential of group educational programs. Further, he sees educational programs as a way of involving faculty in student life and promoting student affairs as a key player in the education of students at Midstate.

His staff, however, is skeptical, because in the past, they had put an enormous amount of time and effort into educational programs, with very few known positive outcomes. Further, they argued that one-shot educational programs had little potential for learning. After extensive discussions, the vice president and his staff agreed to try again, but only if the programs were based on a systematic assessment of student needs and assessed to determine their effectiveness in terms of desired student learning outcomes.

Step 1: Define the Problem

The vice president for student affairs saw educational programs as important to student learning; his staff, however, questioned their effectiveness based on their past experience. Neither had any evidence that programs were effective or ineffective other than poor attendance in the past. Further, there was no systematic assessment of student needs on which to base programs.

Step 2: Determine the Purpose of the Study

One purpose of this study, flowing from the problem, is the systematic assessment of student needs, as discussed in Chapter Nine. However, here we focus on the second purpose of the study: to assess the effectiveness of group educational programs.

Step 3: Determine Where to Get the Information Needed

Students who attended group educational programs were the primary source of information about program effectiveness.

Step 4: Determine the Best Assessment Method

A mixed methodology study was decided on, using a brief survey with both quantitative and open-ended items, to provide insight into what students were learning and how they were learning.

Step 5: Determine Whom to Study

All students who participated in all group educational program for an entire academic year were studied.

Step 6: Determine How the Data Will Be Collected

Data were collected from students during group educational programs, because to try to collect data after the program usually results in a very low response rate. However, there are other postprogram data collection strategies that might be considered. For example, if participants volunteer their e-mail addresses, they could be invited to link to a Web-based survey and provide responses electronically (see Chapter Eight). Or if they volunteer their telephone numbers, they could provide their feedback at a later date by telephone (see Chapter Seven). But getting data from students at the time of the program is more cost-effective and more likely to yield a higher response rate than other data collection methods.

Step 7: Determine What Instruments Will Be Used

Developing a group educational program assessment instrument was not an easy task. The first issue to be resolved was to determine if one instrument could be used to assess all educational programs. Some staff argued that since each program was unique, the assessment instrument must be tailored to the unique purposes, methods, and outcomes of a program. Other staff argued that if this approach were adopted, considerable time, resources, and expertise would have to be applied to developing one instrument after another for each educational program, and comparisons among programs would be virtually impossible. After considerable discussion, the staff and the vice president agreed to use a one-page instrument for all educational programs, with the option that program sponsors could use the reverse side of the form for items unique to a particular program.

Again, after considerable discussion, the elements of a common educational program assessment were agreed on.

Program Learning Outcomes

Too often program learning outcomes are fuzzy and thus very difficult to assess. There are several possible learning outcomes of a group educational program.

Content Mastery Often a major intended learning outcome of a group educational program is to inform students about a particular topic—so that they know and understand more about a topic and go away more informed. For example, if the program is about sexually transmitted diseases (STDs), the goal might be for participants to know more about how STDs affect one's body, how they are transmitted, how transmission may be prevented, and other relevant information. If content mastery is an intended learning outcome, then the assessment must attempt to verify if students' knowledge was increased as a result of attending the program. Following are some examples of content items (using an agree-disagree format) if a quantitative assessment approach is appropriate:

"I learned more about the topic than I previously knew."

"I now have a better understanding of the topic than I previously had."

"I need to know more about this topic."

Attitude Change Another major intended learning outcome of a group educational program is to change student attitudes. For example, if the program is about alcohol use, the goal might be for students to develop an attitude that alcohol abuse is wrong because it negatively affects both the abuser and those he or she might abuse when intoxicated. All too frequently, student attitudes toward alcohol abuse is that it is fun, harmless, and certainly not something someone makes a judgment about with an abusing friend. So if attitude change is an intended learning outcome, then the assessment must include some evidence of this goal as a result of attending the program. Following are some examples of attitude items (using an agree-disagree format):

"My attitudes about this topic are more positive than before attending this program."

"My attitudes about this topic did not change as a result of this program."

"This program has motivated me to reconsider my attitudes about this topic."

Behavior Change Although it is probably unrealistic to expect that student behaviors will change as a result of attending a single educational program, it may well be a long-term goal. One thing we do know for certain is that increased knowledge and more positive attitudes do not necessarily result in changed behaviors. On the other hand, if behavior change is one of the goals of the program, then it should be included in the assessment. For example, if the program is about academic dishonesty, investigators might want some indication of whether a student is less likely to cheat on an examination than before attending the program. Granted, we are asking students to predict their future behavior, which is very risky business, but we should ask the behavior question anyway, knowing that the results in the short term may be unreliable. Following are some examples of change items (using an agree-disagree format):

"I do not expect to change any of my behaviors as a result of this program."

"I expect to change my behaviors in a positive way as a result of this program."

"This program motivated me to reconsider my behaviors in relation to this topic."

Demographics of Program Participants

It is not likely that investigators will be able to assess group educational programming adequately unless they know something about the students who attended. This is important for two important reasons. First, if basic demographic identifiers (such as gender, race and ethnicity, age, class standing, and place of residence) are gathered, the investigators will be able to determine if the students who attended were the ones who should have been there. For example, if a program is targeted to adult students and only women attend, we know we must take steps to encourage men to attend. Second, to do an analysis of content mastery, attitude change, or behavior change, we may want to know if different groups were affected differently. For example, we may want to know if the learning outcomes of upperclass students differed from first-year students, or younger students differed from older students, or majority students differed from minority students. Third, if we intend to do any follow-up with participants, we will need the names, addresses, e-mail addresses, and telephone numbers of participants. If a topic is a particularly sensitive one where participants may wish to remain anonymous, then their privacy should be respected.

Ideally, the best way to assemble relevant demographic information is to gather student identification numbers from those attending the program and then retrieve the information from institutional records. This approach, however, has several drawbacks. First, it assumes that the institution has a student information system that is easily accessible. Second, it assumes that the information can be merged easily with data from the assessment instrument. And finally, it assumes that the student is informed about what information will be retrieved and how it will be used. A student ID number disclaimer might read:

> *Please provide your student ID number. It will allow us to access other information in the institution's records such as age, class standing, race/ethnicity, enrollment status, place of residence, gender, and other information relevant to this program. Information regarding individuals will be held in strict confidence and will not be revealed under any circumstances.*

More realistic, however, is to gather this information at the time of the program as part of the assessment instrument. At a minimum, one should gather the following information:

- Age
- Gender
- Race or ethnicity
- Enrollment status (part or full time)
- Number of credit hours completed
- Place of residence

There may also be demographic characteristics specific to the program's purposes, which should also be gathered. For example, if the program's purpose is to raise awareness about disabled students' collegiate experiences, you might want to gather more information about participants who are disabled.

Program Format and Structure

The success or failure of a group educational program may well depend on the program format and structure. Too often, we fail to resist the temptation to preach content to students for an hour and then ask for participant

EXHIBIT 17.1

Group Educational Program Assessment

Office of the Vice-President for Student Affairs

Title of Program _____

Date _____

Presenter _____   Sponsor _____

Student ID Number _____   Your student ID number will allow the sponsors to access demographic information from institutional records, such as age, class standing, race/ethnicity, enrollment status, place of residence, gender, and other information relevant to this program. Information regarding individuals will be held in strict confidence and will not be revealed under any circumstances.

Item	Strongly Agree	Agree	Neutral	Disagree	Strongly Disagree
1. I learned more about this topic than I previously knew.	5	4	3	2	1
2. This program has motivated me to reconsider my attitudes toward this topic.	5	4	3	2	1
3. I do not expect to change any of my behaviors as a result of this program.	5	4	3	2	1
4. This program was well organized.	5	4	3	2	1
5. Different points of view were encouraged.	5	4	3	2	1
6. The handouts were helpful.	5	4	3	2	1
7. The facilities were adequate.	5	4	3	2	1
8. The presenter was well prepared.	5	4	3	2	1
9. The presenter challenged me to think.	5	4	3	2	1
10. The presenter maintained my interest.	5	4	3	2	1

Overall, I rate this program: ___ Poor ___ Fair ___ Average ___ Good ___ Excellent

My local residence is: ___ On campus ___ Off campus

My age is: ___ 17–18 ___ 19–24 ___ 25+

My gender is: ___ female ___ male

My ethnic identity is (Check all that apply):

    ___ African American/black   ___ Native American

    ___ Asian American   ___ Hispanic/Latino

    ___ International   ___ White

    ___ Other _____

What did you like most about this program/activity?

How could this program/activity be improved?

Please share other comments you have about this program.

bottom line is that the findings of assessments of group educational programs should be used in two ways: to improve the quality of programs and to demonstrate the effectiveness of group educational programs as an important strategy in promoting student learning.

Step 11: Report the Results Effectively

There are several strategies to accomplish this goal, including writing good summary reports, making sure brief reports are sent to targeted audiences, and making assessment reports available on the Web. Perhaps most important, sponsors and presenters of group educational programs must receive timely and useful reports so that the quality of programs might be improved. (For a further discussion of the use of assessment results, see Upcraft and Schuh, 1996.)

Conclusion

Group educational programs are one of the most used educational vehicles in student affairs but, unfortunately, one of the least assessed, and therefore one of the most criticized. This chapter was intended to encourage the assessment of these programs for the purposes of improving them and to determine how, if at all, they contribute to student learning.

Reference

Upcraft, M. L., and Schuh, J. H. *Assessment in Student Affairs: A Guide for Practitioners.* San Francisco: Jossey-Bass, 1996.

Part Four

Programs and Service Areas

Chapter 18

Assessing Student Academic Success

Lisa R. Shibley, M. Lee Upcraft

PROBABLY NO OTHER ISSUE has been the object of assessment efforts in the past twenty-five years more than student retention. As institutions are threatened by declining enrollments, low success rates of racial and ethnic minorities, challenges to do more with fewer resources, or the need to improve, they have sought more information about what their retention and persistence rates are, why some students graduate (or do not), and what might be done about increasing student retention.

If these studies are done at all, frequently they are done poorly, resulting in misinformation that may lead to bad policy and poor practice. Retention studies often are flawed because there is no clear or realistic definition of *retention* or because they fail to take into account all of the factors that contribute to retention.

This chapter suggests ways of studying student retention (including casting aside that term for the more general term *student academic success*) and focusing on assessing student success in more nontraditional institutions, such as two-year institutions and those institutions with largely commuting, part-time, and adult learners. This chapter also suggests resources available to help design and develop student academic success assessments. (For a model of assessing academic achievement and retention for more traditional institutions, consult Terenzini and Upcraft, 1996.)

Problems Associated with Assessing Student Academic Success

Many problems exist with the ways institutions typically approach learning about student academic success. Let us look at a typical retention study. An institution proudly develops a study, which looks at students entering the institution at a particular point in time and then determines how many of them graduated from this institution four or five or even six years later. These studies also may compare the retention rates of different student groups, such as racial and ethnic minorities, women, disabled students, and adult students. These studies then are used to define retention problems and become the basis for policies and practices designed to improve retention. Worse yet, they become the basis for declaring institutional success (if the graduation rate is high) or institution failure (if the graduation rate is low).

What is wrong with these studies is that, at best, they do not tell the whole story; at worst, they tell the wrong story. Student academic success is determined by the backgrounds, characteristics, and academic abilities of students *before* college as well their experiences *during* college. The most widely recognized and frequently used framework for assessing educational outcomes is Alexander Astin's input-environment-outcome (IEO) model (1991). According to Terenzini and Upcraft (1996), the primary purpose of this model is to identify and estimate institutional influences on student outcomes such as academic success. In particular, this model is a useful tool for identifying those precollege student attributes and college experiences over which institutions have some programmatic or policy control.

Research on student academic success shows that there are many precollege and during-college variables that make a difference. Astin (1991) identified 146 possible input (precollege) variables, including high school grades and admissions test scores, student expectations, career choice, reasons for attending college, religious preference, occupation, education, income, and a variety of demographic characteristics, such as race, ethnicity, age, gender, marital status, and citizenship. Is it any wonder, then, that highly selective institutions that attract homogeneous students from higher socioeconomic backgrounds typically have high retention rates, compared with open admissions institutions with students with diverse academic and personal backgrounds and characteristics? This difference may have as much to do with whom these institutions attract as it does with what they offer once students enroll. The consideration of input characteristics when assessing student retention helps to understand the influence of student's backgrounds and characteristics on their ability to persist.

To assess students' academic success, according to Terenzini and Upcraft (1996), requires finding ways "to take into account" (that is, control) initial differences. Such controls, in a sense, put all students on the same starting line as they begin their college careers. Unless such controls are part of a student academic success assessment, there will be no way to distinguish between outcomes that are attributable to an institution's educational efforts and those that are attributable to students' backgrounds and characteristics.

Astin (1991) also identified eight classifications of environment (during-college) variables that contribute to student success:

- Institutional characteristics (such as type, control, and size)

- Students' peer group characteristics (such as socioeconomic status, academic preparation, values, and attitudes)

- Faculty characteristics (such as favored methods of teaching, morale, and values)

- Curriculum (such as true core and types of requirements)

- Financial aid (such as Pell grants, Stafford loans, or merit awards)

- Major field choice

- Place of residence (such as college dormitory, fraternity or sorority housing, living at home, or apartment living)

- Student involvement (hours spent studying, number of classes taken in different fields, participation in honors programs, participation in extracurricular activities, and relationships with faculty)

Students living in the honors residence hall with frequent contact with faculty outside the classroom may have a greater opportunity to succeed than those who commute forty-five minutes every day for class, have difficulty finding a place to park on campus, and then need to be home at a certain time every day to meet their children as they arrive home from school. Just as we will control for input characteristics of students so we can better explore learning outcomes, we must find ways to control for during college experiences that may influence those outcomes.

The third part of Astin's IEO model is outcomes. For the purposes of this discussion, let us assume that student academic success is a desired outcome. In the example of a simple retention study, it was assumed that there was only one outcome that measured student academic success: whether the student persisted to graduation at the institution. Although this may be one of many appropriate definitions, it is not the only one. Academic success also may embody students' academic achievement (some students may lack the necessary skills or motivation to earn good grades), students' educational goals (some students may enroll only long enough to develop the skills necessary to get a job, with no intent to graduate), students' enrollment patterns (some students may not intend to stay at one institution until they graduate, but rather transfer to another institution, or frequently stop out and reenroll in the same institution), students' interests (some students may be enrolled strictly to pursue their own learning interests, with no intent to graduate), or other student-centered educational intentions. So when institutions restrict their definition of retention to persistence to graduation, they may be presenting an inaccurate picture of how their institution contributes to student academic success.

All institutions should beware of "retention" studies that fail to take into account precollege and during-college characteristics and defines student success exclusively as persistence to graduation. Instead, student academic success should be defined in terms that reflect students' educational goals.

Because there are many nontraditional institutions serving nontraditional students, we are providing a case study of a state-supported, four-year, open admissions, urban commuter institution. The students who attend this institution reflect the diversity of students in both two-year community colleges and some four-year residential institutions. The case study at City College USA provides a framework for operationalizing the steps to assess academic success using Astin's IEO model (1991). (To learn more about Astin's IEO model as an approach to retention studies and how to conduct a student academic success study in an institution with traditional students, see Upcraft and Schuh, 1996.)

A Student Academic Success Assessment Case Study

Toward the late 1980s, attrition rates at City College USA, a state-supported, public, open admissions, commuter institution with about ten thousand full- and part-time students located in an urban setting created great concern. Initial tracking in the early 1990s revealed a 40 percent six-year graduation rate. Enrollment patterns indicated that many students "stopped out" and "stopped in." Some students left midsemester, often without officially withdrawing from courses. The student average age increased from nineteen to twenty-six. The typical student worked at least thirty hours per week off campus or had young children at home, or both. Student matriculation in vocational programs increased, while matriculation of new students in the liberal arts programs declined.

Previous attempts to understand graduation and enrollment patterns proved ineffective. The president, under constant pressure from the trustees to do something about high attrition and low graduation rates, decided that more and better information was needed. She recently asked you to gather such information, which might give some insight into how to solve the problem. She is especially interested in the nature of the student population and any background characteristics or environmental factors that might influence persistence to graduation. You decide to approach this problem by using the steps outlined in "Steps in the Outcomes Assessment Process" in Chapter Ten of Upcraft and Schuh's *Assessment in Student Affairs* (1996).

Step 1: Define the Problem

The problem for this institution is that there is a perception, shared by the institution's trustees and president, that student dropout rates are too high and graduation rates too low. One aspect of this problem may lie in City College's definition of student academic success. It is clear that this institution is not taking into account its mission and the type of students it enrolls. In fact, academic success includes not only persistence to graduation but also academic achievement, students' educational goals, students' interests, and their enrollment patterns. In the case of City College USA, the previous method for determining academic success relied wholly on persistence from semester to semester and graduation rates. Using only attrition rates as a measure of academic success was quite misleading. The institution must not only conduct a study that takes into account students' precollege backgrounds and characteristics and during-college experiences, but must also expand its initial definition of student academic success.

Step 2: Determine the Purpose of the Study

Another way of framing this step is to ask, What information do we need to solve the problem identified in Step 1? As a result of extensive discussions within City College USA by faculty, staff, students, administrators, and trustees, the following questions emerged:

- What are the educational aspirations of our current and prospective students?

- What are the enrollment patterns of our students?

- What precollege characteristics and experiences and during-college experiences influence students' academic success?

Based on these questions, the purpose of the study is to gain greater insight into student academic success, taking into account their educational goals, enrollment patterns, and precollege and during-college variables.

Step 3: Determine the Appropriate Assessment Approach

The case of City College USA requires both a quantitative and qualitative approach. Astin's Input-Environment-Output Model provides the framework for the quantitative part of this study.

Both qualitative and quantitative research methods would provide useful information here. For the purposes of the study, only quantitative data will be collected and used. Qualitative data in the form of interviews and focus groups could uncover insights ranging from the relationship of student-faculty contact, personal or family problems, hours spent studying, and contact with peers to educational goals, enrollment patterns, reasons for leaving the institution, and persistence to graduation.

Step 4: Determine the Outcomes

The outcomes assessed in this study of this study are based on the purposes of this study identified in Step 2:

Persistence to graduation—enrolling until a degree is attained from City College USA

Persistence to job or promotion—enrolling until a better job is acquired but before a degree from City College USA is attained

Persistence to stopping out—discontinuing enrollment but later reenrolling at City College USA

Persistence to transfer to another institution—enrolling until transferring to another institution but before a degree from City College USA is attained

Persistence to personal fulfillment—enrolling in courses until pursuit of a leisure activity or enhancement of one's knowledge in a particular subject like photography or American Revolutionary history is satisfied (with no degree aspirations)

Failure to achieve any outcome—leaving the institution without achieving graduation, job promotion, transfer, reenrolling, or any other educational goal

Step 5: Identify the Input or Control Variables

To determine outcomes, precollege backgrounds and characteristics must be taken into account:

Prior academic experiences and success: High school grade point average; standardized test scores; math, reading, and writing placement scores; and length of time from high school graduation to college enrollment

Demographic characteristics: Age, gender, race or ethnicity, socioeconomic status, citizenship, disability, marital status, number of dependent children or parents, parents' educational level, and veteran status

Educational goals: Persistence to graduation, persistence to job or promotion, persistence to transfer, persistence to personal fulfillment, and stopping out

In most cases, the inclusion of all input variables is not feasible (Astin, 1991). We must choose which among the variables are most influential and are readily available at City College USA. Variables not included should be listed among the limitations of the study.

Step 6: Identify the Environmental Variables

The environmental variables include students' academic and social characteristics. Again, it is not possible to include all environmental variables, so those used in this study are considered most important and readily available for City College USA students:

> *Academic information and experiences:* College grade point average, number of remedial credit hours taken, number of credits earned, major, full-time or part-time status, classroom-related activities, time spent studying, estimation of learning gains, and perceptions of the academic environment

> *Out-of-class experiences:* Hours spent per week in participation in cocurricular activities, working, and attending to family responsibilities; quality of relationships with other students, faculty, and administrative personnel; perceptions of the college environment; place of residence; use of student services and programs

Step 7: Select the Measurement Instruments

Data for most of the precollege (input) variables were gathered from institutional records. Other precollege data were gathered directly from students through the Entering Student Questionnaire published by the National Center for Higher Education Management Systems and the College Board. (Two-year and four-year versions of this instrument are available; see Resources for information about these instruments.) This instrument includes items about student characteristics; academic, career, sociocultural, and personal development goals; degree aspirations, reasons for choosing the college of enrollment; and local institutionally based items.

Data for during-college (environmental) variables were gathered using the National Survey of Student Engagement, published by the Center for Postsecondary Research and Planning at Indiana University. This instrument contains items on student demographics; college activities; academic experiences; time spent studying, working, and providing care for family, and participation in cocurricular activities; perceptions of the college environment; quality of relationships; estimation of learning gains; and local institutionally based items. Because this instrument does not have items about the use of student services, we highly recommend including such items based on their availability at the institution being reviewed.

Data for students dropping out were gathered using the dropout surveys described in Chapter Fifteen.

Step 8: Determine the Population to Be Studied and the Sample to Be Drawn

All students who enrolled for the first time at City College USA in a specific fall semester are defined as the population included in this study, yielding about three thousand students. Because the college does not have the resources to study all of these entering students, a random sample of 1,142 students was drawn (see Rea and Parker, 1997), and these students were asked to participate in the study. A sample of this size should be sufficient to ensure representativeness, reduce the sampling error to about 3 percent, and capture enough participants for appropriate statistical analyses.

Step 9: Determine the Modes of Statistical Analyses

Because this study examines the relationship between several independent variables (precollege and during college) and six dependent variables (persistence to graduation, persistence to transfer, stopping out, persistence to job or promotion, persistence to personal fulfillment, and failure to achieve any outcome), a multivariate analysis is most appropriate (for a discussion of multivariate analyses, see Upcraft and Schuh, 1996). The results will show to what extent, if any, these outcomes are influenced by these environmental variables, taking into account the influence of background characteristics. In his IEO model, Astin (1991) analyzed input characteristics for significance as predictors first. Once the significant input characteristics were identified, he combined those with the outcome variables in the analyses. This is an option here because there are so many variables in the study and not all of them may be significant. In this case, a level of significance will need to be set. For most studies, $p < .05$ is acceptable. However, for a larger sample size, setting $p < .001$ as the level of significance might be a better choice. (Any number of statistical sources can be consulted for an explanation of these statistical tools.)

Step 10: Develop and Implement a Plan for Data Collection

Data were retrieved from institutional records and from students. Data were collected at the time of students' enrollment (using the Entering Student Survey), several times during college (using the National Study of Student Engagement), and when they left the institution for whatever reason (using one of the dropout surveys included in Chapter Fifteen). We recommend that the precollege survey be administered the first time students register for courses at the institution or during orientation programs. There should be a schedule for data collection that follows the cohort through the length of persistence being studied. For this case, students were tracked for six years (two-year institutions should track for four years because of the unique "stopping-out" tendencies of students attending those institutions).

Based on previous enrollment patterns, enrollment data were checked at certain points. Enrollment was checked after the close of the drop-add period during the second, fourth, sixth, and eighth semesters, and graduation data were collected when students registered to graduate. All information was gathered using a telephone survey (see Chapter Seven), but an on-line survey is a possibility here (see Chapter Eight).

If students departed during the semester, data were gathered through an exit interview that included the National Survey of Student Engagement and the exit interview recommended in Chapter Sixteen. Data on students not available at the time of their departure during the semester, or on students who left between semesters were gathered through several methods, including e-mail (ex-students' e-mail accounts were not discontinued until six months after their departure), telephone surveys (where former students' telephone numbers were still viable after they left the institution), and mailed surveys (where former students' mailing addresses were still viable). Regardless of the method used to collect the information, the instruments used were the same.

Step 11: Record the Data in Usable Form

According to Terenzini and Upcraft (1996), there are several ways of converting data to computer files, and how that is done may depend on the available local resources. One way is to enter data by hand from the questionnaires to a data file; a preferable way is to design the questionnaire so that it can be machine scanned into a data file ready for statistical analyses.

Step 12: Conduct the Appropriate Analyses

A multivariate statistical analysis is most appropriate. Using a commercially based statistical package, such as Statistical Analysis Systems (SAS) or Statistical Package for the Social Sciences (SPSS), is recommended. Such an analysis in this study should provide valuable information about student academic success, however defined. It also should provide insight into why students with various backgrounds, educational goals, and collegiate experiences achieve these various outcomes.

For this case, the analysis was a struggle. It was important to categorize students based on type of initial educational goal as a first-year student and follow those students through as an individual cohort. That temptation was resisted because it was likely that important data might be lost. The concern was that the analyses would be too complicated to report. Upon further reflection, it was decided that the multivariate analyses conducted would permit flexibility in reporting the findings in ways that the trustees and the president could understand. So, for example, if it was found that for students with an initial intent to graduate, major and number of remedial credits taken negatively predicted persistence to graduation, the data were described in that manner instead of comparing to students with the initial goal to transfer. In addition, data were analyzed at every time point and provided ongoing reports to the president and trustees. Waiting until the end of the longitudinal study (six years) to analyze the data was not feasible because there was a critical need for results as soon as the second semester. The data were analyzed in a more comprehensive method at the end of the study.

Step 13: Evaluate the Analyses for Policy and Practice Implications

Whatever the results, the next step is to determine what policies and practices should be changed or developed in order to help solve the problem that initiated the study: the perception that student dropout rates are too high and graduation rates too low.

Let us assume that one of the findings is that students who enter the institution with the intention of graduating actually have a persistence-to-graduation rate of 75 percent, taking into account their precollege background characteristics and during-college experiences. This is very different from the 40 percent that was previously believed. Let us further assume that low scores on academic placement tests and failure to use remediation services are statistically significant predictors of dropping out. That tells City

College USA that programs and services designed to help overcome academic deficiencies may need to be strengthened or even required.

Factors that contribute to the academic success of students entering with other educational goals similarly can be identified and implications for policies and practices determined. For example, let us assume that the study found that 85 percent of students who entered the institution intending to transfer but not intending to graduate were successful in transferring to another institution. And let us further assume that living on campus appears to be a statistically significant variable in successful transfers to other institutions. As a matter of policy, then, the institution might want to focus on helping commuting students make a successful transfer to another institution.

Step 14: Develop a Strategy for Using the Results

Strategies for how to use assessment results are dictated by several factors, including the original purpose for the study and other institutional factors. In this study, the findings should be distributed widely to vested stakeholders, especially the board of trustees, who were pressuring the president to do something about low retention rates, and to the leaders of various administrative and academic units for whom these results may have implications.

Conclusion

Too often institutions have a limited or no understanding of student academic success because they do not conduct serious studies at all, or they do them poorly. This chapter has presented some ways of assessing student success, primarily by focusing on what students' educational goals were as they entered college, taking into account precollege and during-college variables that affect student academic success. The model presented was designed to include not only traditional institutions but also those with students and enrollment patterns for whom traditional models of assessing academic achievement are inadequate.

References

Astin, A. W. *Assessment for Excellence: The Philosophy and Practice of Assessment and Evaluation in Higher Education.* San Francisco: Jossey-Bass, 1991.

Rea, L. M., and Parker, R. A. *Designing and Conducting Survey Research.* (2nd ed.) San Francisco: Jossey-Bass, 1997.

Terenzini, P. T., and Upcraft, M. L. "Assessing Program and Service Outcomes." In M. L. Upcraft and J. H. Schuh, *Assessment in Student Affairs: A Guide for Practitioners*. San Francisco: Jossey-Bass, 1996.

Upcraft, M. L., and Schuh, J. H. *Assessment in Student Affairs: A Guide for Practitioners*. San Francisco: Jossey-Bass, 1996.

Chapter 19

Assessing First-Year Programs

Jennifer L. Crissman, M. Lee Upcraft

EACH YEAR THOUSANDS of new students enroll in college and begin what is known as the first-year experience. Typically students face this experience with a number of concerns. For traditional students, it may be the thoughts and fears of having a roommate or worrying about whether they will be able to handle the requirements of college work. For students from historically underrepresented groups, it may be the fear of experiencing culture shock or being discriminated against. For disabled students, it may be concern about how their disability will affect their adjustment and transition to college life. Commuters may feel alienated and cut off from campus life and unsure of how to become an integral part of the campus. Women students may be concerned about their personal safety. Returning adult students may be anxious about doing academic work after being out of high school for many years or worrying about balancing work and family responsibilities. For institutions, the first-year experience is about helping students to succeed both academically and socially, and it is about retention. In order to survive, colleges and universities must retain the students they admit.

We know from extensive research that the first year of college is extremely important in students' success in college (Upcraft and Gardner, 1989; Tinto, 1993). This year is a time of transition and adjustment to the social and academic demands of college and a time when the likelihood of dropping out is greatest (Upcraft and Gardner, 1989; Tinto, 1993). The research also tells us that entering students' most critical transition period occurs during the first two to six weeks of the first semester (Levitz and Noel, 1989). Of the students who drop out during their first semester, half do so during the first six weeks (Myers, 1981). Tinto (1993) reports that the largest proportion of institutional leaving occurs during the first year and before the beginning of the second year.

Most institutions of higher education devote considerable time and energy to helping new students make a successful transition to college by a process termed *front loading*: "putting the strongest, most student-centered people, programs, and services in the freshman year" (Levitz and Noel, 1989, p. 79). Common types of front-loading programs include orientation programs (preentry and extended), first-year advising and monitoring of academic performance, precollege testing and assessment, first-year seminars, and programs that cluster students by courses and residences. All of these efforts are more effective if they are concentrated in the first semester of enrollment (Upcraft and Gardner, 1989).

So there is a flurry of activity designed to help students make a successful transition to college. But are these activities effective? Do they in fact help students succeed academically and socially? And how do we know? This chapter presents an overview of assessing first-year programs and works through a case study about an orientation problem using the steps in the assessment process outlined in Chapter Two.

A Model for Assessing First-Year Programs

The comprehensive model for assessment in student affairs presented in Chapter One can serve as a guide when considering how to assess orientation programs.

Know the Backgrounds and Characteristics of Entering Students

Orientation programs should be based on a profile of students entering the institution. How is this group represented by gender, race and ethnicity, age, marital status, disability, and other defining characteristics? What is their level of academic preparation, and will some students need to improve their academic skills? Although such information is almost always a part of institutional databases, often these data are not presented in concise, readable reports that are useful to first-year student program planners and policy makers and to faculty.

Assess Entering Students' Needs

Assessing the needs of students is a crucial activity in the overall assessment process. This is especially critical for first-year students because programs based on these needs must be planned and what is offered must meet those needs. What academic and personal needs must be met if students are to make a successful transition to college? How do student affairs staff know what those needs are?

One important source for identifying first-year student needs is the research literature on this topic. For example, Upcraft and Gardner (1989) suggest a useful framework for considering first-year student needs: (1) developing academic and intellectual competence, (2) establishing and maintaining interpersonal relationships, (3) developing identity, (4) deciding on a career, (5) maintaining personal health and wellness, and (6) developing an integrated philosophy of life.

A second source for identifying first-year student needs is to ask students themselves. Although this is an effective way of determining needs, it is best done after they have been enrolled for a while rather than at the onset of their enrollment. For example, focus groups with new students can ask them to reflect on their experiences during the first few weeks and discuss what the institution did or might have done to help them during this time.

Assess Entering Students' Satisfaction with Orientation Programs

Even if orientation programs are based on systematic studies of entering students' needs, a particular institution's students' needs will not be met if the programs offered do not meet their needs. There must be systematic studies of students' satisfaction with the orientation programs offered, focusing on what was done well and what might be done to improve. The generic program evaluation instrument presented in Chapter Seventeen may be useful. Also, this chapter offers an example of a quantitative assessment instrument specifically targeted to student satisfaction with orientation programs. (For a more detailed discussion of assessing student satisfaction, see Chapter Ten.)

Assess Orientation Outcomes

Ultimately the worth of an orientation program must be measured by whether the orientation efforts resulted in students' making a successful transition to college, doing well academically, meeting their educational and personal goals, and persisting to graduation. (For a more detailed discussion of assessing outcomes, see Chapter Eleven in this book and Terenzini and Upcraft, 1996.)

Assess the Climate for First-Year Students

An orientation program should introduce the new students to a safe, receptive, and inclusive environment. For example, first-year women students should feel safe at night and feel that they are valued members in the classroom. Students of color should feel accepted both socially and academically as part of the community. Students of a different sexual orientation should feel that the campus is a safe place to be open about their sexual orientation. We must assess the campus climate and determine how it will affect new students. (See Whitt's chapter in Upcraft and Schuh, 1996, for a more detailed discussion of assessing campus cultures and climates.)

Assess Compared to Accepted National Standards

The Council for the Advancement of Standards (CAS), formed in 1979, is a clearinghouse of standards for professional associations and organizations. In 1986, CAS, along with the National Orientation Directors Association, published the Standards and Guidelines for Student Orientation Programs, a document that contains thirteen parts that cover topics such as mission, ethics, funding, legal responsibilities, and assessment. In 1988, the *Student Orientation Programs Self-Assessment Guide* was published with eighteen goals for orientation programs, regardless of the size or mission of an institution. Mullendore and Abraham (1993) conclude that the CAS standards have been a useful tool in comparing, assessing, and improving orientation efforts. (For a more detailed discussion of CAS standards, see Miller, 1996.)

Assess Cost-Effectiveness

Cost benefit analysis is difficult to do; nevertheless, all orientation programs must be assessed to determine if the benefits students receive are worth the cost. For example, can we place a price on students' successful transition to college or on their academic success? An institution makes a commitment to students when it accepts them. How much should it be willing to pay up front to help make the new students' transition to college a successful one so that they may continue their education and persist to graduation? And where should the funding come from? Institutional budgets? A general orientation fee? Student fundraisers? Fees for selected orientation programs? (For a more detailed discussion of assessing cost-effectiveness, see Chapter Thirteen.)

An Orientation Case Study

Mid Size University (MSU) is a public institution of eight thousand students. It offers a comprehensive, mandatory, four-day orientation program before classes begin in the fall semester for its twenty-five hundred incoming new students. The new students attending MSU are predominantly eighteen years old, living on campus, and ranked in the top 10 percentile of their high school graduating class. The orientation program comprises academic programs during the day and entertainment every evening. Some examples of the academic programs held during orientation include meetings with academic advisers to discuss registration requirements; workshops to discuss the curriculum and major requirements; workshops on academic policies; and sessions on test-taking strategies, stress management, and personal health and wellness issues. Evening entertainment has included a dance, a hypnotist, and scavenger hunts.

The vice president for student affairs has received some informal feedback that entering students skipped many of the academic programs during the day, went to the evening activities for a short while, and then left to go to the off-campus parties (thanks to the upper-class orientation leaders' telling the new students where the parties were being held). She also has received comments that even when students do attend programs, they are not at all satisfied with them. They do not seem to hit the mark as far as students are concerned.

The vice president wants to know why entering students are not attending orientation programs and why they seem to respond so negatively when they do attend. She wants a systematic assessment to answer these questions.

Step 1: Define the Problem

MSU is spending considerable time, money, and resources planning programs for orientation, yet many new students are not attending the events; moreover, those who do seem to be very dissatisfied with them. The problem is the suspicion that because of nonattendance and student dissatisfaction, the intended goals of orientation programs appear to be unmet, and therefore ineffective in helping students make a successful transition to college and to fulfill their educational goals.

Step 2: Determine the Purpose of the Study

The first purpose of this assessment, given the problem, is to determine why the students did or did not attend the workshops and sessions during the four-day orientation program and what might be changed or improved to increase their attendance. The second purpose is to determine, in a more systematic way, what the level of student satisfaction is with the current orientation program and what might be done to improve this satisfaction.

Step 3: Determine Where to Get the Information Needed

Because the complete four-day orientation program will be assessed, information is needed about everyone involved in the program. Therefore, the entering class of new students (those who attended and those who did not), the upperclass orientation leaders, the student affairs and academic affairs professionals, and other campus administrators who planned or presented workshops will be included in this study. To retrieve this information, the director of orientation will provide a complete list of entering students to determine which ones participated in the program and which did not. The director also will provide a list of the upperclass orientation leaders and the professional presenters.

Step 4: Determine the Best Assessment Method

Patton (1990) states, "Quantitative and qualitative methods involve differing strengths and weaknesses and constitute alternative, but not mutually exclusive, strategies for research. Both can therefore be used in the same study" (p. 14). Based on Patton's observation, a combination of quantitative and qualitative methodologies should be used for this assessment.

A qualitative approach will be used to deal with the attendance problem because it permits the use of detailed observation by the person doing the assessment and the accumulation of data in depth and detail. It is also consistent with Maxwell's (1996) focus on qualitative methodology. He states, "Qualitative researchers need to ask questions about the meaning of events and activities to the people involved" (p. 59). In order to find out why students are attending (or not attending) orientation events, students will be interviewed in a focus group setting, because focus groups provide an effective and efficient way of getting at this information.

The assessment could begin by conducting focus groups of the entering students who did and did not attend the four-day orientation program. To allow the students some time to absorb the impact of their orientation experience, focus groups should occur sometime after the midsemester examinations. Focus groups could be conducted first with students who attended orientation programs to determine why they attended and simultaneously with the new students who did not attend any or only parts of the orientation programs and find out why they did not attend.

Students may not be the only sources of information about this problem. There could be focus groups with student orientation leaders to get their perceptions on why students did or did not attend. And finally, it would be beneficial to conduct focus groups with the professional staff who conducted workshops or programs during orientation. (For further details on how to design and conduct focus groups, see Chapter Four.)

The level of student satisfaction is probably best determined using a quantitative approach. Upcraft and Schuh (1996) state that quantitative studies "give us a very firm foundation for describing and analyzing what 'is,' and offer some insight into 'why' it is the way it is" (p. 85). To gain more insight into student satisfaction with orientation programs, participants could complete an instrument that evaluates the activity at the end of each workshop, session, meeting, or event. This machine-readable instrument would include demographic information about the new student attending the program, as well as his or her level of satisfaction with the specific program and the presenters. The instrument could also accommodate any comments that could not be expressed through the quantitative items on the instrument. (See Exhibit 19.1.)

Step 5: Determine Whom to Study

The attendance dimension of this study will look at the new students who attended the orientation programs, the new students who did not attend the program, upperclass orientation leaders who assisted with the program, and student and academic affairs professionals who presented at orientation. The satisfaction part of the study will include all students who actually attended orientation programs, so sampling will not be necessary.

As Upcraft and Schuh (1996) state, it is rarely possible to include the entire population in a study. Since this assessment study deals with twenty-five hundred new students, a sample of the whole population of new students must be selected for the focus group interviews. To identify the type of sample wanted for this part of the study requires going back to the second step in the assessment process and looking at the purpose: to determine why the students did or did not attend orientation programs. To answer this question, we must gather of sample of students who attended these programs and another sample of students who did not. For students who attended one or more programs, we will use purposeful sampling, "a strategy in which particular settings, persons, or events are selected deliberately in order to provide important information that can't be gotten as well from other choices" (Maxwell, 1996, p. 70). Students who attended one or more orientation programs can be identified from the quantitative instrument they filled out after each orientation program, and from that group, students can be invited to participate in focus groups. Students who did not attend any programs will also be invited to participate in another set of focus groups, also a form of purposeful sampling. As the study is conceived, it is unknown exactly how many groups will be conducted. That will not be determined until the point of redundancy or saturation is reached with each set of participants. Morgan (1998) observes that the number of groups will typically range from three to five. (For further information on qualitative sampling, see Chapter Three.)

Because there are so many fewer upperclass orientation leaders and professionals who presented during orientation than first-year students, all twenty-five leaders and thirty-five professionals will be invited to participate in focus groups.

Step 6: Determine How the Data Will Be Collected

To collect the qualitative information, there will be five focus groups for new students who attended one or more orientation programs, five focus groups of new students who did not attend any orientation programs, one focus group of upperclass orientation leaders, and one focus group of administrators, faculty, and staff who made presentations. Each focus group should be composed of approximately ten to fifteen persons. To make sure that no information is overlooked or forgotten, the interviews will be tape-recorded. (For a more detailed discussion of conducting focus groups, see Chapter Four.)

To gather the quantitative data for the assessment, the program evaluation questionnaire will be distributed after every workshop, session, program, or event during the four days of orientation. This procedure should yield a very high percentage of the population of entering students attending these programs and events.

Step 7: Determine What Instruments Will be Used

To gather the qualitative data within the focus groups, an interview protocol must be developed for each group of people consisting of standardized, open-ended questions that will retrieve the information needed for this study. Using open-ended questions, as discussed by Upcraft and Schuh (1996), means there are no prescribed answers (those that can be answered yes or no). Following are some examples of the interview protocol for the new students attending orientation, students not attending orientation, upperclass orientation leaders, and professionals:

Interview Protocol for Students Who Attended Orientation

1. Why did you attend orientation programs?

2. If you did attend some orientation programs, why did you skip others?

3. Why did many students fail to attend orientation programs?

4. Any other comments?

Interview Protocol for Nonattendees

1. Why didn't you attend any orientation programs?

2. What advice would you give to orientation planners to improve attendance?

3. Any other comments?

Interview Protocol for Orientation Leaders and Presenters

1. Why do you think some students attended one or more orientation programs?

2. Why didn't many students attend orientation programs?

3. What might be done to improve attendance?

4. Any other comments?

The instrument used to gather the quantitative data for this assessment will be a machine-scored program evaluation questionnaire that will ask new students who attended one or more orientation programs how they evaluated those programs, using a five-point Likert scale (see Exhibit 19.1). It will also ask students to provide demographic information about themselves.

Step 8: Determine Who Should Collect the Data

In determining the answer to this question, the debate becomes whether someone from within MSU should collect the data or if someone outside the institution should conduct the study. For the attendance part of this study, the director of orientation, with the help of a few upperclass orientation leaders, two faculty members, and one administrator, will collect the data. The director of orientation will organize the focus groups but will have the faculty members and administrator run the groups, with the help of orientation leaders. It should be easy for the director of orientation to contact all the necessary people to participate in the focus groups since she had already asked them to participate in the orientation program. However, by asking faculty and an administrator to run the different focus groups, she establishes more credibility for the assessment study. Had she conducted the focus group interviews herself, there could have been, at the very least, a perception of bias and, at worst, actual bias. Further, focus group members might not be as honest or as forthcoming if the director of orientation conducted the interview. By having others conduct the groups, students may be more inclined to speak openly, honestly, and freely.

For the satisfaction part of the study, data will be collected from those who participated in the program at the time of the program.

Step 9: Determine How the Data Will Be Analyzed

The data analysis for the qualitative aspect should be ongoing throughout the study so that the director of orientation can explore with later participants issues or points raised by early participants (Lincoln and Guba, 1985; Miles and Huberman, 1984). For the attendance part of the study, once all focus group interviews are completed, the audiotapes should be transcribed.

EXHIBIT 19.1

Orientation Program Evaluation Questionnaire

Office of the Vice-President for Student Affairs

Title of Program _____   Date _____

Presenter _____   Student ID Number _____-_____-_____

	Strongly Agree	Agree	Neutral	Disagree	Strongly Disagree
1. I now know much more about the topic of this program.	5	4	3	2	1
2. I learned more about the skills I need to make a successful transition to college.	5	4	3	2	1
3. I am now more confident about making a successful transition to college.	5	4	3	2	1
4. I now know more about where to get help on the topic of this program.	5	4	3	2	1
5. The presenter(s) were well prepared.	5	4	3	2	1
6. The presenter(s) communicated effectively.	5	4	3	2	1
7. The presenter(s)were knowledgeable.	5	4	3	2	1
8. The presenter(s) promoted participant participation.	5	4	3	2	1
9. The presenter(s) encouraged different points of view.	5	4	3	2	1
10. I would recommend this program to other first-year students.	5	4	3	2	1

11. Overall, I would rate this program: ___ poor ___ fair ___ average ___ good ___ excellent

12. My local residence is: ___ on campus ___ off campus

13. My age is: ___ 17–18 ___ 19–24 ___ 24+

14. My gender is: ___ female ___ male

15. My ethnic identity is (check as many as apply):
 ___ African American/black ___ Native American ___ Asian American
 ___ Hispanic/Latino ___ International ___ White ___ Other _____

What did you like most about this program/activity?

How could this program/activity be improved?

Please share other comments you have about this program.

Do you have suggestions for other programs/activities? Please indicate on back.

Note: *Inclusion of your student ID number will allow the sponsors access to demographic information, such as age, class standing, race/ethnicity, enrollment status, place of residence, and other information relevant to this program. Information regarding individuals will be held in strict confidence and will not be revealed under any circumstances.*

Upcraft and Schuh (1996) note that in focus group interviews, speakers are sometimes difficult to identify. To prevent this from occurring, the director should ask one or two orientation leaders to attend the interviews to make observations and take notes. The faculty member or administrator can facilitate the focus group interviews while the orientation leaders take observational notes. Notes also taken by the faculty or administrator of their impressions of the interview, the participants, and other observations derived from the interview can and should be incorporated into the data analysis.

Once transcription is complete, the director should code the responses, that is, rearrange the data into categories that facilitate the comparison of data within and between these categories and that aid in the development of theoretical concepts (Strauss, 1987). For example, after reading the transcripts of the students who did attend orientation, certain themes emerged: the advising and registration sessions were extremely helpful, the tour of campus (in the scavenger hunt) was fun and informative, meeting with faculty in small groups was beneficial, and spending four days on campus before classes helped make the students feel more at home.

The director should highlight quotations by the students that correlate with these specific themes. This same practice of reading through transcripts, finding common themes, and finding supporting quotations should be done with the remaining focus group transcripts.

For the satisfaction part of the study, data collected using the computerized program evaluation questionnaire will be machine entered into a data file ready for statistical analysis. This file will include demographic information about the students attending the programs, as well as student satisfaction as measured by items using the five-point Likert scale. At a minimum, descriptive analyses of each item should be reported, preferably in percentages. More sophisticated analyses, based on respondents' demographic characteristics (such as by gender, race or ethnicity, or place of residence), might also be desirable.

Step 10: Determine the Implications of the Study for Policy and Practice

What the study reveals will determine the implications. The goal is to find out why students attend or do not attend orientation programs and then determine what policies, practices, or programs need to be changed or eliminated. More specifically, the entire orientation program should be changed to reflect strategies for improving attendance. Also, the results of the satisfaction study should be used to reflect strategies for improving the quality of orientation programs and to ensure that all entering students have an equal opportunity to benefit from them.

The focus group interviews and the evaluation of workshops should provide a better picture of students' and administrators' thoughts, feelings, and opinions of orientation. From those comments, it will be the responsibility of the director of orientation to revise the program in order that more students will attend and be satisfied with the program.

Step 11: Report the Results Effectively

Upcraft and Schuh (1996) provide several suggestions for communicating the findings of a study. To begin, they advise that a "typical report, regardless of the length and intended audience, should include an executive summary, the purpose, design, results of the study, and any recommendations" (p. 26).

It is important that those who are conducting this study write a report and present the findings to the vice president for student affairs. She was the one who heard rumors of the poorly attended programs. She was also the one who identified the problem and decided that orientation must be assessed. Therefore, the qualitative and quantitative findings must be summarized in a clear, concise way and presented to her. Once she has the report, she may choose to disseminate these findings to the council of trustees, the president, or her staff of student affairs professionals. She may use the quantitative findings in the form of graphs, charts, and graphics, while using powerful quotations from students to discuss the qualitative findings.

Conclusion

This chapter provides a model for assessing first-year programs, as well as an example of two problems relating to orientation programs: attendance and satisfaction. There are many other ways of assessing first-year student programs, the most important of which might be demonstrating a relationship between students' participation in orientation programs and the achievement of desired educational outcomes. (See Chapter Eleven in this book and Terenzini and Upcraft, 1996, for outcomes assessment models.)

References

Council for the Advancement of Standards for Student Services/Development Programs. *CAS Standards and Guidelines for Student Support Services/Development Programs.* Washington, D.C.: Council for the Advancement of Standards for Student Services/Development Programs, 1986.

Council for the Advancement of Standards for Student Services/Development Programs. *CAS Standards and Guidelines for Student Support Services/Development Programs: Student Orientation Programs Self-Assessment Guide.* Washington, D.C.: Council for the Advancement of Standards for Student Services/Development Programs, 1988.

Levitz, N., and Noel, L. "Connecting Students to Institutions: Keys to Retention and Success." In M. L. Upcraft and J. N. Gardner (eds.), *The Freshman Year Experience: Helping Students Survive and Succeed in College.* San Francisco: Jossey-Bass, 1989.

Lincoln, Y. S., and Guba, E. G. *Naturalistic Inquiry.* Thousand Oaks, Calif.: Sage, 1985.

Maxwell, J. A. *Qualitative Research Design: An Interactive Approach.* Thousand Oaks Calif.: Sage, 1996.

Miles, M. B., and Huberman, A. M. *Qualitative Data Analysis: A Sourcebook of New Methods.* Thousand Oaks, Calif.: Sage, 1984.

Miller, T. K. "Measuring Effectiveness Against Professional Standards." In M. L. Upcraft and J. H. Schuh, *Assessment in Student Affairs: A Guide for Practitioners.* San Francisco: Jossey-Bass, 1996.

Morgan, D. L. *Planning Focus Groups.* Focus Group Kit No. 2. Thousand Oaks, Calif.: Sage, 1998.

Mullendore, R. H., and Abraham, J. "Organization and Administration of Orientation Programs." In M. L. Upcraft, R. H. Mullendore, B. O. Barefoot, and D. S. Fidler (eds.), *Designing Successful Transitions: A Guide for Orienting Students to College.* Columbia, S.C.: National Resource Center for the Freshman Year Experience, University of South Carolina, 1993.

Myers, E. *Unpublished Attrition Research Studies, St. Cloud State University.* St. Cloud, Minn.: St. Cloud State University, 1981.

Patton, M. Q. *Qualitative Evaluation and Research Methods.* (2nd ed.) Thousand Oaks, Calif.: Sage, 1990.

Strauss, A. *Qualitative Analysis for Social Scientists.* New York: Cambridge University Press, 1987.

Terenzini, P. T., and Upcraft, M. L. "Assessing Program and Service Outcomes." In M. L. Upcraft and J. H. Schuh, *Assessment in Student Affairs: A Guide for Practitioners.* San Francisco: Jossey-Bass, 1996.

Tinto, V. *Leaving College: Rethinking the Causes and Cures of Student Attrition.* (2nd ed.) Chicago: University of Chicago Press, 1993.

Upcraft, M. L., and Gardner, J. N. (eds.). *The Freshman Year Experience: Helping Students Survive and Succeed in College.* San Francisco: Jossey-Bass, 1989.

Upcraft, M. L., and Schuh, J. H. *Assessment in Student Affairs: A Guide for Practitioners.* San Francisco: Jossey-Bass, 1996.

Chapter 20

Assessing Campus Recreation Programs

CAMPUS RECREATION PROGRAMS often include quite a diverse array of activities, including intramural sports, individual fitness programs, club sports, and outdoor recreation activities such as camping and hiking. As campuses continue to develop the physical facilities and staff to organize and support these programs, questions can arise as to just how effective these programs are. These programs often require swimming pools, exercise equipment, playing fields, indoor driving and shooting ranges, and other specialized facilities, so it becomes quite clear that campus recreation can require a tremendous investment of resources. Because the programs are quite diverse and can occur in many places around the campus, simply keeping track of who participates in which programs can be a challenging task. No matter how popular with students, faculty, and others, a recreation program needs to provide evidence that it is achieving its objectives. This chapter provides a model for assessing recreation programs and presents a case study and a potential solution to the problem presented in the case.

Problems Associated with Assessing Campus Recreation Programs

Assessing recreation programs can be difficult for a variety of reasons. Recreation programs can play host to hundreds of thousands of users in a year, occur in a wide number of places, have clientele who are difficult to identify, and have massive budgets. As a consequence, a wide range of assessment problems can occur in assessing recreation programs.

A place to start in looking at challenges relating to assessing recreation programs is that under the recreation umbrella typically are a variety of facilities: swimming pools, gymnasiums, weight-lifting rooms, tennis courts, golf courses, playing fields, and so on. Because these facilities are so different from one another, conducting a meaningful assessment to determine satisfaction with facilities, for example, can be a daunting task. Contrast an assessment of user satisfaction with facilities in the recreation area with virtually any other area of student affairs. With the exception of a student union, the dynamics of assessing satisfaction with facilities are much simpler in other areas, for obvious reasons. So simply measuring perceptions of facilities makes recreation program assessment difficult.

A second problem has to do with defining the clientele of the facility. Not all students use the facility. There is no captive audience like one would find in a residence hall system. Some students bring guests. At times, the facility may be made available to visitors to the institution. Some colleges, particularly metropolitan institutions, encourage students to bring their families to the recreation facility. Multiple users are quite common, and conducting a systematic assessment of their perceptions of the recreation program is a daunting task.

A third problem is that not all users participate in all programs offered in a recreation facility. Some participate in intramural sports. Others just lift weights or swim. Still others participate in outdoor recreation programs but never use the gyms or pools. This means that assessments need to be quite specialized, since it may be difficult to identify students who participate in many of the programs and activities offered by the recreation program.

A fourth problem has to do with assessing the financing of the recreation program. On some campuses, tuition money or money from the state may help support the operation; on others, only fee money and fees for service support the program. In some instances, the facility may have no debt, while other campuses may have a facility with substantial debt. These exigencies make it difficult to compare budgets across institutions.

Although these problems can be overcome with creative thinking and careful planning, they make assessment of recreation programs challenging.

A Model for Assessing Recreation Programs

Assessing recreation programs is a complex task since the recreation program can include many activities, programs, and services. Besides having substantial responsibilities for facilities management, recreation can include intramural sports, individual fitness programs, outdoor recreation, club sports, and even cheerleaders and mascots. Elements of the program can reflect the kind of complexity one might encounter in managing a health club or tennis center—overseeing intercollegiate sports as well as keeping a vast clientele happy with programs and services.

Assessment can play an important role. Consider the following elements of a comprehensive assessment model for recreation programs and services. We will use the term *center* as being synonymous with recreation facilities, programs, and services.

Know the Background and Characteristics of Users

Typically the users of a recreation program extend far beyond students and can include faculty, staff, graduates, student family members, and others who may have an association with the institution. The following questions are crucial in sorting out who uses the facility:

- Which students use the facility?
- What are the demographics of these students?
- How many people are repeat users?
- Who uses the facility in what way, that is, how many participate in intramurals, club sports, individual fitness programs, and so on?
- Which students do not use the recreation center?

Investigators should always be careful not to have too narrow a user base, and as a consequence, keeping a profile of who does not use the center is important. The advent of "smart" identification cards and card readers can facilitate the process of identifying recreation center users. Rossi, Freeman, and Lipsey (1999, p. 192) ask these important questions: "Are there targets who are not receiving services? Are members of the target population aware of the program?"

Assess the Needs of Students and Other Clients

As recreation programs evolve, are there specific needs of users that are not being met? Are these needs realistic given the institution's mission and resources? On some campuses, providing indoor tennis courts is expected; on others, such a facility would be luxury. What are the needs of nonusers? Would more students use the recreation center if different facilities or programs were available? (See Chapter Nine for a detailed discussion of assessing student needs.)

Assess User Satisfaction

Satisfaction assessment is very much a part of the Total Quality Improvement programs that many institutions have implemented, and the responses provided by users are extremely useful in developing an agenda for improvement. Users can identify strengths and weaknesses of the program, areas they recommend for improvement, and specific steps that might be taken to facilitate improvement. (See Chapter Ten for a more detailed discussion of assessing student satisfaction.)

Assess Student and Other Cultures

Several aspects of a recreation center might generate an interesting cultural assessment. Among these are club sports teams, which mirror other intercollegiate teams in many respects, and spirit squads, which include cheerleaders and mascots. Students who participate in club sports or as members of spirit squads spend tremendous amounts of time together, including traveling to road games and events at neutral sites off campus, and as a consequence they develop their own culture. These groups of students lend themselves to analysis using a cultural lens.

Assess Outcomes

If participation in recreation programs is supposed to facilitate student growth or some other desired educational outcome, then data must be generated to support or refute this assumption. This may be the most important of all the forms of assessment, since many programs and services exist to facilitate outcomes. If purported outcomes do not result from participation in recreation programs, then the whole rationale offering them can be called into question. Critical to assessing outcomes is determining what outcomes are intended, given a particular recreation program. This question must be answered first if outcomes are to be assessed. (See Chapter Eleven in this book and Upcraft and Schuh, 1996, for a further discussion of outcomes assessment.)

Assess Comparable Institutions

The use of peer institutions for assessment purposes is a common approach. In the case of a recreation center, the major challenge will be to make sure that the philosophy undergirding the recreation program is similar across institutions. Even if the enrollment of two institutions is the same, if one is a residential campus and the other is a commuter institution, their recreation programs very likely will be substantially different. At a residential campus, for example, it is much more likely to see tremendous participation in intramural competition; at a commuter campus, students may use the recreation center more along the lines of a health club. The National Intramural-Recreational Sports Association (NIRSA) has a number of resources available for assessment purposes. More information about these resources is available at NIRSA's Web site, http://www.nirsa.org.

Assess Using Nationally Accepted Standards

The standards developed by the Council for the Advancement of Standards (Miller, 1997) can be used by institutions to conduct studies with these standards as benchmarks against which to judge their programs. We believe that this form of assessment works best when combined with other forms identified in this chapter. We do not advocate that assessments of this kind be the only ones undertaken.

Assess Cost Effectiveness

This is a particularly salient form of assessment for recreation programs. Since facilities exist off campus in many communities that provide for recreation, campus leaders need to determine from time to time just how competitive the cost of operating the recreation center is on a per student basis compared with membership in a health club. A good means of determining the cost per student on campus is to calculate the cost per full-time-equivalent student. This cost can be compared with that of memberships in off-campus facilities, the data for which can be determined by making a few telephone calls. If there are additional costs for taking classes or using special facilities, such as court time for tennis courts, this should be noted for both the campus recreation center and the off-campus facilities.

Financial support for these programs often comes from student fees and fees for service. At some institutions, tuition revenues may be dedicated to support recreation programs as well. Regardless of the source of the funding, recreation staff need to make sure that the cost of operation is competitive. They also must ensure that users are satisfied with the programs, services, and facilities offered. In this context, consider the following case study.

Recreation Program Effectiveness Case Study

Local College (LC) is a metropolitan institution that draws students primarily from the urban area it serves. Many of the students are returning adult learners with families. The students often work long hours to pay for their education and support their families, and they generally do not have time to participate in a wide array of student activities. Nevertheless, the campus has decided to develop its recreation program.

The approach LC has taken has been to put an emphasis on individual recreation rather than intramural competition. To be sure, students still form teams and compete in intramural leagues, but many students, especially the returning adult learners, tend to use the individualized fitness programs, such as aerobics classes, free swimming, and jogging at the indoor track.

LC has decided to attempt to keep entire families engaged in support of their student's educational endeavors. As a consequence, family members are able to use campus facilities for modest fees. In the case of the recreation center, family members are welcome to use the facilities at certain times of the week, and special activities are planned for children. The recreation program has enjoyed tremendous success according to anecdotal evidence, but the recent election of the student senate has raised a cause for concern.

In this election, a party advocating a reduction in student fees (the primary source of support for many student services, including the recreation program) captured a majority of seats in the senate as well as the student body presidency. This group is demanding greater accountability for the use of student fees. It intends to make sure that every student fee dollar is spent in such a way that students can be assured that their money is well spent. Since the student senate has a substantial voice in how student fees are being spent, this is not an idle threat. The student senate has to approve an annual fee budget before fees can be set each year, and although the LC president can make changes in the budget, historically she has chosen not to do so.

Rather than waiting to be asked to provide information that will sustain the quality of the recreation program, the director has decided that an assessment process should be undertaken to determine just what the perceptions of the recreation program are.

Step 1: Define the Problem

The problem at LC is that the student government leaders are seeking accountability measures. These students have decided that fees are too high, and they want to make sure that all students are receiving appropriate return on their annual investment.

Step 2: Determine the Purpose of the Study

The study has at least two elements to it. The first has to do with whether the funds expended on this activity, the recreation program, represent a good use of student fees. One way of looking at this problem is to determine if this enterprise is cost-effective. If the operation is not cost-effective, then funding might be cut.

The other element has to do with user satisfaction. Are students and other users satisfied with the programs and service provided by the recreation center? Even if the recreation center is cost-effective, if users are not satisfied with its services and programs, funds might be cut. As a consequence, the second aspect of this assessment will have to be conducted as well.

Step 3: Determine Where to Get the Information Needed

Two kinds of studies need to be conducted. One set will deal with whether the recreation center is cost-effective, and the other has to do with user satisfaction. To deal with the cost-effective dimension of the work, determining what cost-effective means is the next step. In this case, it could mean determining if the recreation center is cost-effective compared with health clubs and other similar facilities in the community. Remember that most of LC's students are from the area, and using a health club in town, the YMCA, or a similar facility is a reasonable alternative for them.

The other information that would be useful, although perhaps less important than a local comparison, would be the costs to students to support the recreation center at LC compared with the costs charged to students at peer institutions. This approach is less important primarily because local exigencies can have a significant impact on funding on various programs and activities. For example, if the debt service has been retired on a building, its annual costs very well may be less than on a building that has to cover substantial debt. If gifts have been received that provide endowment support for various activities, such as club sports, that too would affect the funding formula.

Collecting the local information is simple. Calls can be placed to the major health clubs and other facilities in town that offer recreational activities and programs to determine what their annual membership fee is, along with other fees that might be incidental to special programs or activities, such as participating in classes. These costs can be compared with the annual cost charged to students in their fees to determine how competitive the fees are. For example, if the average annual membership fee for health clubs in town is $100 and the amount dedicated to supporting the recreation center per credit hour of enrollment is $2, then the annual cost to each student is $48, assuming that the typical load is twenty-four hours per academic year. In this example, then, the cost of the recreation center is a bargain, assuming that the facilities are equivalent. Conversely, if the cost of an annual membership at a health club is $100 per academic year but the amount per credit dedicated to supporting the recreation center per credit is $5, then students taking a typical load will pay more than the membership fee at a health club. If the facilities, services, and program are equivalent, then the comparison would not reflect favorably on the recreation program.

Collecting information from comparable institutions can be done fairly quickly and easily. Telephone calls to the peer institutions can be placed, and the data can be collected quickly.

The other dimension of this assessment is the extent to which users are satisfied with the quality of services, programs and facilities. These are collected from the users themselves and can be done both quantitatively and qualitatively.

Step 4: Determine the Best Assessment Method

Multiple methods will work very well in this study, which has several dimensions to it. We have described how the data related to cost effectiveness can be collected. The annual cost to students for their support for the recreation center can be compared with the cost of membership in local health clubs through a simple canvass of the costs of the local health clubs by making telephone calls and setting up a grid that might include basic services such as size of gymnasium, availability of a swimming pool, racquet ball courts, and so on. The same approach can be taken with comparing the costs across peer institutions. A telephone inquiry will provide the basic data.

On the other dimension of this project, the extent to which users are satisfied with services, a quantitative survey can be used to collect basic data, and this can be followed up with focus groups and individual interviews. The quantitative dimension of the study can be used to help develop an interview protocol for the focus groups.

Step 5: Determine Whom to Study

We have determined that the cost effectiveness dimension of this assessment will be accomplished by studying local health clubs and peer institutions. That is straightforward and will be completed fairly easily.

All students are potential all of them, unless one were conducting this assessment at small college. LC is not a small institution, so a random sample of the student population will be drawn for the quantitative study. The exact number is a matter of debate, but if the student population were 10,000, we would recommend drawing a sample of 1,550 students. Sample size is always an issue in quantitative studies. (Rea and Parker, 1997, provide some excellent ideas on this topic.)

After the quantitative study has been completed, focus groups will be conducted to examine in depth those issues that emerge. Again, student users of the facility will be studied.

A decision has been made not to include in this study individuals who use the center who are not students. The reason is that the issue at hand has to do with the value received from the expenditure of student fees. Were the presenting problem different, faculty, student family members, or others who use the center might be studied. In this case, though, the nature of the problem has limited the study.

Step 6: Determine How the Data Will Be Collected

The first part of this assessment is to determine the cost effectiveness of the recreation center using two groups for comparison purposes. For health clubs and other local facilities, telephone calls can be placed. For the peer institutions, telephone calls can be placed, or inquiries can be made using e-mail communications. Either way, the data that are being collected are straightforward and relatively simple.

The other part of the inquiry is more complex. The survey needs to collect quantitative information that will help determine the extent to which students are satisfied with the programs, services, and facilities of the recreation center. The data can be collected using a questionnaire administered over the telephone or through a mail-out process. Our strong preference is to use the telephone process rather than the mail. While somewhat more expensive, the use of the telephone is faster and in many respects more accurate (see Rea and Parker, 1997).

The second part of the satisfaction study will involve conducting focus groups with students. The number of groups to study is an issue for which there is no easy answer (Merriam, 1998). Our general advice is to keep conducting groups until the data become redundant. At the point of redundancy, one can have confidence that the range of responses to the questions raised has been identified. For this study, five or six groups may very well be enough, but that will not be determined until the data are being collected.

Step 7: Determine What Instruments Will Be Used

The first part of this study is so simple that it hardly needs an instrument. In seeking data from the local health clubs and similar facilities, a person can call and ask the price of an annual membership. The follow-up question is, "Are there other fees people must pay for special benefits, such as aerobics classes?" If there are additional fees, then the investigator can ask what the amount is and their purpose, such as for an additional $25, members can take unlimited aerobics classes.

The satisfaction survey is more complex. In administering a questionnaire over the telephone, the caller has to be careful not to ask too many questions so as to sustain the attention of the respondent. Exhibit 20.1 contains a suggested telephone interview protocol.

EXHIBIT 20.1

Recreation Programs Satisfaction Interview Protocol

My name is [name of interviewer]. May I speak to [name of respondent]?

I work with the recreation center at LC. You are one of the randomly selected LC students to be called for this voluntary four-minute survey on student satisfaction with our recreation center. Please be assured that your responses are confidential and are reported as summarized data used in future planning efforts by the institution. No individual data will be identified. You may choose not to answer specific questions. You may also see the survey results in about three weeks. If you have any questions, contact [name of contact] in the recreation center [address] or by telephone [telephone number], or by e-mail [e-mail address].

I hope you will take this opportunity for your voice to be heard. Are you willing to participate?

First, please indicate whether you strongly agree, agree, neither agree nor disagree, disagree, or strongly disagree with the following statements:

Item	Strongly Agree	Agree	Neutral	Disagree	Strongly Disagree
1. I know about the recreation facility at LC.	5	4	3	2	1
2. I participate in intramural programs at LC.	5	4	3	2	1
3. I am a member of a club sports team at LC.	5	4	3	2	1
4. I participate in individual workout programs at the recreation center.	5	4	3	2	1
5. I am satisfied with the services available at the recreation center.	5	4	3	2	1
6. I am satisfied with the facilities of the recreation center.	5	4	3	2	1
7. I am satisfied with the staff at the recreation center.	5	4	3	2	1
8. For the cost charged to my student fees, I consider the recreation center a good value.	5	4	3	2	1

9. How often do you use the recreation center?

___ More than once per week

___ Once per week

___ Less than once per week but more than once per month
___ About once per month
___ Less than once per month
___ Never

10. What, if anything, do you find most valuable about the recreation center?

11. How might the recreation center be improved?

12. Any other comments?

The data collected using this instrument will set the agenda for the qualitative study. In the quantitative version of the inquiry, basic information about student perceptions is being collected. We also could aggregate the data based on frequency of use. We might find that frequent users were happier with the facilities than infrequent users. The qualitative part of the study can tell why.

The data from the telephone interviews can be used to help shape the focus group protocol. If it turned out, for example, that students reported not being very happy with staff members, as inferred from a mean score below 3.0 for question 7, then this issue could be examined in the focus groups. Exhibit 20.2 contains a suggested interview protocol for such focus groups.

We urge, in the strongest terms possible, that those planning an assessment conduct a pretest of the quantitative instrument and the interview protocol. The pretest may reveal that the questions will need to be revised, and if the revisions are extensive, then additional pretesting may be necessary (Rea and Parker, 1997).

EXHIBIT 20.2

Recreation Center Interview Protocol for Focus Groups

Welcome to our session. The purpose of this session is to learn more about your perceptions of the recreation center. I am very glad that you have taken time out today to visit with us. This session is being tape-recorded so that I can make sure to be as accurate as possible in writing my report. I will be preparing a report for the college's recreation center, but I want to assure you that I will not attribute anything you say directly to you. Please understand that you may leave the group at any time and that your participation is strictly voluntary. You have a form in front of you that I ask you to sign before we move ahead. It indicates that you understand the voluntary nature of your participation and that you may leave at any time. Do you have any questions at this point? OK, let's move ahead.

1. Please tell us how often you use the recreation center.

2. Why do you use the recreation center?

3. What do you see as the recreation center's strengths?

4. How might the recreation center be improved?

5. What else would you like to tell us about the recreation center that I have not asked?

Step 8: Determine Who Should Collect the Data

An assessment of this type, which is being conducted to determine the value of a program and very well may determine its future, cannot be conducted solely by insiders. People outside the recreation center staff will need to be involved in addition to recreation center staff. We suggest that the chair of the assessment committee come from a unit other than the recreation center and that some neutral parties be involved, such as faculty members or others from across the campus.

One strategy that might be investigated would be having members of the student government association involved in the assessment process. Realistically, not all of them will be interested in or be able to participate in an inquiry of this type. But even if just a few participate, that will give the results credibility in the eyes of the student government association.

Step 9: Determine How the Data Will Be Analyzed

The data collected from the health clubs and similar facilities in the area can be reported on a case-by-case basis. That is, membership at Club A costs $100 per year with additional fees of X for the following services, membership at Club B costs $90 per year with additional fees of Y for the following additional services, and so on. Similarly, the data from the peer institutions can be reported on a case-by-case basis, although some definitions might need to be included. For example, the cost per full-time student at College A is $50 and the building debt is paid in full; the cost at College B is $75 per student, which includes $10 per student to retire the building debt. A grid can be developed for recording and analyzing these data.

The data from the telephone survey will be compiled and analyzed using typical quantitative techniques. This would mean developing measures of central tendency, disaggregating data by frequency of use as well as by race, gender, and year in school, which presumably would lead to a level of analysis that would be sufficient for this study.

The qualitative analysis would include using the constant comparison method (see Glaser and Strauss, 1967), which is designed to identify themes, patterns, and trends in the data. These themes, patterns, and trends would contribute to the overall picture of the relative student satisfaction with the recreation program.

Step 10: Determine the Implications of the Study for Policy and Practice

This assessment was conducted primarily to determine the cost effectiveness of and user satisfaction with the recreation center. The first part of the study was to determine if the cost to students of the recreation center was comparable to, greater than, or less than alternatives available to students attending LC. The second part of the study was to determine the level of satisfaction that students indicated with the recreation center's programs, services, and facilities.

As a consequence of this study, it is possible that funding to the center could be reduced based on a variety of factors. Students might approve a funding level that would result in less net revenue for the recreation center. It is also possible that the data will reveal that the current level of funding is appropriate, given the potential costs to students if they were to pay for a membership in a health club. Or it might turn out that the operation of the recreation program is regarded so well and is so cost-effective that additional funding might be indicated.

Step 11: Report the Results Effectively

The campus community will be awaiting this report and perhaps other assessments of other programs and services. Without question, the student leaders will be interested in learning more about the quality of this operation, since it may be the focus of a budget cut.

Several versions of the report ought to be produced. A short executive summary would set out the results of the study in abbreviated form, along with potential recommendations for practice, which might include different funding formulas. A more complete report should be available to anyone who requests it, and the complete report should be sent to the students in addition to the executive summary.

In addition to sending the report to the students and others involved in the funding process, a meeting ought to be requested with student leaders or time should be sought on the senate's agenda to deliver the report. This will provide an open hearing during which the findings can be presented.

Conclusion

This chapter presents an example of how multiple methods and multiple assessments could be conducted to deal with a significant threat to the recreation program. The chapter has not considered what might happen if the report were unfavorable. What if the data revealed that the recreation program was not competitive in price? What if students reported great dissatisfaction with the recreation center? In these cases, changes should be implemented regardless of the political situation because students deserve the very best programs, services, and facilities possible. Our assumption is that such would not be the case, but if negative data were revealed, then the leadership of the recreation center should address these problems. In this case, the report might turn into a blueprint for action and improvement.

References

Glaser, B. G., and Strauss, A. L. *The Discovery of Grounded Theory.* New York: Aldine, 1967.

Merriam, S. B. *Qualitative Research and Case Study Applications in Education.* San Francisco: Jossey-Bass, 1998.

Miller, T. K. *The Book of Professional Standards for Higher Education.* Washington, D.C.: Council for Advancement of Standards in Higher Education, 1997.

Rea, L. M., and Parker, R. A. *Designing and Conducting Survey Research: A Comprehensive Guide.* (2nd ed.) San Francisco: Jossey-Bass, 1997.

Rossi, P. H., Freeman, H. E., and Lipsey, M. W. *Evaluation: A Systematic Approach.* (6th ed.) Thousand Oaks, Calif.: Sage, 1999.

Upcraft, M. L., and Schuh, J. H. *Assessment in Student Affairs: A Guide for Practitioners.* San Francisco: Jossey-Bass, 1996.

Chapter 21

Assessing an Office of Financial Aid

FINANCIAL AID plays an important role in the recruitment process and also is important in making sure that students persist to graduation (Willcox, 1991). Financial aid typically can be divided into three distinct areas of support: grants, loans, and work-study. Financial aid programs are provided by a variety of sources, including the institution, as well as the state and federal governments, but little investigation of financial aid and its ramifications has occurred (Huff, 1989). Given the importance of financial aid, key questions can be asked about its effectiveness: Who receives financial aid? Does aid make a difference in persistence to graduation? What kinds of aid programs (grants, loans, or work) are more effective than others? Do students repay their loans as is required by the federal government? In this chapter, problems associated with assessing an office of financial aid are reported, followed by a model for assessing financial aid programs and a case study about a financial aid program.

Problems Associated with Assessing an Office of Financial Aid

When it comes to their money, people can be passionate. Students are no different. They view financial aid, especially government programs, as an entitlement, and anything that gets in the way of their receiving their aid in the expected amount, on time, creates problems. Because of the potentially supercharged atmosphere related to money, assessing financial aid can be challenging.

The first problem, and perhaps the most complex in assessing an office of financial aid (OFA), is that students may not understand the rules and regulations that govern the financial aid process. The amount of flexibility that the staff in the office have at their disposal can be quite limited. If forms are incomplete or students do not comply with various regulations, the staff may not be able to serve students as well as they expect. Students may assume, incorrectly, that the reason they do not receive the amount of aid they expect is due to staff incompetence or worse. In actuality, the problem could be the process itself.

A second problem is that financial aid is seasonal work. There are times during the academic year when service cannot be provided to students as quickly as they would like. Simply adding staff to handle the rush may not solve the problem, since the work is highly technical. Training a person to handle financial aid problems is far more complicated than, say, adding a staff member to distribute parking decals.

A third problem is that decisions about who will receive departmental scholarships and activity awards rarely is made by the OFA, but the office may have to handle the administration of the scholarship. So if a student expects a scholarship to be renewed and it is not, it is likely that the OFA will be placed in a position of having to explain, and perhaps defend, a decision that someone else in the institution made.

A final problem is that the department is bound by federal regulations in administering federal programs. Staff have to explain these regulations, whether they appear to make sense or not, to students. These regulations can be extremely complex and can change from year to year depending on decisions that regulators make. Students may interpret such explanations as reasons the OFA gives just to give them grief. Assuredly this is not the case.

A Model for Assessing Financial Aid Programs

The road map provided in Chapter One for assessing various student affairs offices and programs serves as an approach for assessing financial aid programs.

Know Who Receives Financial Aid and How Much Aid Is Received

A good place to start in the assessment process is to know the financial needs of students, and this can be provided by an analysis of the federal forms (the Free Application for Federal Student Aid [FAFSA]) that students file when they apply for federal assistance. It is important for institutional planners to know whether students have substantial financial needs (as measured by eligibility for Pell grants, which are federal entitlements) or needs that can be met through loan programs. Some students who receive aid in effect have no need; they receive merit scholarships for their academic ability (for example, National Merit Scholars), because of their special talents (for example, musicians or athletes), or for other reasons (to meet a state labor shortage in the area of teaching mathematics, for example).

Beyond having a sense of the needs of students in the aggregate, other basic questions about financial aid programs are important. How many students receive aid? What kinds of aid do they receive? What is the ratio of grants to loans to scholarships on campus? What is the average debt load graduates must pay? How do the institution's merit aid programs compare with peer institutions?

Assess Student Needs

Students begin the financial aid process by filing the Free Application for Federal Student Aid. Student needs will be measured to a great extent by formulas provided by the federal government. The cost of attendance, however, will be determined to a great extent by institutional charges. Accordingly, private institutions typically have a higher cost of attendance than, say, public community colleges. If the institution has a policy whereby the financial needs of all students who are offered admission are met, does the institution have adequate resources to meet this policy?

Assess Student Satisfaction with the Financial Aid Office

Students who receive aid will have an ongoing relationship with the OFA, not just from the perspective of filing forms and receiving money but also from the point of view that the office can provide useful information to students related to their financial management. Students who receive loans will receive a briefing from the OFA about their obligations under federal loan policy, which they must acknowledge in writing. The quality of this interaction between students and office staff could be the focus of a satisfaction survey. Other forms of satisfaction also can be measured. Does the office encourage students to participate in work-study programs rather than accept loans? Does the office encourage students to work long hours at off-campus jobs, to the potential detriment of students' engagement on campus (U.S. Department of Education, 1998).

Satisfaction surveys can be difficult to conduct in financial aid offices. At times, students can have unrealistic expectations for what aid officers can do for them, given the relatively narrow bounds established by federal regulations that limit the flexibility they are allowed to exercise in aid administration. As a consequence, students may be unhappy with the aid office when, in reality, their dissatisfaction should be focused elsewhere.

Assess the Extent to Which Financial Aid Facilitates Persistence

Financial aid historically was a tool designed to help students gain access to their institution of choice (Coomes, 1996). Contemporary aid programs are designed to help students persist. If that is the case, how do the persistence rates of students who participate in various aid programs compare with students who do not? Are these students as likely to graduate? This issue is especially important when examining the effect of loan programs, so an assessment might be conducted to determine the relative persistence of students who do not participate in loan programs with those who do.

Use Professional Standards

The Council for the Advancement of Standards in Higher Education (CAS) has prepared a series of standards for the operation of the office of student financial aid (Miller, 1997) that can be useful in preparing a self-study. In addition, federal programs are audited regularly by the federal government to make sure that they are administered in compliance with federal regulations. Although the audits are not the same as conducting a self-study, they do provide an examination of financial aid administration using accepted standards. In this case, the federal government, in effect, established an industry standard.

Financial Aid Case Study

City Area Community College (CACC) serves the local population in many ways. It provides continuing education for residents, works with local industries in employee training, engages in strategic economic development with the local economic development organizations, and, most important, provides the first two years of education for students who are seeking a baccalaureate degree. Many students enroll at City because they cannot afford to move away from home for four years. They complete their general educational requirements at City and then transfer to one of the baccalaureate degree–granting institutions in the state.

The Office of Student Financial Aid (OSFA) at City plays an important role in making sure that appropriate resources are available for students to achieve their educational goals. In many cases, students rely on grant and loan programs to cover the cost of tuition, fees, and books, and many of them work long hours off campus to take care of living expenses. It is important for students that funds are available at the time of registration so that they can pay their tuition and fees. By law, City cannot officially count students as being enrolled until their tuition and fees have been paid. Students are permitted to attend class on an unofficial basis; state appropriations, however, are awarded to City based on a formula related to the number of credit hours students are enrolled in officially, so City has to collect its money.

Students have been complaining with increasing frequency about the bureaucracy, lack of responsiveness, and red tape at the OSFA. They report that it is becoming increasingly difficult to receive their aid on a timely basis, which means that they cannot enroll for classes, and City's enrollment is affected negatively. The OSFA staff counter that regulations for the various programs have become more complex, and if these directives are not followed, funds for aid programs could be cut back.

The vice president for student affairs, in whose division OSFA is located, wants to determine the level of service being provided to students by OSFA. A group is being appointed, and funds are available to conduct assessment.

Step 1: Define the Problem

CACC has a real dilemma. Until students collect their financial aid each semester and officially enroll in class, the institution cannot count student enrollments, which affects the amount of state aid the college receives. Students claim that they are unable to collect their aid money because of the bureaucracy of the financial aid office. The aid office, conversely, claims that increased regulations and greater accountability have required it to make sure that every regulation and procedure is followed, lest the college be penalized for sloppy handling of aid programs.

The problem is complex and requires substantial knowledge and expertise related to the administration of aid programs. Most people in the college have opinions about the operation of the financial aid office, but no one on campus has the expertise to understand completely the requirements of financial aid administration. What is known is that this situation cannot continue because CACC is being affected adversely by the late enrollments.

Step 2: Determine the Purpose of the Study

On the surface, this situation looks as though it is calling for a study of student satisfaction with the financial aid office, but the situation is more complex than that. More precisely, what is necessary is a study of student satisfaction within the context of financial aid regulations. For example, how well are students served who file applications on time and follow procedures exactly? How well are students served who file forms late, provide incomplete information, fail to complete the requisite amount of academic work each semester, or for some other reason fall outside the norm?

Another dimension of the study could include an analysis of the staffing patterns and functions of the office. The CAS standards could be helpful in this inquiry, as could external consultants.

Step 3: Determine Where to Get the Information Needed

The information required for this study will need to come from several sources. Without question, students who use the office of financial need to be included in the satisfaction study, so a list of all students who use the office needs to be compiled from institutional sources as a means of defining the population. Beyond this, a review needs to be conducted of the procedures of the office and the extent to which it is complying with all regulations without being oppressively burdensome in dealing with students. In short, what this study requires is a determination as to whether the office is complying with all regulations while serving students as quickly and accurately as possible. This information will come from office files studied in the context of financial aid regulations.

Step 4: Determine the Best Assessment Method

The problem presented in this study lends itself to a multiple method approach. To begin the study, student satisfaction with the office needs to be assessed. That can be done using both a quantitative and a qualitative approach. Let us assume that approximately five thousand students receive some form of aid each year at CACC. From this group, a telephone survey could be conducted with a random sample of students to get an overall sense of their reaction to the quality of service they have received from OSFA. Another option would be to mail surveys out to students, but for reasons stated elsewhere in this book, we recommend using a telephone survey approach when querying large data sets in quantitative studies.

The responses of the students to the quantitative survey will form the basis for the development of several focus groups to conduct an in-depth exploration of the issues that emerge. The data generated by the qualitative study will add richness to the inquiry.

Step 5: Determine Whom to Study

The determination is to study the students at CACC and conduct a review of the various processes of OSFA. Since it is not feasible to study all 5,000 students, we think drawing a random sample of 1,350 will be adequate (Rea and Parker, 1997).

Typical case sampling (Patton, 1990) will be used to identify participants for the focus groups. Enough students will be invited for focus groups of six to ten participants each (Morgan, 1998). Another possibility would be to identify students who are ready to leave CACC with large debt loads (see Huff, 1989). The focus groups will be conducted until the responses of the students become redundant, which is a key in qualitative data collection and analysis (Merriam, 1998).

Step 6: Determine How Data Will Be Collected

For the quantitative portion of the inquiry, we recommend strongly that telephone interviews be conducted rather than using mailed surveys. Telephone interviews are more expensive, but they can be conducted more quickly and are likely to yield a much higher level of participation. The baseline information will come from telephone surveys.

Qualitative information will be collected in focus groups with students drawn from a list of all of those who have received loans through OSFA. Trained interviewers assisted by another person who will take notes and handle the details of this form of assessment will conduct these interviews.

The third aspect of this inquiry is to review office procedures, the handling of files, the responsiveness of staff to student needs, and so on, which will need to be conducted using institutional records. Investigators will also apply the CAS Standards as appropriate to the OFSA and employ consultants to assist in this process.

Step 7: Determine What Instruments Will Be Used

To gather the quantitative data, a protocol needs to be developed for those conducting the inquiry. It is difficult to ask open-ended questions over the telephone, so we recommend using a structured questionnaire. Exhibit 21.1 contains a suggested interview protocol.

The follow-up to the quantitative study is to conduct a series of focus groups and build on what is learned through the telephone questionnaire. An interview protocol for the focus groups will be developed based on what has been learned. Exhibit 21.2 contains a general protocol that might be used with the focus groups.

Other specific questions could be asked based on the data generated by the telephone interviews. Before the questionnaire is administered to the telephone respondents or the protocol is used with focus groups, both need to be pilot-tested, that is, field-tested with individuals who are potential respondents. (Rea and Parker, 1997, provide more information about this process.) Although the items may seem unambiguous to the investigators, this process is essential; under no circumstances should it be skipped.

EXHIBIT 21.1

Financial Aid Office Telephone Interview Protocol

My name is [name of interviewer]. May I speak to [name of respondent]?

I work with the Office of Student Financial Aid at CACC. You are one of the randomly selected CACC students to be called for this voluntary seven-minute survey on student satisfaction with student financial aid. According to our records, you have received aid from this office. Is that correct? Please be assured that your responses are confidential and are reported as summarized data used in future planning efforts by the institution. No individual data will be identified. You may choose not to answer specific questions. You may also see the survey results in about three weeks. If you have any questions, contact [name of contact] in the Office of Student Financial Aid, [address], or by telephone [telephone number] or e-mail [e-mail address].

I hope you will take this opportunity for your voice to be heard. Are you willing to participate? First, please indicate whether you strongly agree, agree, neither agree nor disagree, disagree, or strongly disagree with the following statements:

Item	Strongly Agree	Agree	Neutral	Disagree	Strongly Disagree
1. I know where to find the OSFA on campus.	5	4	3	2	1
2. The office hours for OSFA are convenient for me.	5	4	3	2	1
3. Generally I do not have to wait long to get help at OSFA.	5	4	3	2	1
4. I find the staff at OSFA are interested in me.	5	4	3	2	1
5. I get accurate information from OSFA.	5	4	3	2	1
6. My financial aid arrives in time for me to register for classes at CACC.	5	4	3	2	1
7. I am satisfied with the service I receive from OSFA.	5	4	3	2	1
8. My friends who use OSFA are satisfied with the level of service at OSFA.	5	4	3	2	1

9. What, if anything, do you find the most helpful about the OSFA?

10. How might OSFA be improved?

11. Any other comments?

EXHIBIT 21.2

Financial Aid Office Focus Group Protocol

Welcome to our session. The purpose of this session is to learn more about your perceptions of the Office of Student Financial Aid. You have been chosen randomly from among students who use OSFA. Is that correct? I am very glad that you have taken time out today to visit with us. This session is being tape-recorded so that I can make sure to be as accurate as possible in writing my report. I will be preparing a report for the Office of Student Financial Aid, but I want to assure you that I will not attribute anything you say directly to you. Please understand that you may leave the group at any time and that your participation is strictly voluntary. You have a form in front of you that I ask you to sign before we move ahead. It indicates you understand the voluntary nature of your participation and that you may leave at any time. Do you have any questions at this point? Let us move ahead.

1. How often do you use the services of the Office of Student Financial Aid?
2. How important is it for you to receive financial aid to attend CACC?
3. How has the staff at the office treated you?
4. What do you tell your friends about the office?
5. What are the strengths of the OSFA?
6. How might OFSA be improved?
7. What have you not told me about the office that you think I should know?

Step 8: Determine Who Should Collect the Data

In the first part of the study, which is concerned with student satisfaction, the data can be collected by a combination of insiders from the OSFA and outsiders from other offices on campus or students. After a bit of training, interviewers can place the telephone calls to collect the quantitative data. They will need to heed the principles defined elsewhere in this book on collecting data through the use of the telephone, but once they have these guidelines in mind, it will not be difficult to collect the data.

Similarly, collecting the data through the focus groups can be accomplished after training has been provided. Conducting focus groups is somewhat more complex and sophisticated than one might think. We urge that two people take part in the data collection process: one to serve as the leader of the group and the other to handle administrative details, take notes, and address any concerns that might arise while the group is in session.

The second part of this inquiry, to determine the extent to which the OSFA is serving students well, is complex and requires special expertise. In this aspect of the assessment process, we would urge that at least one independent consultant be brought to campus to lead the inquiry. A team of at least three senior financial aid officers is preferable but more expensive. The inquiry will be accomplished primarily through reviewing documents in the OFSA, although students as individuals might be interviewed. Although others on campus might participate in the review, the expertise required to determine the appropriate response of the OSFA to individual cases is substantial. The outside expert will have to determine the appropriate questions to ask in reviewing files and possibly interviewing students. Nonetheless, there is no other credible way to get at this dimension of the problem. External consultants also can be used in applying the CAS Standards to the OSFA.

Step 9: Determine How the Data Will Be Analyzed

The data from the quantitative portion of the study can be analyzed using the typical measures of central tendency, including calculating means, medians, and modes. Because each respondent was chosen from the CACC's financial aid database, in order to make sure that all respondents were recipients of loans, investigators know the financial aid packages that they received. Investigators might disaggregate the respondents by calculating a mean size of loan and then comparing the responses of those who received smaller loans with those who received larger loans in order to determine if their perceptions were different. The responses of those who received grants and loans might be compared with those who received loans to determine if any differences existed.

The qualitative data will be analyzed using the typical constant comparative method (Glaser and Strauss, 1967). Data are analyzed as they are collected, and then patterns, trends, and themes are identified.

The analysis of the second part of this study is more complicated. To set the stage for the study, the consultants should receive a charge that outlines exactly what the purpose of their inquiry is. From the inquiry will come guiding questions for their work. Data need to be generated to answer the questions, and the questions can be used in the document analysis. (For more information about document analysis, see Chapter Three. Also consult Whitt, 1992, and Merriam, 1998, for further information about document analysis.)

Step 10: Determine the Implications of the Study for Policy and Practice

This inquiry identifies the importance of a crucial student service for the college. This is not a study examining a campus luxury. Rather, the functioning of this office affects the very health of the college.

If the findings from the quantitative and qualitative satisfaction study indicate that students are unhappy with how they are treated, then immediate interventions will be necessary. Among these would be additional training for staff and possibly a thorough review of the effectiveness of the leadership of the unit.

The other part of the inquiry, the review of files and possible follow-up interviews to determine the effectiveness of the unit, similarly is crucial. If the study finds excessively rigid applications of regulations, failure to exercise flexibility for individual students, breakdown of administrative procedures, or worse, the leadership of the office would be in question almost immediately, because no college can afford to have its students treated badly along those lines. The future of CACC is riding on the findings of the study, so decisive action would be necessary if the worst is uncovered.

Step 11: Report the Results Effectively

As is the case for most other assessments, a series of reports regarding student satisfaction should be generated and tailored to the needs of the office or officer receiving the report. An executive summary would be satisfactory for senior officers; a more complete report would be appropriate for the vice president who ordered the study and administrators of the financial aid office.

The second part of the study is more sensitive, and care needs to be taken in providing copies of it to many offices. We tend to view the use of consultants as a process whereby a specific person is hired to provide a specific report for a specific officer of the institution. In this case, the vice president hires the outside consultants. We would recommend that a complete report be provided for the vice president along with an executive summary. This person can decide who else should have copies of the report, which is a much sounder strategy than having the consultant try to decide who should receive a copy of the report.

Conclusion

This chapter has provided an overview of how assessment might be applied to an office of student financial aid and addressed a difficult problem illustrated by the case study. Financial aid is an aspect of most student affairs divisions that provides a crucial service; for many students, the financial support provided is the difference between their being able to attend the institution and having to enroll elsewhere, or perhaps not going to college at all.

References

Coomes, M. D. "Student Financial Aid." In A. L. Rentz and Associates, *Student Affairs Practice in Higher Education*. Springfield, Ill.: Thomas, 1996.

Glaser, B. G., and Strauss, A. L. *The Discovery of Grounded Theory*. New York: Aldine, 1967.

Huff, R. P. "Facilitating and Applying Research in Student Financial Aid to Institutional Objectives." In R. H. Fenske (ed.), *Studying the Impact of Student Aid on Institutions*. New Directions for Institutional Research, no. 62. San Francisco: Jossey-Bass, 1989.

Merriam, S. B. *Qualitative Research and Case Study Applications in Education*. San Francisco: Jossey-Bass, 1998.

Miller, T. K. (ed.). *The Book of Professional Standards for Higher Education*. Washington, D.C.: Council for the Advancement of Standards in Higher Education, 1997.

Morgan, D. L. *Planning Focus Groups*. Thousand Oaks, Calif.: Sage, 1998.

Patton, M. Q. *Qualitative Evaluation and Research Methods*. (2nd ed.) Thousand Oaks, Calif.: Sage, 1990.

Rea, L. M., and Parker, R. A. *Designing and Conducting Survey Research*. (2nd ed.). San Francisco: Jossey-Bass, 1997.

U.S. Department of Education. *Profile of Undergraduates in U.S. Postsecondary Education Institutions, 1995–96: With an Essay on Undergraduates Who Work.* Washington, D.C.: National Center for Education Statistics, 1998.

Whitt, E. J. "Document Analysis." In F. K. Stage and Associates, *Diverse Methods for Research and Assessment of College.* Alexandria, Va.: American College Personnel Association, 1992.

Willcox, L. "Evaluating the Impact of Financial Aid on Student Recruitment and Retention." In D. Hossler (ed.), *Evaluating Student Recruitment and Retention Programs.* New Directions for Institutional Research, no. 70. San Francisco: Jossey-Bass, 1991.

Chapter 22

Assessing Admissions Programs

THERE MAY BE NO other aspect of a division of student affairs more important to an institution than the office of admissions. Although admissions as a department may be part of various organizational structures on campus, a common locus for this function is the division of student affairs or another unit that has a close relationship with the student affairs division (Hossler, 1996). The success or failure of the admissions office affects virtually every aspect of the institution for obvious reasons. Successful admissions offices attract a sufficient number of the right kinds of students to provide a steady stream of undergraduates who are successful in achieving their educational goals. Lack of success on the part of this office can result in too few students or too few of the kinds of students the institution is interested in enrolling. If too few students enroll in the institution, a budget shortfall may be the result, since tuition represents 18.4 percent of income for public institutions and 42.4 percent of income for private institutions (U.S. Department of Education, 1997). Most institutions count on a certain amount of tuition income each year to balance their budgets; when a shortfall results, difficult choices have to be made to keep the budget in balance.

The qualitative aspect of admissions is just as important. If students who are unable to be successful enroll at a given institution, classroom discussions may be uneven, costly remedial assistance may need to be provided, and in the worst case, students will drop out, resulting in an undesirable graduation rate. The classroom atmosphere can be affected adversely if some of the students can follow the planned learning activities, while others lack the background or skills to follow. Morale plummets, and faculty will point to the admissions office for not doing its job consistent with institutional expectations. This chapter discusses problems associated with assessing admissions, presents a model for assessing admissions, and presents a case study.

Problems Associated with Assessing Admissions

Several problems are associated with assessing an office of admissions. Not the least of them is that an important group to assess is the students who express interest in the institution but ultimately do not enroll. Their reasons for deciding not to attend the institution can be extremely valuable in developing strategies to improve the yield rate. Since these students choose not to enroll, several problems arise. First among these is that they are difficult to locate. Presumably they have chosen to attend another institution, so finding them will require a bit of detective work. Even the most diligent sleuth may not be able to find these individuals without the help of their parents, who may not want to disclose where they enrolled.

Even if these students can be located, there is no guarantee that they will cooperate. They have cast their lot with another college, and they may not want to give up any of their time in helping a college they rejected. The level and interest of these individuals in participating in a study will be limited at best.

Another issue related to assessing admissions is that on some campuses, different offices handle different types of admissions. One office may handle the process for students who are applying directly from high school, another handles transfer admissions, and still another receives international applications. Yet another might be responsible for graduate admissions, although typically that is handled by academic departments and has a variety of other concerns associated with it (Woolston, 1995). In any event, to conduct a comprehensive assessment of admissions would require a review of several departments. That adds complexity to the process.

Finally, assessing admissions, even if one is looking at the admission and enrollment of first-time college students, can involve several departments. Decisions that students make to attend a specific college can encompass a variety of factors, many of which are not controlled by the admissions office. Included in this can be availability and attractiveness of student housing, interaction with faculty and academic advisers, availability of financial aid, and location of the campus. This constellation of factors adds to the complexity of assessing admissions and should be taken into account when conducting an assessment.

A Model for Assessing Admissions

Chapter One presented a comprehensive model for assessment in student affairs. Many of the elements of this model apply to an office of admissions.

Know the Background and Characteristics of Applicants

Perhaps as much as any other student service or program, admissions is a numbers-driven operation. How many inquiries are received? How many of the inquiries result in applications for admission? How many students who apply for admission are admitted? How many students who are admitted enroll?

These questions apply not only to entering first-year students but also to transfer students. Moreover, disaggregating the data is useful in analyzing the success of admissions programs. Are students of color underrepresented in the applicant pool? Are women more or less likely to enroll at the institution? Are students who plan to pursue certain majors more or less likely to enroll? Is distance a factor in converting admissions to enrollments? The number of questions related to tracking potential is almost infinite. As a consequence, admissions needs to have a sophisticated database that can be manipulated to answer virtually any question, and in a hurry.

Assess Student and Other Clientele Needs

What kinds of information do students need to make an informed decision about applying for admission? What kinds of information are useful to present at a college fair? What format for a campus visit meets the needs of potential applicants best? Are articulation agreements in place so that transfer from community colleges is accomplished with a minimum of duress?

Is the right information provided to parents? Are they able to have their questions answered accurately and completely? Sometimes other clients include guidance counselors and school administrators. Are their opinions solicited regularly? Do the so-called feeder high schools have an opportunity to provide feedback to the admissions office?

Assess Student and Other Clientele Satisfaction

The same questions explored by needs assessment can be examined by satisfaction assessment. After needs are articulated, are they met satisfactorily? Whether students enroll or not, do they feel positively about their interaction with the office? Having satisfied students is very important because they will have siblings and friends who may choose to consider the institution or the specific recruited student may choose to transfer in the future.

Assess Outcomes

The outcome of the recruitment process is how many students enroll in the institution, a quantitative perspective. A qualitative perspective is equally important: are the students who enroll sufficiently able academically to be successful at the institution and graduate? Some institutions, because of their philosophy, history, or other reasons, have to enroll a certain number of students to be successful, and they may pay less attention to the students' academic accomplishments. Others have to enroll a certain number of students who are especially able. For them to have just the appropriate number of students is insufficient.

Assess Comparable Institutions

How does the admissions operation compare with peers? Does it attract a similar number of inquiries? Is the conversion rate from inquiries to applications to admission to enrollment about the same, better, or worse? To a certain extent, such data for some schools are the academic equivalent of trade secrets, but assuming one could collect the data, they would provide a useful form of comparison.

Use Nationally Accepted Standards for Assessment

As is the case for other student services, standards have been published by the Council for the Advancement of Standards in Higher Education (Miller, 1997) so that one can compare a specific admissions office with a set of standards. Other resources are available from the American Association of Collegiate Registrars and Admissions Offices (http://aacrao.com) and the College Board (http://www.collegeboard.org). Nationally accepted standards are particularly useful for an internal study but should not be the only assessments conducted.

Determine Cost Effectiveness

Often we refer to this form of assessment in the context of comparing the services of a given program with those in the private sector, such as comparing a visit to the student health center with a visit to the local immediate care clinic. In the case of admissions, however, the measure of determining cost effectiveness may have more to do with the cost of recruiting each student to come to the institution. This cost can be calculated and a determination can be made as to whether the recruitment process is cost-effective. In the final analysis, however, if the institution is able to attract the kinds of students it wants in sufficient numbers, it is unlikely that many complaints will be voiced about the cost.

The following case study illustrates how to conduct an assessment for an office of admissions. The problem is one that demands an immediate response; the institution's health may be in jeopardy if action is not taken.

An Enrollment Case Study

Easternmost College is a private institution with a long history of providing an excellent liberal arts education. Easternmost, however, has found it increasingly difficult to attract students to the campus. Optimally, enrollment should be approximately twelve hundred, but the current enrollment is eleven hundred. As a tuition-driven institution, the college has had to increase tuition at a rate far greater than the inflation rate, but no one is quite sure if that has affected the college's enrollment. The past three years have been especially difficult. The college has received a large number of strong applications for admission and has admitted a highly promising entering class, only to be disappointed by the small number of students who accept the offer of admission and enroll. No one is quite sure why this attrition occurs, but the president has decided that it is time to find out. The president has appointed a blue ribbon team to do this work, and ample resources to conduct the study have been provided. The goal is to determine why sufficient numbers of students are applying for admission at Easternmost College but ultimately enrolling elsewhere.

Step 1: Define the Problem

The problem at Easternmost College is that enrollment has been lower than projected, and the consequence has been that student tuition has generated less income than has been budgeted. To add to the problem's complexity, although strong students apply for admission, they do not accept offers of admission. This last-minute decision on the part of some admitted candidates not to enroll at Easternmost has resulted in fewer students, who are needed to balance the budget. A study needs to be conducted to determine why prospects who have been admitted at Easternmost enroll somewhere else.

Step 2: Determine the Purpose of the Study

The purpose of the study, at least initially, is to determine why students who have been admitted to Easternmost College choose not to enroll there. Upon determining this reason, it is possible that the inquiry might lead in other directions. For example, it might be that the financial aid package offered by Easternmost is not competitive with peer institutions, in which case an analysis of this aspect of the recruitment process might be necessary. It may also be that students who are offered admission choose not to enroll after visiting the campus. If this is the case, then an assessment of the campus visit program would be warranted.

Step 3: Determine Where to Get the Information Needed

Existing campus databases will provide some of the information needed. For example, the databases contain such information as the high school academic records, Scholastic Aptitude Test scores, financial aid information, and other information about students who apply for admission to Easternmost. This information can be used to develop profiles of students who enroll and those who choose not to enroll. This analysis will help in understanding the characteristics of the students who enroll and those who do not but will not explain why students choose to enroll at Easternmost or elsewhere. If consultation is desired from external organizations, two resources worth investigating are Noel-Levitz (http://www.noellevitz.com) and the Educational Testing Service (http://www.ets.org).

Probably the best source of information for this study is the students who chose not to enroll at Easternmost. There may be other sources of information with useful views on this subject, including the parents of students who chose to enroll elsewhere, members of the admissions staff, and perhaps others who will emerge as the inquiry is undertaken. But securing information from individuals who enroll elsewhere can be very difficult to accomplish, since it can be difficult to discern where these students are enrolled and what their identifying information is (for example, telephone number, street address, e-mail address). Nonetheless, this work is absolutely crucial, so the data must be secured.

Let us assume that approximately two hundred prospective students had excellent potential to enroll at Easternmost in the current academic year but did not. The college still has the home addresses and telephone numbers of these students. The best way to determine their college address and telephone number is to call their parents and ask for the information. Since the number of students is manageable, this information ought to be sought for every student.

Step 4: Determine the Best Assessment Method

Normally we believe that multiple methods provide the best approach to conducting an assessment project. In this case, however, if the students who form the population are scattered all over the region, the chance of getting them together in one place for interviews is remote at best. Therefore, the traditional qualitative approach probably will not work.

Nevertheless, the data that will help the committee best understand why students enrolled elsewhere will be words rather than having individuals complete questionnaires with Likert-type scales. The approach that is likely to work best is to conduct fairly structured interviews over the telephone. This will not be easy, but the alternative approaches, such as mailing out questionnaires to the respondents, are not likely to yield the data needed.

Step 5: Determine Whom to Study

The obvious group of people to study consists of individuals who were admitted to Easternmost College but enrolled at another institution. The data set consists of two hundred people, and the objective is to find usable information about as many of them as possible. Every person in the population is included in the study.

Another group of students to work with would be those who enrolled in Easternmost the previous fall. There will be ten focus groups of approximately twelve Easternmost first-year students, selected randomly; if necessary, more groups will be conducted until the point of redundancy. (For more information about conducting focus groups, see Chapter Four.) The information from these students is not as important as the data from those who did not enroll, but they provide a useful group for comparison purposes. It is possible that they were dealt with differently (and better in their eyes) than those who chose to enroll elsewhere.

Step 6: Determine How the Data Will Be Collected

Because the prospects chose to enroll elsewhere, some method of collecting data has to be used other than conducting focus groups. The decision is to contact these students over the telephone and conduct structured interviews with them. An alternative might be to contact them by e-mail and ask that they reply by e-mail. There are problems with this approach, however, not the least of which is that it is difficult to personalize an interview in the event certain information was revealed that demanded a specific follow-up question. In this case, the interaction between interviewer and subject makes more sense than using electronic data collection techniques.

Step 7: Determine What Instruments Will Be Used

No instrument exists that will meet the needs here, so Exhibit 22.1 contains a suggested telephone interview protocol. A somewhat less structured protocol (see Exhibit 22.2) could be developed for the Easternmost students who participate in focus groups.

EXHIBIT 22.1

Interview Protocol for Students Enrolling Elsewhere

My name is [name of interviewer]. May I speak to [name of respondent]?

I work with the Office of Admissions at Easternmost College. According to our records, you accepted admission to Easternmost but did not enroll here. Is that correct? We are conducting a voluntary seven-minute survey to determine why you did not enroll at Easternmost. Please be assured that your responses are confidential and will be reported as summarized data used in future planning efforts by the institution. No individual data will be identified. You may choose not to answer specific questions. You may also see the survey results in about three weeks. If you have any questions, contact [name of contact] in the Office of Admissions, [address], or by telephone [telephone number] or e-mail [e-mail address].

I hope you will take this opportunity for your voice to be heard. Are you willing to participate? My first question is at what institution, if any, did you eventually enroll? _____

1. How did you initially become interested in enrolling at Easternmost College?

2. What led to your decision to apply for admission to Easternmost?

3. You were admitted by Easternmost but chose to enroll elsewhere. What led to that decision?

4. When you think back about your interaction with Easternmost, how would you say you were treated?

5. What did you like most about Easternmost?

6. Were there things about Easternmost that you did not like?

7. Is there anything I should have asked you about Easternmost but have not?

Step 8: Determine Who Should Collect the Data

The members of the committee charged with sorting out this important institutional problem are likely to be involved in collecting data from the individuals who did not enroll at Easternmost. This will take a large number of telephone calls, perhaps as many as two hundred, which will take some time. To supplement the individuals from the committee, it is likely that a group of students could be recruited to help.

Many campuses have telephone banks used for annual fundraising campaigns. These banks provide an effective means of developing a team approach to making this large number of telephone calls. Assuming that each call might take as much as ten minutes, it is likely that collecting the data will take several nights of work.

No matter who is involved in collecting the data, these individuals will need to undergo training in how to conduct a good telephone interview and some simple rules for telephone interviewing. (Chapter Seven provides information about preparing people to conduct telephone interviews.)

EXHIBIT 22.2

Focus Group Interview Protocol for Currently Enrolled Students

Welcome to our session. The purpose of this session is to learn more about why you chose to enroll at Easternmost. You have been chosen randomly from among Easternmost students to participate in this focus group. I am very glad that you have taken time out today to visit with us. This session is being tape-recorded so that I can make sure to be as accurate as possible in writing my report. I will be preparing a report for the college's Admissions Office, but I want to assure you that I will not attribute anything you say directly to you. Please understand that you may leave the group at any time and that your participation is strictly voluntary. You have a form in front of you that I ask you to sign before we move ahead. It indicates that you understand the voluntary nature of your participation and that you may leave at any time. Do you have any questions at this point? OK, let's move ahead.

1. Please describe the process you went through in choosing a college.

2. What led to your decision to enroll in Easternmost?

3. Had you not enrolled in Easternmost, where would you have gone, and why?

4. As you think back about your interactions with the staff you dealt with from Easternmost, what things about them did you like the best? The least?

5. How might the Easternmost admissions process be improved?

6. What else do you think I should know about the recruitment process that I have not asked you?

Thank you for your participation.

Step 9: Determine How the Data Will Be Analyzed

The data will be analyzed using an approach whereby those involved in this process (the members of the committee) will be looking for themes, patterns, and trends from the respondents. From the telephone interviews, such patterns as the factors that led the students to apply for admission at Easternmost but enroll in other institutions and that which they found most attractive in the process by which they were recruited will be crucial. In addition, their reports of interaction with Easternmost faculty and staff will be important. (More information about data analysis is discussed by Manning, 1999.)

From the Easternmost students, the factors leading to their enrollment at Easternmost will be identified, and the reasons they chose not to enroll elsewhere also will be considered. A comparison of the factors important to the Easternmost students and those who enrolled elsewhere will be useful in the analysis.

Step 10: Determine the Implications of the Study for Policy and Practice

This assessment was conducted for serious reasons. The fiscal health of college is in disrepair, and some answers need to be identified in a hurry to determine how the college can get back on track. Based on what is learned from the information gathered from the students who enrolled elsewhere and perhaps some useful data generated by students who did enroll at Easternmost, the strategies employed in the recruitment process will be modified, perhaps drastically.

Other approaches might also have to be modified. Maybe the root cause of the problem is how financial aid is packaged. Perhaps orientation programs need modification. Maybe students were unable to identify the courses they wanted to enroll in and decided to go elsewhere. Perhaps the residence hall assignment process is antiquated. Whatever the reason or reasons may be, Easternmost's future is on the line, and change is necessary.

Step 11: Report the Results Effectively

The college will be anticipating the results of this assessment anxiously. The structure of the report may be less crucial than would be the case of other assessments that have been conducted for less dramatic reasons. Nevertheless, those preparing the report should not deviate from the approach we recommend: focus on the results and recommendations for practice. Clearly the methodologies are important, but they can be discussed in an appendix to the report.

This is the kind of report that is likely to have a wide audience. We recommend that an abridged version of the report be distributed widely, again with a focus on the results and recommendations for practice. Reference can be made as to where to get a copy of the full report, although probably only a few people will request the lengthy version.

Conclusion

This chapter reports an example of a critical problem that is addressed through an assessment. Easternmost College has serious problems that need immediate attention. Our view is that the assessment approach described will provide useful information that can be used to analyze and correct the situation.

References

Hossler, D. "From Admissions to Enrollment Management." In A. L. Rentz and Associates, *Student Affairs Practice in Higher Education*. (2nd ed.) Springfield, Ill.: Thomas, 1996.

Manning, K. "Conducting Constructivist Inquiry." In K. Manning (ed.), *Giving Voice to Critical Campus Issues*. Washington, D.C.: American College Personnel Association, 1999.

Miller, T. K. (ed.). *The Book of Professional Standards for Higher Education*. Washington, D.C.: Council for the Advancement of Standards in Higher Education, 1997.

Rea, L. M., and Parker, R. A. *Designing and Conducting Survey Research*. (2nd ed.) San Francisco: Jossey-Bass, 1997.

U.S. Department of Education. *Digest of Education Statistics, 1997*. Washington, D.C.: National Center for Education Statistics, 1997.

Woolston, V. "International Students: Leveraging Learning." In A. S. Pruitt-Logan and P. D. Isaac (eds.), *Student Services for the Changing Graduate Student Population*. New Directions for Student Services, no. 72. San Francisco: Jossey-Bass, 1995.

Chapter 23

Assessing Residence Life Programs

BECAUSE OF THE MANY different goals and programs typical of residence life programs, assessment can become quite complex. For example, some would see residence halls primarily as an orderly, safe, quiet place where students live, eat, study, and sleep. Others would assert the primacy of the educational function of residence halls: a laboratory where in-class learning can be extended and practiced and out-of-class learning such as interpersonal relations and leadership development can be developed. Still others would emphasize the community aspect of residence halls: where residents learn to build, maintain, and enhance a caring, supportive, and equitable climate among residents.

There are many reasons for assessing residence halls. First, institutions with residence halls devote a lot of time, effort, and resources to residence life programs, often because they believe not only in providing a safe and orderly living environment, but also because there is ample and persuasive evidence of the educational impact of residence hall living, both academically and socially (Pascarella and Terenzini, 1991). This evidence, however, may not have much credibility at any particular institution unless it is also locally confirmed.

Second, since almost all residence life programs are supported through students' room-and-board fees, maintaining acceptable occupancy levels becomes an important cost factor. Student satisfaction with the living environment may well determine if they return to the halls or decide to live elsewhere. And if residents' living needs are not being met, they will move on to other living accommodations. When occupancy declines, room and board rates increase.

Third, at many institutions, most, if not all, first-year students live in residence halls. In fact, some institutions require traditional-aged first-year students to live in residence halls for at least two semesters. Thus, residence life programs become a critical factor in helping students make a successful transition to college. A successful transition is not only a decided benefit to students, but also to the generation of tuition revenue for the institution.

So regardless of the primary purpose of residence life programs at a particular institution, there are excellent reasons for developing and maintaining a comprehensive assessment effort. This chapter suggests several ways of assessing residence life programs within the assessment model presented in Chapter Two and then presents a case study on residential impact.

A Model for Assessing Residence Life Programs
Track Use of Facilities and Programs

Keeping track of who is living in residence halls and where they are living is not a problem, because room assignment systems typically have ample information not only about building, floor, and room assignments, but also other information, such as gender, disability, age, class standing, enrollment status, and major. The problem is that this information is seldom aggregated in ways that are helpful to residence life staff in making decisions, considering policy, or solving problems. There are some practical reasons that this information should be more readily available.

First, this information can be useful in developing programs that meet students' needs. For example, the staffing, programming, and even physical facilities needed to meet the needs of an all-first-year student floor or building will be quite different from what is needed on a floor or building with, say, upperclass science majors. Unfortunately, often this information is not available at all, or is collected by individual building or floor staff well after residents have moved in. It would be particularly useful, for example, for residence hall staff to have a profile of floors and buildings well in advance of initial occupancy for planning and programming purposes. Such a profile might include the information shown in Table 23.1.

The students in Winslow House present a somewhat different mix from residents in general: far more older, upperclass, science students; more diversity by race or ethnicity; and virtually no difference by gender. This information, if available in a timely fashion (before or early in the semester), can be enormously useful to the resident assistant and professional staff.

Second, knowing whom residents are and where they live can be useful in assessing the advantages and disadvantages of various floor or building programs. For example, should first-year students be housed together

TABLE 23.1

Resident Profile of Winslow House

Item	All Residents	Winslow
Class standing		
First-year students	43.2%	14.6%
Sophomores	33.5	19.1
Juniors	13.3	41.3
Seniors	10.0	25.0
Age		
18	40.0	12.5
19	31.6	15.5
20	11.1	38.7
21	7.3	21.3
22+	10.0	12.0
Gender		
Male	55.0	50.0
Female	45.0	50.0
Major		
Science	33.1	63.1
Nonscience	44.2	29.5
Undecided	22.7	7.4
Disability		
Abled	97.2	95.4
Disabled	2.8	4.6
Race or ethnicity		
African American	4.5	1.6
Asian American	6.4	10.6
White	71.4	68.1
Hispanic	4.5	2.1
Native American	0.5	0.0
Multiracial	2.7	4.7
No response	10.0	12.9

or dispersed throughout all buildings and floors? Do floors or buildings with certain resident profiles have different damage and vandalism problems? Are coeducation floors or buildings better living environments than single-sex options? Are living-learning environments conducive to academic success? Such assessments are not possible unless the institution knows, in the aggregate, where students live and whom they are.

Assess Residents' Needs

Assessing residents' needs is important for two reasons. First, although many institutions require students to live in residence halls, seldom does this requirement extend beyond the first year. If there is a mismatch between what is being offered and what is needed, residents will opt to move elsewhere rather than stay in residence halls. Because lower occupancy rates mean higher room and board rates, every effort must be made to ensure that residents' needs are being met.

Second, systematic assessment of student needs can help determine what programs and services are offered. For example, as pointed out in Chapter Seventeen, nothing is quite so frustrating for residence hall staff than to plan a program that no one attends, in part because there was a weak connection between the program and student needs.

There are three primary ways of assessing residents' needs. The first is to infer such needs from the floor and building profile, based on what is known from the literature and research on college students. For example, floors and buildings with high percentages of first-year students will likely have residents who need help in making a successful transition to college. The literature would suggest focusing on helping first-year students make interpersonal connections with other students and develop skills necessary to achieve academically. Floors and buildings with a high percentage of seniors will likely have residents who are making transitions to the world of work or graduate school. The literature would suggest focusing on helping these residents with job placement and graduate school decisions. Because the end of the sophomore year is typically the time when students must select a major, floors and buildings with high percentages of sophomores may want to be focused on career decision making.

The second way is to use a commercially available, general-purpose needs assessment instruments to compare resident and nonresident responses; floor, house, and building responses; and demographic characteristics such as gender, race and ethnicity, class standing, and age. This method also allows institutions to compare their residents' responses to other comparable institutions. Providing this information in a timely fashion is critical.

The third way of assessing residents' needs is to gather data on needs from residents through focus groups and individual interviews. This is probably best done on a floor-by-floor, building-by-building basis by residence hall staff, and as soon into the first semester as possible, preferably within the first two weeks. Exhibit 23.1 contains a suggested focus group interview protocol for assessing residents' needs. (For a more complete discussion of assessing student needs, see Chapter Nine.)

The protocol can be administered by each resident adviser (RA) on his or her floor, thus allowing the RA to hear firsthand what residents want and need. A difficulty is that residents may be reluctant to be entirely candid with a person who has some degree of authority over them. An alternative is to have an RA gather data from another floor and then share the data with that floor's RA. A third alternative is to have professional staff gather needs data. Whatever method is decided, it is critical that the information be collected and analyzed early in the semester. It is also a good idea to repeat the needs assessment process every semester.

EXHIBIT 23.1

Residence Hall Focus Group Interview Protocol

Welcome to our session. The purpose of this session is to learn more about the needs of residence hall students at this college. You have been chosen randomly from among residents on this floor to participate in this focus group. I am very glad that you have taken time out today to participate. This session is being tape-recorded so that I can make sure to be as accurate as possible in summarizing your comments. I will be reporting the findings of our conversation to the Office of Residence Life, but I want to assure you that we will not attribute anything you say directly to you. Please understand that you may leave the group at any time and that your participation is strictly voluntary. You have a form in front of you that I ask you to sign before we move ahead. It indicates that you understand the voluntary nature of your participation and that you may leave at any time. Do you have any questions at this point? OK, let's move ahead.

1. As you think about this year, what issues or problems do you personally expect to deal with?

2. As you think about this year, what kind of floor and building activities would be helpful to you? To this floor and building?

3. What kind of living environment do you hope will develop on this floor and in the building?

4. What do you expect of your resident assistant?

5. Any other comments?

Thank you for participating.

Although these examples are primarily from the programming aspects of residential life, student needs regarding physical facilities, food services, and parking should also be assessed.

Assess Residents' Satisfaction

Resident satisfaction with their living environment is especially important for residence life operations, for the same reasons that student needs assessment is critical. Resident satisfaction will determine whether residents choose to stay or move elsewhere, thus creating less competitive room and board rates. Resident satisfaction can also be an indicator of the quality of services and programs, and thus assessing satisfaction can be a key factor in improving quality.

There are three primary ways of assessing residents' satisfaction with their living environments. The first is to use a commercially available instrument that measures overall student satisfaction, analyzed by residents and nonresidents. The second is to use a commercially available instrument designed to measure students' satisfaction with their residential environment. The third way is to gather data on student satisfaction from individual interviews and focus groups, on a floor-by-floor, building-by-building basis. Using a variation of the introduction to the focus group for assessing residents' needs, Exhibit 23.2 contains an interview protocol.

In assessing student satisfaction, it may be more important to have the information gathered by residence hall staff, but not in floors or buildings where they have a vested interest. Residents' responses will inevitably gravitate to individual staff, especially their own RAs. It is only natural that residents will be reluctant to criticize their RA if that is the person who is collecting the data.

Timing is also important. There must be enough time elapsed for residents to form opinions about their living environment, but the information should come soon enough to make necessary changes. We suggest that the

---

EXHIBIT 23.2

Interview Protocol for Assessing Resident Satisfaction

1. What do you like about living on this floor or in this building?
2. How might this living environment be improved?
3. Any other comments?

first round of satisfaction assessments should occur during the first semester just after midsemester exams and then again at the beginning of the second semester.

Residents' satisfaction with physical facilities, food services, and other residence related issues should also be assessed.

Assess Residential Environments

Residence halls are more than just a collection of individual students pursuing their various educational goals. Floor and building climates develop that can influence residents' educational and personal success (see Chapter Twelve). There are three major ways of assessing residential climate. The first is to use commercially available instruments that measure student perceptions of overall campus climates or the perceptions of specific aspects of the collegiate environment, such as the climate for women, the intellectual climate, or the climate for diversity, analyzed by place of residence.

The second way is to use instruments specifically designed to measure residence hall and floor climate. Climate and environment studies can be highly useful in developing an overall picture of student life.

The third way is to gather data directly from residents through focus groups and individual interviews. Again, using an adaptation of the introduction to the resident needs focus group, Exhibit 23.3 contains an interview protocol that is simple yet gets at basic residence hall climate issues.

These data are probably best collected by staff with no vested interest in the particular floor or building being assessed.

Assess Outcomes

There are two basic ways of determining if residence halls are having an impact on student learning or other student outcomes. The first is to do a comprehensive, longitudinal study of the many factors that contribute to

---

EXHIBIT 23.3

Interview Protocol for Assessing Residential Climate

1. How would you describe the overall climate on this floor and in this building? [Prompts might include the study climate, the interpersonal climate, and the climate for any particular subgroup, such as women; first-year students; gay, lesbian, and bisexual students; or racial and ethnic minorities.]

2. How might the climate on this floor be improved?

student learning, taking into account relevant precollege and during-college variables, making sure that residence is included as a during-college variable. This will yield some general findings on the influence of residence halls on selected student outcomes. (See Chapter Eighteen for a model of student outcomes assessment.)

The second way, suggested in Chapter Eleven, is to ask residents directly what they have learned and how, if at all, the residential experience contributed to that learning. Using an adaptation of the introduction to the focus group that measured residents' needs, Exhibit 23.4 contains an outcomes assessment interview protocol.

Compare Performance Across Organizations

Upcraft and Schuh (1996) hold that the key to comparing performance across organizations (sometimes referred to as benchmarking) is to make sure the organizations chosen are truly comparable. Give the great diversity among residence life programs, if a particular policy, practice, program, service, or facility is being benchmarked, it is important to choose truly comparable programs.

Probably the most frequently benchmarked item is the room and board rate. No institution can afford to get too far out of line with comparable programs in comparable institutions. Other issues to benchmark are staffing patterns, cost effectiveness, facilities, and discipline policies and practices.

Use Professional Standards to Assess

The Council for the Advancement of Standards has issued standards (Miller, 1996) that may be helpful in determining if residence halls are meeting minimal standards in terms of mission, goals, policies, funding, programs, services, and other dimensions.

EXHIBIT 23.4

Outcomes Interview Protocol for Residence Hall Students

As you think about your college career so far,

1. What have you learned? [If prompts are needed, see the outcomes model suggested in Chapter Eleven.]

2. How, if at all, has your residential experience contributed to this learning?

3. How might residence halls have done a better job of contributing to your learning?

Assess Cost Effectiveness

Because room and board constitutes a major portion of students' total college costs (in some instances exceeding tuition and books), providing cost-effective residence halls with competitive room and board rates is essential. Rates must be within the price range of prospective and current residents, as well as competitive with other housing options both within and outside the institution. (See Chapter Thirteen for ways in which cost effectiveness may be assessed.)

A Residence Life Case Study

You are newly appointed as the director of the residence life department at Doitall, a large, major, Research I state university. The department is large and complex, with hundreds of staff responsible for thousands of students. During your on-campus interview, you heard some concerns expressed about the quality of life in the residence halls and the level of supervision provided. Some people thought that the residence halls were out of control: the study atmosphere was terrible, abusive drinking was out of hand, staff were unavailable or incompetent, and the facilities were being torn apart by unruly students. Students, however, seemed satisfied; there were few complaints, and occupancy was stable from year to year. Residence hall staff took strong exception to the assertions of their critics, who included some very powerful faculty and administrators.

About a month after you were on the job, you were summoned to the office of the vice president for student affairs for a meeting with two senior professors, one of them a distinguished professor of engineering and the other the chair of the business management department. Both were reputed to have great influence with the president. These faculty charged that they believed the residence halls were out of control: students could not study in their rooms when they wished to, and often they were too tired to participate in class since they were kept up all night by the noise. Moreover, they attributed poor performance on exams to students' inability to study in chaotic residence conditions.

The professors said they had repeatedly voiced their concerns to the previous residence life director, but they felt all he did was try to distract them with a lot of administrative mumbo-jumbo. In their strongly voiced opinion, the time for delay and phony explanations was over; it was time for action. They made it clear that this mess needed to get cleaned up soon or they would ask the president to hire someone who would. They declared the meeting over and left. The vice president reminded you that not only did these faculty have considerable influence with their faculty colleagues, but the president as well. The vice president then turned to you and said, "Now what?"

Step 1: Define the Problem

Clearly there are many problems inherent in this case study, not the least of which is a political problem: these complaining faculty are well connected with their colleagues and the president. However, their assertions about the quality of life in residence halls are completely anecdotal. But so are the reactions of students and staff. So the problem is that there is no systematic evidence of what is really going on in residence halls. Are they chaotic places where little studying is done and little sleeping is possible? Is alcohol abuse causing significant problems? A well-designed, systematic study of the overall quality of life in the residence halls could provide accurate information on which to base action. If the faculty members are right, then certain actions become viable. If the staff is right, then the vice president has data to refute the faculty members' allegations.

Step 2: Determine the Purpose of the Study

The purpose of this study is to gather information from students about the quality of life in residence halls. Information is needed on the following issues:

- Study atmosphere
- Alcohol use and abuse
- Enforcement of rules
- Educational programming
- Intellectual atmosphere
- Physical facilities
- RA performance

Step 3: Determine Where to Get the Information Needed

The quality-of-life information will be gathered directly from students living in residence halls.

Step 4: Determine the Best Assessment Method

Under ordinary circumstances, a mixed methodology study would be appropriate using both a quality-of-life instrument and an interview protocol for focus groups. However, certain other factors intervened. First, both of the complaining professors, as well as the president, had great respect for quantitative data and viewed qualitative data as "subjective." (See Chapter Two for a discussion of the political dimensions of assessment.) Second, since there was an urgency to produce this study, it was decided that a quantitative study could be done more quickly than a qualitative study. And finally, there was an excellent commercially available instrument that touched on most of the issues at question.

Step 5: Determine Whom to Study

Since residents are a somewhat captive audience with a vested interest in the outcomes of the study, it was decided to include all eight thousand residence hall students in the study rather than any form of sampling. It was believed that the study would be more credible if the entire residence hall population was studied. Further, distribution and retrieval of data were more easily accomplished because resident assistants distributed and retrieved the survey from residents. If managing such a large data set became a problem, then a random sample of one thousand residents would be also acceptable.

Step 6: Determine How the Data Will Be Collected

At first, the idea of putting the instrument in the mailboxes of each resident was considered, but previous experience with this form of data collection had yielded disappointing response rates. Both Web-based and telephone surveys were also considered, but given the length of the instrument (it took about twenty minutes to complete), these options were discarded. Instead, RAs held floor meetings to explain the purposes of the study and distributed the instrument to each resident, asking that it be returned directly to the RA within forty-eight hours. RAs followed up with residents who did not return the instrument.

Step 7: Determine What Instrument Will Be Used

The Association of College and University Housing Officers–International and Educational Benchmarking, Inc., *Resident Satisfaction Survey* was selected for many reasons. First, it is commercially available, psychometrically sound, and developed under the sponsorship of a credible professional organization. Second, it has been used by several institutions, so comparison of local with national results from comparable institutions is possible. Third, the purposes of the instrument fit fairly well with the issues under consideration. And finally, it is possible to add local items to the instrument.

The instrument contains the following sections:

- Demographic information
- Grade point average
- Hours studied per week
- Hours worked per week
- Residence hall staff
- Residence hall life
- Residence hall environment
- Residence hall services
- Safety and security
- Dining services
- Alcohol use and impact
- Overall satisfaction

Step 8: Determine Who Should Collect the Data

RAs distributed and collected the instruments directly from residents.

Step 9: Determine How the Data Will Be Analyzed

The first level of analysis was to determine if the usable sample was representative of the residence hall student population. Also, in addition to a description of the overall results, the data were analyzed in two other ways. First, comparisons among responses from various subgroups were made, including gender, class standing, race and ethnicity, age, and disability. Second, comparisons among various residence hall buildings and floors were also made, including floors with special programs such as honors floors, special academic interest floors, and learning communities.

In this case study, several findings were relevant. First, there was little evidence to support the faculty members' allegations that residence halls were chaotic places where students were unable to study and sleep. In fact, just the opposite was the case. Second, it turned out that residence hall students at Doitall University were more satisfied and reported fewer problems than students at most other comparable institutions. Third, it was clear that students who lived on floors with academically related themes, such as academic interest floors and learning communities, were more positive about their living experience than other students. Finally, there appeared to be no differences by class standing, gender, age, and race and ethnicity. But disabled students were not nearly as positive as other students and were clearly dissatisfied about a number of issues.

Step 10: Determine the Implications of the Study for Policy and Practice

The primary reason for conducting this study was to provide information to the vice president and president about the quality of life in residence halls in order to answer allegations asserted by two powerful and influential faculty members. From this study, the vice president was able to report that, on the whole, there was little to support those allegations. The study did suggest some areas for improvement, which the vice president asked the residence hall director to consider in reevaluating residence halls policies and practices.

Step 11: Report the Results Effectively

Because the two faculty members had been quite vocal about their criticisms (including writing a column in the student newspaper), the reporting of the study was vigorous and comprehensive. The president and the two faculty members were given an executive summary in advance of a press conference in which the results of the study were released. The report included many actions steps that were going to be taken based on the results, including a reevaluation of the needs of disabled students. It was also announced that this study would be replicated each year to determine trends and changes in student perceptions.

Conclusion

This chapter provides a blueprint for a comprehensive assessment of residential life programs, with an emphasis on an overall quality of residential life. In some ways, assessing residence hall programs is less complicated than assessing many other student services and programs because of a captive audience and because there are many commercially available instruments to assess various aspects of residence life (see the Resources section at the end of this manual). On the other hand, assessing residence hall programs is more difficult than assessing other student services and programs because of the multifaceted nature of residence life and because residence hall assessments are often driven by political considerations beyond the control of residence halls and assessment professionals.

References

Miller, T. K. "Measuring Effectiveness Against Professional Standards." In M. L. Upcraft and J. H. Schuh (eds.), *Assessment in Student Affairs: A Guide for Practitioners*. San Francisco: Jossey-Bass, 1996.

Pascarella, E. T., and Terenzini, P. T. *How College Affects Students: Findings and Insights from Twenty Years of Research.* San Francisco: Jossey-Bass, 1991.

Upcraft, M. L., and Schuh, J. H., *Assessment in Student Affairs: A Guide for Practitioners.* San Francisco: Jossey-Bass, 1996.

Chapter 24

Assessing College Unions

VIRTUALLY EVERY college or university has some type of student center or college union facility. They may vary by physical facilities, programming emphasis, and services offered, but college unions often are the center of student, campus, and community life, particularly on campuses with significant commuter populations. This chapter identifies some of the problems associated with assessing college unions, presents a comprehensive model for assessing college unions, and offers an assessment case study based on a typical college union problem.

Problems with Assessing College Unions

Although virtually all campuses have college unions, they often vary greatly from campus to campus, making the development of an assessment approach applicable to all campuses quite difficult. A starting point is to identify seven major functions typically associated with college unions, adapted from Yates (1992), some or all of which are evident on today's campuses:

Food facilities: cafeterias, snack bars, coffee and ice cream shops, fast food areas, bakeries, restaurants, private dining rooms, food and beverage vending machines, banquet rooms, pubs

Leisure-time facilities: amusement machine areas, billiard and table tennis tables, bowling lanes, card and table games, craft centers, exercise rooms, boat houses, ice rinks, outing centers, darkrooms, rifle ranges, swimming pools, TV lounges

Revenue-generating areas: banks, textbook stores, gift shops, specialty bookstores, mailrooms, public parking areas, duplicating services, guest rooms, ticket sales offices, travel agencies

Social and cultural facilities: art exhibit galleries, auditoriums, theaters, ballrooms, browsing libraries, music listening rooms

General lounges: commuter facilities, lockers, chapels, day care rooms, study lounges

Service facilities: computer labs, campus and pay telephones, meeting and conference rooms, coat check rooms, solicitation booths and counters, postal services, copy machines

Office areas: offices for student government, student organizations, alumni, student activities, yearbook, radio, and campus newspaper

Of course, there may be great overlap among these functions. For example, a copying center or day care facility may generate revenue, a general lounge may also serve as a TV lounge, and food services may also be lounging areas. The assessment problem is complicated by these many and often overlapping functions.

Many college union professionals would argue that college unions are much more than just a collection of services and facilities. They would assert that unions are also instrumental in student learning and student development, and often they are an integral part of a campus's sense of community. The Association of College Unions–International (ACUI) publication, *Task Force 2000 Final Report* (1990), advocated both a student development and a community development perspective. Any assessment approach must include these outcomes as well.

A second problem is the lack of a captive audience. For residence halls, counseling centers, health services, and career services, individual students are identified as service users, and thus assessment efforts can focus on the needs, satisfaction, and outcomes of these users. But college unions typically do not have captive audiences that are easily identified. Rarely can we identify by name individuals who eat in the food services areas, relax in lounges, ask questions at information desks or by telephone, use computer labs, or buy tickets at the ticket sales office. Alternate assessment approaches are needed to overcome this disadvantage.

A related problem is that unions serve not only students but also faculty, staff, administrators, the local community, parents and family, and the general public. Thus, assessments must be focused not only on functions but on the wide array of users. For example, it may be as important to assess community needs as campus needs, or faculty needs may be as important as student needs, depending on the scope of union offerings.

A fourth assessment problem is the changing diversity of students. For example, a commuter-based campus may need lounges, study space, lockers, and food services, whereas a residentially based campus may require meeting rooms, student government offices, and entertainment facilities. Campuses that are successful in attracting racial and ethnic minorities must ensure that the physical and cultural environment of the union is welcoming and supportive. Whenever there is a shift in the mix of students, college union programs, facilities, and services must change to meet students' changing needs.

A fifth assessment problem is the changing preferences of students. According to Bookman (1992), the lifestyles and values of the campus community have changed, with direct implications for college unions. Among the changes are a greater emphasis on leisure time, the expectation of one-stop shopping, the movement toward a more "grab-and-go" eating pattern, increased access to computers as a learning and communication resource, access to copying and desktop publishing services, and an increased use of debit and credit cards. Perhaps more than most other student affairs functions, the effectiveness of student unions depends on knowing and responding to student and other clientele changing preferences.

Finally, unions are under increasing pressure to generate revenue and become profit centers for the institution. In general, this means moving toward contract services (food courts filled with franchised food services), convenience facilities, game rooms, and initiating fees for services previously offered without charge, such as use of pool tables or fees for meeting rooms. Greater emphasis on student unions as profit centers means pressure to move away from high-maintenance and low- or no income-producing services and facilities. As this pressure mounts, union administrators sometimes may have to choose between generating revenue and meeting student needs.

For all these reasons, college unions present an assessment challenge.

A Comprehensive Model for Assessing College Unions

Track Use of Programs, Facilities, and Services

Tracking the use of facilities and services in a college union is difficult, because to gather such information at all times in all locations would disrupt the use of such facilities and services substantially. There are, however, alternative ways of assessing use that overcome this handicap.

Time-Sliced Assessments

It is possible to gather reliable and useful data on the use of programs, facilities, and services by doing so periodically. For example, if it becomes important to know how many persons use informal lounges, whom they are, and how they are using those facilities, it is possible to count and observe use over a typical day in three or four typical weeks. If knowing what type of information is sought over the telephone is important, over a typical day in three or four typical weeks, clerical and professional staff could keep a count of the number and types of calls and ask callers for some demographic information such as their status (student, faculty, staff, general public, and so forth), gender, age, race and ethnicity, or other pertinent information. (If demographic information is asked for, callers must be informed about why this information is being gathered, how it will be used, and the confidentiality parameters. See Chapter Thirty-Two on the ethics of assessment for a more complete discussion of informed consent.)

General Use Surveys

Another approach is to include a services and facilities use section in more general college union surveys. For example, Educational Benchmarking, Inc., in collaboration with the ACUI, offers a general college unions instrument focusing on student learning, leadership, programming, services, and other union functions. Or a telephone or Web-based survey of a random sample of users could be used to determine the demographics of users.

Focus Groups

Focus groups can be useful in gathering information from students. For example, it is possible to put together focus groups of college union users and probe the frequency and type of their use, paying close attention to the demographics of the respondents. It might also be possible, based on the results of time-sliced assessments, to construct focus groups of typical nonusers in order to gain insight into their reasons for not using union facilities and services.

Group Educational Programs Assessments

Keeping track of students and other users who participate in more formal educational programs (such as leadership development and student government–related activities) is a bit easier than other forms of assessment, because it is possible to retrieve relevant information about participants. (See Chapter Seventeen for details on assessing group educational programs.)

Assess User Needs

There are several ways of assessing user needs in relation to student unions. Unions can be part of comprehensive student needs assessment surveys (see Chapter Nine) or focus groups (see Chapter Four). Needs assessments can be done using commercially available or locally constructed surveys, and focus groups can be used to assess students' needs specific to college union offerings. Given the changing diversity and lifestyle preferences of today's students, student needs assessments are critical to the effectiveness of college unions and should be conducted at least annually.

Assess User Satisfaction

For most of the college union functions described above, customer satisfaction is the key to their success. If users are dissatisfied, they will go elsewhere, especially if the services offered are also available elsewhere on campus or in the community. In many ways, assessing student satisfaction is a cornerstone of assessing college unions. Because of the wide variety of college union functions, multiple approaches are recommended and should be done systematically and frequently.

Brief Customer Satisfaction Forms

Short (no more than three or four questions) and easily completed (closed-ended questions) instruments are likely to yield greater returns than longer, less user-friendly approaches. For example, many of the major franchised food service providers have customer satisfaction forms based on these parameters that can be used as well by college union managers. These same forms can be used to assess user satisfaction with other union facilities, such as leisure-time facilities, social and cultural facilities, and general lounges.

General Satisfaction Surveys

College unions are sometimes included in general campus satisfaction surveys (see the Student Opinion Survey published by American College Testing). The ACUI also publishes a student satisfaction survey. Because of the differences among college unions, locally developed instruments may be more useful (see Chapter Five), using telephone-based or Web-based data collection procedures (see Chapters Seven and Eight, respectively).

Focus Groups

Focus groups can also be helpful in getting at user satisfaction (see Chapter Four). Because so many different constituents use college unions, it may be useful to design focus groups by user type as well as function.

Educational Programs Assessments

When college union facilities are used to offer educational programs, the generic instruments suggested in Chapter Seventeen may be helpful.

Assess Outcomes

College unions are not typically focused on student outcomes in the usual sense of attributing certain developmental or academic outcomes to participation in college unions programs, services, and facilities. The exception might be specific student development programs, where more systematic assessments of impact are certainly feasible. However, because many unions focus more on services and facilities, in a sense user satisfaction is often the desired outcome, and it can be inferred from student satisfaction assessments.

If there are certain union programs with specific intended learning outcomes, two options are available. First, along the lines suggested in Chapter Seventeen, students can be asked what they learned and how they learned it, given specific learning outcomes. Second, if a comprehensive, longitudinal study of student success is conducted (see Terenzini and Upcraft, 1996), union programs, facilities, and services could be included as one of many during-college experiences that may affect student outcomes.

Assess Campus Environments and Cultures

College unions sometimes assert that their services, programs, and facilities are a part of developing a sense of community for institutions. Unions can be the physical and human hub of student, faculty, and staff communication, interaction, and support. The ACUI asserted just such a proposition in its *Task Force 2000 Final Report* (1990), which argued that the college union serves as the community center, offering services, conveniences, and amenities needed in daily campus life and providing the source for the building of community through its organization, programs, and facilities.

This most admirable and important goal is somewhat difficult, but not impossible, to assess. One way is to make sure that participation in campus union services, programs, and facilities is included whenever more global assessments of campus environments or student cultures are studied. Another approach is to ask students and other users directly through individual interviews or focus groups, using questions such as, "How, if at all, does the college union contribute to the overall sense of community at this institution?" or, "How might the college union make a greater contribution to the overall sense of community at this institution?"

Compare Performance Across Organizations

Upcraft and Schuh (1996) note that the key to comparing performance across organizations (sometimes referred to as benchmarking) is to ensure that the organizations chosen are truly comparable. Given the great diversity among college unions, if a particular policy, practice, program, service, or facility is being benchmarked, it is important to choose truly comparable unions.

Use Professional Standards to Assess

The Council for the Advancement of Standards in Higher Education (CAS) has recently published revised standards for college union and student activities functions. These standards suggest that college union professionals provide students opportunities for their intellectual, personal, social, leadership, cultural, and civic development. They further suggest that programs must take into account individual differences and reflect campus demographics (Council for the Advancement of Standards in Higher Education, 1998). CAS also provides self-assessment guides that may be helpful in the overall assessment process.

Assess Cost Effectiveness

College unions are business ventures that must be efficiently and effectively administered. Often budgets are in the millions of dollars, so assessing cost effectiveness is no ordinary task for most union administrators. Add to this the increasing pressures to become more financially self-sufficient and develop more revenue-generating operations, and the importance of assessing cost effectiveness becomes critical. (Chapter Thirteen discusses a model of assessing cost effectiveness that is applicable to college unions.)

A College Union Case Study

Upandcoming Comunity College is a two-year commuter institution with about five thousand full-time students and three thousand part-time students. Upandcoming has never had a centralized college union facility. The typical union functions—a bookstore, two cafeterias, three amusement machine areas, a craft center, two exercise rooms, a bank, an art gallery, a computer lab, and student government offices—are spread all over campus in various campus buildings. Virtually no place is available on the campus for students to congregate between classes, and student organizations must meet in classrooms, competing with faculty for available space. Although there is a director of student unions, the geographical distance among various functions makes the coordination of programs, services, and facilities difficult and creates enormous facilities management problems. Further, the development of a sense of campus community is stifled because there is no central place for students and faculty to congregate and interact. Although enrollments are expanding, college administrators believe the lack of a centralized student union is a major reason that students choose other institutions.

President Goforit is very interested in building a centralized union facility that could become the hub of campus life and serve as an excellent incentive for more students to enroll. He is, however, an academic by training, and he is under pressure to expand classroom and faculty office facilities as well. Therefore, he needs more evidence that a student union is needed and will be used if built. He wants more information before he takes on the task of raising the funds necessary to build a new facility.

Step 1: Define the Problem

There is some anecdotal evidence that the current union operation at Upandcoming Community College has some serious problems, and the president has responded by asking for more information as he considers a new, centralized facility. He is feeling the heat from his admissions office to add a facility that will contribute to recruitment and enrollment efforts. Both students and faculty believe Upandcoming lacks a real sense of community. But there is no information on the current use of union facilities and little information about user satisfaction with the current union facilities, services, and programs. Moreover, no systematic study of the campus climate has ever been conducted. Without this information, it is likely that the president will not commit the funds to build a new facility.

Step 2: Determine the Purpose of the Study

It is clear that Upandcoming needs more information about the current use of all union functions, as well as student and other user satisfaction with current functions. Therefore this study has two purposes:

1. Determine the current use of all union functions by students, faculty, staff, the community, and the general public.

2. Determine the satisfaction of students, faculty, staff, the local community, and the general public with current union functions and a sense of campus community.

Step 3: Determine Where to Get the Information Needed

For the first purpose (determine current use), current records of various union functions may provide some information, but it is probably necessary to get more systematic and comparable information from all current union functions. The retrieval of this information may vary slightly from function to function, but all units will be expected to produce such information.

For the second purpose (satisfaction with current union functions and a sense of community), information will be gathered directly from all users and potential users: students, faculty, staff, the local community, and the general public.

Step 4: Determine the Best Assessment Method

For tracking the use of unions functions, a quantitative approach is preferred, because specific, numerical information is required when recording and analyzing numbers and types of students. For assessing user satisfaction, a combination of quantitative and qualitative methods probably is appropriate, because there is a need for quantitative information on the extent of satisfaction or dissatisfaction with union functions as well as why users are satisfied or dissatisfied.

Step 5: Determine Whom to Study

At Upandcoming Community College, faculty, staff, students, the local community, and the general public use the union facilities. Therefore, a stratified random sample of each group should be drawn, making sure that within each group, participants are adequately represented by gender, age, race and ethnicity, part-time and full time enrollment status, and other relevant factors (see Upcraft and Schuh, 1996, for more specific information on sample size, margins of error, and other sampling issues). For faculty, staff, and students, samples can be drawn from institutional records. However, the local community and general public present a different kind of sampling problem because there are no institutional records for these constituents. In this case, a convenience sample may be the only option. That is, local community and general public users are identified and asked their opinions. In the college union setting, this may involve simply identifying users at the point of use, determining if they are from the local community or the general public, giving them a sense of the purposes and goals of the study, and asking them to provide information on the spot or at some later date by telephone or e-mail. After data are collected, it is then possible to describe those samples and determine if they are generally representative of the general population. As Upcraft and Schuh (1996) point out, convenience sampling is neither purposeful nor strategic, and its limitations must be identified in any reporting of the results of the study.

Step 6: Determine How the Data Will Be Collected

Information about users is probably best gathered with periodic time-sliced assessments. Each union function should be asked to keep track of how many and who uses union facilities, services, and programs during several typical days over several typical weeks. Telephone contacts as well as physical presence of users should be included.

Under normal circumstances, focus groups of various users would probably be the best approach. However, this is an exclusively commuter population, and our experience has been that commuters are reluctant to take the time to participate in focus groups because of their other commitments (often family and work) and their reluctance to return to the campus once they leave for the day. A Web-based survey (see Chapter Eight) is certainly an option, but because some commuters do not have Web access except when on campus, a telephone survey (see Chapter Seven) is probably the better option.

Step 7: Determine What Instruments Will Be Used

For tracking use, there should be a common format required of all union functions. In this instance, in addition to numbers of users, the following demographic characteristics should be collected from users:

- Gender

- Race or ethnicity

- Age

- Enrollment status (full time, part time, or not enrolled)

This information is purposefully brief, because user tolerance for more complete information will be low, especially if the information is gathered over the telephone. Because the information will be collected by union function, the type of function being used will be self-evident. There may also be instances where other demographic information is vital (for example, facilities managers may want to know about use by disabled students), but it should be kept to a minimum.

For user satisfaction, a telephone survey instrument will be used (see Chapter Five on instrument development and Chapter Seven on developing telephone interview protocols). In this instance, we suggest the interview protocol in Exhibit 24.1.

Step 8: Determine Who Should Collect the Data

For determining use, professional staff or trained student employees from each of the functions should gather the information directly from users. Volunteers should be avoided, because of the level of expertise and accountability required to collect this information.

EXHIBIT 24.1

Telephone Protocol for Union Satisfaction

My name is [name of interviewer]. May I speak to [name of respondent]? I work with the Union Program at Upandcoming Community College. We are conducting a voluntary seven-minute survey to determine user satisfaction with our student union. Have you used this facility? If so, we would like to ask you a few questions. Please be assured that your responses are confidential and are reported as summarized data used in future planning efforts by the institution. No individual data will be identified. You may choose not to answer specific questions. You may also see the survey results in about three weeks. If you have any questions, contact [name of contact] in the Student Union Office, [address], or by telephone [telephone number] or e-mail [e-mail address].

I hope you will take this opportunity for your voice to be heard. Are you willing to participate?

1. How often do you use the following college union functions and if used, what is your level of satisfaction?

   Responses to use: 0: Never   1: Once a semester   2: Once a month   3: Once a week

                  4: 2–3 times a week   5: Every day

   [If answer is never, skip to next function. If used, ask for level of satisfaction.]

   1: Very unsatisfied   2: Unsatisfied   3: Neutral   4: Satisfied   5: Very satisfied

	Responses	
Function	**Use**	**Satisfaction**
Bookstore	____	____
Computer lab	____	____
Craft center	____	____
Cafeterias	____	____
Art gallery	____	____
Exercise rooms	____	____
Amusement machines	____	____
Bank	____	____
Student government offices	____	____
Other (please specify)		
_____	____	____
_____	____	____

2. Please comment on how union functions at Upandcoming might be improved.

3. The college is considering adding new functions that are often included in campus unions at institutions comparable to Upandcoming. Please indicate the importance of the following union functions not currently offered.

Function	**Important**	**Neutral**	**Not Important**
Coffee shops	____	____	____
Informal lounges	____	____	____
Study lounges	____	____	____
Meeting rooms	____	____	____

EXHIBIT 24.1

Telephone Protocol for Union Satisfaction, continued

Function	Important	Neutral	Not Important
Copying services	____	____	____
Ticket sales offices	____	____	____
Gift shop	____	____	____
Auditorium	____	____	____
Ballroom	____	____	____
Library	____	____	____
Alumni offices	____	____	____
Student newspaper offices	____	____	____
Campus yearbook	____	____	____
Commuter lounge	____	____	____
Other (please specify)			

4. Do you support building a centralized college union facility at Upandcoming?

____ Yes   ____ No   ____ No opinion

5. If so, how should this building be funded? (Indicate as many as apply.)

____ Borrow the money

____ Use current college fiscal resources

____ Impose a special union building tax each semester until the building is paid off

____ Impose user fees for services rendered

____ Increase tuition

____ Seek private donors

____ Other sources (please specify)

6. Any other comments about the proposed new union building?

7. Please indicate the following information:

Gender:	____ Male ____ Female
Age:	____ Under 18 ____ 18–22 ____ 22–25 ____ Over 25
Enrollment status:	____ Full-time student ____ Part-time student ____ Not enrolled
Race/ethnicity	
(Check all that apply)	____ African American ____ Asian American ____ Hispanic
	____ White ____ Native American ____ Other _____

For the telephone survey, trained student employees or volunteers are appropriate, consistent with recommendations provided in Chapter Seven.

Step 9: Determine How the Data Will Be Analyzed

For tracking who uses services and programs, descriptive data should be compiled showing the number of users, type of use, and the characteristics of users. Inferential statistics can be used to determine if there are differences among users by characteristics. For example, it may be important to know if there is a statistically significance difference in use of facilities between part-time and full-time students. (See Terenzini and Upcraft, 1996, for more detailed information on conducting statistical analyses of quantitative data.)

In this case study, several findings were relevant to the problem. Current use was moderate to low for students, with the exception of the bookstore and the computer lab. Use was very low for faculty, the local community, and the general public, yet the need for union functions among all groups was very high.

Improvements centered on locating all unions functions in one location, and virtually all respondents supported building a centralized college union facility. As might be expected, most respondents, but especially students, favored funding the new facility by borrowing money, seeking private donors, or using current college financial resources rather than increasing tuition or imposing user fees for services rendered. There was some moderate support among students (about one-third) and stronger support among other groups for a special union building tax to fund a new union building.

Step 10: Determine the Implications of the Study for Policy and Practice

The primary reason for conducting this study was to provide President Goforit with information needed to determine if a centralized student union building should be built. From the study of current use, the president should be able to determine if current facilities are adequate to meet current student demand. From the satisfaction survey, he should be able to determine if students are satisfied with current union functions and which additional functions might meet student needs. The information gathered should be specifically targeted to the impending decision.

Step 11: Report the Results Effectively

Upcraft and Schuh (1996) note that writing a good report of assessment findings may be as important as conducting a good study. They recommend using a brief format that focuses specifically on the findings of the study in relation to the problem, writing multiple reports to targeted audiences, and making specific recommendations based on the findings. In this instance, because the president commissioned the study, he will most likely want the full report, introduced by an executive summary. (Details on how assessment reports should be written and implemented are discussed in Schuh and Upcraft, 1996. Chapter Seven in this book provides a model for reporting telephone surveys.)

In this case study, after consultation with all the groups affected, the president decided to build a new union facility, funded by a development campaign specifically targeted to this project, borrowing some money, and making up the difference with a special union building fee for students.

Conclusion

Compared to student affairs units with more captive audiences, assessing student unions is more difficult and complicated, yet nevertheless extremely important. Enormous amounts of human, budget, and facilities resources are devoted to college unions, so we must expect that critical questions will be asked about mission, use, need, cost, and effectiveness. Union staff must devote more time and energy to assessment than they have in the past. The very future of college unions may depend on it.

References

Association of College Unions–International. *Task Force 2000 Final Report.* Bloomington, Ind.: Association of College Unions–International, 1990.

Bookman, M. "Funding College Unions in the Year 2000." In T. E. Milani and J. W. Johnson (eds.), *The College Union in the Year 2000.* New Directions for Student Services, no. 58. San Francisco: Jossey-Bass, 1992.

Council for the Advancement of Standards in Higher Education. *The Book of Professional Standards for Higher Education.* Washington, D.C.: Author, 1997.

Terenzini, P. T., and Upcraft, M. L. "Assessing Program and Service Outcomes." In M. L. Upcraft and J. H. Schuh, *Assessment in Student Affairs: A Guide for Practitioners.* San Francisco: Jossey-Bass, 1996.

Upcraft, M. L., and Schuh, J. H. *Assessment in Student Affairs: A Guide for Practitioners.* San Francisco: Jossey-Bass, 1996.

Yates, M. C. "The College Union Facility of the Future." In T. E. Milani and J. W. Johnson (eds.), *The College Union in the Year 2000.* New Directions for Student Services, no. 58. San Francisco: Jossey-Bass, 1992.

Chapter 25

Assessing Health Services

Margaret E. Spear

COLLEGE AND UNIVERSITY health services exist in two worlds: the world of higher education and the world of health care. In these contexts, the college health service must manage change successfully if it is to survive and grow. Meaningful assessment is a critical part of this process.

During the twentieth century, college health moved from a reactive approach to a proactive one. For most of the century, college health professionals focused on the clinical treatment of illnesses. The biomedical disease model defined an approach in which physicians provided convenient, campus-based outpatient and infirmary care to sick students. In the past twenty years, the college health model has changed significantly to emphasize education and the prevention of disease and disability (De Armond and others, 1991). This newer model supports early intervention, quality assurance, cost effectiveness, and the involvement of student customers. It also values the importance of being connected to the broader campus community (American College Health Association, 1993).

We can best understand health behaviors and health status today within a social context. Thus, it is not enough simply to see disease and illness on the campus as the responsibility of the college health service. Rather, health interventions must include modifying community norms, behaviors, and attitudes. As the scope of health service practice grows, so do the assessment challenges (Jackson and Weinstein, 1997).

The nature of college health practice will continue to change in response to changes in the student body. Demographic shifts in the college student population will affect individual as well as community health issues. With a traditional student body, the provision of basic acute primary care and community preventive health services may be relatively simple. It is much more difficult to provide and evaluate services for a student body whose members are primarily older than twenty-five, have children, hold jobs, and carry greater financial burdens. Similarly, the service and concomitant assessment issues become increasingly complex for a more ethnically, culturally, and socioeconomically diverse population.

Within this changing situation, the current reality of health services in higher education is one of great pluralism. Of the 15 million students enrolled in institutions of higher education, 80 percent attend schools that offer direct health care services (American College Health Association, 1993). At a small college or community college, the health service may consist of a registered nurse who provides basic first aid, personal health advice, and limited outreach educational services. At the other end of the spectrum, a large university may provide comprehensive, multidisciplinary primary care services delivered by physicians, nurse practitioners, nurses, and others. These services might include a full complement of ancillary services, including lab, x-ray, physical therapy, and pharmacy. Some larger health services provide specialty care, such as orthopedics, dermatology, and optometry and even complementary therapies like massage, acupuncture, and chiropractic services.

Similar to the range in scope of services, the facilities that house campus health services vary considerably. The solo registered nurse at a small college may work in a one- or two-room suite in a classroom or administrative or residence hall building. A comprehensive, accredited university health service may be in a modern, multimillion-dollar, fully equipped ambulatory health care center (for patients who can ambulate and are not ill enough to require hospitalization).

Predictably, financial issues and challenges have emerged in the context of the rapid growth of managed care and the competition in higher education. Previously fully funded by general funds or prepaid student health fees, health services have developed a myriad of funding models to respond to the increasing demands of financially strapped parent institutions on the inside and those of managed care on the outside. Increasing numbers of students have no insurance or inadequate insurance. Of those with insurance, more are enrolled in managed care organizations. The costs of providing medical care continue to rise (albeit at a lower rate than in the 1970s and 1980s). Between 1987 and 1990, a national survey found that the institutional share of funding for health services decreased from 45 to 16 percent, while the portion of budgets funded by fees for service increased from 34 to 63 percent (Brindis and Reyes, 1997). University administrators are asking for increased efficiency. They are considering a range of radical solutions, including outsourcing, carve-outs, and simply closing down campus-based services. In this climate, it becomes even more important to be able to measure and track the cost effectiveness of various service models.

Finally, there are basic attitudinal issues within the campus academic and administrative community. The provision of a range of student services in institutions of higher education rests on several philosophical assumptions. The primary assumption is that student development enhances learning and that personal circumstances and the out-of-class experience affect the learning process. These notions, fundamental to the foundation of student affairs, may conflict with the belief that the academic mission is preeminent. This leads to a profound ambivalence about student services in general and college health services in particular. Whereas some may believe that student health is important to developing healthy individuals who are effective and productive in their academic pursuits, others question whether this matters at all. Reflecting this ambivalence, many college health centers "exist at the periphery of the campus rather than at its heart" (Jackson and Weinstein, 1997, p. 237). College health and campus decision makers need to pose some difficult questions and define goals for the health status of the institution—its students, faculty, staff, and community. What is the value of a healthy student body? Why is it important? Who is responsible for health? Is responsibility individual or collective? What is the relationship between the health of students and that of faculty and staff (Patrick and others, 1997)? Answering these questions requires accurate, meaningful assessment methodologies and strategies. This chapter discusses challenges in health services assessment, presents a comprehensive plan for assessing health services, and identifies steps in the health services assessment process through the use of a case study.

Problems with Assessing Health Services

A number of particularly challenging issues must be addressed in assessing college and university health services. These relate to the nature of ambulatory primary health care evaluation and the great variation in service models.

Ambulatory health care is by nature difficult to evaluate because there is often a long latency period between the therapy or intervention and its consequences. This is particularly true with preventive interventions. Effectively treating or preventing high blood pressure, obesity, or smoking may all reduce an individual's risk for a heart attack later in life. However, given the mobility of college students, the outcome for this group is very difficult to track and demonstrate. Similarly, community-based health interventions such as efforts to reduce smoking or binge drinking are even more difficult to evaluate. Because of the barriers to long-term outcome evaluation, it is important to evaluate the process of care and identify short-term or intermediate outcomes that can be assessed more easily.

The great variety of health services staffing, facilities resources, and funding models creates special evaluation problems. The level of service provided will be determined in part by the type of staff employed. In a setting with a registered nurse, basic first aid, triage, and simple protocol-based interventions will be appropriate. In a large, multidisciplinary, accredited clinic, a more comprehensive level of care would be expected. Each of these settings will determine in part the kind of assessment that is needed. A visit in each of these settings may be very different. The process of care as well as the outcomes of care may vary. Similarly, "productivity" expectations may vary considerably for different professionals in different practice settings.

Diverse funding models create challenges as well. It is important to identify costs accurately in order to measure cost effectiveness, but this is very difficult to do. While cost per visit or the cost to treat a certain problem may be of interest, the comparability of such data in different settings may not be valid. One health service may be entirely self-supporting, and thus its costs include salaries, benefits, and maintaining the physical plant. Another's budget may include only operational costs. Comparing cost per visit in these diverse settings will be very misleading.

The confidentiality of the medical record results in some unique assessment challenges, many of which can be overcome. Most data needed for assessment do not rely on the patients' identity so that data analysis will not violate confidentiality. For longitudinal evaluations of individual cases, the research design will need to accommodate confidentiality mandates. Finally, chart review for the purpose of quality-of-care assessment must be done in a way that protects client and provider identity; the results of such review must be reported without any identifiers.

Despite these many challenges, it is essential for health service and student affairs leaders to develop meaningful assessment strategies. With such strategies, a health service will be able to demonstrate its value to the institution as well as the quality of its service to students.

A Comprehensive Model for Assessing Health Services

Based on the model presented in Chapter Two and the factors just noted, I suggest the following approach to assessing health services.

Track Patient Use, Demographics, and Types of Problems

Student health services usually keep records of appointments and other encounters and so probably track this information in some way. It is helpful to know, over time, how many visits there are for a given service per year. Changes may help inform decisions about resource allocation. It is also important to be able to count and track unique encounters. What percentage of the student body accesses health services during a given year? What proportion of the student body never uses on-campus health services? Such information can sometimes identify access issues and indicate the need for in-depth analysis.

For more complex health services, it is important to track service contacts by department. How many students were referred for laboratory testing, x-rays, or physical therapy? If there is a health service pharmacy, how many prescriptions did it fill? As with the clinical visit information, following such data over time can and should inform strategic decision making. In addition, it is an important component of meaningful utilization review. For example, of all students seen for ankle injuries, what percentage have x-rays done? How does this compare with established standards of care?

However, it is not enough simply to count heads. Rather, it is important to have demographic data about the students served, such as age, race, marital status, semester standing, and sexual orientation. A comparison of such demographic data on health service contacts to that of the population covered can determine if certain groups of students are underserved.

Information about the nature of the clinical encounter can be useful in planning and resource allocation. By using standard diagnostic codes (International Classification of Diseases; Medicode, 1999) and procedure codes (Current Procedural Terminology; American Medical Association, 1999), it is relatively simple to track patterns over time. With the increasing use of computerized systems for clinical practice management and patient records, it is important to think about assessment as a priority in choosing such systems. Well-designed practice management and computerized patient record software have the potential to simplify data collection and analysis. A good practice management system will provide simple yet comprehensive reports.

Assess Individual and Community Health Needs

Describing the aggregate health issues (needs, risks, and behaviors) for a campus population is very important. The emphasis on community health for institutions of higher education is consistent with national public health strategies. Along with the establishment of national health objectives in *Healthy People 2000* (U.S. Public Health Service, 1990), *Healthy Campus 2000* (American College Health Association, 1992) established a series of health objectives for adolescents and young adults. These objectives define behavioral goals relating to safety (car and bicycle), diet, tobacco and alcohol use, rape, suicide, sexual activities, and violence. These priorities should guide campus-based population assessment. Although it is not always clear what behavioral standards are appropriate, we can at least begin to identify process measures, mediating variables, and intermediate outcomes as an appropriate evaluation strategy (Jackson and Weinstein, 1997).

A number of instruments and methodologies should be considered. For example, the Core Alcohol and Drug Survey was developed in 1990 to assess the nature, scope, and consequences of students' drug and alcohol use, as well as students' awareness of relevant policies. It was designed to be inexpensive, easily administered, of high quality, statistically reliable, valid, and comparable to other surveys in the field. Currently, two versions of the survey, a short (two pages) and a long (four-page) form, are available. The longer survey includes questions relating to broader issues of sexuality, campus violence, institutional climate, perceptions of campus. and extracurricular activities (Core Institute, 1998).

In the spring of 1999, the American College Health Association (ACHA) piloted the National College Health Assessment (NCHA) survey, which evaluates a range of individual belief, behavior, and knowledge parameters. It will be further refined and should be available for general use in spring 2000. The goal of this project is to create a college-appropriate health assessment instrument that will provide specific data to individual institutions and aggregate national data on health factors that may affect academic performance and retention. This instrument should be a useful tool for colleges and universities that want to assess systematically the health status of the institution—its students, faculty, and staff. If it is successful, the ACHA's NCHA survey will help achieve the following goals:

- Generate incidence rates for specific health problems.

- Plan programs and service delivery modes.

- Prioritize student needs.

- Allocate resources.

- Design effective intervention strategies.

- Identify protective and risk factors to academic performance.

- Measure progress toward national health objectives.

This assessment can help institutions define their community health vision and measure the extent to which the institution meets the goals of the American College Health Association (1999a).

Assess Student Satisfaction

Student satisfaction surveys are an important part of a comprehensive student health services assessment plan. Several different approaches to student satisfaction will be complementary if used appropriately.

Periodically, perhaps every two to five years, a campuswide survey drawing on a random sample of students should be administered. Such a broad-based assessment will provide valuable information on nonusers as well as the users who are more often surveyed. This type of survey can ask nonusers why they have not used the campus health service and provide important information about access and scope of service. In addition, surveys can ask students to prioritize different types of services, and the results can help guide decision making. An example of such a survey that might be adapted to suit local needs is contained in Exhibit 25.1.

User surveys also are of value and can be general or focused in nature. A general satisfaction survey should be regularly administered to all users for a short but representative time period. The same survey, used yearly, can demonstrate change (improvement or decline) in perceived quality. It is also possible, and in some settings advisable, to measure importance and satisfaction for the same parameters of services. This will help define what is most important to students and provide student input into resource allocation decisions. The survey contained in Exhibit 25.2 is an example of a user satisfaction survey that could be adapted to any college health services. Patients are asked to complete the survey immediately after treatment and return it to a central location in the health service. Both overall results and results by type of treatment can be analyzed.

If information beyond the analysis of responses by treatment area is not required, specific functional areas can develop narrower, issue-driven customer surveys on an as-needed basis. For example, if the wait time for an appointment for HIV testing is getting longer and health services is not sure how important a factor that is for students, a brief survey can be developed and used. Similarly, if a change has been instituted in a particular area, a focused user survey will help assess the impact of the change. Function-specific user satisfaction surveys can be adapted from the general user satisfaction survey contained in Exhibit 25.2.

EXHIBIT 25.1

Health Services Student Survey

1. Please rate the frequency with which you use the following sources of information when deciding where to go for medical care:

Source of Information	Use Frequently	Use Occasionally	Never Use
Student directory	_____	_____	_____
Telephone directory yellow pages	_____	_____	_____
Residence hall staff	_____	_____	_____
Family members	_____	_____	_____
Home physician	_____	_____	_____
Friends	_____	_____	_____
Insurance information	_____	_____	_____
Student newspaper	_____	_____	_____
Internet	_____	_____	_____
Other (please identify) _____	_____	_____	_____
_____	_____	_____	_____

2. Please indicate where you have received health services during your enrollment at this institution (check all that apply):
   ____ College health service
   ____ Local physician
   ____ Local health care facilities
   ____ Your own family physician
   ____ Other (please identify) _____
   ____ Haven't yet needed health services

3. Please indicate which of the following college health services you are aware of (check all that apply):

Service Offered	Am Aware of	Did Not Know Existed
General medicine	_____	_____
Emergency care	_____	_____
Women's health	_____	_____
Immunization clinic	_____	_____
Pharmacy	_____	_____
Physical therapy	_____	_____
X-ray	_____	_____
Laboratory	_____	_____
Student insurance	_____	_____
Ambulance	_____	_____
Nutrition clinic	_____	_____
HIV counseling/testing	_____	_____
Drug/alcohol intervention program	_____	_____
Telephone consultation service	_____	_____

4. How did you become aware of the service(s) you checked in item 3 (check all that apply):
___ Student handbook
___ Student newspaper
___ New student orientation
___ Other students
___ Health service brochures
___ Student directory
___ Residence hall staff
___ Academic adviser
___ Faculty
___ Health service Web page

5. Do you know whom to contact if you had a health concern or problem?
___ Yes   ___ No   ___ Uncertain

6. How important are the following when you seek health services?

Item	Not Important	Important	Very Important
Location	___	___	___
Cost	___	___	___
Hours of operation	___	___	___
Confidentiality	___	___	___
Timely scheduling of appointments	___	___	___
Quality of care	___	___	___
Competence of health care providers	___	___	___
Waiting time	___	___	___
Availability of health care needed	___	___	___
Friendliness of environment	___	___	___
Sensitivity of staff to my needs	___	___	___
Other (Please specify)			
_____	___	___	___
_____	___	___	___

7. When was the last time you used our college health service?
___ Never used   ___ Within the last year   ___ 1 year ago   ___ 2 years ago
___ 3 or more years ago

If you have used our college health service, please proceed to question 9.

If you have *never* used our college health service, please answer question 8.

8. If you have never used our college health service, please indicate the reason(s) for not doing so (check all that apply):
___ No need
___ Inconvenient location
___ Insurance mandates other care sources
___ Inconvenient hours
___ Cost
___ Desired services not offered
___ Concerns about privacy
___ Long wait to get an appointment

EXHIBIT 25.1

Health Services Student Survey, continued

___ Concerns about staff sensitivity to my needs
___ Prefer care from family physician
___ Unaware of services
___ Concerns about language barrier problems
___ Concerns about confidentiality
___ Level of care needed not provided
___ Quality of care not acceptable

If you answered question 8, please proceed to question 12.

9. How many times have you used our college health service in the past 12 months?
___ Never ___ Once ___ 2–5 times ___ 6–10 times ___ More than 10 times

10. At your last visit to our college health service, how satisfied were with the following items?

Item	Very Dissatisfied	Dissatisfied	Neutral	Satisfied	Very Satisfied	Not Applicable
Location	____	____	____	____	____	____
Cost	____	____	____	____	____	____
Hours of operation	____	____	____	____	____	____
Confidentiality	____	____	____	____	____	____
Timely scheduling of appointments	____	____	____	____	____	____
Quality of care	____	____	____	____	____	____
Competence of health care providers	____	____	____	____	____	____
Waiting time	____	____	____	____	____	____
Availability of health care needed	____	____	____	____	____	____
Friendliness of environment	____	____	____	____	____	____
Sensitivity of staff to my needs	____	____	____	____	____	____

11. How might our college health service be improved?

_____
_____
_____
_____

12. Are you covered by health insurance?

___ Yes (Please indicate plan name) _____

___ No

___ Don't know

If you answered no to question 12, please skip to question 16.

If you answered yes to question 12, please answer questions 13–16.

13. If you answered yes to question 12, please indicate the type of insurance plan:

___ Health maintenance organization (HMO)

___ Preferred provider organization (PPO)

___ Other (please specify) _____

___ Don't know

14. Do you know how to submit a medical bill to your insurance carrier for reimbursement?

___ Yes ___ No

15. Do you use a third-party pharmacy card issued by your insurance plan to purchase medication?

___ Yes

___ No

Don't know

16. Because of our commitment to providing quality health care that does not discriminate against a person because of age, ancestry, color, disability or handicap, national origin, race, religious creed, gender, sexual orientation, or veteran status, we are asking you for the following information. **Providing this information is voluntary, anonymous, and confidential, and you may refuse to answer any of these questions.**

Gender: ___ Male ___ Female

Age: ___ Under 18 ___ 18–22 ___ 22–25 ___ Over 25

Number of credits earned: ___

Academic status: ___ Undergraduate ___ Graduate

Residence: ___ On campus ___ Off campus

Sexual orientation: ___ Heterosexual ___ Gay male ___ Lesbian female

                             ___ Bisexual male ___ Bisexual female ___ Transgendered

Race/ethnicity (check as

many as apply):   ___ African American ___ Asian American ___ Hispanic/Latino

                             ___ White ___ Other (please specify) _____

Citizenship: ___ U.S. ___ Other (please specify) _____

Disability?   ___ Yes ___ No

If yes, please indicate

type of disability and

check all that apply   ___ Visually impaired/blind ___ Mobility impaired

                             ___ Hearing impaired/deaf ___ Learning disabled

                             ___ Other (please specify) _____

EXHIBIT 25.2

Health Services User Satisfaction Survey

In keeping with our mission of providing patient-centered, quality health care to the clients we serve, your opinion is important to me. Please take about five minutes to complete this anonymous survey regarding your visit today to our health center. Indicate the appropriate responses, and deposit the survey in the collection box at the entrance to our building. Completion of this survey is completely voluntary, and you may refuse to answer any question. The information you provide will be helpful in our ongoing effort to improve our services. Please do not add your name or sign this form. Thank you!

Dr. I. M. Able, Director, College Health Services, [telephone number], [e-mail address]

PLEASE WAIT UNTIL YOUR VISIT IS COMPLETED TO COMPLETE THIS FORM

PLEASE INDICATE WHERE YOU RECEIVED CARE TODAY:

___ General medicine

___ Emergency care

___ Women's health

___ Immunization clinic

___ Pharmacy

___ Physical therapy

___ X-ray

___ Laboratory

___ Student insurance

___ Ambulance

___ Nutrition clinic

___ HIV counseling/testing

___ Drug/alcohol intervention program

___ Other (please indicate)

Please use the following scales to tell us how important each of the following health service attributes is to you. Then rate how satisfied you were with that attribute during today's visit:

Importance: 5 = very important; 4 = important; 3 = somewhat important; 2 = unimportant; 1 = very unimportant

Satisfaction: 5 = very satisfied; 4 = satisfied; 3 = neutral; 2 = dissatisfied; 1 = very dissatisfied.

Attribute	Importance	Satisfaction	No Basis
Access and Physical Layout			
Phone system			
1. Ability to reach proper area	5 4 3 2 1	5 4 3 2 1	0
2. Length of time waiting on hold	5 4 3 2 1	5 4 3 2 1	0
Scheduling and appointment			
3. Convenience of appointment	5 4 3 2 1	5 4 3 2 1	0
4. Wait time between scheduling appointment and date of appointment	5 4 3 2 1	5 4 3 2 1	0

Attribute	Importance	Satisfaction	No Basis
Locating proper area			
5. Directions given	5 4 3 2 1	5 4 3 2 1	0
6. Signs in building	5 4 3 2 1	5 4 3 2 1	0
Appearance of facility			
7. Cleanliness	5 4 3 2 1	5 4 3 2 1	0
8. Comfort	5 4 3 2 1	5 4 3 2 1	0
Quality of Care			
Receptionist staff			
9. Courtesy	5 4 3 2 1	5 4 3 2 1	0
10. Promptness	5 4 3 2 1	5 4 3 2 1	0
11. Response to questions	5 4 3 2 1	5 4 3 2 1	0
Nursing staff			
12. Courtesy	5 4 3 2 1	5 4 3 2 1	0
13. Promptness	5 4 3 2 1	5 4 3 2 1	0
14. Response to questions	5 4 3 2 1	5 4 3 2 1	0
15. Explanation of procedures	5 4 3 2 1	5 4 3 2 1	0
16. Directions for follow-up care	5 4 3 2 1	5 4 3 2 1	0
Clinical staff (physician, nurse, physician's assistant)			
17. Courtesy	5 4 3 2 1	5 4 3 2 1	0
18. Promptness	5 4 3 2 1	5 4 3 2 1	0
19. Response to questions	5 4 3 2 1	5 4 3 2 1	0
20. Explanation of diagnosis/ procedures	5 4 3 2 1	5 4 3 2 1	0
21. Response to questions	5 4 3 2 1	5 4 3 2 1	0
22. Directions for follow-up	5 4 3 2 1	5 4 3 2 1	0
Privacy			
23. When interacting with staff	5 4 3 2 1	5 4 3 2 1	0
24. When examined by clinician	5 4 3 2 1	5 4 3 2 1	0
Wait time			
25. Length of wait time to see clinician	5 4 3 2 1	5 4 3 2 1	0

26. How long did you wait from the time of arrival/appointment to time seen by clinician?
____ hours ____ minutes

Overall Impressions

27. Please indicate your overall level of satisfaction with the quality of services you received from our health service:
____ Excellent ____ Good ____ Average ____ Fair ____ Poor

28. Would you recommend our health service to a friend? ____ Yes ____ No ____ Undecided

29. Would you return to our health service in the future? ____ Yes ____ No ____ Undecided

EXHIBIT 25.2

Health Services User Satisfaction Survey, continued

30. What might be done to improve our health services?

31. Any additional comments?

32. Because of our commitment to providing quality health care that does not discriminate against a person because of age, ancestry, color, disability or handicap, national origin, race, religious creed, gender, sexual orientation, or veteran status, we are asking you for the following information. **Providing this information is voluntary, anonymous, and confidential, and you may refuse to answer any of these questions.**

Gender:	___ Male ___ Female
Age:	___ Under 18 ___ 18–22 ___ 22–25 ___ Over 25
Number of credits earned:	___
Academic status:	___ Undergraduate ___ Graduate
Residence:	___ On campus ___ Off campus
Sexual orientation:	___ Heterosexual ___ Gay male ___ Lesbian female
	___ Bisexual male ___ Bisexual female ___ Transgendered
Race/ethnicity (check as many as apply):	___ African American ___ Asian American ___ Hispanic/Latino
	___ White ___ Other (please specify) _____
Citizenship:	___ U.S. ___ Other (please specify) _____
Disability?	___ Yes ___ No
If yes, please indicate type of disability and check all that apply	___ Visually impaired/blind ___ Mobility impaired
	___ Hearing impaired/deaf ___ Learning disabled
	___ Other (please specify) _____

THANK YOU AGAIN!

Assess Clinical Processes

Volumes have been written on the challenges of defining and assessing the quality of clinical services. Assessing the process of clinical services is based on the assumptions that certain procedures and treatments are standard and if these are followed, the outcome will generally be better. In a college health setting, this will be done in large part through the systematic review of clinical records. Clinicians will need to agree on the appropriate standard of care and then evaluate, using clinical record review, whether the standard has been met. It is important to look at situations that are high risk (for example, an abnormal Pap smear follow-up), high volume (common problems such as infectious diseases including strep throat and urinary tract infections), and very unusual (a patient death or unexpected or other very serious outcome). This assessment will need to be done by medical professionals in accordance with standards set by professional organizations (Accreditation Association for Ambulatory Health Care, 1999; Joint Commission for Accreditation of Healthcare Organizations, 1998).

Assess Outcomes

Outcome assessment similarly is complex. In the clinical arena, it is important to track the extent to which individuals treated for specific problems recover and return to classes and their pre-illness level of functioning in a timely manner. This review can proceed retrospectively or prospectively. Constraints of confidentiality will determine the methodology to some extent. As with process assessment, outcome assessment is generally done through chart review. However, patient follow-up interviews can be part of outcome evaluation.

For example, an evaluation of the quality of care provided to students with ankle injuries could include chart review and a follow-up telephone call. The chart review would evaluate whether the clinician took a complete history, did the appropriate examination and diagnostic testing, and recommended a suitable treatment plan. Two weeks and again six weeks after the visit, a telephone call to the patient would be made to ask how the patient was doing and to assess the degree to which he or she had recovered.

Assess Campus Climates and Environments

As suggested in Chapter Twelve, assessing campus climates or environments can provide useful information for student programs, services, and facilities. Social norm theory tells us that what is normative behavior for the group or community will have a major impact on individual behavior. To create a healthy campus, a college health service must assess and understand communitywide risks, beliefs, and knowledge so that it can design appropriate interventions. Hence, it is critical for college health professionals to understand many factors about the campus climate, particularly the norms relating to alcohol, tobacco, and other drugs; diet and exercise; sexual behaviors; sexual assault; and other forms of violence. The Core Alcohol and Drug Survey and NCHA surveys were designed in part to accomplish this type of community health assessment.

Make Comparisons with Other Health Services: Benchmarking

Benchmarking is increasingly relevant in institutional and organizational assessment and planning. In addition, both of the agencies that accredit ambulatory health care services now mandate that the organization develop some sort of report card of critical indicators, which will enable it to compare itself to similar institutions.

In recognition of the importance of benchmarking activity, the ACHA in 1997 appointed a work group that developed a limited number of benchmarks for college health:

Number of student users of student health services as a percentage of total students. This benchmark, which looks at the level of service provided to the students of the college or university, provides a quantitative measure of the share of the student health market held by the campus health service.

Number of student patient visits per total student enrollment and number of nonstudent patient visits as a percentage of total patient visits. This benchmark provides a measure of the utilization of the student health service by the student population of the campus and by other populations.

Number of student patient visits per full-time equivalent (FTE) health care provider; number of nonstudent patient visits per FTE health care provider; total patient visits per FTE health care provider; and number of total visits per FTE health care provider. This benchmark seeks to measure the efficiency of the student health service providers.

Cost per patient visit. This benchmark looks at the cost of providing health services for students on a per-visit basis and is therefore a rough measure of cost effectiveness.

Number of total patient visits per gross square foot of facility space. This benchmark is an estimated measure of the adequacy of the student health service physical facility.

FTE health education staff per student. This benchmark is a measure of the level of health education staffing.

FTE mental health professional in student health services per student. This benchmark is a measure of the adequacy of mental health staffing for health services that provide mental health counseling.

Number of Pap smears per enrolled female student. This benchmark is a measure of the extent to which the student health service has made preventive health service available to all eligible female students and also to the subgroup of women who use the health service for any reason.

Number of students in full compliance with the ACHA recommended prematriculation immunization practices for two doses of measles vaccine, hepatitis B, and purified protein derivative (PPD) screening as a percentage of students. This is a measure of the effectiveness of the institution's prematriculation immunization requirements.

The benchmarking project also yielded detailed definitions to ensure as much consistency as possible.

The ACHA benchmarks will probably evolve because what is relevant in 1999 may not be as important in 2010, so it is critical for institutions to continue to engage in dialogue about what benchmarks are valid. It is also very important to identify truly comparable institutions. It will not be helpful or convincing for a small, rural college of twelve hundred students to compare itself to a large, urban university with a student body of twenty thousand (American College Health Association, 1999c).

Measure Effectiveness Against Professional Standards: Accreditation

Accreditation is a voluntary process through which an organization is able to measure the quality of its services and programs against nationally recognized standards. The certificate of accreditation is a symbol to others that the organization is committed to providing high-quality care and that it measures up to relevant professional standards.

Interestingly, professional standards for health services are not included in a substantive way in the standards of the Council for the Advancement of Standards in Higher Education. On the other hand, the ACHA has provided comprehensive standards and guidelines for college health since 1961. The most recent edition appeared in 1999 (American College Health Association, 1999b). In addition, two private agencies provide comprehensive standards for ambulatory health care services: the Joint Commission for Accreditation of Healthcare Organizations (JCAHO) and the Accreditation Association for Ambulatory Health Care (AAAHC).

Both JCAHO and AAAHC have a comprehensive and detailed set of standards for all areas of health service policy and practice. Administrative standards address governance, administration, rights of patients, quality improvement, risk management, and facilities issues. Clinical standards describe the elements needed to ensure the highest quality of care, excellence in clinical record keeping, and documentation. The accreditation standards define expectations in the areas of infection control, research, teaching, professional development for staff, and customer service. Specific guidelines have been developed for different aspects of service delivery, including comprehensive primary care, urgent and emergency care, overnight care, and occupational health services (Accreditation Association for Ambulatory Health Care, 1999; Joint Commission for Accreditation of Healthcare Organizations, 1998).

The standards and guidelines provide strong mandates for an organization that chooses to become accredited but can also provide guidance to those that do not choose to become accredited.

Assess Cost Effectiveness

Cost effectiveness issues are always critical to the survival and improvement of college health services. Chapter Thirteen provides a full description of assessing the cost effectiveness of health services.

A Health Services Case Study

Oakberry State College is a midsized state-supported primarily commuter institution, which has increased its enrollment by about 50 percent in the past ten years, primarily because of new on-campus residence halls. As a consequence, Oakberry now has approximately three thousand students in residence and about five thousand commuters.

Oakberry's health service was designed to meet the needs of an older, commuting population and offered limited health services. The health services were provided by a nurse practitioner director, a registered nurse, and a physician who saw patients on-site one half-day per week and provided telephone consultation and backup. Most students sought health care from community providers; they relied on Oakberry's health service primarily for minor ailments and emergency referral.

As enrollments increased over a ten-year period, student demands on health services increased. Younger residential students who had never sought care in the community expected more. They had health problems and expectations that were different from those of their commuting colleagues. Even the addition of another registered nurse five years ago had little impact. Despite an increase in staff, students were not seen in a timely manner, staff felt overburdened, and it was the impression of some that quality of care was suffering. Moreover, residential students demanded a more comprehensive type of care than commuters did.

The health service director asked the vice president for student affairs for an additional registered nurse to handle increased student demand for services. The vice president was reluctant to fund yet another staff member without a more thorough review of health services. Some thought Oakberry should get out of the health services business altogether and encourage students to join one of two managed care networks in the community. Others argued that Oakberry should provide more comprehensive health services to meet the expanded needs of residential students.

A comprehensive review of health services would involve many things: looking at patient use, determining cost effectiveness, considering other health care options, benchmarking with other comparable institutions, measuring student satisfaction with current services, assessing student needs, assessing quality of care, and other assessment strategies.

Step 1: Define the Problem

As enrollments at Oakberry increased and students changed, health services remained virtually unchanged The vice president correctly has asked for a thorough review of health services before she will commit additional resources. The problem is that in order for the vice president to determine the future of health services at Oakberry, she must first know the health and health service needs of students. After that initial assessment, other assessments may be necessary (for example, satisfaction, quality of care, cost effectiveness), but the beginning point of solving this problem is to assess the health needs of Oakberry students.

Step 2: Define the Purpose of the Study

The purpose of this study is to assess the health and health care needs of students at Oakberry State College.

Step 3: Determine Where to Get the Information Needed

Information about the health care needs of students can be gathered primarily from two different information sources: current health service records and students themselves. The type of health records kept will determine the best source of information. Appointment logs, billing records, or a computerized information system can all, in slightly different ways, provide a demographic profile of current users and their presenting health problems. Students can provide information about themselves through surveys or participation in focus groups or individual interviews.

Step 4: Determine the Best Assessment Method

Two different assessment methods could be used for the needs assessment part of this study. A thorough analysis of the demographics of current users and their presenting health problems will provide valuable information about the health problems of current health service users. However, an aggregate picture of the health needs of all students—health service users and, more important, nonusers—will require different methodologies.

A survey of a randomly selected population will provide one type of information, and individual and group interviews will complement that information. All three methodologies are worth pursuing at Oakberry.

The NCHA will help describe the aggregate health needs, risks, and behaviors for Oakberry students. It can provide incidence rates for specific behaviors or concerns and identify major significant risks and problems. Such information will help prioritize the health needs of the campus population.

In addition, focus groups and individual interviews will augment survey data with more detailed, contextual information. For many other needs assessments, focus groups alone might suffice, but some personal health care needs may be better communicated in a private, individual, and confidential setting, so individual interviews will add to what is learned in focus groups.

Step 5: Determine Whom to Study

Selection of focus group and individual interview participants will be extremely important. Representation of different groups of students will be especially important, given the changing demographics of Oakberry students. The following types of students should be included:

- Commuters
- Resident students
- Women
- Men
- Adult students

- Racial and ethnic minorities
- Students in each year (first, second, third, fourth, graduate)
- Health service nonusers
- Health service users

There should be at least one focus group and a minimum of three individual interviews for each of these categories. As reported in Chapter Four, each focus group should consist of five to ten participants.

Step 6: Determine How the Data Will Be Collected

Because of the confidentiality of student health records, health service personnel will collect data from current health service records. Data will be collected directly from students through audiotapes of focus groups and individual interviews.

Step 7: Determine What Instruments Will Be Used

As noted in Step 3, the actual source of the data will depend on the administrative systems in place at the college. Often appointment or billing records are the best source of this information. If absolutely necessary, clinical records can be the source. Abstracting the information from the clinical chart would be very inefficient and labor intensive, however.

Whatever the source, all of the benchmarking described earlier in this chapter should be charted:

- Total clinic visits per year
- Unique patient encounters per year
- Top ten diagnoses of patients seen with numbers for each diagnosis
- Number of visits in each clinical department (for example, walk-in clinic, appointment clinic, women's health)

For each of these components, demographic information should be obtained on patient age, racial or ethnic identity, marital status, class standing, and off-campus compared with on-campus status.

The focus group and individual interview protocol should include the following questions:

"What are your current health care needs?"

"How, if at all, are these needs being met?"

"What health services should this institution provide?"

"To what extent and in what way—that is, prepaid fee versus fee-for-service—would students be willing to pay for health services?"

"Any other comments about your health care needs?"

Step 8: Determine Who Should Collect the Data

Health service personnel must collect data from current health service records. For the focus groups and individual interviews, this issue becomes more complicated. Health service personnel are best equipped to interpret what students are saying about their health care needs and to probe for additional information, but they have a personal stake in the outcome of the study, so they may unintentionally interpret student comments in a biased way.

We recommend using health service personnel for individual interviews, because students may share confidential information. We also recommend using health service personnel to conduct focus groups, but with two additional requirements. First, a trained, upperclass student with knowledge of health services should be co-leader of the group. Second, when the transcripts of the focus group discussions are analyzed, there should be a broad representation of interpreters: health service personnel, students, other student affairs staff, faculty, and administrators.

Step 9: Determine How the Data Will Be Analyzed

Data gathered from health service records will be analyzed and summarized according to the format suggested above. Data from individual interviews and focus groups will be analyzed according to guidelines suggested in Chapter Four. Because of confidentiality concerns, someone who understands the meaning of medical confidentiality should transcribe audiotapes of individual interviews and the focus group sessions. Interpretation and analysis should be done from the transcripts.

Step 10: Determine the Implications of the Study for Policy and Practice

Several conclusions were reached regarding the health care needs of Oakberry students. From the analysis of health care records, it was obvious that use and types of problems varied a great deal by student demographics. Students of traditional age, living on campus, women, and whites were much more likely to use campus health services than were older, commuter, male, and minority students. Further, the types of problems they had were different. The findings of the focus groups and individual interviews confirmed these differences, which included the scope of services needed and potential sources of funding.

Based on this and other information produced by this study, the vice president appointed a task force of staff, students, faculty, administrators, and community representatives. The task force will move beyond this study to conduct a comprehensive assessment focusing on quality of care, scope of service, delivery models, and cost effectiveness and will make recommendations for the future.

Step 11: Report the Results Effectively

Upon seeing the results of the study, the vice president realized that a public and inclusive dialogue was needed to build a consensus on how to deliver health care to students. Summary reports were sent to various stakeholders, including the president, and task force members were instructed to conduct individual and group meetings with students, faculty, local health care providers, administrators, and health services personnel.

Conclusion

The situation at Oakberry State College is not unusual and illustrates how college health is a rapidly changing field, responding in large part to the changes in higher education and health care. By approaching the problem systematically and using basic evaluation methodologies, an initial needs assessment made clear what had to be done. Although the preliminary assessment and the further work of the task force would require significant time and other resources, the investment was a valuable one. A complete understanding of the health needs of the campus as well as a thorough analysis of the processes and systems of health care delivery at the college will help campus leaders make the best decisions for the future.

References

Accreditation Association for Ambulatory Health Care. *Accreditation Handbook for Ambulatory Health Care.* Skokie, Ill.: Accreditation Association for Ambulatory Health Care, 1999.

American College Health Association. *Healthy Campus 2000: Making It Happen.* Baltimore, Md.: American College Health Association, 1992.

American College Health Association. "College Health: A Model for Our Nation's Health." *Journal of American College Health*, 1993, 42, 77–78.

American College Health Association. *The American College Health Association National College Health Assessment, Pilot II, 1999: User's Manual.* Baltimore, Md.: American College Health Association, 1999a.

American College Health Association. *Guidelines for a College Health Program: Standards Division Workgroup.* Baltimore, Md.: American College Health Association, 1999b.

American College Health Association. "Recommended Benchmarks and Data Definitions for College Health." Unpublished document. Baltimore, Md.: American College Health Association, 1999c.

American Medical Association. *Current Procedural Terminology CPT.* (Standard ed.) Chicago: American Medical Association, 1999.

Brindis, C., and Reyes, P. "At the Crossroads: Options for Financing College Health Services in the 21st Century." *Journal of American College Health,* 1997, *45,* 279–288.

Core Institute. *Core Alcohol and Drug Survey User's Manual.* (6th ed.) Carbondale: Student Health Programs, Southern Illinois University, 1998.

De Armond, M., and others. "College Health Toward the Year 2000." *Journal of American College Health,* 1991, *39,* 249–252.

Jackson, M. L., and Weinstein, H. M. "The Importance of Healthy Communities of Higher Education." *Journal of American College Health,* 1997, *45,* 237–241.

Joint Commission for Accreditation of Healthcare Organizations. *1998–1999 Comprehensive Manual for Ambulatory Care.* Chicago: Joint Commission for Accreditation of Healthcare Organizations, 1998.

Medicode. *Physician ICD-9-CM.* Salt Lake City, Utah: Medicode, 1999.

Patrick, K., and others. "Principles for Assuring the Health of College Students: A California Perspective." *Journal of American College Health,* 1997, *45,* 289–293.

U.S. Public Health Service. *Healthy People 2000: National Health Promotion and Disease Prevention Objectives.* Washington, D.C.: U.S. Department of Health and Human Services, 1990.

Chapter 26

Assessing Career Services

Jack R. Rayman

IF STUDENTS ARE ASKED which of the many student services are most essential, placement services would probably rank high on their list, especially if they are seniors. If students with career indecision are asked (especially when pressures to select a major are bearing down on them), career counseling would be high on their list. And parents are now asking institutions with growing bluntness, "What exactly are we paying for?" and they measure the quality of higher education in terms of their children's ability to land secure and well-paying jobs (Pew Higher Education Roundtable, 1994). Clearly in the minds of students and parents, the need for career services is very high, although often cyclical. This chapter describes some of the problems associated with assessing career services, offers a comprehensive model to assess the very diverse and often segmented career services that exist in colleges and universities, and provides a case study.

Problems with Assessing Career Services

The first problem with assessing career services is defining them. There are probably as many definitions as there are institutions of higher education, ranging from comprehensive career development and placement services to one-person job placement operations. Rayman (1993) has identified seven broad career services functions:

> *Career planning and counseling:* individual career counseling, individual career assessment, computer-assisted career counseling, group career counseling, courses for credit, and others

Placement: on-campus recruiting, job listing services, placement advising, placement skill development workshops, résumé referral services, career days and job fairs, placement library, and others

Career programming: outreach programming and seminars, special topics workshops, programs for special populations (minorities, the disabled, women, gay, lesbian and bisexual students), experiential education programming, and others

Information support: placement library, career information, Web site information on employers, employer advisory boards, professional staff library

Communications: printed materials including office brochures, placement manuals, newsletters, radio and television spots, e-mail help addresses, telephone- and Web-based delivery systems of all types

Professional development and training: professional development and training programs for undergraduate and graduate student workers, part-time employees, clerical staff, professional staff, employers, and others

Assessment: postgraduation follow-up studies, employer satisfaction studies, evaluation of various career services functions, and others

Thus, it is likely that assessment of career services will not be one global assessment but rather a series of assessments based on individual functions and using multiple approaches. The most common misconception regarding the assessment of career services is that there is a definitive answer to the question, "What is your placement rate?" If nothing else, this chapter will demonstrate how simplistic and inappropriate that question is when applied to today's comprehensive career services.

Second, career services are sometimes centralized, sometimes decentralized into academic colleges and departments, and sometimes a combination of centralized and decentralized (Bechtel, 1993; Herr, Rayman, and Garis, 1993). Generally centralized career services are more easily assessed than decentralized services, whose purposes, functions, policies, and practices may vary substantially from college to college or department to department. For example, one academic unit may emphasize job placement, while another may focus on cultivating relationships with prospective donors through the placement process.

Third, career services may have varying reporting channels, including business services, student affairs, and academic affairs (Herr, Rayman, and Garis, 1993). Assessments may be substantially influenced by the explicit or implicit values inherent in each of these reporting channels. For example, student affairs is most likely to emphasize developmental outcomes, while academic affairs may be more interested in job placement, especially in the case of academic departments that are subject to accreditation guidelines. Since assessment always begins with defining the problem, the problem may vary according to reporting channel, and thus the whole assessment agenda may be quite different.

Fourth, at many institutions, individual and group career planning and counseling may be administratively separated from career placement services. For example, many comprehensive counseling centers include career planning and counseling, while placement services are often stand-alone units with no direct integration with career development. Thus, the assessment agenda may be quite different depending on where career development and career placement services are offered.

A Comprehensive Model for Assessing Career Services

Track Client Use of Services

Keeping track of who uses career services and programs is relatively easy with career placement services and individual and group career development services. More difficult is keeping track of who attends educational programs and who accesses career information. Nevertheless, the numbers of students using these services can be tracked through the use of technology (such as Web site counters and electronic counters) and with the support and commitment of a staff that understands the value of tracking all client services. Although accounting for the number and types of students who participate in broad career services areas (such as counseling, placement, and programming) may seem a rather dull and unimportant task, the careful examination and analysis of these summary data can lead to helpful and even startling conclusions with significant implications for service delivery. For example, here are some conclusions that can be drawn from the career services annual report of an actual university based on simple client tracking of service utilization (Pennsylvania State University, 1999):

> Despite the fact that the ratio of women to men enrolled at the university is nearly exactly fifty-fifty, women are more prone to use career counseling services in a ratio of about 65 percent to 35 percent.

> On the basis of their enrollment ratio, minority students are much more likely to use career services than majority students are.

Approximately 70 percent of the job interviews conducted on campus are for business and engineering students, in spite of the fact that business and engineering students account for less than 40 percent of the total enrollment.

The most frequently requested workshop topics are résumé preparation, interview skill building, and job search strategies.

Alumni seek career counseling in nearly the same numbers as do first-year students.

Contrary to conventional wisdom, liberal arts students are no more prone to seek individual career counseling than are engineering students.

Men are more than twice as likely as women to register for on-campus recruiting, yet women constitute more than half of the undergraduate population.

More than 100,000 hits are recorded on the Web page per month.

These and the many other conclusions drawn from simple tracking procedures have significant implications for service delivery, office policy, staffing, and resource allocation. The key here is that even these basic records can help document the demand for services, discover problems with regard to service delivery, and develop policies and practices to address these issues. A basic tracking system should be the cornerstone of every career services evaluation system.

Assess Career Planning and Counseling Needs

Career services needs are in a constant state of flux, so constant attention must be given to assessing client needs. How do we know what career information is needed? How do we know the career counseling needs of students? How do we know what group educational programs to offer? How do we know the needs of employers who screen, interview, and hire the institution's graduates? In this section these and other questions will be considered as they apply to the six broad service areas; then specific suggestions and concrete examples of how these needs can be assessed will be provided.

One of the most useful and least obtrusive ways to assess the career planning and counseling needs of students is to keep systematic records of client presenting problems. At many career centers, brief walk-in or intake counseling is offered. A record is kept of each intake session indicating the presenting problems, the recommended services, and the referral made. This information is entered into a computer at the end of each day, and a cumulative daily, monthly, and yearly record is produced. Examination of such simple but systematic intake records is especially valuable in determining what the most common presenting problems are, what day of the week and what weeks and months of the year problems are most like to arise, and the most frequently requested and provided services. Exhibit 26.1 contains a sample intake form completed for each client by the intake counselor.

Two other common ways to assess career counseling needs are by survey (telephone, e-mail, or mail) and by means of focus groups. Both forms take considerable planning, time, effort, and resources if they are to be done well, but both can yield useful results. Generally formal survey and focus group needs assessments of counseling and planning are conducted on an occasional basis only, for two reasons. First, experience has shown that there is a consistent student demand for these vital services and that this demand does not vary much over time. Second, with any survey of clients who have voluntarily availed themselves of counseling services, there is the issue of breach of confidentiality. That is, clients are guaranteed confidentiality when they elect to enter a counseling relationship. The simple act of identifying counseling clients for the purpose of conducting a survey or focus group itself constitutes a breach of confidentiality. Therefore, client needs assessments should be conducted sparingly and only when there is a compelling need to assess.

Assess Placement Needs

Because the need for placement assistance is usually assumed, little systematic needs analysis has been done in this area. Graduates of colleges and universities must go somewhere after graduation: full- or part-time employment; graduate, professional, or proprietary school; or some alternative placement such as the military, the Peace Corps, or retirement. Because of the wide range of possible placements, the type of placement assistance can vary greatly depending on the clientele being served. For example, a high percentage of the graduates of Ivy League institutions go on to graduate and professional school, and nearly all the graduates of associate degree technical programs go directly into the workforce.

Even within the same institution the placement aspirations (and therefore placement needs) of graduates vary widely. Graduates of engineering and business schools are predominantly career oriented, with 80 to 90 percent securing immediate full-time employment, while graduates of liberal arts schools are much more inclined to go to graduate or professional school (up to 80 percent at some institutions). Nearly all the graduates of colleges

EXHIBIT 26.1

Intake Career Counseling Form

Visit date: _____

Gender: ___ Male ___ Female

Age: ___ Under 18 ___ 18–22 ___ 22–25 ___ Over 25

Major: _____

Race/ethnicity (indicate all that apply):

___ African American ___ Hispanic ___ Asian American ___ White ___ Native American

___ International ___ Other (please specify) _____

Current status: ___ Undergraduate student ___ Graduate student ___ Alumnus or alumna

___ Faculty/staff ___ Employer ___ General public

If currently an undergraduate student, indicate total number of credits earned (not including
this semester): ___

Have you received services here before? ___ Yes ___ No

If yes, when? _____

Telephone: (   ) _____   E-mail address _____

Concerns: Check all that apply

___ Career planning	___ Job search
___ Decision about major	___ Résumé preparation
___ Internship	___ Graduate/professional school application
___ Summer job	___ Vocational/occupational information
___ Interview skills	___ Employer information
___ Correspondence (for example, letters of application, essays)	___ Other (please specify) _____

Disposition:

___ On-site intake assistance; no further referral needed

Referral to (check as many as apply):

___ Individual career counseling	___ Placement library
___ Career information center	___ Career exploration CD (for example, DISCOVER)
___ Workshop/educational program	___ Mock interview
___ On-campus recruiter scheduling	___ Career Services Web page
___ Summer jobs listing service	___ Other (please specify) _____
___ Referral to another campus agency (please specify) _____	

of science who aspire to be scientists must go on to graduate or professional school; to be a scientist requires an advanced degree. Although a small number of institutions conduct occasional student surveys or focus groups to ascertain the placement needs of their students better, most institutions assume that assistance of some sort with placement after graduation is desirable, and nearly every college and university in the nation provides some form of placement assistance. Generally survey or focus group needs assessments of placement services will focus on what type of placement services are needed rather than on whether placement services are needed.

Assess Career Programming Needs

The career programming needs of college and university students vary depending on placement, career planning, and counseling needs. In effect, career programming is a function of the career center that exists to meet the placement, career planning, and counseling needs that have been identified in some way.

There are three principal ways that career services practitioners determine what programs to provide: on the basis of theory, on the basis of prescription, and on the basis of customer survey results.

Theory

Many career centers offer certain programs because the theoretical literature regarding student career development suggests that such a program would be desirable developmentally. For example, Super's theory of career development (Super, 1957) suggests that all individuals go through a career life stage called exploration. In that stage, individuals systematically explore their own personal values, interests, abilities, and aspirations (internal exploration), and they also explore the many career options available to them (external exploration). On the basis of theory, then, we would expect that career centers should be offering an array of workshops, classes, and seminars that assist students in conducting systematic self-exploration. Such programs are often titled "Career Planning," "Starting Early to Plan for Career Marketability," or something similar. Similarly, internships, externships, career fairs, and cooperative education are useful means of assisting students to explore the world of work.

In a sense, theory provides a map of expected human behavior and needs that help career services offices to determine what programs will have utility for clients. (For a more detailed discussion of how theory should guide practice in the career center, see Rayman, 1993, Chapter One.)

Prescription

Externally determined standards like those of the Council for the Advancement of Standards in Higher Education (CAS) or the National Association for Colleges and Employers (NACE) are often the basis for the establishment of certain programs and services. For example, if the CAS Standards suggest that career centers should offer student workshops on résumé preparation, job search strategies, and interview skill building, most career centers will be predisposed to offer such workshops (programs) to their clients. Similarly, at times a dean, vice president, legislator, or other politically powerful individual will prescribe or require that a program be offered for political or other reasons. Often these prescribed programs have utility and are desirable—but sometimes they are not.

Survey

The most effective way that programming needs are determined is through the types of survey and evaluation described in previous sections of this chapter. Any assessment of career services needs will result in a determination that certain career programs are necessary to facilitate the delivery of placement services. In a 1999 survey of the most frequently requested (by students) programs at Pennsylvania State University, the following emerged as being most in demand (and presumably most needed):

- Orientation to Career Services (How to Take Advantage of the Services Offered)
- Career Planning for Undecided Students
- Job Search Strategies
- Résumé Preparation
- Interview Skills
- Internship and Summer Job Search
- Cover Letter and Other Correspondence
- The On-Site Interview: What to Expect
- Job Search for International Students
- Applying to Graduate and Professional Schools
- Multicultural Career Issues
- Finding a Job Abroad
- Making the Most of Career Fairs
- Career Issues for Women

Assess Information Needs

Information needs are similar to programming needs in that access to information is a by-product of the assessment of placement and counseling needs. The services offered are career placement, career counseling, and planning. Some form of information system must support these services. In years past, the major source of career information consisted of those career resources found in the career library: books, magazines, periodicals, professional association newsletters, chamber of commerce reports, corporate annual reports, Department of Labor publications and resource materials, and others. Today nearly all these materials are available on the World Wide Web. Indeed, the primary informational resource for today's career center is access to the Web for staff, students, and employers alike.

To my knowledge, there are no formal assessment devices for determining the information and information technology needs of a career center, but the following are strategies that some career centers have used to assess their information needs:

Benchmarking, that is, comparing the institution's information needs and system to those of peer institutions

Hiring an outside consultant

Forming a quality management team consisting of career center staff and faculty and staff from other units within and outside the college or university

Assess Communications Needs

Two basic communication needs exist within career centers. The first of these is the need for every staff member to have rapid, direct contact with multiple computer-based data files internal and external to the university. This is the institutional communication sometimes known as a management information system (MIS). High-quality, timely information is so crucial to the career services enterprise that many recent benchmarking and external review initiatives within the profession have focused on MIS infrastructure. In general, this need can be filled only if every staff member is equipped with a high-end personal computer fully loaded with word processing and spreadsheet software and full Internet access. Recent NACE surveys (Collins, 1998) indicate that more than 90 percent of NACE members are adequately equipped by this definition.

The second major communications need is for a sophisticated means of advertising and promoting career services and programs to the career center's customers, principally students and employers. To fill this need, most centers employ a comprehensive range of alternative communication strategies: student newspapers, placement manuals, career center newspapers, radio and TV spots, mass e-mail, chat rooms, individually directed e-mail, group orientation sessions, brochures, flyers, computer-based telephone messaging systems, and Web pages, among others. Recent surveys suggest that student newspapers continue to be a powerful communications tool, while Web pages and e-mail systems that push information to clients are becoming increasingly popular (Collins, 1998). As technology continues to change, assessment will play an important role in ensuring that career centers communication systems keep pace.

Assess Client Satisfaction

Student satisfaction with services and programs is the key to quality improvement. Nowhere is this more true than in a customer-focused enterprise such as career services. The techniques available for assessing client satisfaction vary in terms of their formality, complexity, and convenience, but a wide range of techniques must be employed if career services are to improve continuously. (See Chapter Ten for a more thorough discussion of assessing satisfaction.)

Advisory Boards

Advisory boards are not often thought of as elements of a strategy to assess client satisfaction, but if they are effective, they will assist in performing this function. Student advisory boards are the most important of such mechanisms, but many career centers also employ faculty and employer advisory boards as well. The key characteristic of advisory boards is that they are usually made up of consumers of the services of the career center. As such, their members interact with and relate to their peer consumers frequently and are thus in a position to represent views beyond their own about the quality of, appropriateness of, and satisfaction with career center services. Individual members, because of their dual role as both consumer and advisory board member, usually take a positive approach to providing feedback to center staff. Their vested interest in ensuring that the center provides the very highest-quality career service makes them a key source of satisfaction feedback.

Program Evaluation Forms

Another useful method of assessing client satisfaction is through the continuous and ongoing use of program and presenter evaluation forms. The generic group educational program evaluation presented in Chapter Seventeen (see Exhibit 17.1) can be adapted to evaluate career services programs. These forms have the advantage of a high response rate, particularly if the presenter stresses the importance of evaluating programs and the form is distributed and collected at the end of the program.

Recruiter Checkout Surveys

Corporate recruiters represent a crucial source of feedback about the quality and character of various elements of the on-campus recruitment process. Key among these elements are:

- The number of no-shows for interviews

- Students who might benefit from assistance with interview skills

- Suggestions and comments pertinent to placement service and accommodations

- Suggestions pertinent to the relevance of the curriculum in various academic programs

- General comments and suggestions

Feedback from such surveys provides useful support for planning changes in training programs, the curriculum, and placement policies and procedures. An example of a typical recruiter checkout survey is contained in Exhibit 26.2.

Suggestion Boxes

No one should ever overlook or undervalue this obvious and perhaps simplistic means of assessing customer satisfaction. In my experience, some innovative and useful ideas result from placing a suggestion box in high-traffic areas within the career center and providing users with easy-to-use forms with which to provide their suggestions (see Exhibit 26.3). Moving the suggestion box from one service area of the center to another from week to week or month to month has a tendency to stimulate user input. A modern version of the suggestion box is the electronic or virtual suggestion box, set up by inserting a suggestion form in the career center Web page that allows students to provide suggestions and feedback from remote locations.

Spot Evaluations

From time to time it is useful to identify a random sample of service users (students, employers, faculty, staff, or alumni), and send them customer satisfaction surveys by direct mail. Such spot evaluations can be extremely useful in evaluating the effectiveness of various existing services and modifying and improving services in accordance with client perceptions and expectations.

EXHIBIT 26.2

Recruiter Checkout Form

Your evaluation of our job placement service is very important to us so that we may continue to improve its quality. Please be assured that your responses are confidential and will be reported as summarized data used in future planning efforts by the institution. No individual data will be identified, and your participation is strictly voluntary. You may choose not to answer specific questions. You may also view the results by checking our Career Services Web page (http://www.careerservices.edu). We hope you will take this opportunity for your voice to be heard.

Company name _____

Recruiter name _____

Visit date _____

1. Please indicate any student who did not appear for his or her scheduled interview (without prior notification).

   Student Name   **Major**   **Interview Date and Time**

2. What was most impressive about your best interview?

3. Any suggestions pertaining to this institution's academic programs? Feel free to mention specific programs or majors.

4. Any other comments?

5. Which of the following helps you in recruiting students to your company (check all that apply)?
   ____ Participating in career fairs   ____ Sponsoring activities for departments
   ____ Participating in on-campus recruiting   ____ Sponsoring activities for students
   ____ Offering internships/co-ops   ____ Offering scholarships in departments
   ____ Placing ads in the student newspaper   ____ Offering grants to career services
   ____ Placing ads in the career services newsletter ____ Research collaboration with faculty
   ____ Meeting with faculty   ____ Holding general information sessions
   ____ Holding campus social events   ____ Personal correspondence with students
   ____ Holding meetings with student organizations ____ Guest lecturing in classes
   ____ Other (please specify) _____

6. Please indicate your use of the following recruiting methods for finding candidates for full-time positions:

Recruiting Methods	Never Use	Sometimes Use	Often Use	Always Use
Career fairs	_____	_____	_____	_____
On-campus recruiting	_____	_____	_____	_____
Internships/co-ops	_____	_____	_____	_____
Job postings (hard copy)	_____	_____	_____	_____
Job postings (Web)	_____	_____	_____	_____
Faculty referral	_____	_____	_____	_____
Other (please specify)				
_____	_____	_____	_____	_____
_____	_____	_____	_____	_____

7. How do this institution's candidates compare to candidates from other institutions?

Criteria	Worse Than Most	About the Same	Better Than Most	Not Applicable
Grade point average	_____	_____	_____	_____
Co-op/intern experiences	_____	_____	_____	_____
Extracurricular activities	_____	_____	_____	_____
Preparation for interview	_____	_____	_____	_____
Interview skills	_____	_____	_____	_____
Preparation in major	_____	_____	_____	_____
Relevant prior job experience	_____	_____	_____	_____

8. What, if anything, makes this institution stand out among schools at which you recruit (check as many as apply)?

____ Quality of academic programs   ____ Ease of recruiting process

____ Intern/co-op programs   ____ Responsiveness of Career Services staff

____ Variety of recruiting opportunities   ____ Geographical proximity

____ Facilities   ____ Efficiency of operation

____ Other (please specify) _____

Thank you for your assistance. We appreciate your interest in our students and look forward to your next visit to our campus.

EXHIBIT 26.3

Career Center Suggestion Box Form

WE'D LIKE TO DO A BETTER JOB!

Please give us your comments and suggestions

Date _____   Semester _____   Department _____

Which of the following career services did you use?

____ Intake counseling	____ Group counseling
____ Individual career counseling	____ Placement library
____ Career information center	____ Career exploration CD (such as DISCOVER)
____ Workshop/educational program	____ Mock interview
____ On-campus recruiter scheduling	____ Career Services Web page
____ Summer jobs listing service	____ Other (please specify) _____

Which of the services you used were the most helpful, and why?

Which of the services you used were the least helpful, and why?

How might career services be improved?

In general, how would you rate Career Services?

____ Poor ____ Below average ____ Average ____ Good ____ Excellent

If you would like to discuss your suggestions with us, please indicate the following information:

Name _____   Telephone _____   E-mail _____

Thank you for your suggestions.

These one-shot random satisfaction surveys are easy and inexpensive to administer, and if they are well designed and carried out within two weeks of the date services were rendered, they usually result in a high response rate. Alternatively, spot satisfaction surveys can be carried out by e-mail or telephone. Telephone surveys are more labor intensive but usually result in a very high response rate, and they allow for some give and take between the customer and the person conducting the survey.

Assessment by Walking About

Many management gurus (Slater, 1994; Garfield, 1992; Peters and Waterman, 1982) have advocated that a key to excellence is getting close to the customer. I know of few better means of assessing customer satisfaction than for the director and other staff members to get out on the front line, mingle with the customers (students and employer representatives), and listen to what they are saying. Often the best front-line position for feedback is that of the office receptionist or clerk. Few other experiences provide greater insight into the needs of customers than a short walk in the shoes of the customer or the front-line service purveyor.

Assess Client Outcomes

Perhaps the most important yet least addressed aspect of career services (or any other student service for that matter) is that of assessing client outcomes. How do the career services provided affect clients in the world at large? Do students who use career services perform better in the world of work than those who do not? Do career services have a positive effect on retention? Are students who use career services more likely to secure appropriate employment?

The most universally assessed outcome is the placement rate. Did graduates who were seeking employment secure employment? Nearly all career services use some type of simple follow-up study to secure this basic information. Career services follow-up surveys of graduates seek to determine two facts: what did the student do after graduation, and what services did the student use to accomplish that end? Thus, it is possible to conclude what percentage of graduates secured appropriate full-time employment, what their average starting salary was, and what percentage of them used the on-campus interviewing process to find their job. This is about as far as most career center–conducted postgraduation surveys go, but even these modest outcome studies can be invaluable when a comprehensive analysis is done by college, major, gender, ethnicity, or other parameters. By using the same methodology year after year and examining the data in these many different ways, meaningful longitudinal comparisons can be made that are helpful not only to prospective and enrolled students but to faculty, staff, and administrators as well.

A small number of career centers have begun to probe beyond simple placement rate to determine what impact the experience of higher education has on student success after graduation and what elements of the higher education experience (formal class experience, out-of-class activities, seminars, workshops, internships, cooperative education) had the largest impact on that behavior. (See Chapter Sixteen for a full discussion of post-graduation assessment and Chapter Eleven for assessing outcomes.)

Use Professional Standards to Assess Career Services

It may be useful to evaluate career services against external standards. In the case of career services there are two widely available sets of external standards: the CAS Standards (Council for the Advancement of Standards in Higher Education, 1997) developed by a consortium of student affairs professional associations (including the American Counseling Association, the American College Personnel Association, and the College Placement Council) and *Professional Standards for College and University Career Services* established by the National Association of Colleges and Employers (1998). The two sets of standards are remarkable similar, and either provides a useful benchmark against which career services can be compared. Both professional associations have developed user-friendly evaluation workbooks that make the evaluation task reasonably reliable, straightforward, and easy. Evaluation against either set of standards can be done by an external reviewer, internal staff, or both.

Compare Performance Across Organizations

There are two increasingly common methods of comparing performance across organizations: benchmarking and external reviews. These two techniques are enjoying increased popularity because of their value in assessing and comparing career centers along the seven functional areas specified by Rayman (1993) in terms of staffing, cost effectiveness, salary structure, funding sources, organizational structure, use of technology, reporting lines, and even office title.

Benchmarking

NACE has been conducting benchmarking surveys on behalf of its members for the past several decades. The results of its most recent survey appear in the winter 1998 edition of the *Journal of Career Planning and Employment*.

Although NACE has attempted to enhance the benchmarking value of its survey results to individual institutions by breaking it down by institutional size, the relatively low response rate (26.8 percent) limits its use as a benchmarking tool. Nevertheless, there is much to be learned from the NACE Career Services Surveys, and NACE is to be commended for continuing to support this effort. Perhaps the most valuable aspect of the survey is the picture that emerges from a comparison of current survey results with those of past surveys (1975, 1981, 1987, 1991, and 1993). Then, as Collins (1998) points out, "the evolution of the profession emerges in stark relief." These trends are knowledge that all career services directors must have.

Perhaps more useful to individual career centers are the regionally and individually conducted benchmarking surveys that have become quite common. For example, institutions belonging to the Big Ten Athletic Conference have done several benchmarking surveys in the past decade. Similarly, other conferences and associations of institutions with similar visions, missions, goals, and size have found benchmarking to be a valuable assessment tool. Clearly benchmarking will continue to be an important assessment tool for college and university career centers.

External Reviews

External reviews have become a popular assessment tool, especially if there is a perception that a career center needs to alter its mission, goals, and staff significantly. If the members of the review team are credible professionals, external reviews (assessments) can provide a powerful stimulus for change and service enhancement. Several of the regional NACE associations have established external review committees with the charge of conducting career center external reviews on request. The use of external reviews as an assessment tool will undoubtedly continue to increase.

Career Services Case Study

Career services at Maxwell State University are comprehensive and centralized. Like most other land grant institutions, Maxwell State has a large enrollment in the colleges of engineering, business, science, and agriculture. In fact two-thirds of the total enrollment of twenty-four thousand students at Maxwell State are in these four colleges. The career center, which is well established and supported by central administration, primarily provides services in placement, counseling, and programming.

For the past five years, the volume of traffic at the center has been stable. Annually more than five hundred different employers visit the campus and conduct approximately fourteen thousand on-campus interviews. The counseling staff of the center has been conducting about four thousand individual counseling appointments per year, and the programming staff has been reaching approximately ten thousand students through outreach programs. Student, faculty, and employer perceptions of the center have been quite positive.

Last year in an attempt to improve service and enhance efficiency, the center purchased and implemented a new Web-based information system (WBIS) that allows students to obtain career information and schedule job interviews using the Web. For example, a student may learn more about a particular career by going to the career services Web site and linking to a careers data bank. If the student wants more information about a prospective employer, that same Web site links to the Web sites of approximately five hundred companies. Students can even schedule their own job interviews and arrange for site visits. Further, if a student needs help in developing a job résumé or preparing for a job interview, the Web site has software that meets these needs. It is even possible to access a career decision-making software package from this Web site.

The system has been well received by students, who can now access many of these career services remotely from computer terminals located across campus or their own computers. Students seem pleased with the convenience of the new system, but in general, there has been a decline in student use of career counseling and student attendance at outreach programs. Further, there has been 20 percent decline in the number of students who sign up for on-campus interviews.

The close association between the implementation of the WBIS and the onset of these disturbing trends seems more than coincidental, yet the staff are uncertain about how to proceed.

Step 1: Define the Problem

The problem is that there appears to have been a decline in the use of career services (counseling, outreach programs, and on-campus job interviews) since the implementation of the WBIS. These trends are particularly disturbing because the primary mission of career services is to help students with career decisions and match them with prospective employers in ways that meet both employer and student needs.

Although there is some reason to believe that there is a cause-and-effect relationship between these trends and the implementation of the new WBIS, there has been no systematic assessment to determine if in fact they are related.

Step 2: Define the Purpose of the Study

The purpose of this study is to determine what relationship, if any, the implementation of the new WBIS has to the documented decline in the use of career services.

Step 3: Determine Where to Get the Information Needed

Undergraduate students who have used career services will be the primary source of information for this study.

Step 4: Determine the Best Assessment Method

Most often quantitative methods are better used to determine what is happening, and qualitative methods are better used to determine why it is happening. In this case, however, given the sampling and data collection problems described below, a quantitative approach was used to determine why these trends were occurring.

Step 5: Determine Whom to Study

Determining whom to study on the surface seem relatively simple: select a sample of students who accessed career services in traditional ways (scheduling appointments with career counselors, attending career outreach programs, and scheduling on-campus job interviews) and compare their reasons for choosing this alternative with a sample of students who accessed these same services from the WBIS. The problem is that although there are reliable ways of identifying students who used traditional services, there is no way of identifying individual students who accessed the WBIS. The WBIS could calculate how many students used the system and when they used it but could not identify individual students or the reasons for their use.

Although there was no ideal solution, the decision was to select a fairly large, random sample of approximately three thousand undergraduate students, knowing that most of them would not have used career services at all. Sometimes it is necessary to cast a fairly large sampling net in the hope of snagging a few appropriate subjects—in this instance, those who had used career services.

Step 6: Determine How the Data Will Be Collected

Several alternatives were considered, but in the end a Web-based survey was selected for several reasons. All students at Maxwell have computer accounts and e-mail addresses, increasing the likelihood of a good response rate. Further, the large sample size made telephone interviews or mailed surveys prohibitively expensive. (See Chapter Eight for more specific information on Web-based data collection.) The data were collected toward the end of the spring semester. This time period was chosen because data collection is much more difficult if the time span covered is more than one academic year.

Step 7: Determine What Instruments Will Be Used

Exhibit 26.4 contains the Web-based survey that was used to gather information from students in the sample. This survey is traditionally formatted so that it may be used as either a telephone or mailed survey. (For information regarding formatting Web-based surveys, see Chapter Eight.)

Step 8: Determine Who Should Collect the Data

The computer consultant hired by the career services center sent out the survey and compiled the responses, under the direction of the associate director of career services.

Step 9: Determine How the Data Will Be Analyzed

The data were analyzed by using the Statistical Package for the Social Sciences data analysis statistical package. Comparisons of responses were made by demographic characteristics as well as by WBIS users, non-WBIS users, and users of both. About six hundred usable responses were returned, which analyses revealed were representative of Maxwell students. Although this 20 percent response rate is small, the anticipation was that most of the three thousand students sampled would not have used career services at all. The response rate was high enough to allow for comparisons by demographic characteristics.

Step 10: Determine the Implications of the Study for Policy and Practice

The results of this study were quite interesting. First, the level of satisfaction of those who used WBIS and those who used traditional services was about the same. Second, there were many students who used both, depending on the service offered. For example, students needing career counseling were much more likely to use a career counselor rather than the career decision-making software. On the other hand, students who needed only simple information tended to use the WBIS more than traditional career services.

EXHIBIT 26.4

Career Services Web-Based Survey

Thank you for linking to this Web site to participate in a survey designed to improve the quality of services offered by the Office of Career Services and to compare traditional career services with those offered by our new Web-Based Information System (WBIS). You are one of the randomly selected Maxwell students to be contacted for this voluntary five-minute survey. Please be assured that your responses are confidential and are reported as summarized data used in future planning efforts by Career Services. No individual data will be identified, and you may choose not to answer specific questions. You may also see the survey results in about four weeks on the Career Services Web site (http://www.careerservices.edu). If you have any questions, please contact [name] in Career Services at [address], or by telephone [telephone number] or e-mail [e-mail address].

    I hope you will taken this opportunity for your voice to be heard.

1. Have you used career services during this academic year (fall or spring semesters)? ___ Yes ___ No
If you clicked "No" on this question, please click here to return the survey. ___

2. During this academic year (fall and spring semesters), which career services have you accessed, using non-WBIS services, and if used, what is your level of satisfaction? (If none, click here ___)

Service	Very Dissatisfied	Dissatisfied	Neutral	Satisfied	Very Satisfied
___ Accessed information about employers	___			___	___
___ Scheduled a job interview	___	___	___	___	___
___ Submitted a job application	___	___	___	___	___
___ Submitted my résumé to a prospective employer	___	___	___	___	___
___ Accessed information about careers	___	___	___	___	___
___ Accessed information about majors	___	___	___	___	___
___ Accessed career-decision-making counseling	___	___	___	___	___
___ Accessed information about the Career Services Center	___	___	___	___	___
___ Accessed help in writing a résumé	___	___	___	___	___
___ Accessed help in developing interview skills	___	___	___	___	___
___ Other (please describe)					
_____	___	___	___	___	___
_____	___	___	___	___	___

EXHIBIT 26.4

Career Services Web-Based Survey, continued

3. During the past academic year (fall and spring semesters), which WBIS career services have you used, and if used, what was your level of satisfaction? (If none, click here ____)

WBIS Service	Very Dissatisfied	Dissatisfied	Neutral	Satisfied	Very Satisfied
____ Linked to employer Web pages	____	____	____	____	____
____ Scheduled a job interview	____	____	____	____	____
____ Submitted a job application	____	____	____	____	____
____ Submitted my résumé to a prospective employer	____	____	____	____	____
____ Accessed information about careers	____	____	____	____	____
____ Accessed information about majors	____	____	____	____	____
____ Accessed the career-decision-making software program	____	____	____	____	____
____ Accessed information about the Career Services Center	____	____	____	____	____
____ Accessed the résumé preparation software program	____	____	____	____	____
____ Accessed the interview skills software program	____	____	____	____	____
____ Other (please describe)					
_____	____	____	____	____	____
_____	____	____	____	____	____

4. If you accessed any career services using WBIS during this academic year, why did you choose the WBIS? (Click on all that are appropriate)
   ____ More convenient
   ____ Greater accuracy of information
   ____ Access to more information
   ____ Took less time
   ____ More privacy
   ____ More personal control
   ____ Dissatisfaction with traditional Career Services
   ____ Other (please describe)

5. If you did not access career services using WBIS during this academic year, why not?

___ Didn't have computer access to WBIS

___ Didn't know about WBIS

___ Didn't know how to use WBIS

___ Prefer services delivered by people, not computers

___ Tried once but got frustrated

___ Other (please specify)

6. Any additional comments?

7. Please tell us a little about yourself

Gender: ___ Male ___ Female

Class Standing: ___ First year ___ Second year ___ Third year ___ Fourth year

Residence: ___ On campus ___ Off-campus apartment ___ Home

Major: (Please indicate) _____

Race/ethnicity (check all that apply):

___ African American ___ Asian American ___ Caucasian ___ Hispanic ___ Native American

___ Other (please specify) _____

Thank you for your help.   **Click here to return survey** ___

Click to clear form

Second, convenience, accuracy, and time saved were the primary reasons students used WBIS, and personalized attention was the overwhelming reason students preferred traditional career services. Third, computer access was not a barrier to nonuse, much to the relief of those who feared that some economically disadvantaged groups would be excluded from receiving WBIS services. And finally, in general, men, upperclass students, and majority students were more likely to use WBIS than other groups.

Through a careful analysis of the data, it was determined that students who used WBIS were much less likely to access career services through traditional delivery modes. Thus, it appeared that the implementation of WBIS was related to the decline in student use of career counseling, outreach programs, and placement services. But the fact that overall there were no differences in the satisfaction level between WBIS users and nonusers somewhat relieved the concern that students were somehow being shortchanged by using the WBIS.

Because users, nonusers, and users of both delivery systems had been identified, further studies with each of these cohorts became possible.

Step 11: Report the Results Effectively

This study was not reported to the general public, because it was felt that the results were very preliminary, and much more study was needed before any conclusions could be drawn. A report was compiled and made available to the career services staff and administration, as well as the vice president for student affairs. A plan for further study was developed that included individual interviews and focus groups of several of the cohorts identified by the study.

Conclusion

I have asserted elsewhere (Rayman, 1999) that pressures to cut costs have "forced career centers into a range of activities to justify their existence as never before. Assessment, focus groups, benchmarking, external reviews and other means are increasingly being employed to demonstrate the efficacy of career services. We have entered an era of accountability never before experienced in higher education. If we wish to survive this era, we will need to do a better job of advocacy and we will also have to become more efficient and innovative in our use of existing resources." Thoughtfully designed and executed assessment strategies will be the cornerstone on which the career centers of the new millennium will be built.

References

Bechtel, D. S. "The Organization and Impact of Career Programs and Services Within Higher Education." In J. R. Rayman (ed.), *The Changing Role of Career Services*. New Directions for Student Services, no. 62. San Francisco: Jossey-Bass, 1993.

Collins, M. "Snapshot of the Profession: Results of the 1997 Career Services Survey." *Journal of Career Planning and Employment*, 1998, 58(2), 32–36, 51–55.

Council for the Advancement of Standards in Higher Education. *The Book of Professional Standards for Higher Education*. Washington, D.C.: Council for the Advancement of Standards in Higher Education, 1997.

Garfield, C. (1992). *Second to None: How Our Smartest Companies Put People First*. New York: Avon Books, 1992.

Herr, E. L., Rayman, J. R., and Garis, J. W. *Handbook for the College and University Career Center*. Westport, Conn.: Greenwood Press, 1993.

National Association of Colleges and Employers. *Professional Standards for College and University Career Services*. Bethlehem, Penn.: National Association of Colleges and Employers, 1998.

Pennsylvania State University. *Career Services Annual Report.* University Park: Pennsylvania State University, 1999.

Peters, T. J., and Waterman, R. H. *In Search of Excellence: Lessons from America's Best-Run Companies.* New York: Warner Books, 1982.

Pew Higher Education Roundtable. "To Dance with Change." *Policy Perspectives,* 1994, *5*(3), pp. 1A, 12A. Philadelphia: Institute for Research on Higher Education.

Rayman, J. R. (ed.). *The Changing Role of Career Services.* New Directions for Student Services, no. 62. San Francisco: Jossey-Bass, 1993.

Rayman, J. R. "Career Service Imperatives for the Next Millennium." *Career Development Quarterly,* 1999, *48,* 175–184.

Slater, R. I. *Get Better or Get Beaten: Thirty-One Leadership Secrets from GE's Jack Welch.* Burr Ridge, Ill.: Irwin, 1994.

Super, D. E. *The Psychology of Careers.* New York: HarperCollins, 1957.

Chapter 27

Assessing Counseling Services

Dennis Heitzmann, Kenneth L. Nafziger

PSYCHOLOGICAL COUNSELING centers face a serious and continuing dilemma. In spite of the substantial number of students on college and university campuses who are seeking treatment for serious psychological problems (Gallagher, 1999; Levine and Cureton, 1998; Pledge and others, 1997), counseling centers across the country have been under enormous pressure to contain costs, do more with less, and demonstrate their value to the institution.

Levine and Cureton (1998) make a compelling case for the existence of the "frightened student." Student respondents to their national survey cited fear of victimization, violence, and instability, as well as emotional, sexual, and financial problems. The reality is that more students in college today than ever before are suffering from serious emotional conditions that run the full spectrum of diagnostic disorders. According to Archer and Cooper (1998), "Compared with students in the past, students today arrive on campus with more problems as a result of dysfunctional family situations, with more worries and anxieties about the future and about the serious problems facing them in modern society, with an increased awareness of their own personal demons, and with a greater willingness to seek psychological and psychiatric help" (p. 6). The bottom line is that students are coming to college overwhelmed and more damaged than those in previous years. It comes as no surprise that students are seeking counseling services in record numbers. Consequently, in the absence of significant additional funding and staff, waiting lists for treatment in college counseling centers seem to be a sign of the times. The need for psychological services has never before been greater.

With increased demand for counseling services comes the challenge of fiscal reality on our campuses. Even in a robust economy, it is incumbent on administrators to demonstrate sound fiscal management and any unit's worth from an economic standpoint. Certainly during leaner economic periods, and even today, reports that collegiate administrators are reducing or even eliminating psychological services are not surprising. The questions are all too familiar. Just what responsibility does an institution have to students whose problems interfere with their ability to develop academically and socially? In any case, what systematic evidence is there (other than scattered anecdotal reports) to demonstrate that students who receive psychological services actually get better? And if they do, are they better students? In sum, what value is added to the lives of students and to the institution at large by the presence of counseling services?

On the whole, counseling centers have adapted well to these pressures. Long-term therapy has been significantly curtailed and replaced by shorter-term therapy and off-campus referrals for students with chronic or entrenched problems. Group therapy, a treatment of choice for many students, also provides an efficient alternative to more expensive individual services. Intake procedures have been streamlined to ensure immediate accommodation for students in crisis and to expedite referrals to individual therapy and groups. "Quality improvement" and "customer satisfaction" have become more comfortable additions to the clinician's lexicon. Nonetheless, despite improvements in clinical service delivery systems, there remains a compelling need to demonstrate the inherent value of a center's programs and services, not only in support of individual students but also in support of the mission of the institution. This chapter outlines responses to these institutional pressures, demonstrates programmatic methods to evince the continuing value of counseling centers on campuses, and presents a case study.

Problems with Assessing Counseling Services

In certain respects, assessing counseling services presents more challenges than almost any other student service. For instance, in order to maintain credibility with clients, the centerpiece of any counseling center must be the ethical (and legal) commitment to confidentiality. Thus, any approach to assessment must first respect that principle. The resultant limitations to program assessment are clear: certain types of information about clients will simply not be available. To illustrate, if we are assessing the effectiveness of a leadership program for student leaders, we can bring them together in a focus group and ask key questions about their leadership training experience, with little or no concern about the anonymity or confidentiality of those participating. The same would not be true for clients who received individual therapy without seriously violating basic principles of confidentiality.

Second, there may be a difference of opinion between therapists and the institution regarding the essential purposes and goals of therapy in a collegiate setting. Many good therapists would argue that their goal is to enable clients to recover from their troubled states and to become mentally healthy individuals, irrespective of the impact on their enrollment status. Many good administrators, on the other hand, would argue that colleges are educational institutions, not rehabilitation agencies, and the primary purpose of therapy should be to enable students to go to class, succeed academically, and persist to graduation.

Third, there has been a long tradition in many counseling centers to cooperate with faculty research projects. While such collaborative efforts may well engender solid collegial relationships and inform relevant research in the fields of clinical, social, and counseling psychology, there may be no immediate or clear impact on the improvement of counseling services for students. Given a paucity of discretionary time for research and assessment projects, centers must carefully balance the selection of studies that would most likely provide useful information in support of the center's mission, while cooperating in faculty-based research.

Finally, because waiting lists are sometimes long and the pressures to provide treatment and ancillary activities are great, assessment is usually assigned a lower priority. When faced with the choice to deal with a student in crisis or to analyze some client assessment data, no competent therapist would compromise the student in pursuit of the data. On the other hand, in the absence of current and continuing systematic evidence of the effectiveness of a counseling center, the very existence of the center could be brought into question. The reality remains that sometimes counselors must do the things they must do in order to survive and thrive, so that they can do the things they want to do: serve the best interests of students. Counselors may be confident that they make important contributions, but they must demonstrate that they do so through data management, action research, and accountability studies.

All things considered, it behooves a counseling center to conduct assessments that demonstrate its worth to the institution in providing the highest-quality services to students. We believe it is possible to conduct such studies in ways that resolve the contextual problems. The emphasis in this regard is on practical assessment—assessment that demonstrates the value-added contribution of a counseling center to various audiences, studies performed in a timely and cost-effective manner, and assessments that are packaged to appeal to often disparate audiences with different questions about the relevance and effectiveness of a counseling center. Finally, it is important that assessment be pursued without compromising the services being delivered to student consumers.

This chapter provides an array of assessment initiatives: initiatives that may be of utilitarian value in response to a mandate, initiatives that allow a center to anticipate questions about a center's functional value, and initiatives that serve to assure students (and the institution) that they are getting the very best return on their investment in counseling services.

A Comprehensive Model for Assessing Counseling Services

Although we are affiliated with a large, public, research institution, we believe that virtually all of the elements of the model we present can apply to smaller sites as well. Client demographics, student clinical needs, satisfaction surveys, outcome research, assessing campus climates, benchmarking, and adhering to professional standards are no less important to counseling services in smaller colleges and universities than they are to large, comprehensive, research institutions. All of the material presented in this chapter may be customized to the unique and special needs of mid- to small-sized counseling services. Moreover, given the model and some creativity, the assessment program may apply to any institution where counseling may be defined as psychological, counseling, career choice and planning, or academic advising.

Track Client Demographics and Types of Problems

Unlike some other student affairs units that are more limited in identifying student users (such as recreation facilities and student unions), counseling centers can identify their clients, describe their demographic characteristics, and categorize their various psychological problems. Such information can be used in several ways, but tracking usage statistics is particularly relevant. For most centers, systematically collecting clinical data and reporting in aggregate form is the most important form of assessment information to be made available. Inherent in the data are answers to myriad questions of interest to proponents and critics alike. For instance, an academic dean who is worried about anecdotal reports of distressed students may wish to know the proportionate number of students from his college who have sought counseling services. The director of a center for women students may wish to know if there has been a rise in students presenting with eating disorders, so as to suggest programming for her constituency. A vice president for student affairs may need broad-based counseling center data for an upcoming presentation to the board of trustees. A colleague director may want to know about the percentage of the total population of students who are seen annually in counseling.

Sheer numbers of students using counseling services are useful indexes for various reasons. Low numbers may indicate that potential clients do not know about the services, and if they do, they may choose not to use them for reasons about which the counseling center should know more. On the other hand, high numbers and long waiting lists may indicate the need to realign or expand resources to meet increased demand.

Identifying the types of students who use services may provide answers or stimulate compelling questions worth answering. Are users representative of the student population, and if not, which groups of students are underrepresented? For example, it is not unusual for juniors and seniors to use counseling resources at a higher rate than first-year students. Yet student success is very much dependent on a successful transition to college, and it is likely that counseling centers can be a powerful influence during this critical period. Thus, a disproportionately lower number of first-year student clients may suggest that the counseling center should reconsider its services in the light of this apparent missed opportunity.

In considering the establishment of data streams, it is important to note that the data be comprehensive but also tailored to the needs of the target audience. It is valuable to know about varying levels of problem severity among clients at intake if the goal is to improve a clinical service delivery system. However, the dean of the college of engineering may be more interested in knowing about the relative incidence of students seeking services from academic departments under his or her purview.

A useful array of demographic information would include gender, age, racial and ethnic background, nationality, marital status, class standing (first year, sophomore, and so forth), college and major, and primary referral sources. With these baseline data, a director and staff are better prepared to address a rather broad spectrum of potential questions and concerns.

Assess Student Clinical Needs

Fundamental to the success of any treatment modality is the assessment of client needs. The initial diagnostic impression of a student seeking counseling services becomes the basis for the substance and type of therapy. However, assessing the counseling needs of students in the aggregate is a totally different process, and one not usually accomplished by the traditional means, such as needs surveys and focus groups. (It is impossible to imagine a survey in which students are asked what psychological problems they have and how those problems could be solved.) An obvious (and more reliable) approach is to identify these needs by analyzing the types of problems presented by clients and determining what is needed to resolve these problems.

Categorization by client presenting problem can be useful in strategic planning, analyzing trends, and program offerings, as well as budget and human resource allocation. For example, a few decades ago virtually no one sought help for eating disorders. Today a substantial portion of services is devoted to treating students with this concern. In response to this trend, most counseling centers have hired therapists with specialized training in this area, revised staff development efforts to include eating disorders, offered educational programs, and the like. If there is an increase in students with attention-deficit disorder, these students may not only need therapy but may also profit from medication or environmental accommodations. This means that the counseling service must consider a plan to establish treatment responses to include counseling, medication (through a staff psychiatrist or referral), and consultation and advocacy on behalf of the student if the student's needs are to be met.

Assessing student counseling needs, then, most often ensues from an analysis of the aggregate needs that arise in the therapeutic process rather than employing more traditional survey measures. At the very least, some categorization of presenting concerns ranging from a simple "personal, academic, or career" classification may be useful, but more highly differentiated diagnostic categorizations based on the fourth edition of the *Diagnostic and Statistical Manual of Mental Disorders (DSM-IV)* (American Psychiatric Association, 1994) would be more illuminating. The *DSM-IV* has the advantage of being understood in many mental health service settings, but the disadvantage of not documenting certain types of problems specific to counseling centers. Counseling centers that want to take a more site-specific approach may find helpful the multivariate classification system described by researchers at the University of Missouri-Columbia (Heppner, Kivlighan, Good, and Roehlke, 1994). Centers that wish to take a more holistic approach may consider tracking subjective well-being in addition to distress, as advocated by Schlosser (1996). Schlosser's subjective health process model (SHPM) includes a family of related instruments to assess the components of the SHPM. Schlosser's assumption is that counseling may independently improve a client's distress without necessarily addressing issues of well-being. Both lack of distress and positive signs of health are important for students to function optimally in an academic environment.

Assess Student Satisfaction

A systematically administered satisfaction survey affords valuable information about a counseling service. The opportunity to get the direct self-reports of student consumers not only about their experience with counseling but also about their experience with the center in general is a useful planning and accountability tool. Following are the standard items in a consumer satisfaction survey:

- Services received (individual, group, psychiatric, testing)

- Length of wait to see a counselor for a first appointment

- Referral to another agency for continued counseling (if yes, indicate which, and with whom)

- Length of treatment

- Self-reported improvement ratings

- Items related to comfort with and expertise of counselor

- Items related to the ambiance of the center, including reception services, waiting room, and telephone contacts

- Things the counselor did that were helpful or harmful

- Opportunities for open-ended comments, including positive and negative experiences with the center and the services received

Exhibit 27.1 contains a suggested posttherapy evaluation based on these general criteria.

Assessing the outcomes of individual and group therapy has long been a difficult problem for therapists and counseling centers, but recent efforts have been quite encouraging. After Howard, Kopta, Krause, and Orlinsky (1986) brought dose-response studies to the attention of psychologists, efforts have been underway to document changes as they occur over time. Tracking the progress of individual clients helps to address when to terminate and when to refer a client for additional therapy. The use of brief instruments that may be quickly scored by computer or scan sheets (such as the Brief Symptom Inventory, Derogatis and Spencer, 1982, and Outcome Questionnaire–45, Lambert and others, 1996) expedites administering more frequent measures that provide more immediate information to the therapist and the client. An even better approach to documenting outcomes is multisite studies such as those undertaken by the Research Consortium of Counseling and Psychological Services in Higher Education, which recently

EXHIBIT 27.1

Evaluation of Counseling Services

Year: _____   Code # _____

In an effort to evaluate and improve our counseling services, the staff would like you to respond to the following questions. The evaluation form should take about fifteen minutes to complete. All of your responses will be treated confidentially. The form is coded so that we can follow up if you do not respond and so that we can use the code rather than your name in our data analysis. The staff person you saw will not have access to your individual survey. Your answers will be reported only as part of the aggregated group of survey responses, and your identity will not be disclosed, even to your counselor.

1. What type of services did you receive this past year (check all that apply)?
   ___ Intake only (preliminary meeting for evaluation and/or referral)
   ___ Follow-up individual counseling: approximate number of times you met with your counselor (please check one)

   ☐ 1–3 times   ☐ 4–6 times   ☐ 7–10 times   ☐ 11–15 times   ☐ Other _____
   ___ Group therapy
   ___ Psychiatric services: evaluation or medication follow-up

2. Approximately how long did you have to wait to see a counselor for the intake appointment?
   ☐ immediate   ☐ 1–3 days   ☐ 4–6 days   ☐ 1 week   ☐ 2 weeks   ☐ 3 weeks
   ☐ 1 month   ☐ more than 1 month

3. After the intake, how long did you have to wait to see your counselor for your first individual counseling?
   ☐ immediate   ☐ 1–3 days   ☐ 4–6 days   ☐ 1 week   ☐ 2 weeks   ☐ 3 weeks
   ☐ 1 month   ☐ more than 1 month

4. Following your services, were you referred to another agency or person for continued counseling?
   ☐ Yes   ☐ No   ☐ If yes, please specify:
   ☐ Community mental health center
   ☐ Psychology training clinic
   ☐ Private therapist (specify) _____
   ☐ Psychiatric/rehabilitation hospital
   ☐ Private psychiatrist
   ☐ Other _____

(please circle one)	Very Dissatisfied	Dissatisfied	Neutral	Satisfied	Very Satisfied	Not Applicable
5. How satisfied were you with the services you received from the referral agency or person?	1	2	3	4	5	NA

EXHIBIT 27.1

Evaluation of Counseling Services, continued

(please circle one)	Poor	Fair	Good	Very Good	Excellent	Not Applicable
6. How would you have rated your well-being when you started counseling?	1	2	3	4	5	NA
7. How would you have rated your well-being at the end of your counseling?	1	2	3	4	5	NA

(please circle one)	Of No Help	Of Little Help	Somewhat Helpful	Helpful	Very Helpful	Not Applicable
8. Do you feel that the counseling you received was helpful in your remaining at this institution?	1	2	3	4	5	NA
9. Was the counseling you received helpful in improving your academic performance?	1	2	3	4	5	NA

(please circle one)	Poor	Fair	Good	Very Good	Excellent	Not Applicable
10. How effectively were the following diversity issues addressed in your counseling?						
a. Race/ethnicity	1	2	3	4	5	NA
b. Gender issues	1	2	3	4	5	NA
c. Spiritual issues	1	2	3	4	5	NA
d. Disability	1	2	3	4	5	NA
e. Sexual orientation	1	2	3	4	5	NA
f. Other (please comment) _____						

11. If you are not currently using this agency's services, for what reason(s) did you stop (check all that apply)?

☐ I felt counseling had helped me solve the problem.
☐ I felt I could handle things on my own.
☐ I reached the agency's session limit.
☐ My counselor and I agreed I was ready to stop.
☐ My counselor decided it was time to stop.
☐ My counselor was not helpful.
☐ I did not want to work on my concerns at the time.

☐ I was not satisfied with my progress.

☐ Circumstances made it impossible to continue counseling (examples: dropping out of school, moving, schedule problems, end of semester).

☐ I was referred to another agency for counseling.

☐ I preferred counseling elsewhere.

☐ Other specify) _____

COUNSELOR EVALUATION

12a. Did you receive follow-up counseling at this agency (after your intake)?   ☐ Yes   ☐ No

If no, skip to question 20. If yes, we would like you to share your opinion about your counselor's performance by circling the numbers that best fit.

(please circle one)	Poor	Fair	Good	Very Good	Excellent	Not Applicable
12b. How well do you feel you and your counselor worked together?	1	2	3	4	5	NA
13. How capable or expert as a counselor did he or she seem to be?	1	2	3	4	5	NA

(please circle one)	Strongly Disliked	Disliked	Neutral	Liked	Strongly Liked	Not Applicable
14. How well did you like your counselor as a person aside from his or her expertise?	1	2	3	4	5	NA

(please circle one)	Of No Help	Of Little Help	Somewhat Helpful	Helpful	Very Helpful	Did Not Take Tests
15. I found the results of the tests I took during counseling to be:	1	2	3	4	5	NA

(please circle one)	Poor	Fair	Good	Very Good	Excellent	Not Applicable
16. How would you rate your total counseling experience at this agency?	1	2	3	4	5	NA

17. Please describe anything your counselor did that was particularly helpful?

18. Please describe anything your counselor did that was particularly harmful.

19. If you needed further help, would you return to your counselor?   ☐ Yes   ☐ No

EXHIBIT 27.1

Evaluation of Counseling Services, continued

CENTER EVALUATION

(please circle one)	Strongly Disagree	Disagree	Neutral	Agree	Strongly Agree	Not Applicable
20. I felt the information I disclosed would be held confidential.	1	2	3	4	5	NA
21. I would recommend the services of this agency to other students.	1	2	3	4	5	NA

(please circle one)	Very Dissatisfied	Dissatisfied	Neutral	Satisfied	Very Satisfied	Not Applicable
22. Consider the overall services of the agency, not only the person you saw for counseling. How satisfied have you been with the services you received?	1	2	3	4	5	NA

23. Rate each of the following items related to the general services of the agency.

	Poor	Fair	Good	Very Good	Excellent	Not Applicable
a. Initial impression	1	2	3	4	5	N.A.
b. Reception area	1	2	3	4	5	N.A.
c. Forms	1	2	3	4	5	N.A.
d. Reception staff	1	2	3	4	5	N.A.
e. Telephone contacts	1	2	3	4	5	N.A.

Please feel free to add comments about items 20 through 23 above _____
_____
_____

Please take this opportunity to express your feelings, either positive or negative, about your experience with this agency. We encourage you to be completely open and candid since this is the only way we can evaluate ourselves and initiate improvements. Use the back of this sheet if needed.

_____
_____
_____

completed a nationwide survey of clients and their therapists at over one hundred institutions. This collaborative effort at collecting and analyzing data provides useful information that is widely generalizable and assists sites that do not have time to devote to their own programmatic studies. Being part of these studies allows comparing an individual center's results to the aggregate. Consequently, more evidence is accruing for the effectiveness of college counseling centers.

Even if there is credible evidence that the therapeutic process has been successful (by whatever clinical criteria are applied), some critics of counseling centers have insisted on demonstrating the relationship between the therapeutic process and students' educational goals. It is no longer enough to show that clients solved their problems; it must be demonstrated that solving these problems is related to these students' educational progress and success. One very crude (but surprisingly effective) way is to ask them. For instance, a five-point Likert scale from "not a factor" to "a major factor" could be used in response to the following questions:

"Did you feel that the counseling you received was helpful in your remaining at [name of institution]?"

"Did you feel that the counseling you received was helpful in improving your academic performance?"

These two simple items can become powerful tools when significant numbers of students respond that the counseling they received was a major factor (a score 4 or 5 on the item) in improving their academic performance or keeping them at the institution.

Using multi-item scales and multiple measures is even better to reduce mono-operation and mono-method bias (Cook and Campbell, 1979). Researchers at the Iowa State University Counseling Service have begun to document a relationship between scores on the Quality of Life Survey and student retention. Following the lead of Iowa State University, other counseling centers may begin to document such a relationship with the various instruments employed in their own settings.

Assess Campus Climates and Environments

As suggested in Chapter Twelve, assessing campus climates and environments can provide useful information for student services, programs, and facilities. Although it is not the sole responsibility of counseling centers to assess campus climates and environments, it is important for such assessments to be designed and analyzed in ways that provide information useful to counseling centers. For example, if an assessment of the climate for women on campus reveals that women who have been sexually assaulted are reluctant to report such incidents or do not know where to turn for help, the implications for counseling services are substantial and direct. Thus, it behooves a counseling center to have a voice in determining which environmental assessments are conducted, how they are conducted, and how the results are analyzed and used. Although it is not expected that a counseling center will be solely responsible for campus global assessments, it is important to be participants in the development of campus climate surveys and other institutionwide assessments that serve to inform the counseling center while encompassing a broader set of interests.

Compare with Other Counseling Centers: Benchmarking

Having a view to comparable counseling centers is another valuable source of information. Information about client presenting problems, waiting lists, new therapies, assessment practices, scheduled and kept client sessions, size of staff, budget allotments, salaries by position and length of experience, and the like can be useful in strategic planning, professional staff development, salaries and administrative practices, and policies and procedures. Two prominent national surveys have been important resources for counseling center directors and their staffs for many years. The College and University Counseling Center Directors Data Bank (Magoon, 1999) and the National Survey of Counseling Center Directors (Gallagher, 1999) provide comprehensive comparative data and information on topics of relevance to any center concerned about its position on various dimensions in relation to comparable centers. Some regionally based organizations offer similar surveys (one is the Big Ten University Counseling Centers Annual Survey). Participation in either or both surveys provides routine annual comparisons, which allow a center to ascertain regularly how it is doing compared to similar settings, to anticipate trends, and to make adjustments accordingly.

Measure Effectiveness Against Professional Standards

Counseling centers are among the core services included in the professional standards developed by the Council for the Advancement of Standards (CAS) (1986). While CAS standards may be helpful to counseling centers, the accreditation process developed by the International Association of Counseling Services (IACS) (2000) is considerably more comprehensive and the accreditation process far more influential. The purpose of the IACS has been "to encourage and aid counseling services throughout the United States and internationally to meet high professional standards, to inform the public about those which are competent and reliable, and to foster communication among counseling services operating in a variety of settings."

For nearly fifty years, IACS has measured hundreds of university and college counseling centers by standards established for collegiate counseling services. The process involves self-study, completion of application materials for review, and an on-site evaluation by IACS representatives. Among the areas that IACS considers are the following:

- Relationship of the center to the university or college community
- Counseling services roles and functions: individual and group counseling and psychotherapy, crisis intervention and emergency services, outreach programming, consultation services, research, and training
- Ethical standards
- Counseling services personnel: qualifications and competencies
- Professional development
- Physical facilities
- Size of staff and workload
- Staffing practices, compensation, and salary

The value of accreditation is fourfold: there are inherent benefits to a staff's common pursuit of the accreditation process; pursuit of accreditation serves as an opportunity to demonstrate openness to review and criticism; a successful accreditation review certifies quality in service delivery; and a well-timed and accurate critique rendered by an accreditation agency can be useful in support of a center's efforts to pursue institutional support for quality improvements.

Finally, for certain mid- to large-sized centers, the development of an internship in professional psychology accredited by the American Psychological Association (APA, 1996) is another way to measure a center's effectiveness in relation to professional standards. Similar to IACS, APA conducts a site visit and requires annual reports on the internship training program at these centers. Although the emphasis is on the center's training activities, implicit within the review is that the center is functioning at acceptable levels in all service delivery areas.

Assess Cost Effectiveness

Certainly many counseling centers have been under enormous pressure to provide more cost-effective services, and in some cases services have been reduced because of budget constraints. Because many of the budget issues are similar to those in health services, readers are referred to Chapter Thirteen.

Off-Campus Counseling Referrals Case Study

The Typical College Counseling Center (TCCC) has experienced many of the same problems as most other counseling centers across the country: increased student demand for services, increasing numbers of more seriously and chronically disturbed students, longer waiting lists, and no additional resources. As a result of this situation, the TCCC set reasonable time limits for treatment, offered more group treatment, and began referring students with chronic, entrenched problems to a for-profit psychological clinic located off campus and staffed by licensed private practitioners. This referral system assumes that TCCC has thoroughly examined this clinic to determine if it is an appropriate referral resource. Exhibit 27.2 contains a form used to gather information about such referral resources.

After a student is seen at intake by a college therapist and if it is determined that the current resources at the TCCC are inadequate to meet the therapeutic needs of that student, then with the signed permission of the student, a referral to the local psychological clinic is made. Records are transferred, and the intake therapist discusses the case with clinic professionals. Follow-up contact may be made after the first appointment, but the reality is that there is no further assessment of whether the client's needs were met.

At a recent counseling center staff meeting, the coordinator of clinical services expressed concern about the TCCC's failure to determine the effectiveness of this referral program. She was concerned that no follow-up procedure was in place to determine if clients were being properly treated. She felt strongly that the lack of systematic tracking of referrals raised serious legal and ethical questions. The director of the center and the staff agreed that an assessment of the referral program should be done within the next three months.

There are many options for assessing this off-campus referral system, including documenting the demographics of students who are referred and their presenting problems, assessing referred student satisfaction, assessing differences in outcomes between retained and referred clients, benchmarking with other counseling centers to compare number and types of referrals, and documenting staff time saved and benefits to students from this referral system. For this particular case study, however, the decision was to focus on comparisons between the posttherapy evaluation of retained and referred clients and reviews of selected cases referred off campus.

Step 1: Define the Problem

When a counseling center refers a student after intake to an off-campus provider, it is assumed that the center has some interest in this client's welfare even after the referral is completed. The absence of systematic evidence

EXHIBIT 27.2

Mental Health Referral Sources Information Survey

Name: _____

Degree: _____

Agency/practice: _____

Title (for example, psychologist): _____

Address: _____

Telephone _____

E-mail: _____

May we give this e-mail address to referrals?   Y   N

Licensure and specialty training (for example, American Association of Marital and Family Therapists or American Board of Professional Psychology): _____

Professional memberships: _____

Sex: F   M   Years of experience: _____   Is your office accessible to persons with disabilities? Y   N

Circle regular hours you provide services: Weekdays   Evenings   Weekends   On Bus Line? Y   N

Populations preferred (check all that apply):

1. ___ Adolescents
2. ___ Adults
3. ___ Athletes
4. ___ Children
5. ___ College students
6. ___ Persons with disabilities

7. ___ Gay/lesbian/ bisexual/ transgendered
8. ___ International
9. ___ Multicultural (ethnic/race)
10. ___ Older adults
11. ___ Other _____
12. _____

Assessments (check all that apply):

1. ___ Cognitive/IQ
2. ___ Learning disabilities
3. ___ Neuropsychiatric
4. ___ Personality
5. ___ Projective

6. ___ Vocational/ Career
7. ___ Attention deficit disorder, attention deficit/ hyperactivity disorder
8. ___ Other ___
9. _____
10. _____

Treatment Modalities Provided

1. ___ Art
2. ___ Brief
3. ___ Couples
4. ___ Children
5. ___ Family
6. ___ Groups, types:

7. ___ Individual
8. ___ Long-term
9. ___ Music
10. ___ Play
11. ___ Other _____
12. _____

Managed Care Panels (Eligible for payment)

1. ___ Aetna
2. ___ BlueCross/ BlueShield
3. ___ Champus
4. ___ Green Spring
5. ___ Health Assistance
6. ___ Horizon
7. ___ Magellan

8. ___ Medical Assistance
9. ___ United Behavioral Health
10. ___ Value Behavioral Health
11. ___
12. ___
13. ___
14. ___

EXHIBIT 27.2

Mental Health Referral Sources Information Survey, continued

Clinical/Treatment Interests

1. ___ Adjustment disorders
2. ___ Attention deficit disorder, attention deficit/hyperactivity disorder
3. ___ Addictions
4. ___ Anger management/violence
5. ___ Anxiety disorders
6. ___ Career concerns
7. ___ Drug and alcohol
8. ___ Eating disorders

9. ___ Grief/loss disorders
10. ___ Health psychology
11. ___ Identity disorders
12. ___ Learning disabilities
13. ___ Men's issues
14. ___ Mood disorders
15. ___ Pain disorders
16. ___ Personality disorders

17. ___ Psychiatric
18. ___ Rape
19. ___ Relationship issues
20. ___ Religious/spiritual concerns
21. ___ Sexual abuse
22. ___ Sexual disorders
23. ___ Sexual orientation

24. ___ Sleep disorders
25. ___ Sports psychology
26. ___ Stress management
27. ___ Trauma
28. ___ Women's issues
29. ___ Other
    _____
    _____

Theoretical Approaches/Techniques

1. ___ Adlerian
2. ___ Behavioral
3. ___ Brief/solution focused
4. ___ Cognitive
5. ___ Cognitive/behavioral

6. ___ Developmental
7. ___ EMDR
8. ___ Existential
9. ___ Feminist
10. ___ Gestalt

11. ___ Humanistic
12. ___ Hypnosis
13. ___ Interpersonal
14. ___ Jungian
15. ___ Psychodynamic

16. ___ RET/REBT
17. ___ Reality
18. ___ Transactional
19. ___ Other ___
    _____

What is your standard fee? _____

Do you have a sliding-fee scale? **Y N**   If yes, what is the fee range? _____

Do clients need to pay up front? **Y N**   Do you submit insurance forms for your clients? **Y N**

Do you collaborate with psychiatric providers and see clients who require psychiatric medications or treatment? **Y N**

Would you be interested in providing a professional development presentation for the counseling center staff? Y N

If yes, what topics might you be interested in presenting (use back for additional space)? _____

_____

Return to Research Coordinator.

of what happens to the client after the referral at the least creates an information vacuum that prevents a center from developing confidence about the value of alternative services for its students. At worst there may be detrimental consequences to the referred client, and some legal ramifications in the event that harm occurs to the client as a result of the referral.

Step 2: Determine the Purpose of the Study

The overall purpose of this study is to determine the effectiveness of the off-campus referral program by determining if referred clients receive effective treatment that meets professional standards from off-campus service providers. Psychological providers who accept referrals from the TCCC should be informed that some of the clients referred to them will receive posttherapy evaluations just as the TCCC clients do.

Step 3: Determine Where to Get the Information Needed

Information will be gathered from two sources: the referred clients themselves and the private service provider's client records.

Step 4: Determine the Best Assessment Method

For information collected directly from referred clients, a quantitative approach will be used. The same posttherapy instrument (see Exhibit 27.1) that retained clients use will be administered to referred clients. For the qualitative study, a review of the records of the private service providers will be undertaken to determine if they are in compliance with usual and customary professional record-keeping practices.

Step 5: Determine Whom to Study

All students who received treatment in residence or at the off-campus clinic during the current academic year will be participants in the quantitative part of this study. For the review of clinical records of those receiving treatment from the off-campus clinic, a random sample of twenty case records will be reviewed.

Step 6: Determine How the Data Will Be Collected

For the quantitative study, data will be collected by paper-and-pencil instruments administered to all student clients, regardless of where they were treated. For the case review, information gathered from a random sample of service providers' client records will be reviewed by the counseling center's clinical staff in the same way as resident clients' records are reviewed, thus verifying appropriate protocols of treatment.

Step 7: Determine What Instrument Will Be Used

For the quantitative part of this study, a posttherapy evaluation instrument will be used. Many examples of instruments used in college counseling centers are available at a Web site provided by the Counseling Center Village at the Office (http://ub-counseling.buffalo.edu/ato.html). Second, a general instrument based on our home site, Penn State University, is included in Exhibit 27.2. Finally, a copyrighted assessment is available from Greenfield and Attkisson (1989) that has been used in programmatic research by the Research Consortium. All of these instruments generally include a measure of satisfaction with the services provided, the physical environment, the professional knowledge and competence of the counselor, the contribution of the service to well-being, the decrease in debilitating symptoms, and the arrangements for crisis interventions if needed. In addition, we recommend asking how much the services contributed to the student's retention in school and the impact on his or her academic performance. One version of this last question is contained in Exhibit 27.1.

For the case review, Exhibit 27.3 contains the quality control guidelines for charting standards by which record keeping and case planning will be evaluated.

Step 8: Determine Who Should Collect the Data

Designated counseling center staff will distribute and retrieve the posttherapy evaluation instruments. One of the issues is timing. Clearly the best results are found if the client is asked to evaluate services as soon after termination as possible. This does not, however, necessarily address long-term outcome, since a three- or six-month follow-up is recommended to confirm how well the client has maintained improvements. Designated counseling center staff will also review copies of the clinical records from the off-campus provider for the case review, allowing for the confidential coding of records as stipulated by ethical guidelines for research by both the American Psychological Association and the American Counseling Association.

Step 9: Determine How the Data Will Be Analyzed

Analyzing the data from the posttherapy evaluation instrument will begin with a comparison of mean outcomes of retained and referred clients. Since the TCCC did the initial intake assessment and referral, a pretherapy Global Assessment of Functioning (GAF) score is available from Axis V of the *DSM-IV* along with a pretherapy score on a standardized instrument

EXHIBIT 27.3

Quality Assurance Checklist

In/Out Policy

All charts are to be returned to the refile bin by the end of each workday. NO EXCEPTIONS. Counselors do not own the charts; they are the property of the agency and should never be taken off the premises or kept in a counselor's office or mailbox overnight.

Any staff member may access the files at any time to pull a chart, but MUST complete an out card for that chart and place it in the designated out card area.

Staff members are NOT permitted to refile their charts. This is to be done by the staff assistants only to minimize the number of loose documents and maximize the completeness of charts.

Condition/Order of Charts:

All records should be kept in chronological order in each section, with the most recent note on top. There are to be no loose papers in the charts at any time, including sticky notes and phone messages. Ideally, these messages should be converted to a brief note and placed in the file. If it is necessary to keep these messages, they must be stapled to a progress note or another sheet of paper to avoid being lost. Papers are to filed *behind* the appropriate tabs, not in front.

Progress notes need to be complete, including the client's full name, the date (including the year), and the counselor's name. There should be no blank lines. Any corrections should be crossed out with a single line and initialed, and the counselor must sign his or her name at the bottom of each note. A signature at the top of the note will not suffice. Black ink should be used when writing notes, because blue ink does not copy or fax well.

Definitions of Each Category:

Progress notes includes ongoing group notes, individual therapy notes, and summaries.

Psych./Medical includes all psychiatric care documents, such as the psychiatric evaluation form, the typed evaluation, labs, blue referral form, and typed progress notes from psychiatric providers. This makes it easier for the psychiatric providers to locate pertinent information that they need for each session.

Psych./Evaluations includes the typed intake evaluation and psychological assessments.

Forms/Correspondence includes the intake form, consultation form, diagnosis and disposition form, authorization to release information form, and copies of any letters sent to or received from students.

Past Records includes any correspondence relating to *outside treatment*. This could be current records, not necessarily past records.

Note: *The categories reflect essential policies, although the procedures may vary from agency to agency.*

(such as the Brief Symptom Inventory or Outcome Questionnaire–45). Because most students referred off-campus are expected to have more severe or longstanding problems, the results should be analyzed using an analysis of covariance with GAF or the pretherapy assessment score as the covariate (Cook and Campbell, 1979). Ideally, the sites could provide periodic assessments during the course of therapy using a standard outcome instrument (for example, the Outcome Questionnaire–45 has been used by the Research Consortium of Counseling and Psychological Services in Higher Education), and dose-response curves could be analyzed using individualized growth curve analysis (see the hierarchical linear modeling approach described by Bryk and Raudenbusch, 1992). It may, however, be unreasonable to expect multiple sites to provide repeated measures at multiple intervals. At least three waves of data collection would be needed for each client in order to provide more meaningful results than the ANCOVA. For simplicity, the ANCOVA is recommended as the more practical and feasible approach.

For the case review, the percentage of notes that included essential items may be recorded by reviewers. The overall percentages may be reported in descriptive statistics, and any differences may be discussed in terms of their practical (as opposed to statistical) significance. We would expect a high level of compliance to quality record keeping in both settings.

Step 10: Determine the Implications of the Study for Policy and Practice

The assessment addresses the concerns about whether referred clients are satisfied with services received and are improved in their psychological functioning in patterns similar to the group of students who are retained for treatment at the TCCC. The results of studies such as this one can provide compelling evidence to support the TCCC administration's efforts to improve referral practices. Since it has become increasingly common for college counseling centers to use community providers in certain instances, it is incumbent on each center to demonstrate the ease and efficiency of referral, verify that linkage has occurred between the private provider and the student clients, and gauge the level of satisfaction and improvement experienced by the referred client. Moreover, the qualitative review of records will reassure the TCCC that professional record-keeping protocols are being followed by community clinical service providers. Ultimately the counseling center will be better able to convey to all concerned parties that when a referral is made, it is being done in a safe and efficient manner in the best interest of the student.

Step 11: Report the Results Effectively

Both TCCC staff and those at the referred agency should receive a report of the quantitative assessment and case reviews. The availability of a written report would serve as a starting point for follow-up discussions on existing practices and recommendations for improvement. Ideally, discussions related to the results would yield closer liaison between the center and referral sources and improved services for students referred to the community. Annual report data should indicate not only the percentage of students who are referred off campus but also the degree to which referred students report both satisfaction with services received and improvement in functioning.

Conclusion

In spite of the fact that counseling centers have captive audiences for which extensive records are kept, assessing counseling centers is a unique process compared to most other student services. Although the task is challenging, this chapter has presented many ways in which counseling center effectiveness can be assessed within the constraints of confidentiality and other ethical considerations.

Undoubtedly, student self-reports on the impact of counseling on retention and academic performance provides the TCCC with a strong argument for adequate funding to continue to serve students while supporting the institution in tangible ways. To retain students at a considerable savings to the institution and contribute to a student's academic performance underscores the important role that the counseling center plays in service to the university's mission. Continuing improvement efforts and the ability to demonstrate a value-added contribution to the university allow any center to maintain and improve its important role on campus.

References

American Psychiatric Association. *Diagnostic and Statistical Manual of Mental Disorders.* (4th ed.) Washington, D.C.: American Psychiatric Association, 1994.

American Psychological Association. *Guidelines and Principles for Accreditation of Programs in Professional Psychology.* Washington, D.C.: American Psychological Association, 1996.

Archer, J., and Cooper, S. *Counseling and Mental Health Services on Campus: A Handbook of Contemporary Practices and Challenges.* San Francisco: Jossey-Bass, 1998.

Bryk, A. S., and Raudenbusch, S. W. *Hierarchical Linear Models: Applications and Data Analysis Methods.* Thousand Oaks, Calif.: Sage, 1992.

Cook, T. D., and Campbell, D. T. *Quasi-Experimentation: Design and Analysis Issues for Field Settings.* Boston: Houghton Mifflin, 1979.

Council for the Advancement of Standards for Student Services/Development Programs. *CAS Standards and Guidelines for Student Services/Development Programs.* College Park, Md.: Council for the Advancement of Standards for Student Services/Development Programs, 1986.

Derogatis, L. R., and Spencer, P. M. *The Brief Symptom Inventory: Administration, Scoring, and Procedures Manual—I.* Baltimore, Md.: Clinical Psychometric Research, 1982.

Gallagher, R. P. *National Survey of Counseling Center Directors.* Alexandria, Va.: International Association of Counseling Services, 1999.

Greenfield, J. K., and Attkisson, C. C. "Steps Toward a Multifactorial Satisfaction Scale for Primary Care and Mental Health Services." *Evaluation and Program Planning,* 1989, *12,* 271–278.

Heppner, P. P., Kivlighan, D. M., Good, G. E., and Roehlke, H. J. "Presenting Problems of University Counseling Center Clients: A Snapshot and Multivariate Classifications Scheme." *Journal of Counseling Psychology,* 1994, *41,* 315–324.

Howard, K. I., Kopta, Krause, M. S., and Orlinsky, D. E. "The Dose-Effect Relationship in Psychotherapy." *American Psychologist,* 1986, *41,* 159–164.

International Association of Counseling Services. *IACS Accreditation Standards for University and College Counseling Centers.* Alexandria, Va.: International Association of Counseling Services, 2000.

Lambert, M. J., and others. *Administration and Scoring Manual for the Outcome Questionnaire (OQ-45.2).* Stevenson, Md.: American Professional Credentialing Services, 1996.

Levine, A., and Cureton, J. S. *When Hope and Fear Collide: A Portrait of Today's Student.* San Francisco: Jossey-Bass, 1998.

Magoon, R. *Data Bank: College and University Counseling Centers.* College Park: University of Maryland Counseling Center, 1999.

Pledge, D. S., and others. "Stability and Severity of Presenting Problem at a University Counseling Center: A Six-Year Analysis." *Professional Psychology: Research and Practice,* 1997, *29,* 386–389.

Schlosser, B. "New Perspectives on Outcomes Assessment: The Philosophy of Subjective Health Process Model." *Psychotherapy,* 1996, *33,* 284–304.

Chapter 28

Assessing Greek Life

ONE OF THE MOST perplexing aspects of student life at virtually any institution that has fraternities and sororities is their role in the life of a campus. Members of these organizations are criticized regularly for behavior antithetical to the purposes of higher education in general, and substance abuse problems are reported widely in the literature as well as the popular press (Whipple, 1998). To their credit, however, members of Greek letter organizations have longstanding commitments to philanthropic endeavors as collegians, and graduates frequently are extremely active supporters of their alma mater through their service and their treasure.

Because of the pressure placed on these organizations, their advisers, and campus administrators, it is clear that assessment may play an important role in strengthening fraternities and sororities. A number of documents have been published regarding standards for these organizations (Shonrock, 1998), but evidence that indicates that these proposals have had an influence on curbing the abusive behaviors that occur too often in these organizations still is lacking.

Assessment activities can be very useful in demonstrating the extent to which initiatives to improve Greek life are effective. Moreover, a body of literature exists that indicates that Greek life does not contribute to the academic purposes of higher education (Pascarella and Terenzini, 1991; Astin, 1993; Kuh and Arnold, 1993), and for these organizations to remain viable, steps need to be taken to recast Greek organizations as learning communities (Whipple and Sullivan, 1998).

This chapter identifies problems associated with assessing fraternities and sororities, provides a model for assessing fraternities and sororities, and then presents by a case study with an analysis of an approach to address the situation presented.

Problems Associated with Assessing Greek Life

Some special problems are associated with assessing Greek life. Among these is that these organizations are private and secret in nature. If any assessment being conducted does not have the sincere, wholehearted cooperation of the leadership and the members, the chances that it will be meaningful are reduced. In times of duress, members of Greek letter organizations can take almost a passive-resistant approach to cooperating with the institution, and trying to accomplish anything meaningful in the way of an assessment can be extremely difficult. For example, if the members will not complete questionnaires or participate in focus groups, the study may be doomed to fail.

Not only the collegians can be difficult to work with; members who have graduated but continue to be active in chapters can be as difficult or worse. Although the institution may have some leverage with active members, it has almost no way of securing the cooperation of recalcitrant graduates. If the graduates do not want to cooperate or encourage the collegians not to cooperate in an assessment, the study is in serious trouble.

Another problem for some institutions is that the Greek houses are located off campus, on private property. This means that the relationship between the campus and the Greek letter organizations is no different from the relationship with any other student organization. Again, issues of cooperation arise. If the organization chooses not to cooperate, it will be very difficult to develop meaningful assessments.

From time to time, Greek organizations publish studies that put them in a very positive light. Some of these studies, while poorly done, have the effect of obfuscating the truth. For example, Greeks may publish on an annual basis a report that the all-Greek grade point average is higher than the all-campus average. On the surface that may true, but what also may be true is that during-college variables that affect grade point average may not have been taken into account in the study, including precollege indicators such as American College Testing and Scholastic Aptitude Test scores, high school grades, and socioeconomic status, and perhaps more important, during-college variables such as the number of hours worked per week, major, involvement in campus activities, and place of residence. (For a more thorough list of pre- and during-college variables that are related to student academic success, see Chapter Eighteen.) Often when these variables are taken into account, the comparison of grade point averages reveals a very different story. This campus folklore can be difficult to overcome.

Finally, at some institutions, influential friends and benefactors were members of Greek letter organizations as undergraduates. These individuals may apply pressure on the institution to drop an assessment project before it gets started, particularly if the assessment is likely to reveal negative information about the fraternities and sororities. This sort of problem can be very difficult to overcome.

A Model for Assessing Greek Life

The conceptual perspective on how to assess various student affairs offices and services can be applied to fraternities and sororities as well. This applies to organizations that are members of Interfraternity Council (IFC), Women's Panhellenic Association (WPA), and National Pan-Hellenic Council (NPHC). Although the fraternities and sororities may vary in their purposes, this model can be applied successfully to members of any of these organizations.

Know the Members of the Organizations

Good assessment practice begins with knowing who uses the services and why. In the case of Greek letter organizations, basic information about the members—their demographic characteristics, their grade point averages, their majors, and so on—will be helpful. Normally this information is collected through the submission of rosters and applications to participate in rush activities. Nonetheless, the Greek affairs office should make a point of providing a semester-by-semester list of Greek membership to senior administrative officers in the institution in addition to chapter officers and advisors.

In addition to the demographic summary, trend data can be useful. Are Greek letter organizations growing, shrinking, or staying constant in size? How do the grades of their members compare with the all-campus average? Do they persist at rates consistent with the rest of the student body? This form of assessment typically answers these questions and others.

Assess Student Needs

Needs assessment in the case of Greek letter organizations can be a little difficult to address, since the direct experience of members is affected by what goes on in the individual chapters. Still, a variety of services are provided by the Greek affairs office, such as leadership development experiences; coordination or advising of Greek week activities; advising the IFC, WPA, and NPHC; training and advising the various conduct boards; and so on. Important work also is done with chapter advisers and alumni and alumnae groups in the area. As a consequence, needs assessment can be quite important with the students who are directly served by the office. Additional services and support may be provided directly to the members, and an assessment of these needs would be important in program planning.

Assess Satisfaction with the Greek Affairs Office

Needs assessment and satisfaction assessment go hand in hand. As needs are assessed and interventions and services planned, then client (student, graduate, and so on) satisfaction needs to be assessed. Are advisers available to deal with student concerns? Do they provide support for the organizations? Do they understand the concerns raised by graduates? Do they confer with leaders before making decisions? These questions and others can form the basis of satisfaction assessment.

Besides questions related to the satisfaction with staff and the office in general, specific assessment ought to be conducted related to large-scale initiatives that are supported by the office. Among these would be satisfaction assessments with rush, Greek week, homecoming activities, and scholarship support initiatives. These activities should undergo routine assessment, and using a satisfaction assessment is a solid approach.

Assess the Culture of Greek Organizations

Kuh and Arnold (1993) have provided an excellent model of a study of Greek culture. These kinds of studies are difficult to conduct for a variety of reasons (see Whitt, 1996), but they can be very useful in terms of understanding student life. The factors and conditions that lead to certain behaviors (a strong climate that supports academic excellence or a climate that stresses social activities) can be addressed in such studies. Typically these need to be done by insiders and outsiders, and they can be especially useful if concerns are raised about the quality of life in Greek letter organizations.

Assess the Outcomes of the Greek Experience

One of the concerns expressed about involvement in Greek letter organizations is the extent to which they support cognitive development and academic achievement (Kuh, Branch Douglas, Lund, and Ramin-Gyurnek, 1994). With questions being raised about the Greek experience, one of the ways of determining the effect of the experience is to conduct an outcomes assessment. Holding all precollege experiences constant, does the Greek experience enhance or impede academic development or cognitive growth? Do students who participate in Greek letter organizations develop a view of the world consistent with the institution's mission? Are they more likely to engage in philanthropic activities? These questions and others that can be tied directly to the institution's mission statement can answered through outcomes assessment.

Apply Professional Standards

Miller (1997) served as the editor for the most recent version of the professional standards for student affairs, *The Book of Professional Standards for Higher Education*. Guidelines are provided for fraternity and sorority programs and are very useful in conducting a self-study. Among these guidelines is an assertion that assessments be conducted regularly in Greek affairs.

Sorority Life Case Study

Sorority life at Great Plains State University has been one of the most robust experiences for women at the university over the years. Membership has been highly regarded by most and prized by many, and the women have taken an approach that allows any woman to join a sorority on campus as long as she participates in rush and maintains a minimum grade point average. Ten sororities comprise the WPA system on campus, and the average membership is sixty women per house. This system has been quite egalitarian and is highly regarded throughout the region as a model system. Alumnae support has been very strong at Great Plains, and collegians agree that the quality of sorority life appears to be strong. Nevertheless, problems have emerged.

Three years ago, the number of women who held active membership in the sororities began to decline. Rush was as successful as ever before, but women started to drop out of their sororities as early as the second semester of their sophomore year. No specific reason was given other than "lack of relevance" as some of the women reported. Dropping out may mean disaffiliating with the sorority or simply going on an inactive status. In a few cases, women continued their active status but stopped participating in sorority activities, such as attending the weekly meetings and participating in philanthropic activities and social or recreational events.

The local alumnae group expressed concern about this situation because sorority life was such a valuable experience for them. In fact, some alumnae asserted that being a member of a sorority was the defining experience of their college career. Many of the current collegiates find the experience valuable, but they also complain about their chapters' being dominated by powerful alumnae. The alumnae have expressed their concerns to the president informally, and the vice president contacted the dean of students to look into the attention. The Greek adviser agrees but is unsure as to what to do. Clearly some systematic work needs to be done.

Step 1: Define the Problem

Sorority life, long an asset of Great Plains State University appears to be in decline, if one is to believe the alumnae group. The alumnae need to be taken very seriously by GPSU because they have been consistent supporters of sorority life, a long tradition at the university, and strong benefactors of the university. To lose them as supporters of the university would be a major loss in many ways.

The problem, as it is defined, is also manifested in the behavior of the collegians who indicate that sorority life is no longer relevant, and as a consequence, they are comfortable dropping out from active participation in their chapters. The students' behavior illustrates the problem identified by the alumnae. The problem, then, is to determine the factors and conditions that appear to be contributing to a lack of enthusiastic participation by upperclass members of GPSU sororities in their organizations.

Step 2: Determine the Purpose of the Study

Both the alumnae and the upperclass students have identified a problem. The alumnae are concerned about the health of the sororities; the upperclass students are dropping out because of a lack of relevancy in sorority life. They appear to agree on the problem, but are concerned for different reasons. The purpose of the study will be to determine why upperclass women cease to participate actively in their sororities. This will lead, it is hoped, to identifying factors that have created this condition, and as a result will determine what can be done to sustain student interest in sororities. When that occurs, upperclass women may participate more actively in their sororities, which will be a benefit to them, and the alumnae will be happier because of the active leadership that will be provided by these women.

Step 3: Determine Where to Get the Information Needed

The primary source of information for the study is from the upperclass women themselves. If they are dropping out of active participation in their sororities, no one can explain the situation better than they can. Because this may not be a recent phenomenon, a secondary source of information will be the archives of the Greek adviser's office to determine if, in fact, the dropout rate is greater than what the alumnae remember. It is possible that the circumstances have changed only marginally over recent years, so before undertaking a complex study, it would be useful to confirm the assertions of the alumnae. Examining the records in the office can do that quite easily.

Another study could involve meeting with alumnae leaders to determine how the lack of participation of the upperclass students has affected the sororities.

Step 4: Determine the Best Assessment Method

Since we primarily seek the reasons undergirding behavioral decisions on the part of students, a qualitative study is in order. Those who are dropping out of active participation are juniors and seniors, so the data can be gathered from them through the use of interviews or focus groups. Focus groups are more likely to generate a richer discussion and therefore appear to be the logical step.

The data collection method for determining if women currently are dropping out more often than in the past can be done through a study of the records of the Greek adviser, which are available in the central office. Document analysis will help identify if what is asserted has happened.

Information should also be collected from chapter alumnae. Each house has a group of five to seven alumnae who are active supporters of the chapter as advisers, members of the house corporation, financial supporters, or helpers with the rush process. The best way to generate information from this source would be to conduct focus groups with them.

Step 5: Determine Whom to Study

The study will look at all women who drop out of their sororities as juniors or seniors, using the definition cited in the case study. The study will include women who disaffiliate, go inactive, or simply stop participating in sorority events. The Greek adviser's office or the sororities can identify these women. Leaders of the sororities would have to agree to identify those who quit participating in house events. If a sufficient number of these individuals do not agree to participate in the focus groups, an alternative would be to invited recent graduates who fit the profile to participate in the group interviews. Identifying individuals in the geographical region of GPSU could be a challenge, but if even a few could participate, that would contribute to the richness of the study.

Since there is a potential pool of fifty to seventy alumnae, the group is too large to include everyone in the study. Because of this problem, the focus groups can begin with individuals who hold a designated role, such as chapter adviser or member of a house corporation. Groups will continue until the point of saturation is reached.

Step 6: Determine How the Data Will Be Collected

This is a qualitative study, so data will be collected using focus groups and document analysis. The focus groups with the collegians will be conducted until the point of redundancy is reached, as indicated in the literature (see Merriam, 1998, for example). This means that focus groups will continue to be conducted until no new information is developed from the group discussions. It is likely that at least three groups will have to be conducted, but more may be necessary. In designing the study, the investigators are not sure how many women have dropped out of active participation, and this will not be known until the document analysis has been conducted. Without question, representation from each of the sororities is necessary, and it is advisable that several members from each sorority be included in the focus groups.

Data in the archives of the office will be studied to determine if this problem has accelerated in recent years. Although it will be impossible to determine the number of women who were not active participants in their sororities, those who have disaffiliated or failed to stay current as dues-paying members can be identified. If statistical significance is sought, a chi-square analysis could be used.

Information from the alumnae will be collected using the same strategy as was used with the collegiates—that is, continue to conduct focus groups until the point of redundancy is reached. Care will be taken to include alumnae from all the sororities—preferably at least two or three members from each. A minimum of three to four focus groups will be conducted. (For more information on conducting focus groups, see Chapter Four.)

Step 7: Determine What Instruments Will Be Used

We have discussed the approach to collecting data in this qualitative study. This next step is to develop an interview protocol that can be used with the students and the alumnae. The protocol that could be used with the students is contained in Exhibit 28.1.

Other questions may emerge as a consequence of the first focus groups, but this set would provide a good start on gathering the data for the study.

Also, an interview protocol with the alumnae (see Exhibit 28.2) would provide their perceptions of sorority life and why they feel may be on the decline, especially for upperclass students. The protocol could be developed in this fashion.

Two other approaches could be used if more data were needed. One would be to conduct focus groups with women who stayed active in their sororities during their entire undergraduate careers. Their responses could

EXHIBIT 28.1

Focus Group Interview Protocol for Disaffiliated Sorority Members

Good evening. My name is [provide name], and I represent the Office of Student Life at Great Plains State University. The purpose of this study is to learn more about sorority life here. You have been invited to participate in this focus group because you were once a member of a sorority but subsequently decided to disaffiliate. Is that correct?

This session is being tape-recorded so that I can make sure to be as accurate as possible in reporting your comments. I will be preparing a report for the Office of Student Life that will contain recommendations for improving sorority life at GPSU. I want to assure you that your comments are confidential and that I will not attribute anything you say directly to you. You may leave the group at any time, and your participation is strictly voluntary. You have a form in front of you that I ask you to sign before we move ahead. It indicates you understand the conditions under which this study is conducted. Do you have any questions? OK, let's move ahead.

1. Why did you choose to enroll here at Great Plains?

2. Did the reputation of sorority life at Great Plains have anything to do with your decision to enroll? Please discuss.

3. According to our records, you decided to pledge a sorority. Is that correct? Why did you choose to do so?

4. Did sorority life turn out to be what you expected? Why or why not?

5. When you think back on your experiences in your sorority, what were the highlights?

6. According to our records, at some point you decided to cease active participation in your sorority. Is that correct? Why did you make this decision?

7. Knowing what you know now, would you still have pledged a sorority? Please discuss.

8. What would you advise an incoming first-year woman about sorority life?

9. What do you see as the strengths of the sorority system at GPSU?

10. How might the sorority system of GPSU be improved?

11. Any other comments?

Thank you for your participation in this study. The results may be obtained from the Office of Student Life in about six weeks at [address, telephone, or e-mail address].

EXHIBIT 28.2

Focus Group Interview Protocol for Sorority Alumnae

Good evening. My name is [provide name], and I represent the Office of Student Life at Great Plains State University. The purpose of this study is to learn more about perceptions of sorority life at GPSU. You have been invited to participate in this focus group because as an undergraduate, you were a member of a sorority. Is that correct?

This session is being tape-recorded so that I can make sure to be as accurate as possible in reporting your comments. I will be preparing a report for the Office of Student Life that will contain recommendations for improving sorority life at GPSU. I want to assure you that your comments are confidential and that I will not attribute anything you say directly to you. You may leave the group at any time, and your participation is strictly voluntary. You have a form in front of you that I ask you to sign before we move ahead. It indicates you understand the conditions under which this study is conducted. Do you have any questions? OK, let's move ahead.

1. We understand that you have been active supporters of the sororities since your graduation from Great Plains. Is that right?

2. Why have you chosen to continue to be involved in sorority life on this campus?

3. From your experience, how, if at all, has sorority life changed over the past fifteen years?

4. As you see the system currently, what are its strengths?

5. If you were in charge of the sororities for a day and could change everything, what would be the one thing you would not change?

6. How might the sorority system at GPSU be improved?

7. There is a perception that junior and senior women are dropping out of their sororities. Do you share this view? If so, why do you think they are leaving?

8. What else would you like to tell us about sorority life on campus?

9. Any other comments?

Thank you for your participation in this study. The results may be obtained from the Office of Student Life in about six weeks at [address, telephone, or e-mail address].

be compared with the dropouts' to determine what differences, if any, existed between the two groups. Another approach would be to compare the two groups using a quantitative instrument to determine if their experiences as a student was different. The College Student Experiences Questionnaire (Pace and Kuh, 1998) would be a good all-purpose instrument for this activity. The College Outcomes Survey from the American College Testing Program (1993) also would be a possibility. A tool that is available to measure the Greek experience is the Greek Experience Survey, developed at the University of Minnesota. More information about this instrument is available through harrold@tc.umn.edu.

Step 8: Determine Who Should Collect the Data

Members of the student affairs staff, interested faculty, or even active members of the sorority system can collect data. With appropriate training, for example, members of the WPA leadership could team with student affairs staff to conduct the interviews. We think that using two people to conduct a focus group is desirable, since one can focus on leading the group, while the other takes notes, collects consent forms, handles logistics, and otherwise assists as necessary.

A review of sorority membership records would provide assurance that the dropout rate had accelerated recently. The Greek adviser and other members of the student affairs staff could do this work. This probably would not be a good place for students to get involved; although the records may not be confidential in the strictest sense, they certainly are sensitive. Rather than err in the direction of revealing something that should be kept private, the better strategy is not to expose the records to students. If help were needed, it might be possible to involve faculty.

Step 9: Determine How the Data Will Be Analyzed

The quantitative data can be analyzed by developing aggregate summaries for each year and identifying the number of women who participated in sororities, the number who dropped out using the definitions supplied earlier in this chapter, and the resulting attrition percentage. If necessary, chi-square statistics could be computed to determine if a significant difference occurred from year to year.

The qualitative data will be analyzed using the constant comparative method (Glaser and Strauss, 1967). Patterns, themes, and trends in the data will be identified. If a group of collegians is interviewed who continued as sorority leaders throughout their career, the response of these women will be compared with the dropouts. The views of the alumnae and the dropouts need to be compared, with a special emphasis on the question related to the strengths and weaknesses of the sorority system. It is possible that the dropouts and the alumnae see sorority life very differently, and identifying those differences is fundamental to making changes, if changes are warranted.

Step 10: Determine the Implications of the Study for Policy and Practice

Sorority life may be on a slippery slope at GPSU, and alumnae are concerned that the magic of the past may be lost. If the study reveals systemic problems with the sorority system, changes would be in order. One potential approach would be to change the way rush is conducted. This would be a logical conclusion if the dropouts revealed that they did not have enough information about their sorority before they pledged.

It is possible that the data from the office archives will reveal that the current dropout rate is no worse than it has been in previous years. If that is the case, while important information might be learned from the focus groups, perhaps only minor changes will be needed to reestablish the sorority system as a robust force on campus. An educational campaign might be the approach taken with the alumnae. This could consist of a series of meetings with alumnae from each house, looking at the dropout rate, explaining that the dropout rate had not changed, but still seeking their input in addition to what they had suggested from participating in focus groups. If this is the approach, then changing perceptions is the purpose rather than planning fundamental changes in the sorority system.

Step 11: Report the Results Effectively

Although this problem does not have the potential for significant implications for the entire campus as many other cases reported in this book do, the problem is significant. To be sure, the viability of the sorority system is important in the life of Great Plains, but many students might not care if the sororities are sustained. Therefore, reporting the results to a wide campus audience may not be necessary. Nevertheless, members of the student affairs staff would require a summary report, and a copy of the full report should be on file with the Greek affairs office. An executive summary should be sent to the president because she initiated the inquiry. What is significant about this assessment is that the results would be shared with the sorority members and alumnae. The results might be reported to members of these groups through the use of presentations featuring overheads, slides, or other multimedia, followed by question-and-answer sessions or brainstorming activities. If the report included suggestions for change, then these information sessions would be designed in part to seek the concurrence of the members and the alumnae. Other approaches might be tried as well, but this is clearly a different approach to disseminating information to interested stakeholders from those that have been used in other campus assessment initiatives.

Conclusion

Sorority life at Great Plains has deteriorated in the eyes of influential alumnae. Steps need to be taken to determine if this true and, if so, what needs to be done. If their perceptions are incorrect, an educational program would need to be put in place. Regardless of what the data determine, it is clear that the situation cannot continue as it has. Assessment in this case is a necessary step to strengthen a system in jeopardy.

References

American College Testing Program. *College Outcomes Survey*. Iowa City, Iowa: American College Testing Program, 1993.

Astin, A. W. *What Matters in College? Four Critical Years Revisited*. San Francisco: Jossey-Bass, 1993.

Glaser, B. G., and Strauss, A. L. *The Discovery of Grounded Theory*. Hawthorne, N.Y.: Aldine, 1967.

Kuh, G. D., and Arnold, J. C. "Liquid Bonding: A Cultural Analysis of the Role of Alcohol in Fraternity Pledgeship." *Journal of College Student Development*, 1993, *34*(5), 327–334.

Kuh, G. D., Branch Douglas, K. B., Lund, J. P., and Ramin-Gyurnek, J. *Student Learning Outside the Classroom: Transcending Artificial Boundaries*. Washington, D.C.: School of Education and Human Development, George Washington University, 1994.

Merriam, S. B. *Qualitative Research and Case Study Applications in Education*. San Francisco: Jossey-Bass, 1998.

Miller, T. K. (ed.). *The Book of Professional Standards for Higher Education*. Washington, D.C.: Council for the Advancement of Standards in Higher Education, 1997.

Pace, C. R., and Kuh, G. D. *College Student Experiences Questionnaire*. (4th ed.) Bloomington: Indiana University, 1998.

Pascarella, E. T., and Terenzini, P. T. *How College Affects Students: Findings and Insights from Twenty Years of Research*. San Francisco: Jossey-Bass, 1991.

Shonrock, M. D. "Standards and Expectations for Greek Letter Organizations." In E. G. Whipple (ed.), *New Challenges for Greek Letter Organizations: Transforming Fraternities and Sororities into Learning Communities*. New Directions for Student Services, no. 81. San Francisco: Jossey-Bass, 1998.

Whipple, E. G. (ed.). *New Challenges for Greek Letter Organizations: Transforming Fraternities and Sororities into Learning Communities*. New Directions for Student Services, no. 81. San Francisco: Jossey-Bass, 1998.

Whipple, E. G., and Sullivan, E. G. "Greek Letter Organizations: Communities of Learners?" In E. G. Whipple (ed.), *New Challenges for Greek Letter Organizations: Transforming Fraternities and Sororities into Learning Communities*. New Directions for Student Services, no. 81. San Francisco: Jossey-Bass, 1998.

Whitt, E. J. "Assessing Student Cultures." In M. L. Upcraft and J. H. Schuh, *Assessment in Student Affairs: A Guide for Practitioners*. San Francisco: Jossey-Bass, 1996.

Chapter 29

Assessing an Office of Student Conduct

NO OTHER OFFICE, department, or service may be more difficult to assess than an office of student conduct (OSC) since this student affairs function almost exclusively deals with students and clients who are unhappy and do not want to have anything to do with the office. In many cases, students have been referred to the office because they have been involved in an unpleasant incident on campus, as either an alleged perpetrator or a victim. Nonetheless, the OSC plays an important role on campus. It is responsible for enforcing the institution's student code of conduct and also serves to educate students about how responsible adults must act in an orderly society.

"Probably no other specialty area has engendered so much debate, disagreement, and dissension in student affairs" (Fley cited by Dannells, 1996) as the OSC. The matters that this office may deal with range from those that may seem trivial, such as making sure that students understand why parking regulations must be enforced, to addressing serious issues, including matters of civility, assault, or worse (Schuh, 1998). Regardless of the role the office plays in the life of the campus, whether it handles hundreds of cases a year or just a few each month, it must be able to withstand assessment of how it applies the institution's standards to individual cases and whether learning outcomes result from its interventions.

This chapter identifies selected problems associated with assessing an office of student conduct, suggests a model for assessing the OSC, and then presents a case study demonstrating how this office could use assessment.

Problems Associated with Assessing an Office of Student Conduct

The major problem associated with assessing an OSC is that it can be very difficult to secure the cooperation of those involved in cases heard by the office to cooperate in an assessment project. Let us start with alleged violators of campus conduct policies.

It is quite rare for a student not to challenge a charge of violating institutional policy, from parking tickets to more serious circumstances. The process that the accused participates in is adversarial—not necessarily in the strictest legal framework, but more from the perspective that the accused has a point of view, the accuser has a different point of view, and the hearing officer or body has to make a decision that applies institutional standards in the case. At times students are removed from the institution, often against their expressed wishes, or they are severely penalized in other ways. If the purpose of an assessment of an OSC is to seek the perspectives of the accused regarding how this person thought the judicial process treated him or her, it will be difficult to secure cooperation. To be engaged in an adversarial relationship with a student and then turn around and ask the student's point of view about the circumstance creates a difficult assessment climate.

Another problem with assessing an OSC is trying to work with the victims of campus incidents. At least two issues arise. First, these individuals, especially if the situation has been serious, as when they are the victims of assault, may not want to have anything to do with the situation. In some cases, victims withdraw from the institution and can be difficult to locate. Either way, the problem of securing their cooperation can be difficult.

In other cases, the victims may disagree with how the case has been handled or what the decision is regarding the case. These individuals, too, are not going to be willing participants in an assessment of the OSC.

One other problem arises in assessing an OSC. If one is interested in broad student perspectives about the office, it is difficult to secure informed opinions, since much of the work of the office is conducted confidentially. As a consequence, the campus community will not know precisely how cases are handled or what the decision of the hearing body has been about the case. At best, an assessment of student opinion in general will be based on incomplete information. Nevertheless, an OSC can be assessed.

A Model for Assessing an Office of Student Conduct

Various approaches can be taken to assessing an OSC.

Know Who Interacts with the OSC and Why

The OSC runs on data management. Since the office rarely brings charges against students of its own volition, it needs to be able to provide a tracking system for the cases it adjudicates. A tracking system can include such features as these:

- Who initiated the charge (student, faculty member, campus police, residence hall staff, and so on)?

- What rule or policy was allegedly violated (theft, vandalism, assault, and so on)?

- Who was charged with the offense?

- What are the demographic characteristics of the alleged offender (gender, class standing, major, and so on)?

- Did the alleged offender admit or deny responsibility?

- Who adjudicated the situation (hearing officer, conduct board, or someone else)?

- Was the adjudicated decision appealed, and if so, to whom?

- What was the final decision (responsible or not responsible)?

- What was the ultimate sanction?

This information can be kept using a simple database that should be updated periodically—at least once per week if cases are heard frequently or perhaps less often than that if only a few cases are heard each month.

Assess Student Needs

A primary purpose of an OSC is to meet the institutional need of maintaining a lawful and orderly campus environment, consistent with its mission and the laws of the land. However, this issue also reflects one of the goals of the office: to make sure that students understand the institution's conduct standards and the disciplinary process. Do students who are referred to the office understand that the alleged offense is a violation of the institution's conduct regulations? Do they understand the process that the institution follows in adjudicating judicial cases? Do students know where to find the institution's regulations in print? Do they know where to turn if they are charged with a violation? These questions and others provide a way of assessing students' educational needs, before they have been charged with a violation.

Assess Student Satisfaction with the Office of Student Conduct

This may seem like an unusual form of assessment, because typically student satisfaction is thought of as students' enjoying an experience and hoping they will repeat the experience in the future. In actuality, an OSC may make a decision that has an adverse affect on a student (such as being placed on probation or being suspended from the college for a semester). In many instances, the office would prefer not to have an ongoing relationship with the student since that person would be a repeat violator of institutional regulations.

Assessment, then, would reflect different criteria in this case. Examples of the questions that would frame student satisfaction with the OSC include the following:

"Did you understand the charges brought against you?"

"Did you understand the disciplinary process? Was this process followed in your case?"

"Were you referred to someone who could help you with the process?"

"Did you feel that you had an opportunity to present your case?"

"Did you have an opportunity to prepare an appeal if you did not accept the initial decision regarding your case?"

These questions get at the fairness of the process and have nothing to do with how satisfying the experience was for the student. Satisfaction in this instance has to do with the appreciation of the judicial process and does not get at the extent to which the student agreed with the final decision. The objective, rather, is to make sure that each student has a complete opportunity, using the college's regulations, to present a case and be heard.

Assess the Extent to Which the Office Deals with Repeat Offenders and Why

Most offices of this type profess to have an educational effect on students. If that is the case, then theoretically the office will see very few repeat offenders, and students who have been through the judicial process should demonstrate certain types of learning. To determine the answer to the first issue, the office can ask whether the alleged offender has appeared before the office on other charges. If so, the person is a repeat offender. Just exactly what level of repeat offenders is too high is a matter of debate and professional judgment. In the eyes of some, a rate of 15 percent would be too high, while others might not find a 25 percent repeat rate of offenders troubling. In any event, the data ought to be calculated and provided for discussions on campus on student conduct.

The other aspect provides an interesting format for discussion. Because of privacy regulations, focus groups may not be the most appropriate forum for discussions with offenders about what they have learned from their experiences with the office, but individual interviews are appropriate. A month or more after the student's case has been adjudicated, an interview might be conducted to explore what the student has learned from the process, how the student's overall behavior has changed, and what the student would tell colleagues about the office.

Assess the Campus Climate

Campus climate often has an influence on behavioral norms of students (Kuh, Schuh, Whitt, and Associates, 1991). In the case of a campus with a myriad of conduct problems, such as substance abuse, accelerating crime rates, and inordinate numbers of fights, assessment of the campus climate might be in order to help determine the extent to which the climate encourages or at least tolerates persistent violations of campus regulations. Depending on the results, the OSC might develop educational interventions to affect student behavior. At a minimum, this office could conduct the study and determine the appropriate steps to take to correct this situation.

Use Professional Standards

The Council for the Advancement of Standards in Higher Education has prepared a set of standards for this kind of office (Miller, 1997). These standards can provide a framework for a self-study conducted by the office.

Student Conduct Case Study

Southeastern Technical College (STC) is a state-assisted institution that provides an excellent technical education to a student body that hails from the region. Most of the students at the college are in curricular areas related to the application of science to practice situations, such as engineering, design, and agriculture. The students who attend STC tend to be first-generation students, and many have to work to defray their college costs.

STC is known as a place where students work hard. The academic standards are demanding and require a tremendous amount of work. STC also has a campus culture where students play hard on the weekends, especially

Friday and Saturday nights. The local community of Smithville has an accommodating attitude toward students, and on weekends beer flows freely, regardless of student age. The consequence of these weekends is that students get into scrapes on and off campus, and incidents of fights, occasional vandalism, excessive noise when others are trying to sleep, and general rowdiness are filed with the OSC reflecting the previous weekend's adventures.

A group of faculty began to meet informally to discuss this problem. They are concerned about the effect of this behavior on students who do not drink, on international students who do not participate in the revelry yet are a significant percentage of the student body, and the extent to which the climate of the campus is antithetical to the high academic standards the college boasts. In their view, nothing happens to students who engage in this uproarious behavior, and the college appears to be winking at serious problems. Recidivism, in their view, is rampant, which reflects on the ineffectiveness of the OSC.

The faculty group met with the president about this situation and asked that steps be taken to curb this problem. The president, who is aware of the problem, needs more information and has communicated this conversation to the vice president for student affairs, who in turn calls the director of OSC. This is a serious situation, and the problem needs to be assessed.

Step 1: Define the Problem

STC has a problem that appears to result from a variety of factors, not the least of which happens to be the casual attitude toward liquor control laws in Smithville, but OSC is being held responsible for cleaning up the mess. Realistically, one office cannot accomplish the task whatever it is, but since OSC has the responsibility for dealing with student conduct, it has to take the lead on this issue. The president, who is a patient person, understands this, and the vice president for student affairs is supportive of the office and its staff, but information is needed so that a plan can be developed to deal with the problems affecting campus life.

The problem, as it has emerged from several discussions, is that student behavior is out of control over the weekends. The students believe that as long as they work hard during the week and complete their assignments and other class work on time, they should be allowed to do whatever they want on the weekend. This line of thinking has not been challenged until now.

For now, the problem is defined as analyzing and identifying the factors and conditions that have contributed the significant number of conduct problems that occur on weekends. A secondary issue is to determine the effectiveness of OSC in dealing with student conduct problems.

Step 2: Determine the Purpose of the Study

This study has two components. The first part of the analysis is to analyze the student culture that contributes to the student conduct problems that occur on the weekends. For this component, a campus culture study needs to be conducted. The second aspect of the study has to do with what students learn from participating in the student conduct process. This means that an inquiry needs to be conducted with students who have been charged with violations of the student code of conduct at STC. What have they learned from the adjudication process, and why did some repeat their offense, if in fact a large number of repeat offenders are seen by the office?

Step 3: Determine Where to Get the Information Needed

Primarily the data for this study will come from the students themselves. Students will be the best source of information for describing climate. Other sources of information will be the OSC and the campus police department (CPD). Records from these campus agencies will be useful in determining what the data reveal about student behavior.

Step 4: Determine the Best Assessment Method

A multiple method approach to this problem seems to be the best choice. Clearly a study on student culture and campus climate needs to be conducted. The total enrollment of STC is just over four thousand, so a series of focus groups will need to be conducted with the students of STC. From the total enrollment, students will be identified by class for the focus groups. Exactly how many groups will have to be conducted is unknown, because the groups will continue until the point of redundancy is reached; nevertheless, at least three focus groups of students from each class will have to be conducted. More may need to be conducted depending on what is found. (More information about conducting a campus climate study can be found in Caple, 1991, and Whitt, 1996.)

The other assessment method is to conduct an analysis of data in the files of the OSC and CPD. If it turns out that a large of students are repeat offenders, additional work will need to be done to determine why. That too might be handled through the use of focus groups.

Step 5: Determine Whom to Study

Theoretically all students who attend the college could be chosen to participate in the focus groups. A decision is made to stratify students by class (freshman, sophomore, junior and senior) (a variation of stratified purposeful sampling; Patton, 1990) and conduct at least three focus groups with each class. More might be necessary.

The institutional records to study are those in the OSC and CPD. The goal is to determine is how many students are repeat offenders and what happens to students who are charged with violations of campus behavior regulations. The records will be examined for a period of three years, working back from the close of the previous fiscal year. These data are readily available and can be analyzed quickly and accurately.

Step 6: Determine How the Data Will Be Collected

Two studies will be conducted to answer the questions related to this case: a campus culture study and an analysis of various records that are available in the OSC and the CPD.

The student culture study will require a qualitative approach. This can be accomplished most directly through the use of focus groups conducted with students by class standing. These interviews will need to be conducted by trained interviewers who are familiar with this data collection technique. Each focus group will be led by one person, who will be assisted by a person who will take notes and handle the technical side of the interviews, such as collecting subject release forms from the students, tape-recording the interviews, and so on. (Additional information about conducting focus groups is contained in Chapter Four.)

Observations also might be a part of this study. Members of the team conducting the study might want to visit student hangouts and observe student behavior. (Mills, 2000, provides information about observational techniques.)

The other study relates to examining institutional records in order to determine the percentage of recidivism of offenders and the extent to which the repeat offenses are similar to, less significant than, or more significant than the first offenses. For example, if a student was seen for the first time with a charge of disorderly conduct and found responsible, then was seen for too many parking tickets, it would be difficult to establish a linkage between one violation and the other. On the other hand, students who are seen repeatedly for alcohol problems or for problems that result from misuse of alcoholic beverages would represent serious concerns for the campus. An example might be a student who is charged with disorderly conduct resulting from the abuse of alcohol and then becomes a repeat offender as a person who vandalizes a building as a result of alcohol misuse as well. The number of these cases needs to be identified, and an analysis needs to be conducted as to whether these cases result from ineffectiveness on the part of OSC.

This inquiry needs to be conducted using insiders and outsiders, meaning that a person from OSC likely will have to take the lead on the inquiry but that several other people from outside OSC should assist in the process. If it is unclear as to the effectiveness of the interventions of OSC, individual interviews might be held with the student offenders to learn more about why they continued to violate institutional regulations. These interviews would be conducted by people outside OSC, who must be well trained in interview techniques.

Step 7: Determine What Instruments Will Be Used

A campus culture study will be conducted through the use of a series of focus groups with STC students, organized by class standing. The focus groups will be conducted with members from each class until the point of redundancy is reached. A typical interview protocol for these interviews is contained in Exhibit 29.1.

Individual interviews might be held with students who were multiple offenders of campus regulations. Because of privacy concerns, a list of these students' names could not be turned over to those conducting the inquiry. After the names have been identified and a decision has been made to go ahead with interviews (perhaps after finding that 40 percent of all offenses were committed by repeat offenders), the OSC would have to contact the students to determine if they would be willing to participate in the study. Other specific questions may arise after a few students have been interviewed.

Step 8: Determine Who Should Collect the Data

The campus culture audit could involve individuals from OSC as well as others from various offices on campus or faculty. Clearly anyone who conducts a focus group will need to be trained in the technique (Krueger, 1998). After training has been completed, pairs of investigators can gather the data. One good strategy is to pair a member of the OSC with a faculty member or another member of the student affairs staff to conduct the focus groups.

Individual interviews may be conducted depending on what is learned from the analysis of the records. These could be conducted by insiders or outsiders since permission would have been secured from each student who participated in the focus group interview. Training in interview techniques would be necessary. After the training has been completed, interviews from OSC or other aspects of STC could conduct the sessions.

EXHIBIT 29.1

Interview Protocol for Campus Culture

Hello, my name is [provide name], and I represent the Office of Student Conduct. The purpose of our discussion today is to learn a little more about student life at STC and your perceptions about campus life. This session is being tape-recorded, so that I can make sure to be as accurate as possible in writing my report for the Office of Student Conduct. Your remarks here will remain confidential, and I will not attribute anything you say directly to you. Your participation is strictly voluntary, and you may leave the group at any time. You have a form in front of you that I ask you to sign before we move ahead. It indicates you understand the purpose of the study and the nature of your participation. Do you have any questions at this point? OK, let's move ahead.

1. Why did you decide to attend STC?

2. Have your expectations for attending STC been met? Please explain.

3. Tell us a little bit about a typical week for you at STC. Hit the highlights, and tell us what you do.

4. How do you find academics at STC?

5. Let's us move on to the weekends. What generally do you do on weekends?

6. Would you say the way you spend time on the weekends is fairly common for students at STC? Please explain.

7. Have you ever gotten into trouble on campus as a result of your weekend activities? Please explain.

8. Besides what you do on the weekends, what other activities are available?

9. When you arrived on campus, what did the upperclass students say about how they spend their time on the weekends?

10. Are you satisfied with the quality of student life at STC? If not, what needs to be changed?

11. Is there anything about student life at STC that we should have asked you but did not?

Thank you for your participation. A copy of my report can be obtained from the Office of Student Conduct [address, telephone number, and e-mail address] in about six weeks.

Step 9: Determine How the Data Will Be Analyzed

The data from the focus groups will be analyzed using the constant comparative method (Whitt, 1991), and patterns, themes, and trends will be identified. Since the data are collected and analyzed simultaneously, preliminary constructions will be developed as the focus groups are conducted.

Analyzing the information from the databases of the OSC and the CPD will be a little more difficult. To be sure, identifying repeat offenders and their offenses will not be very difficult, but determining if the first offense has any relationship to the other may be very difficult, and determining the influence of the OSC on student learning will be impossible. As a consequence, the data generated from the personal interviews will be important. This phase of data analysis represents a classic situation where the quantitative analysis shows what questions to ask, and the qualitative aspect helps to determine the answers to those questions.

Analyzing repeat offender data can be challenging as a consequence of the Family Education Rights and Privacy Act (Kaplin and Lee, 1997). The names of offenders should not be revealed to any person who does not have an official need to know these names. This problem might be overcome by using a combination of individuals from OSC and those who would have routine access to the information anyway, such as a dean of students, the dean's principal associate, or other individuals in the office of student affairs. Sensitivity to privacy requires that these records not be made public in any way.

Step 10: Determine the Implications of the Study for Policy and Practice

The nature of student life at STC has become a concern for faculty and perhaps others on campus, since it appears as though the student body, or at least some members of it, are out of control on the weekends. This may result in serious alcohol possession and consumption problems, legal issues, vandalism, and a host of other concerns. One cannot be sure from anecdotal evidence if the student culture supports this kind of behavior, and it is time to determine if that is the case. If the conclusion is that the student culture encourages this kind of behavior, then steps will need to be taken to address the issue and curb what may be a situation out of control.

In fact, if the problem is as serious as some believe, the very existence of STC may be threatened. Students not interested in a never-ending weekend party as has been described might choose to go elsewhere to college. Continued problems will arise related to student health, the destruction of property, and, perhaps inevitably, the relationship of STC and Smithville. Potential approaches to addressing a problem of this nature could include partnerships with local community merchants to curb the easy access to alcohol, developing alternative forms of entertainment for students on the weekends, more intensive educational efforts related to substance abuse, and other items that may emerge from the inquiry.

The other piece of this study deals with the effectiveness of OSC. The study may reveal that the impression that the office is ineffective is incorrect. But if it turns out that the OSC has no effect on student behavior and repeat offenses are common, then a thorough examination of the adjudication process would be warranted. Different sanctions might be identified, additional training for hearing officers might be warranted, and a change in the mix of student or faculty involvement as hearing board members might be contemplated.

Step 11: Report the Results Effectively

We recommend that a series of reports be published at the conclusion of the assessment. These would include an executive summary for senior officers of the institution, and reports would be available for selected staff members of the division of student affairs and perhaps interested students such as the officers of the student government association. A full report would be made available for the vice president for student affairs and the OSC staff. The faculty who raised questions about student conduct to the president might receive a shorter version of the report; they may not be interested in the methodology, but it is important to assure them that they could receive a copy of the full report upon request.

A report of this nature has the potential to be volatile politically. As a consequence, the impression should never be created that important findings are being hidden. This assessment may even need to be reported in an abridged version to the student newspaper, since all students on campus may be affected by the findings and potential recommendations for change in conduct codes.

Conclusion

What started out as the concerns of a few faculty members about student life on the weekend has turned into a comprehensive assessment of student culture. These kinds of studies are complex, time-consuming, and expensive. In the case of Southeastern Technical College, the quality of student life may have deteriorated to the degree that a major initiative to change the culture might be indicated. The Office of Student Conduct may be ineffective in dealing with students, and a different approach may be required. This assessment project has the potential to change the complexion of the college, so it needs to be conducted with great care and thoroughness. Anything less will result in actions or inactivity that could have adverse consequences for the student body and the institution as a whole.

References

Caple, R. B. (ed.). "Special Edition." *Journal of College Student Development*, 1991, 32(5).

Dannells, M. "Discipline and Judicial Affairs." In A. L. Rentz and Associates, *Student Affairs Practice in Higher Education.* Springfield, Ill.: Thomas, 1996.

Kaplin, W. A., and Lee, B. A. *A Legal Guide for Student Affairs Professionals.* San Francisco: Jossey-Bass, 1997.

Krueger, R. A. *Moderating Focus Groups.* Thousand Oaks, Calif.: Sage, 1998.

Kuh, G. D., Schuh, J. H., Whitt, E. J., and Associates. *Involving Colleges: Successful Approaches to Fostering Student Learning and Development Outside the Classroom.* San Francisco: Jossey-Bass, 1991.

Miller, T. K. (ed.). *The Book of Professional Standards for Higher Education.* Washington, D.C.: Council for the Advancement of Standards in Higher Education, 1997.

Mills, G. E. *Action Research.* Columbus, Ohio: Merrill, 2000.

Patton, M. J. *Qualitative Evaluation and Research Methods.* (2nd ed.) Thousand Oaks, Calif.: Sage, 1990.

Schuh, J. H. "Matters of Civility on Campus." In A. M. Hoffman, J. H. Schuh, and R. H. Fenske (eds.), *Violence on Campus.* Gaithersburg, Md.: Aspen, 1998.

Schuh, J. H., and Laverty, M. "The Perceived Long-Term Influence of Holding a Significant Student Leadership Position." *Journal of College Student Personnel,* 1983, 24(1), 28–32.

Whitt, E. J. "Artful Science: A Primer on Qualitative Research Methods." *Journal of College Student Development,* 1991, 32(5), 406–415.

Whitt, E. J. "Assessing Student Cultures." In M. L. Upcraft and J. H. Schuh, *Assessment in Student Affairs: A Guide for Practitioners.* San Francisco: Jossey-Bass, 1996.

Part Five

Assessment Issues

Chapter 30

Getting Started

ONE OF THE HARDEST aspects of conducting assessments is getting started. Kaufman and English (1979, p. 175), when writing about needs assessment, describe the situation this way: "Usually, the most difficult part of conducting a needs assessment is obtaining commitment and obtaining approvals and resources to get the job done: *getting going*." A variety of problems can impede getting started on an assessment project. Our view is that these problems must be overcome, or assessment will never be undertaken. And if assessments are not undertaken, a number of results are likely to occur, none of them good.

We divide this discussion of getting started into three parts: discussing problems that impede assessment and how to overcome them, identifying assessment issues that are not negotiable, and finally, describing assessment matters that are negotiable. But first, consider this scenario.

You are the director of residential life at Local College (LC). LC has a fairly small residential population (one thousand residents out of a student enrollment of twelve thousand), and many of the students who attend LC are commuters. Although the vice president for student affairs has been supportive of what you do, this person's interest clearly has been on academic support services and other programs that make enrollment at the college possible for returning adult learners.

You run a good operation. Your budget is balanced, staff members are enthusiastic in their work with students, and many good programs are planned each year for the residents. The food service has received many compliments from students, and parents seem satisfied with the prices. Normally, increases are not much more than the cost of living, and the buildings are in good repair. Your program won a regional award last year, and you generally think things are moving along well.

You have been discussing the future of the college with the director of undergraduate admissions and have learned that the demographics of the area where most of your residents come from (the western part of the state) indicate an eroding number of students who will be going to college. The high schools there are shrinking in size as the populations of small towns contract, and you want to anticipate potential revenue problems by beginning to develop a comprehensive assessment program that will help you identify areas where the residence halls can be strengthened, as well as the assets of your department from the point of view of your students. You know that if things are not improved, your budget base may shrink, and fiscal problems could be just around the corner.

The vice president is not especially worried about the future and says, "Things have always worked out for us." Your staff thinks things are working fine and report not having the energy or expertise to devote time to assessment. You know that assessment will take time and some money, and although your financial situation is adequate, you are not sure that you can convince the departmental budget committee to commit funds to undertaken a comprehensive program. Still, this assessment initiative needs to be undertaken. If you do not start thinking about the future, no one else will. How do you proceed?

Overcoming Barriers to Assessment

The barriers that impede assessment projects need to be managed and overcome, or assessment projects will never get off the ground. Let us look at these in a bit of detail.

No Money

One of the best ways to doom an assessment project is to fall victim to the excuse that no money is available to support the project. As a consequence, goes this line of thinking, the project should be postponed until a more robust budget year ensures that a project can be undertaken.

This excuse will work year in and year out, because as long as assessment is seen as a frill, it will always be supplanted by "more important" budget priorities. Budgeting is a matter of setting priorities as to how funds will be spent, and what is a frill to one person is essential to another.

Assessment does not have to be expensive. The largest expense in virtually any departmental budget is staffing costs, so if staff are given appropriate time to spend on an assessment project, the major portion of the cost of a project can be covered. If consultants are needed, perhaps colleagues on campus have expertise in research design construction or interview protocol development. They might be willing to donate their time or would be willing to trade their expertise for skills that staff in your department may have that would be valuable to another department. If such expertise is not available on campus, perhaps a trade can be arranged with another campus that is geographically proximate. You can help that campus with a project as thanks for receiving help with your project.

The other elements in the project, such as printing, secretarial support, and data analysis, are costs that are manageable. If the department is unable to underwrite these costs, campuses often have small research grants available to faculty members. In a case like this, an arrangement can be developed with a faculty member who needs a site for a research activity. Professional organizations also have grant programs, as do private foundations and governmental units. The expense of the project should never stand in the way of undertaking it.

Lack of Assessment Expertise

Not everyone has had courses in research methods and design, and of those who have had such experiences, it could have been years ago. Further, not all research experts know and understand the differences between research and assessment. So an excuse that one can use to postpone a project or not undertake it at all is that no one in the department has the appropriate expertise to conduct the project.

It is ironic that in institutions of higher education, lack of research expertise can be used as an excuse not to conduct assessments. Research expertise abounds in colleges and universities through graduate students, faculty, and professional staff. When looking for assessment expertise, all one has to do is start talking with faculty colleagues about the rich sites available in student affairs for conducting research and evaluation projects. The unit being assessed can provide the site, and the faculty member can supply the expertise. What may make this particularly enticing is that the department can offer assistance in data collection and analysis, which is attractive to virtually any faculty member wishing to conduct field research.

Another source of expertise is institutional research personnel, if the institution has such an office. Often these staff have the expertise and may also have access to valuable and relevant data that may assist in the assessment process. Yet another often overlooked source of expertise is undergraduate or graduate students. Although the expertise may be more narrowly focused, it can often be helpful when it comes to technical support such as data management and even statistical analysis. Sometimes students are willing to work for free to get some experience in managing and analyzing data.

Lack of Commitment and Support from Leadership

Sometimes unit staff understand the need for assessment, but senior leaders in the division of student affairs do not. As senior leaders deal with broad policy issues, external stakeholders, budget issues, and so on, they may lose touch with the day-to-day challenges of delivering programs and services to students. They will need to be convinced that conducting assessments is in everyone's best interests, including their own.

Strategies need to be developed to convince senior leaders that assessment is something they need to support. Among the approaches would be to assess a program or service that is particularly important to senior leaders—one that is highlighted in annual reports, discussed with parents during orientation sessions, or featured in presentations to the governing body. Perhaps these are programs that are designed to help historically underserved students or programs that advance student leadership skills.

Another approach is to assess a program that will make the senior leader have a positive image. Maybe this is a program for which the senior leader provided additional funding, a program that has received regional or national recognition for excellence, or a program that the president views highly. Within any division, staff know about programs that are highly successful. Why not begin the assessment process by assessing those programs that are going to help the division look good? More areas that are problematic can be assessed later.

Finally, it might make sense to remind the supervisor, and gently, that regional accrediting bodies are asking for more detailed assessment data from institutions undergoing the decennial accreditation process that demonstrate that programs and services have a positive impact on students. An observation that the student affairs division could become a campus leader in the institution's effort to demonstrate how students learn and grow at the campus could be compelling.

Lack of Staff Support

Finally, there can be the problem of lack of staff enthusiasm for assessment projects. Staff may complain that they are busy, have too much to do already, and do not have the energy to put into another initiative. Besides, if this project is undertaken, they say, students will be served less well; they will have to wait several more days before being seen by a counselor, before participating in a workshop, and so on. The irony is that it is often the best and most hard-working staff that are the most resistant, because they are the most resistant to taking time away from their job duties, particularly time with students.

In these cases, staff will need assurance that assessment is a high priority and that they cannot afford not to devote the necessary time to conduct an assessment of the unit's programs and services. Perhaps the department head will need to provide temporary resources to help the unit accomplish its purposes or the assessment project, but hiding behind the excuse that conducting the assessment will result in poorer service for students is unacceptable. Staff must realize that the future of the unit may depend on conducting credible assessments of their impact on students and the institution.

Nonnegotiable Issues

In overcoming these barriers and moving a student affairs organization toward a comprehensive approach to assessment, some issues are nonnegotiable, that is, they must be part of the assessment process, or assessment should not be done at all.

Assessment Will Be Done

Those who are not in favor of conducting assessment studies will develop a host of reasons supporting the contention that assessment studies cannot or should not be done—for example, the timing is not right to conduct an assessment, the costs are too great, the process will detract from the delivery of direct services to students, or staff do not have the expertise to complete a high-quality assessment. Whether to conduct an assessment is not negotiable in our view. Assessment studies need to be done to address a variety of issues identified in this and other books. In the case of our scenario, if the assessment is not done, the department could be in jeopardy in the end. Planning must be undertaken to deal with slowly shifting demographic trends. To get ready for the future, data must be collected on how life in the residence halls can be improved, how students can be retained to a greater degree, and how new initiatives can be accomplished to make the residence halls even more attractive. In short, assessment will help departmental leaders shape the future rather than react to it.

Staff may complain that they do not have enough time, adequate resources, appropriate expertise, or consultation available to get the job done. None of these problems, even if they are real, should stand in the way of conducting assessment studies. Staff need to realize that in the case of the situation outlined at the start of this chapter, the future viability of the department may rest on the assessment projects. This initiative needs to begin now. Compromise is not possible.

Studies Will Have Integrity

Poor studies may be worse than conducting no studies at all. As a consequence, studies must have integrity:

- The purposes of the study are made clear.

- All limitations are identified.

- The methodology of the study is appropriate to the purposes of the study.

- Data must be analyzed consistent with accepted data analysis procedures.

- The study respects the integrity of its subjects.

- Data collected are reported truthfully and completely.

- Conclusions must be supported by the data.

- Recommendations must be consistent with data and conclusions.

- Participants must be treated consistent with human subjects policies and practices (see Chapter Thirty-Two).

- The highest level of ethics will permeate the study (see Chapter Thirty-Two).

There is no question in our minds that most assessment studies will have limitations, and these will need to be identified in the limitations section of the study's report. But even with certain limitations, studies need to be conducted with integrity.

In the case of the scenario, the department head does not anticipate encountering adverse data since things seem to be moving along quite well. But should the data reveal problems with the operation, adjustments may need to be made. If some programs do not measure up to student expectations, then these programs should be improved or eliminated. Finally, if, in working with summer program clients, inadequate services or facilities are revealed, changes will have to be contemplated.

Assessment Will Conform to Institutional Standards

Most institutions have standards for undertaking studies using research methods. This means that a human subjects committee or institutional review board will approve the general approach of the assessment study, review how subjects will be treated, study the letter of invitation to potential subjects, review an interview protocol or survey instrument, and so on. Any deviation from the institution's standards is a major mistake.

The way to make sure that institutional standards are upheld is to be sure to contact the chair of the campus's institutional review board while the study is still in the conceptual stage. If the person heading the assessment team is leading a study committee for the first time, a conversation with the chair can be very useful. So can a frank discussion about institutional standards and expectations. Another useful discussion could be with senior faculty members on campus who are known for their research. Suggestions from them about ensuring a study's integrity is time that is well spent.

Working with a human subjects committee may be a new experience for the director of the program in our scenario. In fact, possibly this person may not even know that such permission must be secured before moving the assessment along since no such committees existed when the person was going to graduate school. Investigators should never fail to secure permission for a study from the human subjects committee. Those who have doubts at any point on the process about how to proceed must be sure to contact the chair for advice. (Further discussion of working with the human subjects committee and other ethical issues is contained in Chapter Thirty-Two.)

At Local College, the focus of the scenario, those responsible for conducting the assessment will need to confer with the human subjects committee to make sure that institutional standards will be met. Also, consultation might be sought with the person responsible for institutional research so that copies of reports from that office can be studied as to form and substance. The study conducted will have to be at a level comparable to the work expected on campus and reflected in these reports.

Multiple Methods Will Be Used

Obviously some studies lend themselves well to a certain type of methodology. Among these are keeping track of users of services where quantitative methods make sense or studying the culture of a student organization where a qualitative approach might suffice. But most projects benefit from using multiple methods. "Combining qualitative and quantitative approaches in the same study simultaneously benefits from the respective advantages of depth and breadth, understanding and generalizability, and closeness to context, as well as standardization across settings" (Berkowitz, 1996, p. 69).

Multiple methods add time and expense to a study and require a broad array of research skills. But we believe strongly that the use of both quantitative and qualitative methods will serve assessors well. Quantitative methods do an excellent job of identifying problems, providing a numerical analysis of the problem, or framing an agenda for additional study. But a study that relies strictly on quantitative methods cannot provide in-depth answers to such questions as how or why something is the way it is. A quantitative study can show that a specific percentage of students regard a service in a certain way (for example, 26.8 percent of all respondents report that the service's operating hours are adequate, but 31.6 percent would prefer different hours). This response does not identify what the change should be. So a qualitative study would provide depth to the assessment. In practical terms, the qualitative dimensions of the assessment might mean that focus groups of service users will reveal that students prefer extended evening office hours and would support an increase in the service fee to extend hours.

The scenario in this chapter would lend itself to assessments that examine student needs, student satisfaction, and outcomes related to student growth and development. In each of these cases, a quantitative study followed by a qualitative study will yield the kind of information on which to develop plans. It is clear that no systematic data are available on the needs of LC's residential students. One possibility is to conduct a quantitative study of what these needs are, using a national instrument or an instrument developed locally. Complementing this approach would be focus groups of residents to learn more about their needs and how they might be met.

A similar approach could be taken to satisfaction. American College Testing (ACT) has an excellent instrument on student satisfaction, as does Noel Levitz, that could be administered to a sample of residents to provide a numeric picture of residents' satisfaction. Focus groups could be employed to follow up on issues that emerge from the qualitative study.

Finally, a variety of instruments could be used to measure the impact of the residential experience on students. The College Student Experiences Questionnaire (Pace and Kuh, 1998) is an excellent instrument for this purpose as the student outcomes instrument developed by ACT. Following the quantitative phase of the assessment, the use of focus groups could be employed to add richness to the assessment project.

We think that almost all studies need to use multiple methods. Developing a study with this understanding in mind will result in richer findings and very likely will lead to changes that will improve services to students and other clients.

Results Will Be Reported

"Knowledge serves little purpose if it is not put to use," Reviere, Berkowitz, Carter, and Ferguson point out (1996, p. 11). We believe that results need to be reported. There may be a temptation to bury the results of a study that do not reflect well on the department or program being assessed. After all, who wants to reveal their weaknesses?

In spite of the risk, results need to be reported. Elsewhere in this book we have indicated that the worst-case scenario should be identified when considering undertaking a study. If the worst case is unacceptable, then it is wise not to do the study, assuming that is an option. In some cases, the politics of the situation will not allow avoiding doing the study. But assuming there is an option, it may be best simply to avoid the study.

If the study is undertaken, the results must be reported. Not reporting the results will cause additional problems. Those involved in the study will wonder what happened? Media, especially the student newspaper, will charge a cover-up and run stories about the study whose results were not reported. In short, the failure to report the results will become the story.

In our scenario, the operation is highly regarded and is working well at the moment. But the results of the study may point to potential erosion of facilities, services, or programs that might make the residence halls less attractive in the future. These problems need to be reported so that accurate plans can be developed.

Reporting unfavorable results takes courage. But these results can be reported with an action plan to remedy the situation. In this way, the report becomes the first step in the development of an improved situation. One other aspect of reporting unfavorable results is worth comment. Conducting an assessment that results in unfavorable findings is discouraging. On the other hand, the willingness of a unit to undertake an assessment conducted with high integrity and then reporting the findings may result in the unit's receiving the admiration of other units, especially those units that are unwilling or unavailable to conduct their own assessments.

Negotiable Issues

In conducting assessments, several issues can be negotiated toward the goal of establishing and maintaining an effective assessment effort.

What Is the Purpose of the Study?

Determining the purpose of the study is the first negotiable item, although there is no other consideration that is more important than a clear specification of the purpose it is intended to accomplish (Hobbs, 1979). Suppose that concerns are raised about the quality of life in campus residence halls. Critics assert that the level of the overall student experience in campus residences is not what it should be. An assessment of the situation is indicated. All interested agree on that as a logical course of action.

But this assessment could take a number of forms. One might be to conduct a satisfaction assessment of the residents. Are they happy with their experiences? Do they find the experience consistent with their expectations. Or an outcomes assessment might be conducted. Does the residential experience result in student growth and development consistent with institutional objectives? How does the growth of residents compare with commuters? Still another possibility might be to conduct a cultural assessment. What are the values of students who live in the residence halls? What do students expect of each other?

In our scenario, the assessment needs to be conducted to provide a basis for future initiatives. But whether the study is a needs assessment, satisfaction assessment, outcomes assessment, or something very different, like an environmental assessment or student culture assessment, is debatable. We have suggested the former rather than the latter, but room for compromise exists because regardless of the type of assessment conducted, positive and negative aspects of the residence halls will be identified. As the planning process moves from assessment to evaluation, issues can be addressed to improve the residence halls for the future.

Any or all of the studies proposed would be appropriate for the assessment of the general presenting problem. The purpose of the study would have to be negotiated to the point where all the interested parties would agree on it. Perhaps conducting something as complex as an outcomes assessment may be more than the campus is ready for the first time an assessment is undertaken. Still, LC wants to know something about how students react to the residential experience, so it might compromise and conduct a satisfaction assessment using a strong, nationally recognized instrument like ACT's student satisfaction survey. Assuming this first study goes well, more complicated studies can follow in the future as members of the campus community get used to assessment as part of the yearly campus routine. What they will not negotiate is whether to conduct the assessment; they can negotiate the type.

Who Will Be Involved?

Who will be involved in the study is the second item that is negotiable. Suppose in the scenario described that one proposal would be to involve those who are critical of the residence halls in the study. Would they have much to contribute? How strong are their research skills? What if they are not involved?

One of the challenges in an assessment is the degree to which those who are critical of the service or program should be involved in the assessment process. Although it is impossible to make a blanket statement about whether critics should be involved to some extent in the assessment process, certainly exploring whether they should be involved makes sense. Without their involvement, there is potential for criticism that the process was not open, that the assessment was structured to generate favorable results for the unit being assessed, and that the recommendations were self-serving. Probably a good place to start is to try to involve as wide a group as possible in the planning phase of the assessment, eliminating some people only when their inclusion is impossible.

In the scenario, LC would probably want people from inside and outside the department. Among the people who may be involved would be students; representatives from admissions, the dean of students office, and financial aid; and perhaps several interested faculty members.

Reviere and Berkowitz (1996) make the case that stakeholders ought to be involved in an assessment process. They report that compromises might need to be struck in terms of scientific rigor, control of the efforts, and potential conflicts among stakeholders. But they concluded, "Even so, the benefits of stakeholder participation outweigh the drawbacks" (p. 209).

What Are the Criteria for Assessment?

The criteria for assessment also are negotiable. This issue deals with how to measure success. In some situations, it is very difficult to determine success. What is a good experience for residence hall students? What is a negative experience? How does one measure student growth? A good example is the experiences that students have in residence halls. Suppose noisy neighbors in the residence halls disrupt a student's life. As a consequence, the student learns how to negotiate with others and deal with this kind of problem, resulting in greater autonomy and self-reliance on the student's part. Is this a good experience? The student encountered an unpleasant situation and was distracted, but it was resolved. The value of the experience is in the eye of beholder.

This example illustrates how the criteria for assessment can be negotiated. If the people conducting the assessment determine that such distractions, regardless of their outcomes, are inappropriate, then learning about these kinds of situations may lead to one form of intervention. On the other hand, if developing more autonomy and self-reliance is an important goal of the program, then the experience was positive. Once the definition of what is desirable has been determined, then the assessment's results can be framed and potential interventions designed.

At Local College, staff in the division of student affairs could form the core of the assessment team. Complementing them would be several faculty with special expertise in research design. It might even make sense to bring aboard some graduate students from the state university located fifty miles away who are studying research methods. They have the potential to be very helpful in this process.

Who Will Conduct the Study?

People in the department being assessed are best equipped to conduct some studies, but other studies are better conducted by a combination of people inside the unit with people exterior to the unit but still members of the campus community. Still others ought to involve people from outside the institution. Expertise certainly is a determining factor in who will be involved in conducting the study.

We believe that people from the unit being assessed should be involved in the study. Generally, doing an assessment without the involvement of people from the unit can cause problems, not the least of which is the claim by those interior to the unit that "those who conducted the study simply do not understand us." And other more subtle claims can be made about the assessment. Moreover, developing recommendations for change generally is difficult without the involvement of the people within the unit. What is important to remember is that often a combination of people inside and outside the unit is the best course of action. Who more precisely will be involved is negotiable.

The LC scenario is not particularly emotionally charged because the assessment is being done for planning purposes. Relatively little or no external pressure is being placed on the director other than self-imposed pressure. Thus, the people who are involved in the assessment likely should be those with the greatest expertise who can contribute to the process. This also might be a good opportunity to educate selected staff about the value of this kind of process. They might also be involved in supporting roles.

What Is the Design of the Study?

A multiple methods approach is clearly the most desirable way to conduct a study. Exactly how a study might be designed, though, is negotiable. And there may be times that the practical situation will not allow for the use of multiple methods. Consider this example.

A unit is under pressure to demonstrate how it contributes to student growth. A governing board meeting is scheduled in six weeks to discuss this issue, along with others, so a study has to be conducted quickly to determine the extent to which the unit contributes to student growth. No one in the unit has the specific expertise to conduct a quantitative study, although several staff have excellent qualitative skills. A qualitative study is conducted, and the results are presented at the board meeting along with some recommendations for practice.

In this example, the design was negotiable to the extent that the expertise of the staff and the time available dictated that a certain kind of study had to be conducted. As long as the study was a good one and had the elements of a good study, the approach was acceptable. In other situations, the design may be negotiable. (Although the design may be negotiable, we do not suggest that the quality or the integrity of the study are compromised.)

Local College can use a combination of qualitative and quantitative methods to conduct the study of residential life on campus. It needs to determine student satisfaction with various services and programs, how cost-effective the department is, and the extent to which the various programs and learning experiences of the department contribute to student learning. Mixed methods will serve this assessment well.

Is Any Consultation Needed?

Whether consultants are needed will be a function of the nature of the assessment, the skills of the staff who are conducting the assessment, the time available, and other specific elements of the study.

Consultants could be identified in one or more of the following areas:

- Research design
- Instrument development
- Data collection
- Data analysis
- Development of various reports
- Presentation of findings

Individuals who serve as consultants may be from the institution or could be external to the campus. For example, a faculty member in sociology or psychology with specific interests in research methods could be helpful. Graduate students in higher education, student affairs, or counseling could participate in the process. To identify potential consultants, taking an inventory of associates in the college is a good place to start. As specific areas of expertise are identified, these individuals can be invited to assist in the development of the project.

No formula exists related to the extent to which consultants are needed, except that if staff do not have the expertise to handle certain elements of the study, then clearly consultation is needed. On the other hand, if those conducting the study have the expertise, then there may be no point in using consultants.

One of the important benefits of using consultants is that once they have agreed to participate in the project, they will be interested in the project's findings. Hobbs (1979, p. 33) points out that "generally, people who have contributed their time and ideas also exhibit greater interest in the results and the prospective courses of action they may imply." Thus, the use of consultants from the institution may have the consequence of developing a corps of allies on the campus that can be very helpful in the process of making changes. (For a discussion of use of consultants, see Chapter Thirty-One.)

How Should Findings Be Interpreted?

What the findings mean is open to interpretation. The discussion section is an appropriate place to interpret what has been found—for example, "This is an appropriate time to mention any subjective and educative reactions of the researcher to the results" (Soriano, 1995, p. 90). Students may interpret qualitative findings differently than staff do. Multiple people may be involved in analyzing the data for multiple audiences (students, staff, faculty, senior administrators, and so on).

Consider the example of the residence hall student who had to negotiate through a situation where the environment was disturbing. The assessors learn that this situation is fairly common, meaning that the environment disturbs students and they have to work with other residents to negotiate their way to improved conditions. Staff believe that this process produces student growth. The assessment reveals that student growth is generated by this approach, but at some cost to students in terms of time and aggravation.

So how does one interpret this situation? Just one issue—that being related to students having to serve as their own advocates when study conditions deteriorate, with staff playing a secondary role but supportive role—can generate substantial discussion and alternative plans. Maybe the solution to the problem is to try to lower the density of the living units by offering more single rooms, or redefine the role of staff, or make physical improvements that will result in the absorption of sound. Is the situation positive or negative? Does it fit with the mission of the institution or the unit? How did this philosophy evolve? Should it continue? These questions and others are open to interpretation and opinion. Perhaps the current approach is just right, but perhaps it is not. From such questions, discussion and debate develop.

In the LC scenario, plans for the future of the residence halls are being developed. How the results are interpreted will be very important, because substantial initiatives may follow, such as facility renovations and changed staffing patterns. Thus, discussions about the findings, perhaps in the form of open hearings with students and staff, may be in order.

What Are the Recommendations for Policy and Practice?

Depending on the findings and the interpretation of them, certain recommendations for policy and practice will emerge. These too are debatable. If the findings of the residential environment study are interpreted negatively, then a variety of possible changes emerge, including articulating a different philosophy of residence hall life, hiring different kinds of staff, providing a different kind of training for staff, or taking a different approach to supervision of staff. Any or all of these different approaches could be implemented if it is determined that changes are necessary. "If larger, more sweeping changes will encounter resistance, start small. Break a large program into smaller, more easily accepted parts. Success from small changes establishes a positive climate for subsequent larger changes and a willingness to examine the future" (Witkin and Altschuld, 1995, pp. 277–278).

To this point in the process, it has been rather smooth sailing for the LC director of housing. But now the most difficult aspect of the process is confronted because implications for practice need to be put in place. Will facility renovations be undertaken? Will a different programming philosophy be adopted? Will room and board rates need to be reduced to remain competitive with off-campus housing, or will they be increased dramatically to pay for new amenities? The wrong decisions on these and other issues could result in long-term problems for the viability of the residence halls. Therefore, these decisions need to be made very carefully and may involve some compromise for the director and the others involved in this process.

Recommendations for policy and practice take the assessment into its next phase: evaluation. If the determination of the assessors is that change is necessary, precisely what the changes should be can vary widely depending on one's perspective, philosophy, and thoughts about the unit's operation.

Conclusion

Getting started in assessment is not easy, but it can be done if the leadership and staff of a student affairs organization have the commitment to developing and implementing a comprehensive assessment program, following the suggestions and guidelines outlined in this chapter. Assessment is no longer a luxury but a necessity, and getting started on the right foot is essential.

References

Berkowitz, S. "Using Qualitative and Mixed-Method Approaches." In R. Reviere, S. Berkowitz, C. C. Carter, and C. G. Ferguson (eds.), *Needs Assessment: A Creative and Practical Guide for Social Scientists,* Washington, D.C.: Taylor & Francis, 1996.

Hobbs, D. "Strategy for Needs Assessments." In L. R. Kaufman and F. W. English, *Needs Assessment: Concept and Application.* Englewood Cliffs, N.J.: Educational Technology Publications, 1979.

Kaufman, L. R., and English, F. W. *Needs Assessment: Concept and Application.* Englewood Cliffs, N.J.: Educational Technology Publications, 1979.

Pace, C. R., and Kuh, G. D. *College Student Experiences Questionnaire.* (4th ed.) Bloomington: Indiana University, 1998.

Reviere, R., and Berkowitz, S. "Building for Future Needs Assessments." In R. Reviere, S. Berkowitz, C. C. Carter, and C. G. Ferguson (eds.), *Needs Assessment: A Creative and Practical Guide for Social Scientists.* Washington, D.C.: Taylor & Francis, 1996.

Reviere, R., Berkowitz, S., Carter, C. C., and Ferguson, C. G. "Introduction: Setting the Stage." In R. Reviere, S. Berkowitz, C. C. Carter, and C. G. Ferguson (eds.), *Needs Assessment: A Creative and Practical Guide for Social Scientists.* Washington, D.C.: Taylor & Francis, 1996.

Soriano, F. I. *Conducting Needs Assessments.* Thousand Oaks, Calif.: Sage, 1995.

Witkin, B. R., and Altschuld, J. W. *Planning and Conducting Needs Assessments: A Practical Guide.* Thousand Oaks, Calif.: Sage, 1995.

Chapter 31

Arranging for a Consultant

TYPICALLY WE DO NOT advocate hiring external consultants to conduct assessment projects. We believe that those who are closest to the situation are better positioned to conduct an assessment than a person external to the campus. But in some situations, hiring an external consultant makes sense. For example, in doing a campus culture study, the perspective of an outsider can be especially useful (Whitt, 1996).

Consultation can take three general forms. One of these has to do with expertise in the specific area of inquiry. For example, if an assessment of the student union is desired, an individual with special expertise in student unions is needed since the leadership of the student union on campus needs help in several areas. The second area of expertise has to do with research methods. Sometimes individuals with specialized expertise are needed, such as a person to conduct focus groups when no member of the staff has the experience with or knowledge about this technique. A third use of a consultant is to conduct assessment workshops for student affairs staff as a way of introducing the whole topic of assessment and building support for its implementation at a particular campus.

There may be times when the expertise necessary to conduct an inquiry requires a person external to the campus. In this book, for example, Chapter Twenty-One presents a case study about the office of financial aid. Part of the assessment plan for that case involved reviewing policies and procedures applied to students through the review of financial aid records. In this case, we suggested that an external person lead the assessment team.

This chapter explains the process by which an external consultant is selected to participate in the assessment process. We present a series of issues that need to be addressed in selecting and working with a consultant.

Do You Need a Consultant?

The first question in this process is to explore whether an external consultant is needed. Two issues need to be considered:

- What about the assessment makes hiring a consultant necessary?

- What special expertise would a consultant bring that is not available on campus?

Frequently campuses hire consultants after concluding that a person external to the campus will have more expertise than is available on campus, including all faculty and staff. In fact, even if the expertise is not available in the division of student affairs, it is possible that faculty members in such disciplines as sociology, anthropology, psychology, or education can make the kinds of contributions necessary to conduct an assessment project. It is important to remember that the time of faculty members is their most precious commodity and that quite typically faculty have only limited resources at their disposal. As a consequence, in lieu of paying a faculty member as a consultant, the office might make some travel money available to the faculty member or some other form of support (such as a summer salary supplement) as compensation for this person's involvement in a project. The faculty member will appreciate this, and the office will find that the cost is far less than hiring an external consultant.

Finding a Consultant

The next issue has to do with finding a consultant. Not everyone is capable of serving as a consultant, and finding a person with some experience dealing with the area in question is essential. Unless a relationship already has been established with a consultant, such as hiring a graduate of the college who has gone on to establish considerable expertise in the area being assessed, one has to rely on several sources for potential consultants. One of these sources is to seek help from professional organizations. At times, these organizations keep files of individuals who report having expertise in certain areas. Although the associations more often than not make no claims about the level of expertise that potential consultants have, they will be able to provide a list of individuals who could be contacted.

The other possible source of recommendations is colleagues. With the use of electronic communications, messages can be sent to a number of colleagues in a hurry seeking recommendations. It is important to make the needs clear in terms of the kind of expertise that is required. Do you want someone who is an expert in design, data analysis, selection of instruments or something else?

Identifying a Consultant

Once there is a list of names of several potential consultants, how do you determine the person to hire? In the beginning, it is important to make contact with all of the potential consultants, determine if they are interested, and ask for résumés, which should include other settings where they have served as consultants. With the names of the institutions, consultants also ought to provide the names of people who can describe what they did at their institution and the level of assistance provided.

The references ought to be checked, especially in the context of what it is that you seek a consultant to do. Just because a consultant has a stellar reputation in the field does not mean that the person has the level of expertise necessary to serve well in a specific role sought by your campus.

Arranging for the Consultant

Once a person has been identified to serve as a consultant, negotiations need to begin to arrive at appropriate terms. These must be determined before the person begins work. A number of items need to be considered.

What Will the Consultant Do?

Will this person lead an assessment process, do training for staff, be on call to handle questions as they arise, some combination of these, or something else? These are very different functions, and some consultants are far more capable of handling some functions well but not others. One of the best ways to arrange for a consultant is that after conversations have been held with the consultant, a follow-up letter is sent so that everyone understands exactly what is expected.

When Will the Consultant Be on Campus?

A time needs to be identified that meets the campus's needs as well as the consultant's. If, for example, a meeting with the senior officers of the institution is necessary, then calendars need to be checked before the dates of the consultant's visit have been determined.

What Is Appropriate Compensation?

Typically consultants charge on a daily basis plus expenses. At first sight, the amount of the person's daily fee may seem high, but this fee encompasses the consultant's preparation for the campus visit or, in the case of a training activity, preparing the training materials before the visit. All of this takes time and is reflected in the consultant's fee. If a report from the consultant is sought, that too will take time and is likely to be the product of several drafts.

One of the best ways to handle compensation is for the campus to provide airline tickets (assuming that the consultant is located farther than driving distance from the campus) so the consultant does not have substantial up-front expenses to cover before being reimbursed. The campus should cover all of the consultant's expenses, including the consultant's mileage to and from airports, meals, lodging, and any other costs. It works to the consultant's advantage to have all meals billed directly to the campus or paid for by the person hosting the consultant. If meals are covered on a reimbursement basis, negative tax consequences will accrue to the consultant, since only part of the cost of the meals may be tax deductible.

What About a Team of Consultants?

If a team of consultants is hired, one person should be designated as the leader and held accountable for making sure that team needs are communicated to the campus. If a report is sought from the team, then the person will transmit the report to the campus. The team leader ought to be compensated at a higher level than other team members since this person has more work to complete than the other team members.

What About Arranging for Payment?

Arranging for payment is the other issue that ought to be settled in advance. A good strategy is to reimburse the consultant for expenses as fast as possible after the consultant has submitted receipts. Payment of the consultant's honorarium should be forthcoming as soon as the work is completed. If a report is sought from the consultant, payment should be made after the report has been received and determined to be consistent with the original agreement. This approach works to everyone's advantage: the consultant can be confident that the report is satisfactory and the campus, by making payment, has indicated that the report is acceptable.

Should a Contract Be Prepared?

The answer to this question depends to a certain extent on how the campus does business with all consultants. But whether a contract or a letter is prepared defining what is required from all parties, it is essential that the arrangements be committed to writing.

What About the Consultant's Schedule?

Depending on the nature of what is sought from the consultant, a well-crafted but not overloaded schedule needs to be prepared. The campus should be mindful if the consultant has traveled more than one time zone and realize that traveling from west to east makes it very difficult to begin work early in the morning. Similarly, if the consultant has traveled from east to west, late evening meetings may be difficult because of the differences in time zones.

Developing a schedule is crucial to the success of the visit. Meetings should not be scheduled every hour. Breaks should be built in the schedule so that the consultant can relax, take a walk, or review notes. If meals are planned in advance rather than ordered from a menu, be sure to check in advance to ascertain whether the consultant has special dietary needs.

One way of wearing a consultant out is to schedule very early breakfast meetings or long dinner meetings. The consultant has had to prepare materials, review notes, and, if an oral report is sought at the end of the visit, organize information in preparing for the next day. Some consultants enjoy lots of social time with the campus community, while others prefer having a bit of private time to collect their thoughts and prepare. The extent to which consultants want to engage in social activity ought to be determined in advance of the visit.

How Will the Consultant's Findings and Recommendations Be Reported?

Although there is no standard format for a consultant's report, the institution should provide some guidance about how to report findings and recommendations. At a minimum, a report should contain some background about the problem that precipitated hiring a consultant, how the consultant went about doing the work (for example, identifying the documents reviewed and a listing of those persons with whom the consultant spoke), what the consultant found to be the facts of the problem, and what recommendations the consultant would make to resolve the problem. The confidentiality of the consultant's report should also be made clear before any work is done. Sometimes it will be a public document, but often it will be a confidential document restricted to a few persons.

What About Involving the Consultant in Other Activities?

One potential aspect of a consultant's visit is for the campus to ask the person to meet with a class or give remarks related to another area of expertise or research. If this is asked of the consultant, then an additional fee ought to be offered, assuming the consultant is interested in this assignment. For example, if the consultant is invited to assist in an assessment project related to student activities but also has conducted research on staff development, he or she might be asked to deliver a presentation on this research. The campus should not assume, however, that the consultant could pull a speech or workshop off the shelf and be ready to deliver it without additional preparation. If the consultant is asked to do something of this nature, additional compensation ought to be offered. Some consultants will not have any concerns about an additional presentation, but others will find it distracting. Without question, an extra presentation will require more energy on the part of the consultant.

Expectations for Consultants

Consultants are not miracle workers. They cannot solve all the problems of the campus in a two- or three-day visit. If the consultant conducts a workshop, then the campus needs to follow through and implement what has been learned in the workshop. If a report with recommendations has been prepared, then it is up to the campus to determine which of the recommendations can be implemented.

Consultants, no matter how quickly they learn about the campus, cannot be expected to solve contextual problems, meaning that it is very difficult for them to help develop strategies to solve political problems, disputes between departments, and so on. Consultants can help identify best practices and good strategies for improvement, but that is about the extent to which they can be helpful. Unrealistic expectations result in little being gained and may have the potential to demoralize the campus.

After the Consultant's Visit

After the consultant has visited the campus and the work has been completed, the campus has to determine how best to use the products of the work. If training has been conducted, staff need to implement what they have learned. If a report has been filed with recommendations, the campus has to develop a timetable to implement those that it wishes to adopt. A call or two for clarification to the consultant is entirely appropriate, but if the contact begins to be ongoing, then a more formal relationship may be sought.

Conclusion

This chapter has identified a number of issues related to the use of consultants. Although it has been framed as advice for the campus, individuals who are interested in doing consulting can use a mirror image. Consultants can play a crucial role in the success of some assessment projects, and the advice provided in the chapter can help facilitate their use.

Reference

Whitt, E. J. "Assessing Student Cultures." In M. L. Upcraft and J. H. Schuh, *Assessment in Student Affairs: A Guide for Practitioners*. San Francisco: Jossey-Bass, 1996.

Chapter 32

Ethical Issues

ONE OF THE MAJOR concerns in any assessment project is that the highest ethical standards guide the activity. Although we have noted elsewhere in this book and other publications (Upcraft and Schuh, 1996) that one might make compromises in the assessment activity, we wish to assert here that one should never make compromises, engage in short cuts, or in any other way fail to uphold the highest ethical standards. This chapter describes the ethical standards that should be applied in assessment activities, presents some documents that are helpful in ensuring appropriate ethical standards, and introduce some ethical scenarios for discussion and reflection.

Kitchener's Principles

Karen Kitchener (1985) has developed a series of principles related to ethics. A brief discussion of them follows based on the work of Canon (1993, 1996).

Respecting Autonomy

This principle assumes that individuals have the right to decide how they wish to live their lives as long as what they do does not interfere with the rights of others. In the context of conducting an assessment, this means that if students do not want to participate in the assessment, they should not be coerced into participating.

There is no question that in the case of some assessments it may be difficult to attract an adequate pool of respondents. This may be especially true when an assessment must be conducted when students have too much else to do, such as during examination periods or just before vacation periods.

It may be tempting to twist students' arms figuratively to participate, but that would violate this principle. Participation in an assessment project should not be a course requirement.

Doing No Harm

Doing no harm means that subjects should never be put at risk. All studies will need approval from the college's Institutional Review Board (IRB), and in the description of the study, the assessor will have to indicate the extent to which potential subjects will be put at risk. If subjects are at risk, this must be acknowledged, and that they may refuse to participate if that is their wish should be explained. Nevertheless, the assessor may claim that the subjects are not at risk and then reveal damaging information.

IRBs are responsible for making sure that research efforts do not pose psychological, physical, or legal harm to participants. They tend to review and approve plans, procedures, and consent forms to be used by organizations external to the college or university as a public service or obligation (Soriano, 1995). Those conducting an assessment should always receive permission from the IRB before collecting data.

Suppose, for example, in conducting a qualitative assessment of the campus's alcohol, a student is referred to not by name but by pseudonym followed by home town and major. If the student is one of just a handful of students from this town and only a few students choose that major, it will be easy to identify the student who has been guaranteed anonymity. If the student is quoted as providing alcoholic beverages to a minor, additional problems could arise. The point is obvious: great care must be taken to make sure that harm is not done to respondents.

Benefiting Others

The general purpose in conducting assessments is to improve agency, unit, or program effectiveness. The driving concern is the welfare of students, clients, or others who benefit from services. Canon (1993, p. 330) makes this observation about benefiting others: "Those in the helping professions assume that the welfare of the consumer comes first when other considerations are equal."

Assessments in student affairs are conducted to improve services and make programs more effective. As a result, assessments are conducted without regard to the consequences. If changes need to be made to ensure that students and other clients are served better, then they will have to be implemented.

Being Just

Whatever those conducting the assessment promise to respondents must be delivered. If this means that an abstract of the results is promised to each of the participants, then it must be provided. This also means that each subject is treated equally. If an incentive is provided to some subjects, for example, the same incentive should be offered to all subjects.

The question of providing an incentive to potential respondents so that they will participate arises from time to time in discussions related to improving the participation rate. One of the strategies we recommend is the development of a partnership with a campus agency, say, a bookstore or snack bar. Each participant then could be provided with a coupon good for a discount on the purchase of an item on campus. This approach spreads the cost of the incentive among several campus departments and keeps the revenue within the institution. We recommend this approach over providing cash to participants or developing an arrangement with an off-campus vendor.

Other incentives that accrue to respondents, according to Soriano (1995), are the sense of moral responsibility or obligation they have to participate in the study or the benefits that will accrue to them by participating in the study. (For more information about recruiting potential participants, see Soriano, 1995.)

Being Faithful

Finally, the assessment process is dedicated to revealing the truth. As we wrote in 1996 (Upcraft and Schuh, p. 294), "Assessment rests on the premise that the process is conducted with scrupulous attention to finding the truth. The very purpose of the assessment is to determine what is true."

Canon adds that this principle also means being loyal and keeping promises. In the case of assessment, a variety of promises are made to all the stakeholders interested in the assessment. The assessment needs to be completed as promised, with reports going to all of those who have been assured that they will receive an accounting of what was found.

Working with Subjects

The heart of the guiding principles that support ethics in assessment has to do with working with subjects. One should never forget that assessment studies are conducted in student affairs primarily to improve the experiences of college students. Students and other members of institutional families form the heart of assessments and should always be treated with the highest ethical standards.

Since assessment studies fall under the broad umbrella of institutional research, the assessor should work with the campus human subjects committee in gaining permission to conduct studies. Permission in this case does not refer to seeking approval for the concept of the study or determining if the study has value. Rather, it refers to the fact that the human subjects committee has approved the approach that the assessor plans to take to make sure that the subjects participating in the study will be protected.

Typically the subjects in assessment studies are not at risk. Pharmaceuticals are not being tested on them, nor are they given lower grades for their courses if they choose not to participate. But there are times when studies could have unpleasant ramifications for subjects if they are not protected. For example, an assessment of the effectiveness of a campus's policy regarding the possession and use of illegal drugs could result in students' revealing that they had used drugs illegally. If this information was reported with student names revealed, the students could find themselves in difficulty. Clearly, protecting the rights of students is crucial in conducting assessment studies.

Commonly the rights of subjects are protected through the use of the institution's human subjects committee (what we have referred to as the IRB). IRBs consist of faculty members and others whose primary responsibility is to review proposed studies to make sure that the rights of subjects are protected. Before anyone is permitted to collect data from subjects, members of the review board have to determine that the rights of subjects are protected. The IRB will review the plan for the study, how the data are collected, and the plan the researcher has to make sure that the rights of the subjects are protected. It may make comments on the letter the researcher has prepared to invite subjects to participate in the study, interview protocols, or other elements of the study. Once permission is provided in writing, the fieldwork can begin. A sample letter that invites people to participate in the study, which should be on the institution's letterhead, is contained in Exhibit 32.1.

Individual campuses may vary in their approach to protecting the rights of human subjects. We urge those conducting assessments to check with the chair of human subjects committee before beginning an assessment project so that the rights of human subjects are protected in planning the project and to make sure that plans do not have to be altered dramatically to conform with campus regulations. Exhibit 32.2 contains a checklist for making sure that the rights of subjects are protected.

EXHIBIT 32.1

Model Consent Form

You are invited to participate in a study of [state what is being studied]. We hope to learn [state what the study is designed to discover or establish]. You were selected as a possible participant in this study [state why and how the subject was selected].

If you desire to participate, you will [describe the procedures to be followed, including their purposes, how long they will take, and their frequency].

[Describe any risks, discomforts, and inconveniences that may reasonably be expected and any benefits to subjects or society that may reasonably be expected.]

Any information obtained in this study in which you can be identified will remain confidential and will be disclosed only with your permission. [If any information will be released to anyone for any reason, state the persons or agencies to whom the information will be given, the nature of the information to be given, and the purpose of the disclosure.]

[Describe any compensation or costs related to the study.]*

Participation in this study is voluntary. Your decision to participate or not to participate will not affect your future relations with [institution or agency]. If you decide to participate, you may withdraw from the study at any time without affecting your status as a [patient, student, or other status].

If you have any questions about this research, please ask me. If you have additional questions during the study, I will be glad to answer them. You can contact me at [name, address, and telephone].†

You will be given a copy of this consent form to keep.

You are making a decision whether to participate. Your signature indicates that you have read the information provided about this study and have voluntarily decided to participate.

_____   _____
Signature of Subject   Date

_____   _____
Signature of parent or legal guardian   Date
[if subject is under 18 years of age]

_____   _____
Signature of Investigator   Date

*If participation of human subjects poses more than minimal risk or involves physical activity, include the following paragraph:

I have been informed and I understand that the college does not provide medical treatment or other forms of reimbursement to persons injured as a result of or in connection with participation in research activities conducted by the college or its faculty. If I believe that I have been injured as a result of participating in research covered by this consent form, I should contact the Office of Research Administration at the college.

†If you are collecting data by means of a mail-out question, you may substitute the following format from paragraph 7 through the end of the document:

You are under no obligation to participate in this study. Your completion and return of this questionnaire will be taken as evidence of your willingness to participate and your consent to have the information used for the purposes of the study.

You may keep this cover letter and explanation about the nature of your participation in this study and the handling of the information you supply.

Sincerely,

_____
Signature of Investigator

Note: *The principal investigator must sign this letter.*

EXHIBIT 32.2

Consent Form Checklist

Items	Yes	No
1. Is the general purpose of the study stated, that is, what the researcher expects to learn? Comments: _____	____	____
2. Is the subject's right to choose indicated? Comments: _____	____	____
3. Is there a statement indicating how a subject was selected as a possible participant? Are the population and number of subjects identified? Comments: _____	____	____
4. Are the procedures to be followed in the study clearly described (time, frequency, nature of information asked, observations, and so on)? Comments: _____	____	____
5. Is there a statement of possible risks, discomforts, or inconveniences that the participants may reasonably expect? Comments: _____	____	____
6. Are any substantial or likely benefits to subjects identified? Comments: _____	____	____
7. Is any standard treatment withheld or alternative procedures disclosed? Comments: _____	____	____
8. Is subject confidentiality explained (for example, use of tapes, photos, data)? Comments: _____	____	____
9. Are subjects' compensation and costs of participating in the study explained? Comments: _____	____	____
10. Is where the subject can contact the investigator to have questions answered indicated? Comments: _____	____	____
11. Is the subject's right to a written copy of the consent form stated? Comments: _____	____	____
12. Is there a statement that expresses that the individual's signature indicates a willingness to participate? Comments: _____	____	____
13. Are appropriate signature and date spaces included? Comments: _____	____	____

Other Ethical Issues

Several other ethical issues are of importance.

Data Access

Who has access to the raw data of the assessment, including completed questionnaires, interview tapes, and documents? It is possible that the assessor's supervisor may want to study the raw data, but if confidentiality has been promised, then the supervisor may not have access to the information. What may be even more difficult is what happens when the information is evaluative in nature, that is, relating to unit leadership. Those who provide the leadership may be curious as to what is said about them. This information cannot be revealed.

Data Ownership

If one of the objectives in agreeing to help another unit with an assessment is to publish an article about the findings, it would be well to determine who owns the data and whether the data can be revealed in the journal article. The information developed in the assessment may seem benign to an outsider, but such may not be the case to members of the unit who do not want the information to be revealed to a wide audience, such as the readership of a journal.

Negotiating an Agreement

Roles in the assessment process need to be discussed and negotiated before beginning the project. The same is true for data ownership. Virtually no situation can be worse than to be unclear about roles in an assessment project and reach an impasse in the middle of it. Exhibit 32.3 contains a sample memorandum of understanding.

Role Conflicts

It is very difficult to evaluate one's own unit without the involvement of outsiders. At times, the person responsible for the unit also may be the person best qualified to conduct the assessment. How is this situation to be handled?

The involvement of others outside the unit can be key to resolving challenges related to role conflicts. So that the leader is also not responsible for leading the assessment of the unit, outsiders can play specific roles designed to resolve conflicts of interest. They can help plan the assessment, collect data, help in the analysis of the results, and assist in the draft of the various reports. This will relieve the pressure on the leader of the unit and help ensure the integrity of the process.

EXHIBIT 32.3

Model Memorandum of Agreement

[Date]

The following document will serve as a memorandum of agreement about the assessment project tentatively titled [project title], hereinafter referred to as "the Project."

1. This agreement is between [name of person commissioning the Project] and [name of person who will do the Project].

2. The purposes of the Project are the following:

    a. _____
    b. _____
    c. _____
    d. _____

3. A preliminary report will be submitted by [name of person who will do the Project] by [date].

4. A final report will be submitted by [name of person who will do the Project] by [date].

5. When the Project has been completed, ownership of the data will revert to [name of the person who will own the data; it can be the person commissioning the Project, carrying out the Project, or a third party. This point is negotiable].

6. [Name of the person who will do the Project] will [or will not] be able to publish the results of the Project without the permission of [name of the person commissioning the Project; this point is negotiable].

7. Permission to undertake the Project from the site's institutional review board will be secured by [name of the person]. In addition, each person who is invited to participate as a subject will have to complete an informed consent form.

8. Upon completing the Project and submitting a final report, compensation for [amount] will be remitted to [name].

AGREED:

_____ _____   _____ _____

Person who commissioned the Project   Date   Person who will do the Project   Date

The codes of ethics of the American College Personnel Association (1997) and the National Association of Student Personnel Administrators (2000), which can be helpful in dealing with ethical issues, are useful sources of information. A list of common ethical mistakes that people engaged in the assessment process make is contained in Exhibit 32.4.

Data Collection

Rea and Parker (1997) note that data should be collected at times convenient to the participants. They also have provided the following guidelines:

More than one adult in the same household should not be interviewed.

Friends or relatives should not be interviewed. If such people turn up in the sampling process, the potential respondent should be turned over to another interviewer.

Interviews should be conducted with as much privacy as possible. This means that if a bank of telephones is used, an adequate distance separates interviewers from one another.

EXHIBIT 32.4

Ethical, Legal, and Human Relations Mistakes Sometimes Made by Educational Investigators

- Forgets to obtain approval for the project from the Institutional Review Board
- Fails to determine who has access to the data generated by the assessment
- Has not prepared answers for questions likely to be asked by site administrators about the assessment
- Compromises the soundness of the assessment design by making changes for the administrative convenience of the institution from which subjects are to be drawn
- Does not follow correct procedures for obtaining informed consent from subjects or their caretakers
- Fails to establish adequate safeguards to ensure the confidentiality of assessment data
- Uses data collection procedures that cannot be defended to critics of the research study
- Establishes good rapport and then loses it by failing to maintain ongoing communications with groups that have a stake in the research project
- Fails to determine data ownership in advance of the data collection
- Fails to resolve potential role conflicts in advance of beginning the project

Source: *Based on Gall, Borg, and Gall (1996).*

Assigned interviews should not be delegated by one interviewer to another.

Interviews should never be falsified.

Ethical Scenarios

Blaxter, Hughes, and Tight (1996) have developed a number of useful scenarios for discussion purposes. A few of them follow, with potential solutions provided in the appendix to this chapter:

Ethical Dilemma 1: You are conducting an assessment of student life. You go to a local establishment that caters to students and encounter two students who are ready to fight each other. Do you intervene?

Ethical Dilemma 2: You are assessing the child care center. In the course of observing staff interacting with children, you see an act that may be abusive to the child. What do you do?

Ethical Dilemma 3: You have been offered a substantial fee to assess the student life office in a college located in a neighboring town. Your college competes heavily with that college for students. Do you accept the invitation?

Ethical Dilemma 4: In assessing the residence life department, you find out from staff interviews that a number of resident assistants do not enforce the college's regulation that prohibits students from drinking beer in the floor lounges. What do you do?

Ethical Dilemma 5: Through a study of life in campus fraternities, you learn that it is common that people attending weekend parties use rohypnol, with the consequence being that unwanted sexual activity occurs. What do you do?

Ethical Dilemma 6: Under the cover of confidentiality, you learn during an assessment of student government operations that certain financial irregularities have occurred. Your informant does not want the situation investigated, since the person's identity will be revealed. What do you do?

Ethical Dilemma 7: In conducting a confidential study of campus organizations, you find that several are engaged in hazing practices, such as having the prospective members routinely clean the kitchen, mow the lawn, and run errands for the active members, which are counter to the college's policy. None of these practices, in your opinion, places students at risk, but hazing is against college policy and you think, although you are not sure, that there might be a state law prohibiting such practices. What are your actions?

Conclusion

This chapter has focused on a number of ethical issues, ranging from how one works ethically with subjects to handling data. One other ethical aspect of assessment needs to be included in this chapter: the need to do the best study possible. Although we agree, in fact often assert, that compromises may be made in developing an assessment project, we also assert that one should conduct the most rigorous study possible. To do anything less would be an ethical shortcoming in the assessment process.

References

American College Personnel Association. *1997–1998 Member Resource Directory.* Washington, D.C.: American College Personnel Association, 1997.

Blaxter, L., Hughes, C., and Tight, M. *How to Research.* Bristol, Pa.: Open University Press, 1996.

Canon, H. J. "Maintaining High Ethical Standards." In M. J. Barr and Associates, *The Handbook of Student Affairs Administration.* San Francisco: Jossey-Bass, 1993.

Canon, H. J. "Ethical Standards and Principles." In S. R. Komives, D. B. Woodard Jr., and Associates, *Student Services: A Handbook for the Profession.* (3rd ed.) San Francisco: Jossey-Bass, 1996.

Gall, M. D., Borg, W. R., and Gall, J. P. *Educational Research: An Introduction.* New York: Longman, 1996.

Kitchener, K. S. "Ethical Principles and Decisions in Student Affairs." In H. J. Canon and R. D. Brown (eds.), *Applied Ethics in Student Services.* New Directions for Student Services, no. 30. San Francisco: Jossey-Bass, 1985.

National Association of Student Personnel Administrators. *Member Handbook.* Washington, D.C.: National Association of Student Personnel Administrators, 2000.

Rea, L. M., and Parker, R. A. *Designing and Conducting Survey Research.* (2nd ed.) San Francisco: Jossey-Bass, 1997.

Soriano, F. I. *Conducting Needs Assessments.* Thousand Oaks, Calif.: Sage, 1995.

Upcraft, M. L., and Schuh, J. H. *Assessment in Student Affairs: A Guide for Practitioners.* San Francisco: Jossey-Bass, 1996.

APPENDIX 32A

Potential Responses to Ethical Dilemmas

Following are potential responses to the ethical dilemmas posed in this chapter.

Ethical Dilemma 1: Fight in the Local Establishment

While observing a fight might provide a vivid description of student life, stopping it makes much more sense. The investigator would not have to stop the fight unilaterally. Rather, a person from the establishment should be called in to stop things before they get out of hand.

Ethical Dilemma 2: Potential Child Abuse

Child abuse can never be tolerated in the name of science. An immediate conference with the senior staff person in charge of the center needs to occur immediately. It is possible that state law may dictate what you must do, and that might include reporting the incident to authorities designed to protect the welfare of children.

Ethical Dilemma 3: Consulting for a Competitor

The honorarium for this service may be tempting, but you never should forget who your employer is. This organization should command your primary loyalty, because in many respects your institution's success will be your success. In this case, it is appropriate to decline the invitation. If you are good at what you do, other invitations will come your way.

Ethical Dilemma 4: Failure to Enforce the Rules

The campus culture will dictate to a great extent your response to this problem. If the campus merely winks at this kind of violation, you might mention to the staff member in charge of the unit that you have observed rule violations and that perhaps closer supervision is warranted. If the campus is very serious about rule enforcement, then it might make sense to speak with a person in greater authority about what you have observed.

Ethical Dilemma 5: Use of Rohypnol at Parties

This situation cannot be tolerated. It needs to be reported immediately to a senior person responsible for these organizations. An alternative is to report the problem to law enforcement.

Ethical Dilemma 6: Financial Irregularities

This situation cannot be overlooked. What you have observed needs to reported to the institutional administrator who has oversight responsibilities for this area of campus life. Confidentiality always has limits for those not protected specifically by law, such as attorneys or physicians. In this case, confidentiality does not protect the person who provided the information.

Ethical Dilemma 7: Hazing in a Greek House

If there is any good news in this scenario, nobody is at risk, since what you have observed was fairly low-level hazing. But national fraternities and sororities prohibit hazing, and many states have laws prohibiting such conduct. You will need to report what you have found to the person who supervises Greek life.

Chapter 33

Strategies for Implementing an Assessment Program

TO THIS POINT we have introduced a wide variety of subjects related to assessment, identified a number of approaches to take in assessing specific issues or departments, and provided information about how to take raw data and turn this information into a blueprint for improvement. To the casual observer, it might seem as though the topic of assessment is so complicated that it would take a team of people working full time to implement an assessment strategy in a division of student affairs. Although we fully acknowledge that assessment takes time, energy, and resources, we also believe that few divisions of student affairs are likely to devote substantial new resources to assessment, even if these resources were available.

As a consequence, we conclude this book with a streamlined approach to implementing assessment activities in a division of student affairs. We believe that this strategy will help in the overall planning of integrating assessment activities in the routine of a student affairs division. This is a logical strategy that takes assessment data and integrates them into long-term planning for the division. For the purposes of this discussion, we are looking at assessment as it applies to a student affairs unit, such as a health service, department of housing, or student activities. It could also be applied to a broader unit, such as enrollment management or auxiliary services, or a more narrowly focused activity, such as leadership development or service-learning. In addition, when we refer to services in this chapter, we are using a very broad definition to include activities, learning experiences, products, and services.

An exceptionally well-developed assessment plan has been implemented at Southwest Texas State University. More information about it can be found at the following World Wide Web site: http://www.vpsa.swt.edu/vpsa/assessment/Assessment_schedule.htm.

Implementing an Assessment Strategy

Seven steps will lead to a comprehensive unit assessment.

Step 1: Examine Your Mission

An assessment ought to begin with this question: Are our activities consistent with what they ought to be given the nature of our division and our campus? We believe that it is entirely possible for student affairs units to lose touch with the mission of the division of student affairs and that of the larger institution. Therefore, the mission of the unit ought to be studied and carefully considered at least annually. A number of questions should be contemplated: Has the institution's mission changed? Is the division of student affairs still operating under the same mission as a year ago? Has the organizational structure changed, and if so, how will this affect our mission? Has the leadership of the institution or the division changed? If so, how might that affect what we are doing in our unit? Andreas (1993) provides advice on how to understand an institution's mission through reading annual reports and presidential speeches and studying planning documents to gain insight into an institution's mission.

It may be comfortable to wait for direction from more senior leaders before reconsidering a unit's mission, but some events clearly signal that a review of a departmental mission in order. Among these are a reorganization of reporting relationships, institutional financial exigency, changes in leadership, and changes in institutional mission. For example, if your institution changed from offering only associate degrees to also offering bachelor's degrees, that would signal a tremendous adjustment for the division of student affairs. Other changes could be less dramatic, such as the division's being assigned a new reporting relationship through the provost rather than a direct reporting relationship to the president. Other actions can have similar consequences, and a change in mission might be in order.

At times, the division may be drifting away from what it was originally constituted to accomplish. If a student affairs division on a residential campus implements additional services for students who do not live on campus, even though they comprise only 3 percent of the student enrollment, it might be time to rethink the wisdom of adding these services. This would especially be the case if they were developed at the expense of previously existing services.

Step 2: Identify Clients, Customers, and Students

The second step is to determine who uses the services, referred to elsewhere in our assessment literature as tracking. We think it is imperative for a unit to know the people it serves. In some cases, this is simple. A director of housing ought to know the number of students who live in the residence halls, as well as demographic information about them, including gender, race or ethnicity, and class standing. A person who operates a student union has a much more daunting task in identifying who uses the facility and why.

For areas where identifying users is difficult, perhaps for one week in the fall and one week in the spring, a strategy can be implemented of keeping track of who uses the facility. That might mean assigning people to every door of the student union and counting the number of people who enter the facility. Taken with cash register receipts, meal counts, and the number of people who use the bowling alley or pool tables, attend movies, buy tickets, and so on, a profile can be developed as to who uses the facility and for what reasons.

Often people get caught up in selecting just the right week for sampling or worrying that the number may not reach expectations. We recommend that until a particular institution has a better way to collect data, using a typical week in the fall and a typical week in the spring is a good strategy. Our thinking is that some data are better than none, and that even if compromises have been made in collecting the information, the staff is better off with a crude profile of who uses the service than having nothing at all.

It is important to remember that some units are designed to serve more than students. Included in the tracking process should be an attempt to identify the range of individuals served, especially if the campus makes special efforts to provide services to graduates, visitors, prospective students, family members of students, and others.

Step 3: Needs Assessment

After determining who uses the services of the unit, the next step is to determine what the needs are of the unit's clients (meaning students and others). A simple but potent question is this: How do you know what the needs of your clients are? Is the portfolio of services offered a consequence of professional judgment, historical record, reading the literature, responding to the suggestion box, or a well-crafted needs assessment project? Our view is that there is no substitute for conducting periodic needs assessments.

The clientele of a unit rarely turns over 100 percent from one year to the next. To be sure, people come and go, but the majority of users return from one year to the next at most four-year institutions. That assertion may not be the case at two-year colleges. For four-year residential institutions, we recommend that a needs assessment be conducted every second or third year. At a commuter institution or community college, the clientele may turn over more quickly than at a residential college, and as a consequence conducting a needs assessment more often might be wise. Our point is that needs assessment probably does not have to be conducted every year, but when it is conducted, it should be thorough and consistent with what has been suggested in Chapter Nine. With a well-constructed needs assessment in hand, planners can be assured that the services they offer are consistent with what students need. And if a needs assessment reveals changes from the past, then plans can be developed to take the service in a different direction.

Step 4: Cost Effectiveness

Assuming that a unit offers the appropriate services, one of the important questions to be explored in the current fiscal environment is whether these services are cost-effective. Cost effectiveness has two dimensions. Do people believe they receive value for the price of the service, and are the services offered at a price comparable to or less than what users can find off campus? Another dimension to this matter, directly related to higher education, is that the competition may be not only a vendor down the street but also a college a thousand miles away that attempts to recruit students from the same population base.

Periodic studies need to be conducted to make sure that services are cost-effective. For some units, comparisons are easy to conduct. The student union can compare the cost of food items with local restaurants to get a sense of how competitive its charges are. The housing office can review ads in the newspaper to compare room charges with local apartments or get on the World Wide Web and review room and board costs at competing institutions.

Other areas might be more difficult to measure, especially if costs include the retirement of debt service at one institution compared to costs at other institutions where there is no debt. Recreation services provide an example where this disparity potentially may exist. Campus A with a new recreation building and substantial debt may have to charge a higher recreation fee than Campus B, with an older facility where the debt has been retired, or Campus C, where the debt service is paid out of other sources.

The cost effectiveness of services related to the perceived value of them is more complex. Focus groups work quite well for this activity. Although we think that annual comparisons of services should be conducted, determining the perceived value of services might be conducted less frequently, since the activity is more complex. It is important to remember, however, that if a service is perceived to provide poor quality, no matter how modest a charge may be, the conclusion will be that the cost is too great.

Step 5: Satisfaction Assessment

After determining client needs and the extent to which services are cost-effective, the next step in an assessment program is to measure client satisfaction with services, programs, and learning experiences. Satisfaction assessment can be linked directly to needs assessment using a unit improvement model. The Total Quality Management (TQM) movement employed a variation on this theme. Whether TQM will ever experience wide-ranging adoption or be thought of as a management fad, the point is that educational organizations, in the highly competitive environment in which they function, need to be confident that their clients are satisfied with that which is offered, or these clients will attend other institutions.

Ensuring client satisfaction is especially important given the development of on-line educational opportunities. No longer can an institution take comfort in its geographical location as insulation against competition. Such thinking as, "We have the only business program for one hundred miles and if students want to study business and stay at home, they'll need to come to us," is flawed. Offerings on the World Wide Web very well might mean that the competition to the local college may be situated a long distance away and is available through the computer in a student's home. The point is this: institutions must be able to ensure that their clients are satisfied with their experiences. Moreover, those experiences need to be consistent with what the institution says it will provide as articulated through its mission statement.

We recommend that a satisfaction assessment be conducted the year after each needs assessment is conducted. If a needs assessment is conducted every third year, then a satisfaction assessment should be conducted the following year. Since this form of assessment is complex and is linked to needs assessment, our position is that a satisfaction assessment need not be annual activity unless the student body had more than 50 percent newcomers each year.

Step 6: Outcomes Assessment

The heart of any assessment program is outcomes assessment. In effect, this is the most important of all assessment activities. Outcomes assessment is both the most complex and the most valuable form of assessment. It is the most useful form of assessment in demonstrating that a service has had an impact on students by contributing to their educational growth and development. We know that out-of-class experiences can have a tremendous influence on student growth (see Pascarella and Terenzini, 1991; Astin, 1993; Kuh, Branch Douglas, Lund, and Ramin-Gyurnek, 1994) and that it is important to demonstrate that the local situation mirrors that which is known about students in a more global sense.

Depending on the nature of the unit, an outcomes assessment might be conducted annually or biannually. Because these studies can be complex and may require the help of a consultant, they need to be well conceived and carefully crafted. The methodology, particularly if one uses a quantitative approach, can be sophisticated. Nonetheless, the consequences of conducting an outcomes assessment can be powerful and can position a unit very well on a campus, especially if the assessment confirms that the unit contributes to student learning and growth.

Step 7: Be Prepared for the Future

Finally, based on all the assessment data that the unit develops, leaders need to be ready for the future. The assessment data can be used to support continuing current programs for the future, making staffing adjustments, planning new initiatives, and so on. Although long-range planning can be challenging and exigencies outside the control of the unit can have a tremendous influence on future activities, the fact of the matter is that long-range planning based on solid assessment projects will position the unit well for future challenges. Assessment data in and of themselves are useful, perhaps interesting, and important in making daily operating decisions. As important, however, is the use of assessment data in long-range planning. It is particularly crucial that assessment data are incorporated into the unit's long-range plan.

A Final Assessment Task: Writing a Good Report

Let us assume that you have been successful in developing a comprehensive assessment program based on this manual. Let us further assume that you have conducted exemplary studies that have followed appropriate ethical guidelines. One would assume that your job is done; in fact, it is only half done. Conducting good studies that yield valuable information for policy and practice is not good enough; the findings and recommendations must be communicated effectively and directed to institutional decision makers in ways that will attract their attention and move them to take action.

As we have pointed out elsewhere (Upcraft and Schuh, 1996), "Nothing is more frustrating than to conduct an assessment study of high quality and then learn, usually over some period of time, that the decision makers failed to act on the study's findings" (p. 275). How does this happen? We believe it is because report writers often assume that the study speaks for itself or that it is inappropriate to write a report that advocates a position or recommended action. There are many assessment investigators who believe that marketing an assessment report is inappropriate or violates investigator objectivity. If assessment were the same as research, this belief might hold water. But as we suggested in Chapter One, assessment is quite different from research in many ways, not the least of which is that the purpose of assessment is to inform policy and practice. In other words, an assessment study fails at its most basic level when recommended actions are omitted.

Assessment reports should, of course, report the study, including its purposes, methodologies, and findings. But an assessment report should also be an advocacy statement, calling decision makers to action. Of course, decision makers can reject the recommendations of an assessment report, but more often than not, they expect some guidance about what action to take.

The formatting of a report can be critical. As we have pointed out, "The most common mistake investigators make is to send a complete and comprehensive report (most often modeled after a typical doctoral dissertation) to all intended audiences. While a comprehensive and complete report should be written, sending the whole thing to everyone is a colossal mistake. It will be intimidating, it won't be read, and, as a result, it will likely have no impact" (Upcraft and Schuh, 1996).

Then what should be done to communicate assessment results effectively? We recommend the following (based on Upcraft and Schuh, 1996):

• Determine the audience. Depending on the study, there is usually more than one audience; it may be students, student affairs staff, the central administration, the chief student affairs officer, the board of control, alumni, the local community, state legislators, or the general public.

• Write summary reports for targeted audiences. A brief summary of the study should be sent to each intended audience, highlighting the findings most appropriate to that audience. For example, what is important to a president may not be important to students, and reports should reflect that fact.

• Write short reports. Short reports, based on the full report, should be no longer than five pages, including a title page and executive summary, which includes the purpose of the study, its design, its limitations (for the typical assessment study, many compromises will be made and should be reported), a summary of the findings, and recommendations for action. It should also refer readers to a source where the full report may be obtained. directing the reader to an office where the full report may be retrieved.

- Write an interesting and readable report. Assessment reports should be "reader friendly" and more casual than a typical research report. Use plenty of headings, keep sentences and paragraphs short, avoid research jargon, and write as clearly as possible.
- Anticipate possible reactions. There are times when the results of a study will be sensitive or controversial and could offend, embarrass, or anger intended audiences. Results that may be controversial must be reported, but if these results are not handled properly, they may well be ignored, so great care must be taken in delivering bad news to decision makers. One strategy is to let them know in advance about the findings, so that they will not be blindsided by a public report. Another strategy is to present controversial results in a balanced way, avoiding pinning the blame on anyone and suggesting possible solutions.

Reporting the findings of an assessment study may be the most important way in which findings are taken seriously and acted on, so investigators should devote much time and discussion to this effort. (For a more complete discussion of reporting and using assessment results, see Upcraft and Schuh, 1996.)

Conclusion

We began this chapter with the observation that this book has presented a tremendous amount of material related to assessment, and short of herculean efforts, the chances that a unit will accomplish every recommendation we have suggested are remote. As a consequence, we believe that the approach we have outlined in this chapter will provide a good road map for an overall assessment plan. That is not to imply that other forms of assessment are unimportant. That is not true. There are times, for example, when assessing the student culture can be very important or using benchmarks for comparison purposes can be instrumental in securing additional resources. Our point is that those interested in developing an assessment plan need to start somewhere and build on a solid foundation to incorporate assessment into the annual work routine.

We are confident that units will benefit from this approach. Institutions will continue to place increasing emphasis on the importance of assessment activities. Those units that undertake this approach will thrive. Those that do not will struggle increasingly to justify their existence. But setting all that aside, the most important reason to undertake an assessment program is that students will be the beneficiaries. Their college experiences will be strengthened, and in the end, improving student experiences ought to be the top priority for all of higher education.

References

Andreas, R. E. "Program Planning." In M. J. Barr and Associates, *The Handbook of Student Affairs Administration.* San Francisco: Jossey-Bass, 1993.

Astin, A. W. *What Matters in College? Four Critical Years Revisited.* San Francisco: Jossey-Bass, 1993.

Kuh, G. D., Branch Douglas, K. B., Lund, J. P., and Ramin-Gyurnek, J. *Student Learning Outside the Classroom: Transcending Artificial Boundaries.* Washington, D.C.: School of Education and Human Development, George Washington University, 1994.

Pascarella, E. T., and Terenzini, P. T. *How College Affects Students: Findings and Insights from Twenty Years of Research.* San Francisco: Jossey-Bass, 1991.

Upcraft, M. L., and Schuh, J. H. *Assessment in Student Affairs: A Guide for Practitioners.* San Francisco: Jossey-Bass, 1996.

Resources

Review of Selected Assessment Instruments

Brian R. Jara

THIS SELECTED ANNOTATED REVIEW is designed to provide information about instruments that may be useful in assessing the services, programs, and facilities discussed in this book. The publishers of these instruments can provide further information for reviewing their purposes, content, and psychometric integrity. Web site addresses are given when available.

We suggest three additional sources for annotated assessment instruments and other assessment publications. The first is the Clearinghouse for Higher Education Assessment. Formerly housed at the University of Tennessee, the Clearinghouse published bibliographies, reviews, and descriptions of selected instruments. Although it no longer exists, readers should refer to the reports cited below.

Two more current resources have been developed: the American College Personnel Association's Commission IX on Assessment for Student Development and the ERIC Clearinghouse on Assessment and Evaluation. Both maintain Web site clearinghouses of a variety of environmental and student development assessment instruments.

Major National Resources for Assessment Instruments

American College Personnel Association (ACPA)
Commission IX Assessment for Student Development
One Dupont Circle
Washington, DC 20036
(202) 835-2272
http://www.acpa.nche.edu/comms/comm09/conm09.htm

American College Testing Program
National Office
2201 North Dodge Street
P.O. Box 168
Iowa City, IA 52243
(319) 337-1000
http://www.act.org

Educational Benchmarking, Inc.
1630 West Elfindale Street
Springfield, MO 65807
(417) 831-1810
http://www.webebi.com

Educational Testing Service
Higher Education Assessment
Rosedale Road, ML 55-L
Princeton, NJ 08541
(800) 745-0269
http://www.ets.org/hea

Noel Levitz Centers
2101 ACT Circle
Iowa City, IA 52245
(800) 876-1117
http://www.noellevitz.com

National Center for Higher Education Management Systems
1540 Thirtieth Street RL-2
P.O. Box 9752
Boulder, CO 80301
(303) 497-0301
http://www.nchems.org

Psychological Corporation
555 Academic Court
San Antonio, TX 78204
(800) 211-8378
http://www.psychcorp.com

University of Missouri–Rolla
Academic Assessment and Student Research
104 Norwood Hall
Rolla, MO 65409-1220
(573) 341-4954
http://www.umv.edu/~assess
http://www.umv.edu/~assess/edpedres/websites.htm

Clearinghouse for Higher Education Assessment

Smith, M. K., Bradley, J. L., and Draper, G. F. *Affective Assessment Annotated Bibliography.* Knoxville, Tenn.: Clearinghouse for Higher Education Assessment, 1993.

Smith, M. K., Bradley, J. L., and Draper, G. F. *A National Survey on Assessment Practices: Results of a National Study on Types of Assessment Instruments Being Used by Various Types of Institutions.* Knoxville, Tenn.: Clearinghouse for Higher Education Assessment, 1993.

Annotated Assessment Instruments

Academic Advising

Academic Advising Inventory: To measure students' perceptions of advising programs along five dimensions: developmental-prescriptive advising, activity categories, student satisfaction with advising, demographic information, and locally generated items.
Student Development Associates
110 Crestwood Drive
Athens, GA 30605
(404) 549-4122

Developmental Advising Inventory: To evaluate the development of young adults across nine dimensions: intellectual, life planning, social, physical, emotional, sexual, cultural, spiritual, and political.
Developmental Advising Inventories
P.O. Box 1946
Paradise, CA 95967
(916) 872-0511

College Student Inventory: To provide advisers with information on students' principal attitudes. Sections on background information, participation in activities, and attitudes toward college. (See Noel Levitz Centers.)

Survey of Academic Advising: To determine student impressions of an institution's academic advising services. Sections on background information, advising information, academic advising needs, impressions of your adviser, additional advising information, additional local questions, and comments and suggestions. (See American College Testing Program.)

Academic Success

Collegiate Assessment of Academic Proficiency: To report the progress of groups of students and determine the educational development of individual students. On a group basis, it reports on students' progress in acquiring foundational academic skills and on differential performance in general education instructional programs within an institution. Modules for reading, writing, mathematics, science reasoning, critical thinking, and optional local questions. (See American College Testing Program.)

SAT II: Subject Tests College Board Achievement Tests: To measure factual knowledge and the application of knowledge in five general subject categories: English, history and social studies, mathematics, science, and languages.
College Board SAT Program
P.O. Box 6200
Princeton, NJ 08541
(609) 771-7600
http://www.collegeboard.org

College Outcomes Survey: To assess student outcomes related to career, emotional, intellectual, moral, physical, and social development, as well as to assess satisfaction with the institution. (See American College Testing Program.)

Graduate Experience Survey, University of Tennessee: To evaluate graduate student outcomes related to academic, intellectual, and social development. Also assesses student satisfaction with the institution. (See Clearinghouse for Higher Education Assessment.)

Graduate Program Self-Assessment: To evaluate graduate programs. There are separate instruments for faculty, enrolled students, and alumni for both the master's and doctoral levels. (See Educational Testing Service.)

Program Assessment Questionnaire: To evaluate undergraduate programs. There are separate instruments for faculty, enrolled students, and alumni. (See Educational Testing Service.)

Student Instructional Report II: To assess the quality of teaching. Local questions can be added, and students can elaborate on their answers to forty-five standard questions. (See Educational Testing Service.)

Alumni

ACT Alumni Outcomes Survey: To obtain student satisfaction feedback and self-reported perceptions of growth in many areas considered important by accrediting commissions and other external agencies. (See American College Testing Program.)

ACT Alumni Survey: To help the institution evaluate the impact that college had on graduates in both two- and four-year institutions. Sections on background information, continuing education, educational experiences, employment history, additional local questions, current mailing addresses, and comments and suggestions. (See American College Testing Program.)

Alumni Survey, University of Tennessee: To survey alumni about their undergraduate experiences, including overall satisfaction, involvement in activities, impact of education, and programs related to major. Also collects employment and background information. (See Clearinghouse for Higher Education Assessment.)

Comprehensive Alumni Assessment Survey: To gather information about alumni, with or without local questions. Sections on employment and continuing education, undergraduate experience, intellectual development, community goals, personal development, community participation, and demographic information. (See National Center for Higher Education Management Systems.)

Long-Term Alumni Questionnaire: To survey alumni who have been away from the institution for more than four years. Sections on background information, educational information, academic goals, career preparation goals, career improvement outcomes, social participation outcomes, personal development outcomes, and employment information. (See National Center for Higher Education Management Systems.)

Recent Alumni Questionnaire: To survey alumni who have been away from the institution for four years or less. Sections on background information, academic goals, career preparation goals, career improvement outcomes, social participation outcomes, personal development outcomes, and employment information. (See National Center for Higher Education Management Systems.)

Survey of Graduates, University of Tennessee: To survey alumni about their undergraduate academic, social, and cultural experiences. Sections on involvement activities, education and its impact, specific programs related to the major, and employment and background information. (See Clearinghouse for Higher Education Assessment.)

Career Services

Career Decision Scale: To assess the level of the student's career indecision and barriers that prevent career decisions.
Psychological Assessment Resources
16204 North Florida Avenue
Lutz, FL 33459
(813) 968-3003
http://www.parinc.com

Career Development Inventory: To assess career development and career maturity based on Donald Super's theoretical model of career development.
Consulting Psychologists Press
577 College Avenue
Palo Alto, CA 94306
(415) 969-8901
http://www.cpp-db.com

Career Decision-Making System, Level 2: To evaluate student characteristics related to career planning. Assesses abilities, job values, school subject preferences, and interests.
American Guidance Service
4201 Woodland Road
Circle Pines, MN 55014
(800) 328-2560
http://www.agsnet.com

Career Development Inventory College and University Form: To assess knowledge and attitudes about career choice for the purposes of designing and evaluating career counseling programs.
Consulting Psychologists Press
577 College Avenue
Palo Alto, CA 94306
(415) 969-8901
http://www.cpp-db.com

College Unions

ACUI/EBI Student Survey: To assess student union user satisfaction with union facilities, services, and programs. (See Educational Benchmarking, Inc.)

Counseling Programs

Consultation Form, Penn State University: To evaluate student background characteristics. Sections on referral information, demographics, academic information, personal information, educational history, medical history, and family history.

Counseling and Psychological Services
Pennsylvania State University
221 Ritenour Building
University Park, PA 16802
(814) 863-0395
http://www.sa.psu.edu/caps

Satisfaction Survey, Penn State University: To assess student satisfaction with counseling services.

Counseling and Psychological Services
Pennsylvania State University
221 Ritenour Building
University Park, PA 16802
(814) 863-0395
http://www.sa.psu.edu/caps

Dropouts

Former-Student Questionnaire: To survey dropout students to determine their reasons for leaving and their reactions to the institution. (See National Center for Higher Education Management Systems.)

The Student Experience—A Look Back, University of Tennessee: To measure opinions of students who dropped out, including the reasons for dropping out, the dropout process, educational outcomes, student relations, peer relations, classroom experiences, future plans, and background information. (See Clearinghouse for Higher Education Assessment.)

Withdrawing/Nonreturning Student Survey: To determine why students leave an institution prior to completing a degree. Sections on background information, reasons for leaving college, college services and characteristics, additional local items, and comments and suggestions. Long and short forms available. (See American College Testing Program.)

Environments

College Student Experiences Questionnaire: To determine how students invest their time and effort in educationally purposeful activities in and out of the classroom; to determine students' perceptions of the institutional environment; and to determine students' self-reported gains in student learning and personal development.

Center for Postsecondary Research and Planning
Indiana University
Smith Research Center, Room 174
2805 East Tenth Street
Bloomington, IN 47408
(812) 856-5824
http://www.indiana.edu/~educ/pprcenter.html

Environmental Assessment Inventory: To provide college counseling center staff with systematic and continuous data about the campus environment, trends in the environment, and impact on students.
Robert Conyne
340 Tangeman University Center
ML No. 46
University of Cincinnati
Cincinnati, OH 45221
(513) 556-3344

Involving Colleges Interview Protocol: To assess student perceptions of campus climate, including mission and philosophy, campus culture, campus environment, policies and practices, and institutional agents.
Center for Postsecondary Research and Planning
Indiana University
Smith Research Center, Room 174
2805 East Tenth Street
Bloomington, IN 47408
(812) 856-5824
http://www.indiana.edu/~educ/pprcenter.html

National Study of Student Engagement: To obtain, on an annual basis, information about student participation in programs and activities that institutions provide for their learning and personal development. Sections on college activities, college environment, estimate of gains, opinions about the institution, and background information.
Center for Postsecondary Research and Planning
Indiana University
Smith Research Center, Room 174
2805 East Tenth Street
Bloomington, IN 47408
(812) 856-5824
http://www.indiana.edu/~educ/pprcenter.html

University Residence Environment Scale: To evaluate different dimensions of student living group environments: relationships, personal development, system maintenance, and system change. It produces ten scores: involvement, emotional support, independence, traditional social orientation, competition, academic achievement, intellectuality, order and organization, student influence, and innovation.
Consulting Psychologists Press
577 College Avenue
Palo Alto, CA 94306
(415) 969-8901
http://www.cpp-db.com

Financial Aid Programs

Questionnaire on Services, Satisfaction, and Expenses: To evaluate students' experiences with financial aid programs and services. Sections on background information, student satisfaction, living expenses, personal expenses, books and supplies, transportation expenses, credit cards, computer usage, employment, and scholarship search services.
Office of Student Financial Aid
Turner Student Services Building, Fourth Floor
University of Illinois at Urbana-Champaign
610 East John Street
Champaign, IL 61820
(217) 333-0100
http://www.oar.uiuc.edu/prospective/ugrad/finan.html

First-Year and Entering Students

Annual Survey of American College Freshmen: To survey students' attitudes and values at the beginning of their first year.
Cooperative Institutional Research Program
Graduate School of Education
University of California, Los Angeles
405 Hilgard Avenue
Los Angeles, CA 90024
(310) 825-1925
http://www.gseis.ucla.edu/heri/cirp.htm

Educational Planning Survey, Penn State University: To collect information about entering students' backgrounds; high school academic and out-of-class experiences; expectations about college, educational, and occupational plans; and reasons for attending college.

Division of Undergraduate Studies
Pennsylvania State University
102 Grange Building
University Park, PA 16802
(814) 865-7576
http://www.psu.edu/dept/dus

Entering-Student Questionnaire: To gain information from entering students at both two- and four-year institutions. (See National Center for Higher Education Management Systems.)

Entering Student Survey: To collect information related to entering students' plans, goals, and impressions. Sections on background information, educational plans and preferences, college impressions, additional local questions, and comments and suggestions. (See American College Testing Program.)

Learning and Study Strategies Inventory: To measure students' strengths and weaknesses in ten areas causally related to academic success: attitude, motivation, time management, anxiety, concentration, information processing, selecting main ideas, study aids, self-testing, and test strategies.
H&H Publishing Company
1231 Kapp Drive
Clearwater, FL 33765
(800) 366-4079
http://www.hhpublishing.com

Perceptions, Expectations, Emotions, and Knowledge About College: To assess students' reactions to personal, social, and academic changes that may occur in a college setting.
H&H Publishing Company
1231 Kapp Drive
Clearwater, FL 33765
(800) 366-4079
http://www.hhpublishing.com

National Center on Postsecondary Teaching, Learning, and Assessment Pre-College Survey: To evaluate the characteristics and educational expectations of entering students. Sections on background information, participation in activities, and perspectives on learning.

National Center on Postsecondary Teaching, Learning, and Assessment
Center for the Study of Higher Education
Pennsylvania State University
104 Charlotte Building
University Park, PA 16801
(814) 865-6346
http://www.ed.psu.edu/cshe/htdocs/research/NCTLA/nctla.htm

Student Adaptation to College Questionnaire: To measure students' adjustment to college, based on the assumption that the college experience places demands on students and requires various coping responses. Sections on academic adjustment, social adjustment, personal-emotional adjustment, and goal commitment and institutional attachment.
Western Psychological Services
12031 Wilshire Boulevard
Los Angeles, CA 90025
(310) 478-0261
http://www.wpublish.com

Student Reactions to College: To measure students' reactions to college, primarily during the first year. Assesses four major areas of student life: process of instruction, program planning, administrative affairs, and out-of-class activities. (See Educational Testing Service.)

Student Satisfaction: The Freshman Experience: To measure first-year students' satisfaction with all aspects of the university. (See Clearinghouse for Higher Education Assessment.)

Survey of Postsecondary Plans: To survey entering students on career and academic plans and goals. (See American College Testing Program.)

Health Services

Lifestyle Assessment Questionnaire: To evaluate how students' personal lifestyle choices affect their overall level of health. Sections on personal data, lifestyle (physical exercise, nutrition, self-care, vehicle safety, drug use, social/environmental, emotional awareness, emotional management, intellectual, occupational, and spiritual), health risk appraisal, and topics for personal growth.
National Wellness Institute
1045 Clark Street, Suite 210
Stevens Point, WI 54481
(715) 342-2969
http://www.wellnessnwi.org

National College Health Risk Behavior Survey: To evaluate college student behaviors that influence mortality and morbidity. Sections on behaviors that result in injuries, use of tobacco, use of alcohol and other drugs, sexual behaviors, body weight/nutrition, and physical activity.
Centers for Disease Control and Prevention
1600 Clifton Road
Atlanta, GA 30333
(404) 639-3311
http://www.cdc.gov

Patient Examination Form: To evaluate doctors, receptionists and reception area, laboratory, nurses, and other aspects of health care environments. (See Clearinghouse for Higher Education Assessment.)

Student Health Services Student Survey: To assess various aspects and functions of student health services.
Office of Planning and Assessment
University of Kentucky
206 Gillis Building
Lexington, KY 40506-0033
(606) 257-1633

Survey of Student Opinions Regarding Campus Acquaintance Rape: To assess students' opinions regarding acquaintance rape. Evaluates students' attitudes and behaviors that may contribute to sexual assault and rape.
Center for Women's Programs
2 Turner Student Services
University of Illinois at Urbana-Champaign
Champaign, IL 61820
(217) 333-3137
http://www.odos.uiuc.edu/women/index.htm

Testwell Wellness Inventory, College Version: A software program to measure physical, emotional, social, intellectual, occupational, and spiritual development.
National Wellness Institute
1045 Clark Street, Suite 210
Stevens Point, WI 54481
(715) 342-2969
http://www.nationalwellness.org

Outcomes

College Outcomes Survey: To assess student outcomes related to career, emotional, intellectual, moral, physical, and social development, as well as to assess satisfaction with the institution. (See American College Testing Program.)

Community College Goals Inventory: To measure reaction to outcome goals. It can be administered to students, faculty, alumni, trustees, or any other groups at the discretion of the institution. Sections on general education, intellectual orientation, lifelong learning, cultural awareness, personal development, humanism, vocational preparation, development preparation, community services, and social criticism. (See Educational Testing Service.)

Small College Goals Inventory: To measure reactions to outcome goals. It can be administered to students, faculty, alumni, trustees, or any other groups at the discretion of the institution. Sections on academic development, intellectual skills, personal development, ethical orientation, cultural awareness, religious orientation, vocational preparation, preparation for lifelong learning, self-understanding, interpersonal skills, and social/political responsibility. (See Educational Testing Service.)

Residence Hall Programs

ACUHO-I/EBI Apartment Survey: To assess apartment dwellers' perceptions of their living environment, including apartment selection criteria; contract or lease; apartment conditions, services, and life; safety and security; fellow apartment residents; and overall satisfaction. (See Educational Benchmarking, Inc.)

ACUHO-I/EBI Resident Satisfaction Survey: To assess residents' satisfaction with their living environment, including the resident assistant, opportunities to participate in hall activities, fellow residents, housing services, study atmosphere, dining services, safety and security, and overall satisfaction. (See Educational Benchmarking, Inc.)

ACUHO-I/EBI Resident Assistant Survey: To assess residents' satisfaction with the RA selection process, expectations, and training; effectiveness in enhancing various student issues; enforcement of rules; RA supervisor; and overall satisfaction. (See Educational Benchmarking, Inc.)

Student Evaluation of Resident Assistant, Penn State University: To measure student reactions to resident assistants. Sections on approachability and availability, sensitivity, discipline, information, and programming.

Office of Residence Life
Pennsylvania State University
135 Boucke Building
University Park, PA 16802
(814) 863-1710
http://www.psu.edu/rl

University Residence Environment Scale: To assess the social climates of student living groups, including involvement, emotional support, independence, traditional social orientation, competition, academic achievement, order and organization, intellectuality, social influence, and innovation. There are two versions: an expected social climate form for students who are entering (Form E) and a form for current residents (Form R).
Consulting Psychologists Press
577 College Avenue
Palo Alto, CA 94306
(415) 969-8901
http://www.cpp-db.com

Satisfaction

College Assessment Program Surveys: To assess personal incentives, opportunities in school to fulfill personal incentives, and perceptions of the culture of the institution. Sections on personal incentives, spirituality, self-esteem, college activities, college/institution culture, satisfaction, commitment to college, common college concerns, and college resources.
MetriTech
P.O. Box 6479
Champaign, IL 61826
(217) 398-4868
http://www.metritech.com/metritech/met_home.htm

College Descriptive Index: To measure student satisfaction with the college experience. (See Educational Testing Service.)

College Interest Inventory: To measure student interest in college curricular areas.
Psychological Development Center
7057 West 130th Street
Parma, OH 44130
(216) 842-2222

Graduate Experience Survey, University of Tennessee: To evaluate graduate student outcomes related to academic, intellectual, and social development. Also assesses student satisfaction with the institution. (See Clearinghouse for Higher Education Assessment.)

Graduate Program Self-Assessment: To evaluate graduate programs. There are separate instruments for faculty, enrolled students, and alumni for both the master's and doctoral levels. (See Educational Testing Service.)

Institutional Goals Inventory: To measure students' perceptions of institutional goals, including outcome goals (academic development, intellectual orientation, individual personal development, humanism/altruism, cultural/aesthetic awareness, traditional religiousness, vocational preparation, advanced training, research, meeting local needs, public service, social egalitarianism, and social criticism/activism). Process goals include freedom, democratic governance, community, intellectual/aesthetic environment, innovation, off-campus learning, and accountability/efficiency. (See Educational Testing Service.)

Institutional Performance Survey: To evaluate institutional performance pertaining to institutional effectiveness, leadership and decision styles, institutional culture, and institutional environment. (See National Center for Higher Education Management Systems.)

Program Assessment Questionnaire: To evaluate undergraduate programs. There are separate instruments for faculty, enrolled students, and alumni. (See Educational Testing Service.)

Student Opinion Survey: To determine student satisfaction with the institution. Sections on background information, college services, college environment, additional local questions, and comments and suggestions. (See American College Testing Program.)

Student Reactions to College: To assess major areas of student life: instruction and classroom experience, counseling/advising, administrative regulations, class scheduling/registration, student activities, studying, faculty contact, student goals and planning, daily living, and library/bookstore. (See Educational Testing Service.)

Student Satisfaction: The Freshman Experience: To measure first-year students' satisfaction with all aspects of the university. (See Clearinghouse for Higher Education Assessment.)

Student Satisfaction Inventory: To measure student satisfaction with a variety of institutional programs and services. Versions are available for both two- and four-year institutions. (See Noel Levitz Centers.)

Student Needs

College Student Needs Assessment Survey: To assist college personnel in assessing the educational and personal needs of college students. Sections on background information, career and life goals, educational and personal needs, additional local questions, and comments and suggestions. (See American College Testing Program.)

Community College Goals Inventory: To measure reaction to outcome goals. It can be administered to students, faculty, alumni, trustees, or any other group at the discretion of the institution. Sections on general education, intellectual orientation, lifelong learning, cultural awareness, personal development, humanism, vocational preparation, development preparation, community services, and social criticism. (See Educational Testing Service.)

Small College Goals Inventory: To measure reaction to outcome goals. It can be administered to students, faculty, alumni, trustees, or any other groups at the discretion of the institution. Sections on academic development, intellectual skills, personal development, ethical orientation, cultural awareness, religious orientation, vocational preparation, preparation for lifelong learning, self-understanding, interpersonal skills, and social/political responsibility. (See Educational Testing Service.)

Index

A

AAAHC (Accreditation Association for Ambulatory Health Care), 211, 355, 358

Academic advising instruments, 487

Academic success instruments, 487–488

Accreditation: assessment principles of, 201, 204–207; assessment strategies for, 207–209; of counseling services, 402–403; evaluators of, 199–200; functional unit, 210–211; general aspects of, 198–199; general criteria and standards for, 200–201e; of health services, 357–358; issues of, 12; nationally accepted standards and, 15; regional bodies governing, 196–198, 197e; starting process of, 209–210

ACHA (American College Health Association), 346, 356, 357

ACUI (Association of College Unions–International), 328, 332

Adler, P., 36

Adler, P. A., 36

Admissions program assessment: comprehensive model for, 304–306; Easternmost College case study on, 306–311; growing interest in, 302–303; interview protocol during, 309e; problems associated with, 303

Advisory boards, 374

Altschuld, J. W., 32

Alumni instruments, 488–489

American Association of Collegiate Registrars and Admissions Offices, 305

American College Health Association, 341, 342, 346, 347, 357

American College Personnel Association, 153, 380

American College Personnel Association Web site, 133

American College Testing (ACT) Program, 133, 148, 422, 448

American College Testing and Scholastic Aptitude Test scores, 414

American Counseling Association, 380

American Medical Association, 345

American Psychiatric Association, 395

American Psychological Association (APA), 211, 403

ANCOVA, 410

Andreas, R. E., 477

Anonymity issues: of mail-out surveys, 76, 77; of telephone surveys, 84

Archer, J., 390

Arnold, J. C., 413, 416

Assessment: of accreditation, 201, 204–207; compared to research and evaluation, 8–9; comparing evaluation to, 4; comprehensive model for, 12–15; difficulties of starting, 441–442; ethical issues of, 464–475; "good enough" rule applied to, 7–8; growing interest in, 3, 16; implementation limitations and, 7; measurement for purpose of, 4–5; negotiable issues of, 449–455; nonnegotiable issues of, 445–449; organizational contexts of, 6–7; overcoming barriers to, 442–445; overview of, 3–9; political context of, 7; resource and time limitations for, 6; strategies for accreditation, 207–209; strategies for implementing, 476–486; student affairs research, 5, 9–12; writing a good report of, 481–483

Assessment barriers: lack of commitment/support from leadership, 444; lack of expertise, 443–444; lack of money, 442–443; lack of staff support, 444–445

Assessment negotiable issues: conduction of study as, 452; consultation as, 453–454; criteria as, 451–452; design of study as, 452–453; determining involvement as, 450–451; determining purpose as, 449–450; interpretation as, 454–455; policy/practice recommendations as, 455

Assessment nonnegotiable issues: on institutional standards, 446–447; integrity of assessment, 446; on methodology used, 447–448; on reporting results, 448–449; that assessment will be completed, 445–446

Assessment process steps: defining the problem, 18–19; determining best method to use, 20; determining data analysis method, 22–23; determining data collection method, 21; determining focus of study, 20–21; determining implications of study, 23;